D1522493

THE SPIRITUAL REVITALIZATION
OF THE LEGAL PROFESSION

THE SPIRITUAL REVITALIZATION OF THE LEGAL PROFESSION

A Search for Sacred Rivers

David Hall

The Edwin Mellen Press
Lewiston•Queenston•Lampeter

Library of Congress Cataloging-in-Publication Data

Hall, David, 1950-
   The spiritual revitalization of the legal profession : a search for sacred rivers /
David Hall.
         p. cm.
   Includes bibliographical references and index..
   ISBN 0-7734-6015-2
   1. Law--Moral and ethical aspects. 2. Religion and law. 3. Lawyers--Religious
life. I. Title.

   K247.6.H35   2005
   340'.023--dc22   2005044500

A CIP catalog record for this book is available from the British Library.

Front cover: Bob Clemenz Photog., Sedona, AZ   WY81-04638.00
Author photo: © David Leifer 2005; David Leifer Photography, Brookline, MA

              The Edwin Mellen Press   The Edwin Mellen Press
                     Box 450   Box 67
                Lewiston, New York   Queenston, Ontario
                USA 14092-0450   CANADA L0S 1L0

                        The Edwin Mellen Press, Ltd.
                        Lampeter, Ceredigion, Wales
                        UNITED KINGDOM SA48 8LT

                  Printed in the United States of America

To my mother,
Ethel Hall
and my father,
Levi Hall

They created the foundation for my spiritual
growth, and they introduced me to the River

Table of Contents

Acknowledgments

This book has been inspired in part by the life and work of various lawyers throughout this country who pursue the practice and study of law according to the highest spiritual values of the legal profession. Space and time will not permit me to mention them all, but the list would certainly include Stu Webb, John McShane, Ozell Hudson, Charles Ogletree, Johnnie Cochran, Rita Pollak, Joseph Allegretti, Nora Bushfield, John Hamilton, Geraldine Hines, J.Kim Wright, Derrick Bell, William Van Zyverden, and countless members of the International Alliance of Holistic Lawyers. Their work and legacy have made writing this book so much easier. Numerous individuals read early drafts of this manuscript and provided enormous insights and feedback that enhanced the quality of this book. I am deeply indebted to John Hamilton, Lucy Williams, Filippa Anzalone, David Phillips, J. Kim Wright, Rita Pollak, Cheryl Conner, William Van Zyverden, Geraldine Hines, and Leonard Riskin. I was blessed to have the careful editing eyes of Alice Alexander who gave her heart and soul to this effort. Lou-Anne Kroutil was also involved in editing an earlier draft. Special thanks to Mary Murphy, my administrative assistant, for her consistent help in preparing this manuscript for publication. I also want to thank the various research assistants who provided valuable help in gathering materials and assisting with footnotes. Rachel Holmes contributed greatly in this regard. I also received valuable assistance from Paul Kular, Brian Giles, Caitlin Palm, and Donovan Dodrill. Various religious leaders shared their insights as I researched this book. Rabbi Wesley Gardenswartz, member of the Islamic Society of Boston, Imam Abdullah Faaruuq, and my Pastor,

Rev. Dr. Leroy Attles were spiritual reservoirs for me on this journey. I am grateful to the following attorneys, judges, therapist and clients who shared their experiences and insights with me as I researched this book. They include, William Van Zyverden, Edward Shapiro, Rita Pollak, Sherri Goren –Slovin, Margaret (Peggy) Peterson, Barbara Bowe, Bonnie Waters, Nancy Brown, Jeffrey Fortang and Geraldine Hines. Conversations with Marilyn Beloff and Julie Macfarlane were very helpful as they discussed their research and unpublished works. Northeastern University, through the financial support of President Richard Freeland, and a Summer Research Stipend from Dean Emily Spieler, made it much easier for me to complete this project. Finally, I would like to thank my wife, Marilyn Braithwaite-Hall, and my children, Kiamsha, Sakile, and Rahsaan, for creating the space in our lives, and making countless sacrifices, which allowed me to devote immeasurable time to this project. Their love, patience, and understanding consistently nurture my river.

Introduction

The picture of the Grand Teton Mountains which appears on the cover of this book embodies the essence and purpose of this journey upon which you are about to embark. Lying in the shadows of these great mountains is a winding river that quietly and majestically flows into some unknown and endless source. The light from the sun at the summit of the mountain shines brilliantly upon the river, giving it new life as it alters and enhances the surrounding terrain. This picture was given to me by a former law student and friend during a challenging time in my life when I had lost my light and my way. Mounted on my wall, the picture served as a constant source of inspiration. Its majesty reminded me of the majesty that dwells within us all, and confirmed for me that I needed to return to the source and power of my own river. Many years later while I was serving as Dean of Northeastern University School of Law, I attended a development conference that was held at the foot of the Grand Tetons. These majestic mountains were more compelling in life than they were in the picture. Though I never saw the winding river on that trip, I had long rediscovered the one that flowed through me. The sun had given new life to my river, and its flow gave me a deeper appreciation of the journey of life. It is because of this river and that journey that I must share this gift with the profession that has given so much to me.

There are many lawyers and clients who feel that the legal profession has lost its way, and lost sight of its majestic mountains and sacred rivers. Lawyers who practice in the trenches of conflict and pain each day are rarely inspired by the majesty of what they do, and aren't often replenished by the sources of power that flow through them. It is my fondest hope that this book will point the way for those who may be lost,

2

inspire those who may be weary, and nurture the sacred rivers that quietly lie in the shadows of the legal profession.

I wrote this book because I deeply believe that these ideas and thoughts are on the minds of many lawyers, law professors and students. On these plain pages are glimpses of the work and yearnings of those who live their lives and conduct their practices and classrooms according to deep spiritual values. Their work and their lives stand as natural reservoirs of hope in desert places. Yet I also wrote this book for those who have distanced themselves from spiritual realities and who feel that there is no room in their practice or lives for this kind of thinking. These rivers of ideas and inspirations are offered with the hope that they will help all lawyers, judges, law professors and students obtain a deeper understanding of our calling within this profession. I also hope that clients and others who encounter lawyers on a regular basis will engage these ideas, for many of the limitations that lawyers impose upon themselves are a product of client expectations. If clients expect lawyers to be narrow- minded, emotionally distant, and to operate as hired guns, then that is frequently the type of person that materializes. Yet, if clients desire and expect caring, sensitive, and thoughtful advocates and counselors who can think with their heads and their hearts, then their yearnings and demands can help usher into existence this new reality.

There are no new major theories or critiques lurking in these pages. There are numerous texts on the religious foundations of law and legal systems. It is not my intent to critique or build on those approaches. This is not an historical analysis of the "theological sources of Western legal tradition," or a critique of how ecclesiastical courts and secular courts originated, overlapped, merged, separated, and yet continued to influence each other. That work has already been eloquently and persuasively done.[1] This is certainly not a call for the reunification of secular courts and religious doctrines. Nor is it an analysis of black letter law encased in religious dogma, standards and scripture. This is an attempt to demonstrate that there is a deep spiritual dimension to the study and practice of law, and to the administration of justice. Our failure to systematically explore and embrace this dimension has had negative consequences for the profession and for those who interface with it. If spiritual insights and developments can offer guidance to other aspects of our lives, then they also can provide lawyers with additional tools and perspectives as we traverse the difficult terrain of law and legal processes.

Some of what you will discover here are insights that have been recorded and embraced by other writers. Yet these insights have not been consistently and systematically applied to the legal profession. So this journey you are about to undertake is a journey of heart and soul, more than it is of the mind. It is a journey of what we know and feel, and a demonstration of our faith in those things we cannot fully explain. I have tried to capture the ideas and issues that I believe those of us in the legal profession need to discuss, and the spirit that we need to embrace. I have tried to weave within these lines a spirit of hope, inspiration and endless possibilities. These are the wings upon which this profession can take flight and soar to new heights.

There are no simple answers to what ails the legal profession. The challenges we face are as varied as the people

4

who practice this craft, and include growing dissatisfaction within the profession, countless ethical violations, and a negative public perception. This book alone cannot address all the challenges and dilemmas that confront us and negatively affect those whom we serve. Hopefully, it will point us in a different direction which has been staring us in the face for years, but is generally overlooked and dismissed. This different path, which many among us are already exploring, will inevitably lead us back to ourselves. It is so easy for lawyers and law professors to externalize the problems that challenge the profession. We feel more comfortable laying the blame at the doorsteps of our institutions, our managers or deans, or with the system in general. Yet every member of this profession has a responsibility to save it from our inadequacies and indifferences, and make it better for future generations.

This book is not intended to be a scathing critique of the legal profession, nor is it an opportunity to air our dirty laundry in public. This is a spiritual love story about law and the role it plays, and can play, in our lives and this society. It is as much a reflection of our beauty as it is of our scars and pain. It is a passionate shout of celebration and a desperate cry for help. The legal profession needs to embrace both aspects of this dual challenge of celebration and self-correction. We must do it for ourselves, and for those who place so much trust in our hands and in our hearts.

The pages that follow contain insights that are not concrete and specific. Some of them would not hold up to scientific rigor. There is no control group that has been used to help me reach these conclusions or to make these claims. This is what I have lived, experienced and observed during my twenty-seven years as a member of this legal profession. The title of my LL.M. thesis at Harvard in 1985 was "A Holistic Model of Legal Education." Some of what I write here is influenced by ideas contained in that paper. The paper was never published, I believe, because I needed to live what I was professing before I claimed to the world that I knew what was missing from the study and practice of law. For the last twenty years I have tried to manifest through my teaching and administration the insights and values that were contained within those pages. Though my journey into this understanding is still in progress, I feel it is time for me to share more broadly these ideas and perspectives.

One notable difference between now and 1985 is the increasing presence of individuals and movements within the legal profession that are embracing perspectives similar to mine. While I certainly was not alone in 1985 in feeling that there was something missing from the structure and practice of law, I am struck by the fact that there are now so many other lawyers who are voicing their discomfort and living out their solutions. Those insightful and dedicated individuals have made it much easier for me to write this book. They are living examples of the "spiritual revitalization of the legal profession" that is the call of this book. They have tasted the bitterness of law without spirit, and have chosen to drink from a well that contains living water. I hope that what I write here not only will capture accurately these individuals and the work in which they are engaged, but also will serve to inspire others to drink from the same well.

By writing this book I have opened a dangerous door that many would prefer to keep sealed. Discussions about spirituality often appear out of place in legal circles, as they do in other parts of our public discourse. The interjection of religious themes into political elections has made many people feel more uneasy and concerned. There is the fear that religious zealots will attempt to impose their beliefs upon us, and that our struggles around political or social issues will not be decided or resolved through thoughtful and dispassionate reasoning, but through dogma and religious doctrines. This is a real and serious fear. We have seen it occur in nations and institutions for centuries. The separation of church and state within the United States Constitution is a major protection against this danger. There is also the belief and fear that discussions about spirituality will divide members of the profession, and thus we should not purposefully and openly invoke concepts that will create separations, schisms and discomfort. There are lawyers and law professors who describe themselves as secular humanists who entered the profession to care for and serve vulnerable people in society. They deeply believe that their work provides them with the greatest satisfaction and connection to others in the profession. The invocation of concepts like spirituality feels intrusive. These are valid concerns that should not be easily dismissed. Sometimes this is merely a disagreement about words and labels, while at other times it reflects serious substantive differences. There is probably nothing I can say in this introduction that will completely address the substantive differences, yet as I try to demonstrate in the book, we can avoid tripping ourselves over the words and labels. Despite the concerns that some may have with my use of the word spirituality, I believe that there is room under this broad umbrella for all who embrace the important and precious commands of this profession.

In the context of this book, spirituality is the intentional decision to search for a deeper meaning in life, and to actualize in one's life the highest values that can be humanly obtained.[2] Those values and beliefs may have their origin in religious traditions, but they also may spring from numerous other precious wells of human experience. In Chapter One I share my list of those highest values and attempt to explain their connection to the practice of law. This list is not absolute or fixed, and various lawyers will, and have, come up with different lists. Certainly this broad definition of spirituality can be twisted and manipulated to include values like greed, selfishness, domination and other negative values. Yet most would agree that the values on this latter list do not contain the highest values that the legal profession should stand for, despite the fact that some use the law to obtain these ends. So in this context, even atheist and agnostic lawyers can be spiritual if they consciously strive to "search for the sacred," and manifest in their lives and work the highest ideals of the profession and life. Though I personally live by a more specific definition of spirituality which is rooted in the Christian faith, it is not my right or intention to impose that perspective on the profession or on individual lawyers. I certainly used and heavily relied on this tradition throughout this book, but I also tried to be respectful and appreciative of various religious and non-religious approaches to spirituality.

Spirituality, as defined, described, and discussed in this book, captures the essence of what all lawyers should be striving to do. Some might argue that if the above proposition is true, then why use a word that can create such tension and resistance. The answer lies in the fact that the deeper one is willing to probe and explore this path, the more one can either grow to appreciate what it stands for, or grow to reject its meaning. One cannot get to either place without engaging the concept. To avoid using it is to succumb to the notion that there is only one way out of this conundrum, and that there is nothing for any traveler to learn on the journey. It is our willingness to engage this concept, as we have engaged other controversial subjects that divided us, that will inevitably lead to a better understanding and a more meaningful sense of oneness within the profession.

Furthermore, despite the fundamental separation between church and state contained in the Constitution, and the long line of cases that preserve this distinction,[3] no impenetrable barrier can be erected between our faiths and our civic and professional responsibilities. Spirituality and religious beliefs are fundamental parts of our social and, for many, personal reality. Some recognize and embrace it; others choose not to believe in this part of reality, or to concede that it is even a reality. Yet these beliefs or lack of beliefs do not eviscerate the existence of faith or lawyers' use of it to help make sense of their lives and their work. The law creates an artificial illusion that we can neatly separate and compartmentalize various parts of our human selves. Though we can to a certain extent, our spiritual realities will and should seep into other parts of our lives, including our professional work. What we must strive to do is find ways to live comfortably with spiritual pluralism in the same way that we struggle with cultural and political pluralism. Our reluctance to embrace this part of our reality only limits our power and ability to enhance our lives and enrich the profession of law.

As the cover picture of the Grand Teton Mountains and the Snake River reveals, I have invited nature to help me on this journey. The symbolism of rivers, mountains and stones will hopefully open doors that we find hard to crack. Buried in the structure of our lives are passageways to deeper understandings and realizations. Hidden within our surroundings and environments are keys to unfolding these passages. Nature always has been a key for unlocking these paths for me. Rivers, in particular, have always touched my soul and inspired me to look within and to appreciate more deeply the people and places that I encounter. There is something majestic and spiritual about the flow of a river. If we gaze upon it long enough, we can become one with its flow. If we are willing to place our hands or feet within its midst, we can feel its smooth serenity as it carries within an eternity of triumphs and tragedies. Not only does it provide a source of life for people, villages and cities, but it also eventually becomes a symbol of the values of the place and the people it sustains. The Nile is more than a body of water in Egypt. Historically, it became the source of life on this side of reality, and a major guide into the eternal life to come. The Jordan River is more than a historical landmark in Judaic/Christian development. It represents the struggle, triumph and spiritual power of oppressed people in their journey for liberation and salvation. The Mississippi River was not just a center of commerce and entertainment for an expanding nation; it represented the culture, music, poetry and praise of people from different backgrounds who had the common experience of the river. The Ganges River in India has a deep spiritual meaning, and in ancient south Indian literature it was described as a force which descended from heaven in order to restore life to the dead. So the river in the context of this book symbolizes the soul and spirit of the legal profession. It represents our connection to each other, and to the divine. It is that invisible, yet tangible, place that gives meaning and purpose to our lives and our work. The river with stones scattered along its bank, and mountains overshadowing its existence, creates a metaphor for understanding how the profession has nurtured its participants, and what we must do in order to discover or return to the ultimate source of law and life. Gretel Ehrlich captured this connection between the river and our spiritual quest in the following passage: "To trace the history of a river or a raindrop...is to also trace the history of the soul, the history of the mind descending and rising in the body. In both, we constantly seek and stumble upon divinity." [4] I hope to take you on a journey down a river that may or may not connect us with the divine, but hopefully will point us to the divinity that exists within us.

It is said that it is difficult to know where a river begins, and so it is with this book. We first glimpse the river moving slowly through the treacherous rapids of definitions and foundations. Chapter One, "On the Wings of Spirit," provides the traveler with a definition of spirituality, an identification of the spiritual challenges facing the legal profession, the illusions of law that entrap us, and an exegesis on the spiritual basis of law. The goal of this section is to open hearts, ease fears, and inspire tired and weary legal souls. The river widens a few miles downstream and we encounter it in full force as it gouges out steep valleys, with majestic mountains watching silently on all sides.

Chapter Two, entitled "A Search for Sacred Rivers," makes the critical distinction between the attorney's personality and the lawyer's soul. The interplay between rivers and stones become clear at this point, with stones representing the classic lawyer personality and the river serving as a metaphor for the lawyer's soul. It is also at this point that the river makes a deep and dangerous drop-off into troubled waters as it discusses lawyers in crisis. The goal of this section is not to air the dirty laundry of lawyers in public, but to indicate that it is often through dramatic personal and professional challenges that some lawyers find their way to the river. Stumbling, battered and bruised, they discover how to handle their pain, and how to deal with temptation as they strive to become and remain ethical lawyers.

Chapter Three, "Practicing Law From the River," takes us to the heart of this search. The river attempts to instruct the inquisitive lawyer about what it means to serve the whole client, embrace the challenge of leadership, and conduct one's practice in a healing manner. The practice of law begins to feel and look different at this juncture, but the stones are still there, serving to remind us of our limitations and inconsistencies, and intensifying our journey. There are no earth shattering theories buried along the riverbank, but there are some different interpretations about the lawyer's and judge's search for truth. As the river leaves the mountains and hills, more tributaries join the river, increasing the volume of water.[5] The flow is less turbulent and the river becomes more familiar now to me, and probably to all the travelers who have ever attended or taught at a law school.

Chapter Four, "Teaching to the River," provides a framework for teaching law so that it systematically nurtures the values and spiritual aspirations of students and professors.

Though this is a familiar part of the river for me, having been a law professor for over twenty-five years, there are some dangerous turns as I reveal my failures, challenges and joys in striving to teach from and to the river. As the river moves downstream the physical parameters of it change, and so do the terrains and the communities that exist on its banks. The land seems barren and desolate. The towns, or what is left of them, appear deserted and neglected. There are still people here, but the river does not provide them with the things they need to survive and prosper, or with the inspiration that they seek. Despite the depressed look of the surroundings and its inhabitants, I am confident that a great people once lived here. They thrived on the river, but for various reasons travelers, commerce and lawyers now come less frequently through their lives.

Chapter Five, "The Social Justice River," explores the challenges, obligations and joys of providing legal services to the poor. This chapter serves to remind lawyers of their legal and spiritual responsibility to serve all of those who live along the river, and those who live in abandoned valleys, isolated from the centers of commerce and business. It also identifies some of the unique challenges for those lawyers who have dedicated their lives to serving the poor. A dramatic occurrence on any river is when the streams of justice and love majestically merge into the same flow. This is the subtle warning and calling of this chapter.

There is a major fork in the river at this point, and it divides into two seemingly separate parts before plunging down a steep mountain and creating a beautiful waterfall. At the bottom of the mountain the waters come together again in order to encounter new streams of practice and overcome old obstacles and dams. Chapter Six, "New Streams and Old Dams," provides various perspectives and approaches to the practice of law that are more value-focused or spiritually centered. Under the banner of holistic forms of practice, the traveler will be exposed to collaborative law, therapeutic jurisprudence, contemplative legal practices, and restorative justice. There are dams, both man-made and natural, that must be overcome if the profession is to reach its full potential. Therefore, cherished practices and policies, such as billable hours, hiring and promotion criteria, are examined through a spiritual prism. Despite the dams, this part of the river becomes very invigorating as the discussion focuses on how various lawyers, from different religious traditions, strive to practice their faiths as they practice law. The river seems to return to its original source and takes on an ancient color and flow as it examines lawyers in sacred texts. The Torah, Talmud, Midrash, Bible, Koran and Bhagavad-Gita are examined for insights into the ancient and sacred role of lawyers, advocates, counselors and judges. This chapter ends by providing some practical steps that lawyers can take to find the river in the "courtroom of divine guidance". The power of prayers, meditation and other spiritual techniques are examined through the experiences and stories of lawyers. As the river enters the lowlands and starts to slow, more streams and bank-side vegetation develops. Numerous trees that thrive in wet conditions clutter the bank, and large rafts of water crowfoot dominate the rushing river.[6] These changes are evidence that the journey has been long and challenging, but still incomplete.

The river now moves to a point where we must temporarily get off, but the river does not stop. Just as rivers have no beginning, they have no end. "When you put your hand in a flowing stream, you touch the last that has gone before and the first of what is still to come."[7] The seventh and last chapter, "Voices From the River," is a poetic reminder of our calling as lawyers. Here the river speaks to us, in its own voice and rhythm. It is calling us to come to her majestic waters so that we can fulfill our mission in life. The river does not speak alone, for the yearning of lawyers who proceeded us are captured in these pages. With the permission of the river, they are trying one last time to help us re-imagine our lives and our work. They are trying to let us know that we have compelling work to do. They are also reminding us that as we do that work we must always be willing to invest in ourselves. The voices from the river want us to embrace the wisdom contained in the Chinese proverb that states, "The mark of a successful [person] is one that has spent the entire day on the bank of a river without feeling guilty about it." My deepest prayer for this project is that you will not feel guilty or disappointed for having spent time with me on the banks, and in the midst of this river that represents the soul of lawyers and the legal profession.

This book, through the invocation of the river, attempts to open a new passageway for lawyers, judges, law students and professors. Some will choose to bathe in and flow with the river, and others will question its existence. For those who enter, I ask that you move with your heart as well as with your head. You may find some revelations, but much of what you find will be confirmations of things you have already felt, experienced or contemplated. Even though the profession has distanced itself from the river, the river still exists within us all.

This may be a journey of uncharted waters for some, and I ask that you embrace and trust the flow. It may take you to places within yourself that have been closed for sometime. But if you are willing to touch those places again, I am confident that you will find precious gems that will help you become a better lawyer and human being. As you go on this journey with me, I ask that you travel in faith. If you already travel the path of spirit and soul, then this will be easy. If you do not, then look for the place along the river that touches you and see if it holds any meaning or insight. If not, then I still thank you for being part of a "river ancient as the world and older than the flow of human blood in human veins." [8]

Chapter One
"On the Wings of Spirit"

Spirituality

When we reflect upon the structure and nature of the legal profession, we generally focus on the concrete and tangible aspects of this reality. Many who practice law, and others who participate in its processes, are of the belief that law is a "spiritless" profession. The traditional structure and practices of both legal education and the legal profession support this belief. Though the legal profession has been blessed with gifted and sensitive individuals who nurtured and cultivated a humanistic approach to their teaching and practice, historically legal educators and practitioners have emphasized and valued rules and doctrines over feelings and emotions. The analysis of the facts from a detached and sterilized perspective was the preferred position and posture for lawyers and judges. Phenomena that could not be easily analyzed, quantified or categorized were quickly dismissed or marginalized within the profession. Therefore, to invoke the concept of spirituality in the law seems antithetical to the dominant practices and culture within law schools and the legal profession.

Spirituality is a hard concept to grasp and a controversial one to invoke. For many lawyers and legal academics it is an extremely hard concept to define and embrace within the confines of our work. We are trained to accept that which is concrete and provable. Our physical bodies we can see, our intellectual energies we can test, but our spirit or soul seems too abstract and otherworldly to spend much time debating and defending. And even if we could define them in a meaningful way, there are serious doubts about what benefits we would derive from this exploration. Despite our training, inclinations and doubts, we must begin to explore systematically and embrace these intangible aspects of our reality. For these ethereal qualities constitute the essence of our being and are symbolic of the place from which we derive our ultimate joy and power. The essence of our moral and divine nature dwells in this intangible world that we spend very little time exploring and discussing.

There is a sacred energy that dwells within these temples we call bodies. It is an integral part of our human nature that we cannot fully comprehend, but which many believe influences our decisions, choices and well-being. This spirit energy is a source for discovering and nurturing our authentic personalities. Our desires to do good things and live meaningful lives derive from and rest on the wings of this spirit energy. From this well springs our need to love and be loved; our quest to find meaning and purpose in our lives and work. Our connectedness to nature, to the past and to the future, moves through this invisible door. In ancient Kemetic traditions this spirit energy was called Maat, which embodies each person's quest for "truth, justice and righteousness."[9] It was the pursuit of these values that determined ones value on earth and in the afterlife. Yet, in carrying out our daily tasks, in striving to fulfill our professional and, sometimes, personal responsibilities, we spend little time reflecting upon and being guided by these sources. Our movements are so orchestrated by the culture of the profession and the norms of various institutions that we often cover up the real source of our joy and meaning. We tend to look for new rules and old laws to cure our professional ailments, when in reality it is our "attitudes and relationships, not rules and standards,"[10] that will have the greatest impact on the legal profession and the people it serves.

It is how we do our work and not what type of work we do, that gives the work meaning. It is not the height and breadth of the legal temples we construct that will bring justice and dignity to the people who enter, but rather the depths of the hearts and souls of those who are the caretakers and guardians of the temple. It is the spirit that we attach to the things we do, and not our spirit in isolation that brings us in compliance with our spiritual or religious commands. In the words of Rabbi Abraham Heschel, "[t]he world needs more than the secret holiness of the individual inwardness. It needs more than sacred sentiments and good intentions. God asks for the heart because He needs the lives. It is by lives that the world will be redeemed, by lives that beat in concordance with God, by deeds that outbeat the finite charity of the human heart."[11] It is the quality of our attitudes, the strength of our relationships, and the righteousness of our actions that stand the greatest chance of revitalizing the profession and making this society and the world a better place.

Yet spirituality is not a panacea for all that ails the profession. It is not an absolute insulator against unethical behavior, nor is it a prerequisite for all good deeds. There are numerous examples of religious zealots who commit horrendous crime and engage in unethical behavior, and there are various individuals who achieve the good life without directly resorting to any religious or spiritual concepts and practices. However, these extremes on the spectrum do not define and capture the reality for most individuals and for most lawyers. The overwhelming center on the spectrum encompasses those who seek to embrace and live by a set of concrete beliefs and practices in order to reach the good life, or to avoid the moral fatalities of life. It is in this large middle group wherein most lawyers fall, and where a more legally-centered definition of spirituality is needed. As indicated in the introduction, the concept of spirituality is used very broadly in the context of this book. In distinguishing spirituality from religion, some authors define it as a process of "seeking personal authenticity, genuineness and wholeness; transcending one's locus of centricity."[12] Others define spirituality as a process of "searching for the sacred, or that which is set apart from the ordinary and transcends the self." [13] Though all of the above characteristics are important to our understanding of this concept, it is this "search for the sacred" that distinguishes spirituality from other intellectual pursuits.[14]

Sacredness directs one to focus on questions of ultimate truth and meaning, the existence of a divine being, or the search for principles that transcend self.[15] Though the culture within which one exists greatly influences one's understanding of what is sacred,[16] the individual's search can have transforming effects upon the individual and the culture. This search for the sacred is critical because spirituality can be neither imposed upon a person, nor obtained without purposeful engagement. We search for many things in life, but the quest for the sacred embraces a different dimension. Just because something is important to an individual, like the practice of law or vegetarianism, does not mean that it embodies a spiritual quest, unless it also contains a search for the sacred.[17] Unless our quest to be a lawyer or a vegetarian serves as a vehicle to help us find the deeper meaning of life, or draws us closer to the divine, or helps us to see the connectedness of the universe, then it is not part of our search for the sacred, and thus is not spiritual.[18] This search for the scared contains four components which are captured in the following quote:

> First the search includes the attempt to identify what is sacred and therefore worthy of devotion or commitment. Second, searching involves the ability to articulate at least to oneself, what one has identified as sacred. Third, efforts at maintaining the sacred within the individual's religious or spiritual experience is part of that searching. Finally, the search includes how the sacred is transformed or modified through the search process itself.[19]

These four aspects of the search will serve as the contours for our exploration of spirituality within the context of the legal profession.

A major challenge of this work is to identify and articulate what is sacred within the practice and teaching of law, and to demonstrate that our quest to embrace and maintain those values will not only transform those of us who are willing to seek, but also will transform our understanding of those values. This search process is holistic in nature because it has an effect on how we feel, think and act within the world.[20] Spirituality connotes more than just an intellectual exercise of remembrance and recitation. It involves the integration of beliefs into the behavior, actions and demeanor of those who believe. Spirituality is that undetectable, yet real, place where intellect, emotions, beliefs and actions merge into a pattern of existence. It is generally believed that in order to obtain and maintain this place of wholeness, a person must engage in various practices and rituals that feed and nurture this integration. However, one's spiritual quest does not immunize one from destructive feelings and emotions. It is a state and process that assists us in making better sense of those feeling and emotions, and ultimately making better choices and rendering wiser judgments.

What is useful about the above definitional approach is that it does not attempt to restrict one to a particular set of religious practices or beliefs, but invites one to examine life, including the practice of law, from a set of sacred principles and values.[21] More importantly, this process of searching for sacred values will hopefully serve as a catalyst that will enable one to actualize those values in one's life and work. This focus on the search for the sacred emphasizes that spirituality is a fluid goal[22] that we must strive constantly to obtain, but which contains evolving levels of understanding and realization. Our paths on this search may be different, but there are these common values, principles, and insights that should be the objective of our search, and serve as the lamplights for our various paths.

What are those sacred values and principles that should be embodied in the spiritual quest of lawyers? One could argue that those values have already been identified and articulated through the American Bar Association's (ABA) Model Rules of Professional Conduct. The Model Rules embrace and highlight values like loyalty, zealousness, confidentiality, competence, avoidance of conflicts, and public service. Though these are important values, they suffer from the twin defect of being too abstract and too rule based. They are structured and conveyed as things "to do or not to do," instead of things to be or to become. The Rules are legal and aspirational in nature, but they are not inspirational in effect. They are stripped of their sacred nature because they are not positioned or intended to lead to some deep or ultimate meaning about law, life, the universe, the divine, or the person. They are regulatory, not transformative. As one scholar in the field of Professional Responsibility notes, " ...referring to lawyers' legal obligation as a matter of ethics suggest that being a good person is primarily a matter of following the legal rules. But one can be a complete sleazeball, from the standpoint of morality, and never violate a single rule in the law governing lawyers." [23]

If this observation is even partially correct, it demonstrates the clear limitation of the Rules and other existing regulatory norms, to serve as the sacred values for this profession. The spiritual quest of lawyers must embrace loftier values that must be pursued and translated into meaningful experiences. One's motivation for pursuing them must emerge from a desire to achieve higher levels of meaning in one's work, yet one's failure to obtain them must not give rise to a sanction from the Bar. These sacred values should not be codified, but must serve as the moral threads that help weave our work into a majestic quilt that can hold the needs, imperfections and dreams of our clients and ourselves. Though each of us can create a defensible list of values, I offer the following seven as the most sacred and redeeming ones for this profession. They are, *Love, Loyalty, Humility, Forgiveness, Service, Faith and Integrity.* These seven broad pillars can serve as the foundation upon which we build and revitalize this profession. They capture the essence of what we are called to do as lawyers, and contain the skills and emotions that are most needed for effective lawyering. These sacred values and principles have little meaning if all we do is declare them, or incorporate them into our personal or institutional mission statements. They reach their full spiritual potential when we internalize and actualize them in our daily work and lives. They also have limited utility if we embrace them at their abstract level without any attempt to apply them to various concrete situations. Each value provides a direct line and a meaningful connection to specific traits, skills, emotions and challenges that lawyers need and confront each day.

Love

The first value that guides us in our search for the sacred is love. From a spiritual perspective, love is a deep, abiding responsibility for the well being of another, regardless of present circumstances, conditions and feelings. Though influenced by feelings, it is not captive to emotions, but springs from a deeper well of commitment and connectedness.[24] It serves as the universal thread that binds us to each other and to the divine. Love is a value that can transcend differences, distances and doubts. Lawyers must cultivate the spirit of love because it serves as the foundation of our calling. It is only because of the existence of human needs that lawyers are necessary in society. Our ability to fully understand and address that human need depends greatly on our ability to embrace and feel connected to the person or persons in whom that need is encased. Though we are trained to commercialize that connection, and thus distance ourselves from the person and the need, it is our genuine and underlying human linkages that enable us truly to be of service to those in need, and to overcome the obstacles that try to prevent us from seeing and serving them.

Love is the source for the compassion and empathy that we need in order to be effective advocates and counselors. Though one can go through the motions of defending and advising clients without operating from this deeper place, we become much more effective when we have a genuine compassion for the work we do, the issues we confront, and the clients we serve. To perform at the pinnacle of our ability and capacity, and to gain the deepest meaning from our work, we must transcend the limits of our own experiences and needs, and touch the heart of others. We must be driven by more than financial rewards in order to achieve our deepest level of satisfaction and self- worth. We realize these experiences by focusing on this fundamental value of love, and actualizing it through our interactions with those with whom we work. This precious value which has been trivialized, maligned and exiled from legal jargon, is the source of our spiritual calling as lawyers. Without love for our work, the people we serve, and the ideals we pursue, we become automated craftspeople without a soul.

For the lawyer, love does not mean that we become so emotionally involved with our clients that we lose our objectivity or violate our professional responsibility. This is not the type of love we seek. To love spiritually gives us more objectivity and allows us to see within the person and not just get trapped by what they present. When we detach ourselves from the person, then we view them so superficially that we cannot honestly serve them. We can serve the problem they present, but not them, we can represent their interest, but we cannot represent them. It is only through the thread of love that we can touch their soul. We tell their story and provide them better counsel when we truly understand and value them. Our role as lawyers and judges, like that of the pastor, priest or rabbi, demands that we see the worth and value in all human beings. We cannot collectively afford to turn people into demons because one of us must eventually serve or defend that person. The American public was horrified by the Maryland Sniper incident in the fall of 2002. Not only were Washington, D.C. and Maryland paralyzed by fear and uncertainty, people across the country began to think twice before they went to shopping malls or stopped at gas stations. As the death toll increased, it became hard to imagine why anyone would engage in such horrible acts. Before the two persons who have now been arrested and convicted were seized, it was very easy to picture in our minds a crazed person, who was devoid of any humanity, as the perpetrator of these acts. As soon as someone real is captured, in addition to the negative things in their background and personality that fits the crime, there is always evidence and stories that point in a different direction. The same people who commit horrendous acts also engage in simple humane deeds. They have people they love, places for which they care, and hobbies they enjoy. Despite our concerted attempt to make them alien creatures who in no way resemble us, they continue to resemble and emerge as the person next door, or the person in our bedroom. Not only must we start erasing the lines that divide us from people who commit evil criminal acts, we must begin to see ourselves as potential perpetrators and victims. It is only through that lens that we may be forced to come to grips with how close we all are to the edge of destructive behavior, and how much more we need to be attentive to our spiritual health, and to that of those around us.

The sacred principle of love does not suggest that persons who have committed wrongs should not be punished for the crimes they have committed, or that they must not compensate those they have injured. Love allows us to see that they are in need of punishment, isolation, rehabilitation or some other correcting force. This is why justice stands right next to love. But the principle of justice does not absolve us of our individual responsibility to try to initiate and achieve various levels of healing within individuals and in society. Certainly those who represent individuals who have committed very heinous crimes may have a difficult time embracing this concept of love in regard to that person. Yet it is critical and essential to do so. The more we dehumanize individuals in our interactions with them, the more we contribute to our own dehumanization, and the more we feed into and contribute to their existing spiritual sickness. Love demands that we see their soul and understand that what stands before us is a polluted river that is overflowing its banks and creating chaos and destruction for all those around it. But it is still a river. It still has the potential to do all the wonderful things that rivers do. We cannot make the change

28

occur, for the river has free will. But we must refrain from polluting it more by treating these persons as if they had no soul. We can contribute to the clean up, to the healing, by pouring our love into it. Love is a powerful purifying agent. It does not work well if a person is not receptive, but each drop opens up another possibility for change.

Even the legal system's most revered goal of justice emerges in large part from this sacred value of love. Robert Solomon in his provocative book, *A Passion for Justice,*[25] argues very persuasively that justice is a natural emotion that emerges out of our engagement with the world. Instead of seeing justice as an artificial, theoretical concept, or as a rationale for punishment, he urges us to understand it as an instinctive emotion that originates from our heart. What feelings emerge from the heart are not just compassion and care, but anger, resentment, and a desire for revenge. Solomon remind us that,

> Our knowledge of justice begins with our experience of our own place in the world; our sense of justice is first of all our emotional response to a world that does not always meet up with our expectations and demands. Our sense of justice, in other words, has its origins in such emotions as resentment, jealousy, outrage, and revenge as well as in care and compassion[26]

But these negative feelings of justice come into existence only because something, or someone, we love has been violated. One of the benefits of our spiritual quest as lawyers, and as human beings, is that it can curtail and contain our negative emotions for justice. Even though the justice feelings of anger, resentment and revenge are certainly understandable and serve a useful role in our human development, they should not serve as the motivating force for the work of lawyers in society. Our quest for justice, which springs from the value of love, must ceaselessly follow this path and return to that ultimate source. If we embrace or ascribe to the vengeance motivation that our clients and others possess, then we cannot fully serve them, or the system that we are sworn to uphold. Our challenge as lawyers is to steer the quest for justice down its highest and noblest path. We are limited in our ability to do this when we are not in search of the sacred principle of love, and able to manifest it in perplexing and horrendous situations. Even when our client's loved ones have been murdered or abducted, we must engage them and the opposite side from a place of love, and we must steer our search for justice down a path that attempts to bring our highest ideals to the forefront.

Some lawyers have interpreted the professional obligation of zealous representation as a command to embrace whatever feelings and emotions the client possesses or wants exhibited. They therefore engage in trial practices, or assume negotiation postures, that are intended to humiliate, intimidate and demean opposing counsel and others. Yet zealous representation is not the antithesis of love, but a command to love. We must cultivate a deep understanding and compassion for our clients in order to zealously represent them. That care and compassion does not release us from our obligation to also deeply respect those who are engaged in this process, even those on the other side. Nor does it mean that we overlook the flaws in our clients' characters, or in some cases, the reprehensible things they may have done. But we must not allow these factors to cloud our view of the work we have agreed to undertake. From the mountaintop of this sacred value, we will find a way to see the problem and the person for who and what they are, and not from some imaginary and idealized perspective. What we will generally see are people drawn toward war, but really in need of peace. Our task, as unpleasant as it may seem, is to be peacemakers[27] in a society and world where too many people are inclined toward war. The wars we must primarily avert are those aimed at destroying the dignity, respect, and spirit of those with whom we have disputes. These wars are conducted with weapons of words, attitudes of disdain, and actions of anger. Though all of these emotions have their place in our lives and work, they should not govern our profession.

Professor Anthony Kronman argues that what is most missing from contemporary lawyers is a deep sense of "practical wisdom."[28] He posits that lawyers have lost the intuitive ability to make sound judgment and good choices for their clients and themselves. If Kronman is right, the answer will not come from experience or intellectual inquiry alone. Wisdom is one of those intangible attributes that cannot be quantified or taught, but we know it when we hear and experience it. Various ancient scriptures[29] suggest that wisdom is a virtue that resides in the heart. When our hearts are cluttered with anger, vengeance, contempt and resentment, then we cannot find the door to our chambers of wisdom. We remain trapped in ideas, theories and facts that keep us from finding practical solutions to complex problems. Love, in its most elevated state, nurtures the heart, releases its shackles, and opens the passageway to wisdom. Certainly our intellectual mastery of various areas of law and aspects of life contributes greatly to our ability to make sound judgments, but we cannot reach this exalted state of wisdom through our intellect alone. We cannot be the type of lawyers our clients and society deserve if we are not able to bring an abundant source of wisdom to our work and to our clients' hearts.

Love is also essential for lawyers because it serves to remind us of the need to care for ourselves. In a profession that demands so much from its participants, it is important that lawyers create the space, and more importantly, the state of mind that encourage us to value and care for ourselves. Love is an outward and inward looking value. Just as we must demonstrate love for our work and clients, we must also display it towards ourselves. When we are not anchored in a pure love that also embraces our genuine needs, then it is easy to overwork and adopt negative coping mechanisms. Not only is this destructive for the lawyer, but also ultimately not beneficial to the client. To usher wholeness into the world, to seek justice wherever it may be hidden, to help heal broken people and broken arrangements and relationships, we must always strive to be whole and healed. Love is the elixir that prepares us to embrace our roles and usher these qualities into the world.

Loyalty

Loyalty is one of the most obvious and readily acceptable values for lawyers. The ABA Model Rules of Professional Conduct embody this value in many of its rules and cannons. At the core of the lawyer-client relationship is a sacred sense of loyalty that the lawyer has to the client. This value permits a lawyer to safeguard secrets and confidences of the client, even when the client admits that he or she has committed a crime.

Loyalty is also at the heart of the conflict rules that are so fundamental to professional ethics. A lawyer is often precluded from suing present and former clients because of this value of loyalty. There are times when a lawyer is precluded from even taking positions that are contrary to the interest of a present or former client. This loyalty value is so strong and pervasive that it may even affect other lawyers within a firm by preventing them from representing individuals who have interests that are contrary to those of a present or former client of a member of the firm.

Despite the sanctity of the loyalty that a lawyer has to a client, there is another aspect of this value that contravenes the interest of the client. The profession and society demand a sense of loyalty from lawyers as well. The confidences and secrets of a client can be revealed when the lawyer is aware that the client intends to engage in an act that could result in bodily harm or death to a third party. Though the lawyer may not even know the person, she has a duty of loyalty to that person's welfare and safety. In addition, the lawyer owes another duty of loyalty to the court. This duty precludes the lawyer from purposely misleading the court, or withholding legal opinions that are relevant to the case, even when those cases are contrary to the position of her client. Though it exists to a lesser extent, there is even a duty of loyalty among and between lawyers that serves as the basis for civility, courtesy and respect. In effect, one could argue that of all the values lawyers are asked to undertake, loyalty is one of the most compelling and pervasive.

From a spiritual perspective loyalty finds its roots in a deeper and more intimate source that extends beyond the confines of the rules of professional conduct. Loyalty in its purest sense is ultimately a deep understanding and commitment to a set of values, principles or ideals. Though those ideals can be embodied in a state, system or institution, they must originate from a more intimate source and place, and for lawyers – like all human beings – loyalty is born inside one's heart and soul. It comes to birth through our ability to embrace and reject values and experiences that occurred in the family, religious institutions, communities, educational institutions, and other socializing processes. Through this process of acceptance and rejection, we develop a sense of loyalty to a certain set of values and to ourselves. It is our ability to "articulate and commit" to these values that gives us a sense of who we are and how we want to live our lives. It is upon this foundation that our professional loyalties must rest. Without this foundation professional loyalties can become twisted and manipulated, and so can we. The more intimate one is with a set of ideals or with a person, the greater the chances are that one will be loyal to that person and to those ideals. What most lawyers need in order to steadfastly comply with the rules of professional conduct is to have a sense of loyalty, before they ever become lawyers, to a set of values that give their lives meaning and purpose. This loyalty is not abstract in the sense that one takes a pledge of allegiance on certain occasions. This loyalty must be a daily encounter and reflection about what is important to the inner soul of the person. It invites us on a journey to the source of our strength on regular basis. In essence, it must be a "lived experience," where each lawyer has a loyalty to the constant search for sacred rivers. For it is only at this level that it becomes easier to reconcile the various forms of loyalty that one must have as a lawyer and those that one must have as a human being. So, in addition to the lawyer's loyalty to clients, courts and society, there must be a deeper sense of loyalty to oneself and to the source of one's strength.

Humility

Humility is the third spiritual value that lawyers must seek, embrace and manifest in our lives and work. It may be the hardest one for some lawyers and law professors to perfect. We are trained to know the right answers and we get paid, sometimes very lucratively, because we hold ourselves out as experts in particular fields, or in regard to certain procedures or processes. A strong part of the legal culture rewards people who can take positions and persuasively defend them to the end. So much of what we teach our students in law school focuses on how to find weaknesses in other people's positions and arguments. This is an essential part of the craft and no one would dare suggest that it has no utility. However, this useful trait, combined with our confident posture, has developed into an unhealthy disease of arrogance. As with all diseases, everyone in the profession is certainly not infected, but the virus is definitely alive and dangerously contagious. There is a high cost associated with this professional illness. It sometimes stands in the way of our resolving disputes in a timely, efficient and constructive manner. It feeds into the poor image that the public has about lawyers, and it probably diminishes some of the respect that some members have for their colleagues. Opposing counsel, judges, and certainly clients are the frequent victims of this overbearing and haughty viral disposition. This problem exists in the legal academy as well as in practice and has been described by one law professor in the following manner: "The complaint is simple: we know less than we claim to know, and we are not as smart as we claim to be. Our theories may be beautiful things to behold..., but they tend to ignore a great deal of messy reality-especially the reality of our own limits." [30] Though it may not cure all that ails us, the antidote for our destructive arrogance is a regular dose of humility.

Humility does not necessitate that we forsake our positions or beliefs, but it does serve as a constant reminder that there are other positions and beliefs that may be as worthy, or better, than ours. It asks that we examine ourselves before blaming others for our failures or those in society. Like love, it grows out of a deep spiritual well that links us to others, and reminds us to respect human beings regardless of their station in life. It demands that we search for and touch the nuances of life's situations, as much as we look for the bright, clear lines. Humility speaks to the lawyer's urgency to reach conclusions and places of finality by urging us to suspend judgments of people, situations and events until we have all the facts and perspectives in front of us. And even then, because we realize that we will never have "all the facts and perspectives," we must proceed with a sense of caution and reticence because there is still much truth to be revealed to us on this journey. This does not imply that lawyers should not make decisions or propose solutions to pressing problems. It only means that we should be reluctant to believe that our answers are fixed and absolute.

Professor William Stuntz captures this aspect of humility when he states, "[h]umility does not counsel inaction, and it is not a posture of indifference. Rather, humility always sees the possibility of its own mistakes. That implies not blindness to errors and injustices that attend the status quo, but awareness that proposed solutions must be tentative, subject to revision as experience dictates."[31] When we embrace the spirit of humility in the teaching and practice of law, we open the heavenly gates of creativity, and we usher in the desperately needed balms of respect, patience and understanding that our students, clients and colleagues deserve and desire. We also create a model and standard that this divisive and conflicted world desperately needs. If lawyers are to be leaders in the society and the world, we must lead in regards to how we approach and resolve conflicts. We must lead in demonstrating that people with vastly different religious, political, racial, gender and sexual perspectives can live and work together. Humility is one of our greatest tools in this leadership role.

Forgiveness

Forgiveness seems like an inappropriate value for lawyers to embrace and pursue. Forgiveness conjures up feelings and images of weakness, spineless self-indulgence and religious repentance. Yet many times it is the lawyer's inability to forgive and understand the power of forgiveness that impedes our success and the fulfillment of our ultimate role. Forgiveness is not a sign of weakness for the lawyer or the client she represents. To the contrary, it is a powerful door that opens up avenues of escape from the vicious cycles of destructive behavior and feelings. It is the fuel that empowers reconciliation and restorative justice. There are various definitions of forgiveness and scholars have debated and elaborated on the numerous descriptions of this concept.[32] I am drawn to the Hebrew word "salach" for forgiveness, which means "to let go,"[33] and thus captures the essence of why this value is so important to lawyers. A lawyer cannot be a healer [34] if she does not possess a profound and deep understanding of the power and importance of "letting go." If lawyers are to help resolve conflicts, disputes and impasses, many of which have deep emotional components, then we must embody and reflect the spirit of forgiveness. But if we have not experienced or witnessed this transformative process in our own lives, then it is difficult to assist or lead our clients to this place.

Sometimes conflicts are not resolved because the client has not "let go" of the hurt, pain or disappointment of the violation or incident. Sometimes conflicts are resolved in form, but the deep underlying harm and injury has never been properly addressed or healed. Forgiveness is the balm that aids in this healing process and serves as a catalyst for breaking through impasses and conceptual barriers. It is also a catalyst for our creative energies. Hidden behind frozen emotions and unrelenting positions, are creative solutions to difficult problems. Our reluctance to "let go" inhibits our ability to think creatively or to structure novel arrangements. To embrace or hold on to the hurt and pain puts the client and the lawyer in a box, when what is needed is "out of the box" thinking and strategizing. To forgive is to release within the universe, and within us, creative juices that spawn effective and innovative solutions to intractable problems.

To forgive or to pursue the spirit of forgiveness in our practice does not mean that we do not hold individuals accountable for their wrongs. Nor does it mean that we remain in, or return to, relationships or business arrangements that are destructive or unproductive. It is the moral and emotional burdens that come along with the violation or breach that must be released. Too often in legal disputes we are not only seeking justice, but we are also seeking moral condemnation and emotional superiority. Though these attributes are normal and certainly to be expected in some situations, they are generally counter-productive in the overall scheme of the case, and in the ultimate health and development of the parties involved. Yet it is very easy for legal advocates to use these tools as levers to achieve their goals or secure a lucrative judgment. Without a doubt, we are charged to accurately and eloquently describe the pain and suffering that our clients have endured because of a violation or breach, but to adequately represent our clients does not demand that we feed into their emotional frigidity for the duration of our relationship with them. In addition to helping them solve the problem, we also must strive to assist them in "letting go" of the hurt and thawing out the frozen positions they carried with them when they first entered our office. For the real power that others have over us is the emotional prison that their actions have invited us to enter. It is natural and normal for us to enter, but it is dangerous and destructive for us to remain there. And from a spiritual perspective, it is unprofessional for lawyers to encourage their clients to remain imprisoned in unhealthy emotional states. This process of "letting go" is a delicate, sensitive, and sometimes slow, emotional and spiritual journey. In order for lawyers to be able to recommend this process of letting go to their clients, they must have experienced and practiced it themselves. Lawyers need this value for themselves as much as they need it for their clients. In our interactions with other attorneys, judges and those with whom we work, we carry around unhealed wounds, unresolved conflicts and disappointments that we encountered long ago. Our vision, professional judgment, and effectiveness are blurred by our inability to release these emotional burdens. A major part of our spiritual quest is to constantly "let go" and cleanse our emotional and spiritual river of those things that pollute and obstruct our ability to fulfill our calling.

Service

Service is a concept and value that lawyers can easily embrace. We readily understand that we are part of a service profession, as opposed to the producer of goods and products. However, in this spiritual context, service is not about what we do but how we do it, and the attitude, values and perspectives we embrace and manifest in the process of our work. It suggests that we are to put the welfare of others before our own. Our reason for being in the role of lawyer is to give of ourselves for the advancement of the client's case and the overall system of law. We must not see our skills and talents as merely revenue enhancing instruments that only serve our selfish desires, but as blessings that we are asked to bestow upon those in need who enter our space. There is a spirit of humility that comes with this value of service. Though we are trained to master concepts, processes and procedures, we must stay in touch with the limits of our own ability and insights. More importantly, we must understand that our abilities and insights do not make us morally superior to those we serve or those we encounter on the street.

This service principle also provides a foundation for the lawyer's pro bono obligation. The services that we dispense as part of this profession are not luxury items that should only be available to those who can afford them. When we take the lawyer's oath, we are agreeing to help ensure that the doors to justice remain open for all in need, regardless of their circumstances or ability to pay. So service in the context of this profession means that some of our talents, skills and abilities should be given away. This is not a choice, like charity, but a moral command that arises from the essential nature of the legal system. We can certainly choose to ignore the command, since no bar association has yet been willing to make this a mandatory rule,[35] but we cannot eviscerate this obligation of its moral power over us. The more we embrace this command, the more we find the true meaning of this calling and find more satisfaction in the work we do. One of the highest spiritual callings is to be of service to those who are in need, but who cannot compensate us for the services we provide.[36] It is at this intersection of genuine need and manifested love that service is born. The more we reside at this divine junction, the more we escape the shackles of selfishness and greed, and the more we experience a blissful joy of meaning and purpose.

Faith

Faith is another critical value in the lawyer's quest for the sacred. It is so critical to our understanding of spirituality that there is an entire section in the book devoted to this concept.[37] Much of the work lawyers do demands that we operate without having all of the facts or information about a case at our disposal. Despite voluminous case law and legal theories that have been developed and recorded, legal processes and decision-making are not an exact science. Therefore lawyers frequently find themselves operating in the dark. For some, this flexibility, discretion and unpredictability leads to a deep sense of cynicism about the process and about law in general. Law and legal processes become a game and winning becomes the overriding goal. Faith in this context becomes a nice platitude that is used by lawyers and clients to reinforce the rightness of their cause or case. The common statement, "I have faith in the judicial system," usually means that the individuals received a favorable verdict, or is a precursor of their intention to appeal the decision. This use and understanding of faith captures only a small portion of the power and necessity of this value to lawyers and the legal profession. Faith, in its deepest and most meaningful sense, involves a sincere and secure belief in the ultimate goodness within the universe and people, and in our ability to make a difference in the world. For lawyers it means a rejection of the cynicism that pervades the profession, and the resurrection of our individual responsibility to change the situations we encounter. To have faith in our clients' ability to benefit from their interactions with us cannot be determined by whether they win or lose. We must begin to believe in them as much as we believe in their case. Having faith in them does not mean that we become naïve and ignore their limitations and weaknesses. It only means that we should not hold them prisoner to those limitations and weaknesses. To have this level of faith requires that we bring more of ourselves to the process, and that we transform sterile business encounters into life affirming relationships. When lawyers operate from this place of faith, it increases the possibility that they will receive more satisfaction from their work.

Faith also becomes the source for creating an island of peace in the midst of this stressful and demanding profession. So much of the stress and depression that lawyers suffer from is born in the fear, anxiety and pressure that they carry around with them each day. The doubts about outcomes, self-worth, control and advancement manifest themselves in subtle, yet harmful ways. Mark Perlmutter in his revealing book, *Why Lawyers (and the Rest of Us) Lie and Engage in Other*

42

Repugnant Behaviors, argues that fear is the cause of so many of the negative characteristics of lawyers. He states, "...lying in litigation arises out of fear. Whether it's fear of humiliation, losing, economic loss, ostracism by our peers, or whatever else, if we didn't fear some consequences of telling the truth, we'd have no need to lie."[38] This fear is not limited to litigation, but is pervasive in the profession and within lawyers. It forces many to do things that they know are inconsistent with their own values and that of the profession. But fear can be so paralyzing at times that even the most gifted lawyers succumb to its power and pull. Perlmutter offers "courage" as the answer to this pervasive and debilitating force within lawyers and others.[39] He demonstrates through actual cases, studies and personal experiences that courage provides numerous benefits for the lawyer who has to confront conflicts on a continuous basis. Courage provides strength in conflict,[40] prevents future conflicts, [41] produces more satisfying results,[42] reduces the cost of conflicts,[43] enhances one's competence and health,[44] brings people closer, and preserves relationships.[45]

Though Perlmutter's definition of courage is both broad and insightful,[46] faith is a more accurate description of the remedy for this disease of fear that plagues the mind and heart of this profession. Courage is an attribute or by-product of faith. Courage is a choice or act; faith is a state of being in the world and a way of perceiving and understanding one's self and life. When we live our lives from a place of faith and nurture it on a daily basis, then we are able to summon courage in moments of internal weaknesses and conflicts, and against strong external oppositions. Lawyers certainly need to be courageous in order to perform their jobs effectively, but faith transcends courage. Faith provides a daily reminder that the source from which our work and calling emerges is pure and divine. It helps us to remember the power contained in the old adage, "Lord give me the strength to accept the things I can't change, the power to change the things I can, and the wisdom to know the difference."[47] To internalize this value places lawyers on a different course of interaction with themselves and with those around them. This new course, called faith, empowers us not just to believe in the legal system, but to believe in the spirit and power of sacred values to prevail over earthly fears. Faith frees us from the prisons erected through our fears of losing, leaving, and not being accepted. It beckons us to look for victories not just in outcomes, but in every interaction. It allows us to serve our clients and society better, because we are in touch with our authentic selves and the authentic purpose of law to ensure that justice prevails in the world.

Integrity

Integrity is essential to the legal profession because so much trust is given to lawyers and judges. This final value contains not only the power to help us live up to the commands contained in the Code of Professional Responsibility, but also compels us to consistently reflect a high level of honesty, dependability and respect in all our affairs and responsibilities. Integrity connotes a sense of wholeness within us and in regard to our relationship with others. This abstract and misunderstood value directs us to be clear about, and consistent with, the values that serve as the anchors for our lives and work. When we live with irreconcilable loyalties, conflicting interests and a fractured sense of self-worth, then we become vulnerable to ethical violations and moments of self-delusion. To remain whole and grounded in this value usually requires more than just our awareness and familiarity with the rules of professional conduct. Integrity does not just require compliance with the letter of the law, but demands that we relentlessly pursue the noblest spirit of the profession. Integrity is also important because it serves as the best and ultimate source of the lawyer's quest for excellence. Though financial compensation, bonuses and promotions are important incentives for our work, the most reliable motivation for our excellence is a deep commitment to internal values. Having internalized a spirit of excellence because it reflects something about who and what we are, we continue to visit this source because it reinforces our sense of self and nurtures that place of wholeness. We visit the source not just to receive external rewards, though they are important, but because we have developed a standard that gives shape and substance to our character. This standard is not a pedestal from which we judge others, but a quiet, reaffirming place from which we assess and motivate ourselves. Integrity is like a sacred blanket within which we wrap our talents, skills and ambitions. Our talents, skills and all of the preceding spiritual values, which the world can easily manipulate and exploit, must be safeguarded from the piercing winds of life. When we take the time daily to reflect on our values and practice them in our lives, we are choosing and weaving the threads that will eventually become a hallowed blanket that others will call our integrity

Though there are many other values that contribute to us living a spiritually-centered life, these seven cornerstones of *love, loyalty, humility, forgiveness, service, faith* and *integrity* capture so much of the essential purpose and calling of the enlightened lawyer. If we could pursue, embrace, and actualize these values in our daily living and practice, we could transform this profession. Many of the challenges and crises that the profession faces[48] are a direct outgrowth of the absence, or minimal presence, of these values. These values help to form and give shape to the river that flows majestically through our lives, and beckons us on a daily basis. Though these values, with the exception of faith, are not discussed separately again in this book they are embedded within the flow of the river, and you will see and hear them as you traverse its rapids. Unfortunately, too many lawyers do not see or hear this river. The walls we have erected around the profession block out its flow and sound. For some, this is acceptable because they genuinely believe that certain aspects of the river are inconsistent with the structure and best practices of the profession. Some lawyers bathe in the river as part of their religious tradition, but are unable or unwilling to allow it to flow into their professional lives. Yet scattered throughout the legal profession are lawyers who not only have torn down the walls that block the river, but also have placed their lives and practices within the midst of its flow. They bathe in it each day. They are subject to its turbulent and swift currents, and are blessed by its rejuvenating and deep presence in their lives. It is their work and journey that will ultimately help to fertilize the banks of this profession.

These lawyers discover and stay connected to the river through various paths. Prayer, meditation, reading, conversation, walks in nature, religious rituals and ceremonies are a few of the practices that lead them to their source of internal power. They have discovered that in order to utilize this internal power, they must pursue it consistently and earnestly. Spirituality is not something that we can just declare, it is something we must practice. Even when we believe deeply in the values listed above, which provide the contours of a lawyer's spiritual quest, we may not be able to manifest them in our lives and work without some process that keeps us focused on them. Just as we must practice the piano daily if we want to master this beautiful instrument, we must seek the river daily if we want to bring its beauty and power to bear in our daily affairs. We must search for it with a sincere heart and a reverent spirit. We must not frantically pursue it because haste does not reveal the essence of the river, which is the essence of our soul. In a sacred text we are reminded that "in your patience possess ye your souls." [49] These spiritual practices reveal our power in incremental, gradual stages. If we are not willing or able to quiet ourselves then we will drown out the sound of the river.

One of the main benefits of pursuing paths that enable us to actualize our spiritual quest is the peace and calm that it brings. There is a peaceful and reassuring energy that emerges from the river. It is a slow moving river that invites and produces slow moving human vessels. It is a meandering stream of life that naturally navigates towards calm winds. The hectic pace of the legal profession can easily draw us away from our personal sources of power and authenticity. We often fail to notice the gems of insight and wisdom that dwell inside and around us because we have conditioned ourselves to overlook these simple, yet profound aspects of life. But if we are truly patient with ourselves and others, and consistently seek love, loyalty, humility, forgiveness, service, faith, and integrity in our lives, we will find the river flowing inside, and we will better detect its movement in others. Patience does not mean that we should not work hard or be demanding of others and ourselves. But our hard work and our demands must emanate from a place of love and respect, and not from a place of contempt and judgment. The river does not judge, and cannot be judged.

Spiritual Resistance

I am very much aware that there is great resistance among lawyers and legal academics to the insertion of spirituality into discussions about law and the legal profession. This resistance stems from various sources and legitimate concerns that must be addressed. Many believe that the walls which separate law and spirit should remain because our profession, like the state, should be free of any hints of religion, divinity or spirituality. I deeply respect that position, and the concerns and the dangers that it is intended to avoid. There is tremendous harm to the society when we try to impose religious or spiritual beliefs on free minds. But I am also aware of the harm that these walls have created inside of us and within the profession. One of the greatest challenges facing the profession is how to engage each other respectfully in meaningful discussions about the spiritual needs of the members of this profession. Just as we grapple with other sensitive and uncomfortable concepts such as race, gender, sexuality and politics, we must open our minds and hearts to this new area of exploration. This quest to explore the intersections of law and spirituality is not driven by a need to interject religious dogma and doctrines into the practice of law. Nor is it intended to justify political actions and decisions with divine interpretations and rationales. This quest is intended to recognize the benefits of the spiritual power and potential that lies within us, because as lawyers we cannot heal if we are broken.

48

There are others who are genuinely offended by the interjection of spirituality into the practice of law because they intellectually do not believe in, or accept the notion of God, religion or a higher consciousness. They fear that the inclusion of the concept is a subversive attempt to insert a dogmatic set of beliefs that will influence policies and decisions. Though history provides enormous evidence to justify and support this fear, it is not the real intent of the river. Spirituality and religion as offered and understood here, should not be used as a club to hold over the heads of those who do not believe, or who do not embrace a particular faith tradition.[50] Spirituality, in its purest sense, is a mirror that points always at the persons holding it, challenging them to live at their highest level of existence, and urging them to love that which exists on the other side of the mirror. Though this has not always been the way many have embraced their religious beliefs, it is certainly the way in which this quest for spirituality within the legal profession should proceed. Other lawyers are skeptical about any claims of progress or advancement through spirituality because they are keenly aware of how much destruction and evil has been done under this banner. Martin Buber eloquently captured this type of resistance towards spirituality on the part of many young people. He wrote;

> It is not difficult to comprehend why many now guard themselves against having faith or confidence in the spirit. For during the past decades the race of man has not, by and large, fared well at the hands of the spirit. For the spirit was not simply silent; it spoke falsely at junctures when it should have had an important voice in history, when it should have told the truth about what was being done or not being done to those who

were making history. On frequent occasions the spirit consented to be a tool when it should have acted on its own capacity of judge and censor. Then again, it has repeatedly retired to a magnificent isolated kingdom of its own, poised high above the world in the realm of circling ideas. Whenever the spirit has done so, it has sacrificed the very factor which makes it legitimate, particularly in crises: its readiness to expose itself to reality, to prove and express itself in reality.[51]

However, the past misuses, abuses or inactions do not subvert the inherent worth or potential of this sacred aspect of reality. They just stand as sobering reminders that spirituality, like a river, can be used for both constructive and destructive ends. So much depends on how man and woman see and embrace it, and how much we are really willing to pay the price that our spirituality extracts. When the river overflows its banks and brings destruction to a town and its residents, we do not blame or reject the river. We try to create better safeguards for the next unfortunate occurrence. To eliminate the force that unfortunately brings about the destructive nature of the river would also eliminate the force that brings the joy, life and peace of the river. In harnessing its power, we expose ourselves to its dangers. As long as the river is carved through land, it will have the potential to bring harm to those who live along its banks. Similarly, as long as the spirit is encased in human flesh it will have the potential and tendency to do harm. That is not a reason to reject it, just a reminder to handle it with care, and never lose sight of both aspects of human nature. There is no immunity or waiver for those who seek to live a spiritual life. It is how we respond in difficult and challenging situations that will give legitimacy to our claim, or feed into the resistance and healthy skepticism that many already possess.

There are many lawyers who are sincere believers in various faith traditions, but are hesitant to engage other lawyers about their beliefs or perspectives. They fear that they will be labeled as "weak," "flaky," or just "different" in an environment where they are striving to be accepted and taken seriously. This is especially difficult for young lawyers who are wrestling with issues of belonging and success. There is the classic concern that if they voice their spiritual or religious beliefs, however mildly, they will be viewed or accused of trying to proselytize and convert others in the office. Some progressive Christian lawyers often hide their religious beliefs because they fear that they will be labeled as a conservative, due to the prominence of conservative Christians in the public media, especially around controversial topics. Some conservative Christian lawyers remain silent about their faith because of the perceived liberal leanings of the legal profession. Likewise, some Jewish and Islamic lawyers feel silenced because they believe that their religious beliefs are still viewed as "alien" in this Christian dominated culture. Though many institutions, especially legal educational institutions, have gone a long way in recognizing and respecting various religious holidays and observances, there is still an implicit agreement that there is an invisible, but constant, line that must not be crossed. For those lawyers who label themselves as "spiritual, but not religious," this topic can make them feel uncomfortable, or even insecure, since so many people interpret spirituality through a religious lens. For some lawyers spirituality and religion are synonymous, but for others they mean very different things. And even within various religious traditions there are numerous denominations, perspectives and sects. This lack of a common language and definition silences many who would otherwise prefer to engage their colleagues in these challenging, but meaningful explorations. So instead of trying to make sense out of this diversity, and sometimes confusion, many choose to remain silent or agnostic.

All of these resistances, concerns and barriers are real, and should not be discarded or minimized.[52] Yet none of them are dispositive of the issue. Unfortunately, we have accepted them as insurmountable obstacles that cannot be overcome. Many of them exist because we have not taken the time to have a direct and informed approach to the matter. Other professions have been willing to embrace these concerns head on and have made important advances in their understanding and inclusion of spirituality within their fields. For example, within the medical profession there is a growing appreciation of the role that spirituality and religion play in the health of patients. Much of this advancement and acceptance by physicians is due to the overwhelming empirical evidence of the benefits of this phenomenon to the overall health of patients. As one medical scholar observed:

> A recent review of more than 1,200 studies of religion and health reported that at least two thirds of the studies evaluated had shown significant associations between religious activity and better mental health, better physical health or lower use of health services.[53]

The fact that polls taken in the last few years indicate that 95 percent of Americans believe in God; that 94 percent of patients admitted to hospitals indicate that their spiritual health is as important as their physical health; and 77 percent also want their doctors to consider issues of spirituality in their care,[54] has forced many physicians to take a serious look at the role of spirituality and religion in the profession. Some have begun to develop and implement spiritual assessment tools that will better able them to incorporate a patient's spiritual beliefs into their medical practice.[55] Even though some medical scholars believe these efforts are premature and would like to see more "compelling empiric evidence,"[56] the debate is at least occurring in a systematic and thoughtful manner. These developments have also led to changes in the curriculum of many medical schools. It is reported that "nearly 50 medical schools currently offer courses in spirituality and medicine." [57] The connection between spirituality and lawyering is not as direct as the connection between spirituality and medicine, since the physician's calling is to directly assist in the healing of the patient's mind and body. Yet this strong evidence from the medical field should remind us as lawyers that this search for the sacred can provide enormous benefits to both us and our clients as we collectively search for wholeness and emotional health.

Even the business world has embraced spirituality and religion with renewed vigor and meaning. Various major corporations have made room in their work days for people to pursue spiritual discussions, prayer services or bible studies. Some companies have made spirituality a fundamental part of their corporate mission. Prestigious business colleges are convening conferences on the topic, and organizational behavioral scientists are exploring and writing about concepts like "organizational spirituality."[58] They are discovering that businesses, organizations and firms have a spiritual component to them which provides enormous benefits to the individual employees as well as to the organizations. These benefits include increased personal fulfillment, balanced and healthy work life, greater capacity to change, increased productivity and performance, and improved creativity and decision making.[59] Though some legal organizations have begun to explore these same connections, it appears to be occurring at a much slower pace. This is due in great part to the resistance discussed above.

My fondest hope is that this book can contribute to reducing some of that resistance by helping to make spirituality a more acceptable area of exploration within the legal profession. Though there are great dangers lurking in the background, there are endless positive possibilities lying dormant right over that invisible line which we are told not to cross. If we cross it in the spirit of the river, and with a solid and meaningful foundation underneath us, we can convincingly and compassionately address the concerns that give rise to the resistances, and create a new space within which this profession can grow and prosper.

The Spiritual Challenge

Even if all were well with the legal profession, there would still be room for a deeper understanding and exploration of spirituality, but the disturbing patterns and challenges occurring within the profession make this exploration unavoidable. The public's perception of the profession is not good. Various studies have demonstrated over time that lawyers rank extremely low in the public's mind with regards to important values such as trust, integrity and honesty.[60] Internally, there are problems ranging from ethical violations and increasing lawyer dissatisfaction, to abnormally high divorce rates and high levels of alcohol and drug abuse. One might argue that this is no different from patterns experienced in other professions. The sad reality is, however, that although these problems exist in other professions, they appear to exist at higher levels among lawyers. And even if the problems are at the same levels as other professions, we cannot afford to view them as standard and acceptable parts of doing business. Like doctors, we are privileged to care for people at their most vulnerable moments. We are the guardians of the legitimacy and integrity of the entire legal system in America, and the legal system serves as the foundation and custodian of this country's democratic form of government. When these disturbing patterns and deficiencies occur within the profession, we plant destructive seeds of doubt and cynicism about ourselves and the entire system of law.

Various studies have demonstrated that a disquieting number of lawyers are dissatisfied with the practice of law.[61] Though many lawyers are paid very well and derive a high level of prestige and access because of their role, there still appears to be something missing for a significant number of them. Long hours, hectic pace, and stressful decisions contribute to high levels of burnout among many members of the profession. As one commentator concluded, "[a]fter five to ten years most lawyers, as evidenced in the North Carolina Bar poll, are so burnt out that they would leave if they could."[62] Even those who find ways to avoid being physically and mentality exhausted from the practice, still do not find enough meaning and personal satisfaction in what they do to justify the long hours and stress. This stress results in mild and serious incidents of depression. A noted psychotherapist who primarily counsels, researches and writes about legal professionals, came to the following conclusion:

> Report after report tells us that lawyers experience psychological unrest at much higher levels than non-lawyers. A survey of 105 occupations showed lawyers first on the list in experiencing depression,...substance abuse is so bad that some attorney disciplinary groups estimate upwards of seventy percent of all complaints against lawyers involve substance abuse; anxiety and obsessive behavior afflict a disproportionately large number of lawyers, sometimes to the point of incapacitation; many lawyers report strong feelings of isolation and social alienation; and upwards of sixty percent of lawyers say they would not recommend the law as a career to their own children. Worst of all, the most common psychological complaint by lawyers are feelings of inadequacy and inferiority in relationships. Lawyers in today's world are lonely, painfully lonely.[63]

This battle with stress and its consequences can begin before the person enters practice. Studies have demonstrated that law students are "almost four times more likely than the general population to suffer from depression and anxiety."[64] What ails the profession ails the academy, since law schools often reflect, emulate and nurture the values and culture of the profession.

56

Various legal scholars have noted this spiritual challenge that plagues the profession. Professor Randy Lee eloquently summarizes these sources in the following quote:

> Evidence of this spiritual crisis abound. Professor Mary Ann Glendon of Harvard speaks of American lawyers who are 'Wealthier and more powerful than their counterparts anywhere else in the world,' and yet 'in the grip of a great sadness.' Dean Anthony Kronman of Yale also speaks of a spiritual crisis, 'disguised by the material well being of lawyers,' which has struck 'at the heart of (lawyers') professional pride.' Professor Richard Weisberg of Yeshiva warns that the legal system has become an ethical vacuum as lawyers demonstrate a willingness 'to substitute wit for judgment, elegance for substance, words for values.' H. Jefferson Powell, professor of law and theology at Duke, notes that lawyers are forgetting their loyalties to the weightier matters of law, justice, mercy, and faith,' to pursue the idols of wealth and power. As they do so, lawyers find themselves more likely to obfuscate than to clarify and more likely to corrode than to build up the common language of law they must share with other generations of lawyers. [65]

Anthony Kronman, in his book, *The Lost Lawyer*, argues that this spiritual challenge is a result of the decline of the "ideal of the lawyer-statesman."[66] Kronman posits that this long discarded ideal contained some key values that lawyers desperately need today. Those values, he suggests, cannot be found in the intellectual realms of legal theories which, in part, have served to undercut the ideal, but must be unearthed from the soul of lawyers. "The ideal of the lawyer statesman was an ideal of character. This meant that as one moved toward it, one became not just an accomplished technician but a distinctive and estimable type of human being – a person of practical wisdom."[67] Kronman goes on to demonstrate how the rise of scientific law reform, in various historical reincarnations, the proliferation of large law firms and their "aggressive commercial tactics," and the caseload crisis in the courts have all converged to marginalize and mystify this defining value of "practical wisdom."

The "Good Lawyer,"[68] under this conception, must now resurrect this "practical wisdom" or prudence, and combine it with "the value of public service and the virtue of civic-mindedness."[69] Yet the enormous drift that has occurred in the profession creates a sense of pessimism for Kronman, and his major advice to lawyers who want to pursue and embrace this lawyer-statesmen ideal is to avoid large firms, and smaller ones in urban areas. His message to law professors, who through their scholarship and teaching methods have contributed greatly to dismantling the common law and its sacred values, is more encouraging. He reminds professors that they have the freedom to "insist on the peculiarity of cases, on their idiosyncrasies, and on the complexity of the world – on its factual complexity, but more important, on its moral and spiritual complexity, on the plurality of incommensurable values that fight for recognition in the law as in other spheres of life." [70] The Lost Lawyer clearly identifies the spiritual crisis and challenge that the profession faces, but falls short of directing lawyers, law professors and judges to a source, perspective, or path where they might discover, nurture and resurrect these precious values of wisdom and public service. Even with Kronman's insightful critique, lawyers remain adrift, knowing that there is a problem and knowing that they are the source of the problem, but finding no river pilot to help set their course.

Many women and lawyers of color find this drift even more unnerving, and find it more challenging to be at peace with their decision to be a member of this profession. In addition to the issues discussed above, they must also balance family responsibilities and cultural differences that often create invisible barriers to mobility, success, and peace of mind. Despite advances made in diversifying the legal profession, we still have a way to go before being "different" becomes an asset and not a burden. For some women, being in a predominantly male environment, which still struggles with the unique needs and perspectives that women possess, can be a stressful experience. The traditional paths to success and advancement do not adequately take into account detours for maternity and child rearing responsibilities. Though many legal organizations have made changes in their policies and practices to address these realities, the dominant culture is still male-oriented, and thus produces various levels of alienation, depression and stress. Some women struggle with feeling welcomed and fully valued among male colleagues who were nurtured in a culture that objectifies and marginalizes women. Their approach to problems, decisions, and the structure of the office can be different and at odds with the dominant male paradigm. So many of these differences are subtle and invisible, which often makes them undetectable from the male eye, but still very real to women who must live with them everyday.

For some persons of color, being in a predominantly white institution can feel as if they are strangers in a distant land. They can speak the language, but they are not always confident that they truly belong. They do not see themselves or the culture that shaped them represented in the seats of power, or even hanging on the walls. There is often an invisible cultural curtain constructed daily through the experiences, habits and nuances of life in the organization. So these individuals are forced to create two lives. In one world they wear the mask, shielding their real feelings and perspectives for fear it will not be appreciated or accepted. In the other world, which becomes smaller due to the enormous amount of time devoted to work, the person attempts to rediscover those aspects of self that bring meaning and connectivity. Thus they migrate between these two cultural worlds, hoping that they will peacefully co-exist, but knowing intuitively that it is almost impossible for them to merge. This dualism, which is a product of race and difference in this country as well as the structure of many legal organizations, places a heavy toll on the productivity and well being of many lawyers of color. The intersection of race and gender make the spiritual challenge of women of color in legal organizations even more difficult. They must grapple with both sources of alienation mentioned above as well as the unique challenge of not fitting completely in the dominant culture or the sub-cultures of white women and men of color. These issues of belonging and diversity have always been a problem within the legal profession, but they have intensified in the last three to four decades with the influx of women and persons of color. We cannot assume that these challenges will automatically take care of themselves, or that diversity training in the narrow sense will make them go away. If the culture of legal organizations is truly to become a welcoming environment where everyone feels appreciated and valued for whom they are, then the soul of the organization must be examined and revived.

In *The Soul of the Law*, Benjamin Sells, a psychotherapist and lawyer, who specializes in counseling legal professionals, makes an observation about the debilitating consequences that flow from the abstraction of law and lawyers.[71] In our culture we have created an abstract image of the law and lawyers that guides our understanding more than our actual experiences. This abstract ideal conjures up certain notions of how the law and lawyers operate within society and our lives. They are both faceless, time-consuming, lacking consistency and integrity, and generally available to the highest bidder. These abstractions come from unreliable sources like television, movies, myths and limited interactions, yet they dwell within the culture and public mind as if they were real and fixed. This problem of abstraction would not be so bad if it only existed within the minds of those who are not part of the legal profession. Unfortunately, they are the dominant mode through which many lawyers identify and understand their role in society. Benjamin Sell eloquently captures the consequences of this abstraction on the lives of lawyers. He writes:

> Whether in terms of feeling like a fungible component in a big law firm machine, or like a sideline spectator of one's own family life, or an amoral technician servicing the bottom line, or like an impostor and fraud, lawyers feel disassociated from daily life - including themselves. I have heard many lawyers describe a feeling of watching their own lives, observing themselves as if there is a deep separation

within them. This separation sets up an inner person, an observer, who feels independent from the lawyer's everyday, habitual self, and who seems to have a perspective on the thoughts and actions of the habitual self.[72]

This separation that Sells observes can, in part, be traced back to law school. Law is generally taught in an abstracted, disembodied and depersonalized manner. Students are subtly, and sometimes directly, instructed to extract their feelings, emotions and themselves from the learning process. Law becomes an objective and sterile process that has very little connection to the person who is learning it. Law becomes a garment that, once understood, can be adorned by the student, but is never absorbed or integrated into the student's life, values, spirit and emotional state in meaningful and healthy ways. Nor does law offer to the student an open invitation to pour her soul and insights into this sacred vessel in order to illuminate it. From its early introduction law resides outside the person. Therefore it should not be surprising that lawyers experience this sense of separation from the practice of law, even though they are engaged in it on a daily basis. This separation does not only exist between the law and lawyer, but also can exist among and between lawyers. To study and practice law in this abstract manner can create a sense of isolation and loneliness. Though lawyers may spend unlimited hours working with other lawyers, their connection to each other can sometimes feel artificial and superficial. These connections grow out of temporary experiences like working on a case, attending the same law school, or living in the same community. All of these connectors can so easily disappear or become less meaningful as time passes. Camaraderie through abstraction has serious limitations. For the vast majority of lawyers there is no common set of beliefs, sacred experiences, or transformative encounters that define their reality as lawyers. It is rare when a person's experience at law school or in a firm or organization provides her with an authentic relationship, imbued with values, ideals and beliefs that help define the person and her role in society. When this does not happen it is up to each person in this separated state to try to find meaning in the role that she has been asked to play in society. Though some are successful at this task, it appears that many find this deeper meaning to be very illusive, if not non-existent.

– This abstraction and separation can create serious psychological and spiritual discord for some lawyers because some of the abstract mandates of law are in conflict with some of the personal desires and emotional vulnerabilities of the person. Law is portrayed as strong and objective, but the person inside the lawyer sometimes feel weak, passionate and partial. Law is rendered as being consistent and predictable, but the person feels contradictory and confused. The law is there to protect, but the person feels vulnerable and unprotected – even from her own feelings. Thus there exists this unresolved tension and dynamic between law and the caretakers of the legal system that can become dysfunctional. Sells captures this impact by indicating that "the very things the Law tries to avoid in its abstract struggle with everyday life are what return in its own life, just as repressed passion can come back as incivility and repressed emotion as ethical breakdown."[73] So we see some lawyers exhibiting the very traits that the law abhors. They are rude, dishonest, and careless. They are also more likely to become victims of various social ills like depression, alcoholism and drug addiction, which the law was in part designed to prevent and curtail. Though no one assumed that laws could prevent or curtail all social ills, its original purpose was to assist in creating order, balance and a sacred equilibrium within individuals and society. And it certainly was not intended to contribute to the creation of social ills among those who were its primary guardians. But unfortunately, to live and engage in the practice of law through its abstracted state has numerous serious consequences for lawyers and for society.

Excessive and intense attachment to form and process also makes it difficult for some lawyers to remain spiritually centered and consistently humane. Many conduct the business of law as if they were representing clones instead of real people. They readily embrace the client's need and tendency to paint or portray the opposition as inhuman. They quickly turn opponents into demons and evil people in order to help their clients appear more like saints and victims. In criminal cases, it is not uncommon for prosecutors to describe defendants as "animals" or "devil like."[74] It is certainly within the bounds of professional conduct and zealous representation to try to demonstrate the severity of the acts committed by the person. Yet we have to wonder what the cost is to the humanity of the legal process and society when we engage in this type of behavior. In divorce cases, it is not uncommon for each side to employ very demeaning, negative and hostile description for the opposing party. Though this technique may contribute to a successful verdict, it comes at a high cost to the parties' future relationship, especially when there are children involved. This process of draining people of their humanity in order to prevail in court is symbolic of how we have drained the law of its spiritual dimensions in order to sell it as a separate, rational and legitimate intellectual enterprise.[75] We have erected these walls around ourselves and around the study and practice of law that prevent us from seeing and appreciating all that law has to offer. These walls keep us from seeing the spiritual dimension and foundation of this great profession. Lawyers must rediscover ways to know law in a personalized and intimate manner, so that the study and practice of law can be imbued with their values, spirit and soul. Without this, the soul of the law and its primary guardians will continue to suffer. [76]

With all of these challenges and many others, it is time for the profession to take a good look at itself and explore new ways by which these dilemmas can be addressed. History teaches us that we can not address these concerns by just passing new rules or working harder. Nor will we change the course of the profession by marginalizing the problems and blaming others. These sins will not be absolved by convening ritualistic meetings and conferences. As Professor Randy Lee states, "there can be no cure for the malaise afflicting the legal profession unless and until individual lawyers and the profession as a whole begin to break down the walls that have separated work from faith, and approach the practice of law as an integral part of the spiritual journey."[77]

This appeal is not just based on unverifiable blind faith, but is supported by numerous empirical studies. Such studies have consistently demonstrated that individuals who have a positive spiritual identity are better able to find more meaning and purpose in life and work.[78] They can more effectively cope with difficult and challenging crises in their lives, and have better interpersonal relationships.[79] There is strong evidence that spirituality and religion are "positively correlated with coping with stress."[80] There is also some empirical evidence that spirituality can serve as a deterrent to substance abuse in certain populations,[81] and overwhelming evidence of its role in recovery from alcohol and drug abuse. [82] So if some of the major challenges facing the profession fall into the categories of dissatisfaction, depression, stress and substance abuse, then not only are we facing a spiritual challenge, but also looking at a spiritual cure.

In order to avail ourselves of this cure, we must individually and collectively go down to the river of our souls and discover the essence of whom we are as lawyers and the reason we were called to this profession, and then begin to envision the type of profession we want to create. There must be a spiritual renewal that comes from the soul of this profession, and thus from the heart of its members. To meet the challenge of today and the potential crisis of the future, we must drink from a deeper moral and ethical well, and we must pursue a healthier and more integrated vision for this profession and ourselves.

The Illusions and Miracles of Law

We live so much of our lives trapped by illusions and seduced by the quest for miracles. There are so many things that we think we need and surround ourselves with that they prevent us from discovering and experiencing our true selves and our true needs. We also live our lives chasing so many dramatic and cataclysmic moments of change that we overlook the small opportunities for self transformation. If we were able to rid ourselves of some of the illusions, then we would create and discover more authentic miracles. The same is true for how we should approach the study and practice of law.

Law holds out to many the grand illusion that it can correct and solve all of the major problems in our lives and in the world. We place so much hope for change, progress and resolution on the law, yet it continues to disappoint us. It disappoints us because it is not capable of living up to the excessive expectations we have placed upon it. We know that it cannot regulate the heart, but we still hope that it will have that effect. We have been warned that it can create as much harm as it alleviates, but we still trust in its power. We hang our hope for a better world and meaning in our own lives around the law. Many entered law school with these illusions. When we begin to realize that there are limitations, contradictions and inadequacies to law and the legal process, we become cynical about its power and role in our lives.

Yet law can be no greater than the people who give it life and meaning. Law cannot do for us what we are not willing to do first inside. It cannot usher in change until we are first willing to change our minds and ultimately our hearts. It can lead the way for those who are struggling with change, progress and resolutions, but it cannot maintain the change for the long run.

Though as new law students and lawyers we quickly abandon the grand illusion of law, we soon develop smaller ones to replace it. We recognize early on that law can not do all that we thought it could or should in the world, but we do believe that it can do a lot for us as individuals. So we live the illusion that being a lawyer will make us smarter, wiser, more accepted, and maybe even financially secure. We create the mini illusion that to be a lawyer we must act, dress and talk a certain way. We wrap ourselves in a blanket of external ideas and concepts so that what we have claimed on the inside will have some external manifestation.

We create the illusion that there is much power that comes with the role and the position we occupy as lawyer. It is out of that illusion that we begin to embrace the relics and trinkets of the profession. If we let those things go, we begin to wonder if our power will go with them. So in order to hold onto our power, we begin to surround ourselves with more and more trinkets. Some will begin to manipulate and exploit others in order to hold onto these illusions of power. Some lawyers believe that their office, brief case and clothes must fit a certain mold or they will not be perceived as being as powerful and influential as they feel they need to be. Some law professors are reluctant to admit that they do not know the answer to a question a student raised because it might destroy the illusion that they are all knowing and powerful. One can see illusions floating in the classroom when students speak out incessantly not to engage their own learning, but to demonstrate that they are smart. We create and sanctify illusions when we pretend that there are qualitative differences between the student who ranks in the 10th percentile and the one who ranks in the 15th percentile. Though more justifiable, it is still an illusion when we think that the student ranked number 1 will be a better lawyer than the one ranked last. Though there are certainly differences in performance that should not be ignored, the major value judgments we make about each person's self worth and potential contribution to the legal profession is what makes this an illusion that we comfortably wrap ourselves within each day.

When we begin to seek more meaning in the practice, instead of ridding ourselves of these illusions, we tend to take on new ones. If we are not enjoying the work we do, or if we are not finding meaning in the practice of law, we sometimes conclude that the organization or firm for which we work is the problem. So we chase our dream in a new location surrounded by new people and a different mission statement. But if we have not discovered or changed our own mission statement, then our newly found heaven will eventually become our old hell. Places and people, like law, cannot give us what we lack inside. They can nurture what we have, but they can not give it to us. If our direction is unclear, if our values are unfocused, if our moral compass is off center, we cannot depend on external forces to set us straight. But the illusion is that if we do all the things that the professional culture tells us to do, then we will not have to worry about these soft internal concerns. Yet it is these soft internal concerns that give us our real power.

A lawyer becomes angry and yells in the courtroom, a managing partner rudely scowls at an associate, a professor intentionally embarrasses a student in class - all because they have embraced the illusion that these things give them power, or hold the keys to success. They probably have used this pattern for some time, and because it generated the expected response, it became a part of their personality. They honor this technique as if it were a hallowed trait that was bequeathed to them. They have wrapped themselves in a pattern that has become so common that they feel there is no other viable and effective way to deal with these types of situations. The illusion has become a reality for them. To consider another way of addressing the situation would appear to be a sign of weakness, a dent in their armor of authority and power. So they and the people around them continue to suffer because the illusion is more comfortable than the truth. The truth is that all of us have wrapped ourselves in patterns of behavior that are destructive to others and ourselves. The truth is that as long as we remain clothed in these illusions we will never discover our true and authentic power as spiritual beings.

So we practice, teach and study law as much out of illusions as we do from a genuine center of our real potential, with many of the things we assume as giving us power, serving only as barriers to self-discovery. Rude behavior, arrogance, elitism, material acquisitions, addictive work habits, manipulation of people and events, and so many other patterns of behavior are standing between some of the lawyers of today and the moral leaders of the future. Many lawyers are slowing down their life styles, changing their practice, engaging in meditation, and praying so that they can discover their true power and potential, and for some, their divine calling.

Though we have built numerous illusions around law, this does not mean that there is not a real potential for us to create miracles in the lives of people and in the world. When we shed illusion we create miracles. Once we are operating consistently from a place of self-discovery and divine guidance, then we are able to help usher into existence things and events that appear to be unexplainable. When a person's life is torn apart by domestic violence, and a lawyer practicing her healing art not only secures a protective order, but also helps to restore a sense of dignity and respect, it is a miracle for that person. When a person has been striving for years to create a business and can not get through the legal maze or secure the funding to make it happen, and a sensitive transaction lawyer shows him how, it is a miracle for that person. It is not a miracle in the sense that we can't explain how it happened, but it is a miracle in the sense that this person's dream was dying and now it lives; the doors of opportunity were once closed, but now they are open. Certain miracles are supernatural, but other miracles come naturally from super people. When lawyers are practicing their craft from a place of excellence, love and compassion, they become super people because they have the power to create miracles in the lives of ordinary people. So buried beneath the illusions of law is the power of miracles. The power lies dormant in the hallowed hallways of law and legal processes. This majestic power waits to be awakened by a spirit that wants to use it for good. Lawyers, by virtue of their training and by the righteousness of their calling carry a key that can unlock the door to the room of miracles. Secreted behind the lawyer's door are small and grand miracles. They can be given out for a price to the highest bidder, or they can be granted to all who earnestly seek them. Lawyers find themselves in the sacred but, at times, unenviable position of choosing how these miracles will be distributed.

In the fast pace life that we sometimes live, lawyers forget that they can be miracle workers. We often see our work as routine business. When we work for those who have stopped believing and needing miracles, we feel as if our calling is nothing more than a supplier of goods for the rich and famous. But we must never forget that we are miracle workers. We must never forget that we carry this sacred key, and that it can unlock doors for many people, not only those who can pay for it. We can help change lives through the work we do. In the right hands, guided by a righteous heart, law can create special moments in the history of humankind. Within its hallowed halls we can put up paintings of freedom, justice and equality, so that those who pass by will not only admire them, but also desire to embrace them. How people respond depends greatly on how well and sincerely we paint the masterpiece. If we paint it with stokes of arrogance and conceit, then we take away from its ultimate beauty. If we paint it with brushes of humility and passion, then we inspire generations to come.

So we must learn to balance the illusion and miracles of law. We must learn to discern between those things we need in order to be effective lawyers, and those things that are mere trappings of our calling. Once we know the difference, then we can devote more of our time and energy into creating small, authentic miracles and less time feeding our illusions. The illusions of power will temporarily make us feel important and make our work feel worthwhile, but there are limits to how much meaning one can derive from illusions. What makes this difficult for many lawyers is that so many people around them have embraced the illusions as real, that shedding them creates a deep sense of vulnerability. Yet in the long run, we will find more peace and personal satisfaction when we discover our true needs as lawyers and as human beings, and pursue those needs with passion and humility. Buried within those genuine needs is the power to create miracles. The first miracle will be the one we create in our own lives and practices.

The Spiritual Basis of Law

It is not uncommon to hear lawyers and judges say while making arguments for a certain interpretation of existing law, that the "spirit of the law demands this outcome." Though these types of arguments and interpretations of law create ambiguity, they are fundamental tools that are frequently used by lawyers and judges. They recognize that there is a dimension to law that can not be captured by black letter words and concepts. Lawyers and judges do not hesitate to invoke "spirit" in this manner because it has become an acceptable method of legal interpretation and argumentation. This use of "spirit" is acceptable because there is a concrete rule or policy that serves as an anchor for the arguments and interpretations, and the reasoning is still restricted to the intellectual domain. Though there is a sense of discomfort when decisions are rendered based on what judges view as the "spirit" of a law or statute, this is a viable and accepted tool for lawyers to invoke.

Though many lawyers are comfortable pursuing the "spirit of the law," most are not comfortable exploring the "spirit in the law." The classical structure and theories of law do not recognize or give voice to non-intellectual aspects of human reality. Despite the strong influence of religion on the early development of law and their seemingly inseparable nature, various legal scholars and educators attempted to drain the spirit out of the structure and practice of law. In order to justify law as a separate discipline and science that could be understood and applied logically and rationally there was a concerted effort to deplete it of feelings, emotions and thus, of its spirit. What Professor Anthony Kronman describes as the "scientific law reform" movement, had as its aim the marginalization or elimination of the common law tradition which resulted in a more sterilized and formalistic vision of law.[83] There also developed a fundamental belief that emotions interfered with the objectivity of the lawyer and judge, and that morality could subvert the rational basis of law. Oliver Wendell Holmes' often cited statement from "The Path of the Law" captures this position: "I often wonder if it would not be a gain if every word of moral significance could be banished from the law altogether."[84] Legal formalism was offered as a closed system wherein law did not depend on other disciplines or aspects of human and social reality for its worth. The interpretation and application of common law doctrine and legal rules became the most sacred part of the study and practice of law. The application of the philosophical concept of positivism[85] to the study and practice of law created a moral and spiritual vacuum. Law became its own morality. The mere existence of law, created through the agreed upon legislative processes, provided a moral covering for law. Appeals to the moral or spiritual foundations of judicial decisions were viewed as less compelling than arguments based on the letter of the law.

This philosophical perspective had a direct impact upon how lawyers saw themselves, and more importantly, it greatly influenced the structure and spirit of the law. Though there have been various philosophical and theoretical movements[86] that have challenged and minimized the dominance of legal formalism and positivism, these anti-spirit movements continue to greatly influence the structure and practice of law today. This exists, in part, because other movements, like realism and critical legal studies, have generally relied on the same scientific weapons of theory[87] and have not addressed directly the matters of the heart. The sterilized casebook method created by Christopher Columbus Langdell at Harvard Law School during the formalism era, is still the primary method through which we teach law students today. "Langdell's goal was to construct a rational scheme for the arrangement of legal doctrine by analytically unfolding the implications of a few foundational ideas. .... By denying the status of law to any decision that could not be independently derived by reason alone, Langdell limited the authority of what is actually in the law to what is rational in it."[88] Though other disciplines are consistently interjected into the classroom and other aspects of human reality are examined, the spiritual foundation of law is not systematically examined or explored. Law students are instructed in a manner and in an environment where their emotions, values and spiritual perspectives are generally very marginal to the primary educational objective. They enter into the practice of law where this pattern and culture continues. The formalistic nature of the practice of law makes it difficult for lawyers and judges to embrace and invoke the "spirit in the law."

The "spirit in the law" or law's spiritual foundation is not rooted in the doctrine and precepts of any particular sacred text. It is captured by a simple, but profound belief in the divine goodness that is woven into the purpose and nature of law, and into the hearts of those who practice and administer the legal system. This dimension of the practice of law encompasses every aspect of our interactions with clients, colleagues, and with ourselves. It is that sometimes dormant, but always very real urge to use law and our lives for the highest human good. The spiritual foundation of law derives from the quest to place within and to extract from the profession those values that will give a greater meaning and purpose to the work we do and to the lives we touch. This spiritual dimension will not re-emerge just because we invoke it. It appears when we live our lives and practice our craft in a manner that is consistent with our most sacred and precious values. It grows out of a universal belief that those who earnestly and honestly seek a connection with the pure, divine and sacred facet of themselves and others will eventually find it.

The most compelling aspect of the spiritual dimension of law is found in the purpose that law serves in society. What law has been called to do in society is fundamentally a spiritual mission. I recognize in making this statement that many trees along the river have been sacrificed to prove the fallacy of this claim. Some have argued that law does not have an essential nature,[89] that its purpose is just to mask underlying economic and political conditions,[90] or that its essential nature is whatever individuals give to it.[91] However, with due respect to all of these positions, and holding aside all of the political motivations that influence so much of what we call law today, at the essence of its purpose, law is put in place in order to direct men and women to realize a higher state of human existence. It attempts to help us recognize the needs of others, and to balance those needs with ours. This is true despite the fact that throughout history law has been used for the opposite end. It attempts to inspire human beings to seek the greater good and not just selfish ends. Law exists in order to reconcile differences that exist between human beings, and to assist them in living together in harmony as opposed to chaos. All of these goals are spiritual in nature. They are the values that most religious traditions seek to cultivate among their adherents. Thus law is not analogous to religion because some of its rules and doctrines are the same, or because of the theological origins of the western legal tradition.[92] Law is analogous to religion because it seeks to do those same things that religion seeks to do. Therefore, those who engage in the practice of law are entitled to see it as something sacred, and not as just another occupation. Those who participate within legal processes and procedures should experience something special and sacred which, regardless of the outcome, creates an opportunity for them to gain a deeper understanding of themselves and life, and assists in the continuous, but illusive quest to create a more harmonious society and world.

So I am arguing that the nature and purpose of law, not laws, is spiritual. This nature and purpose does not vanish because we have viewed, handled and portrayed it as purely material. We have asked it to do things that are more mundane than divine, but that does not distract from its original purpose. Those who are the true caretakers of this precious vessel must strive to restore it to its original calling. Law through its practice and operation must be a blessing to those involved and not a curse. It can be a pathway to self-fulfillment and not just a tool for professional and financial security. This is unlikely to occur unless those who are responsible for the administration of the legal system embrace both the spirit in the law and the spiritual quest that lies, sometimes dormant, within us all.

The law has often been viewed as one of God's instruments on earth to guide human beings through life's journey. It was considered the divine's way of helping us evolve into better human beings, and helping us to overcome our physical and earthly limitations. Law is a sacred vessel, shaped to the contours of human nature. It was fashioned to give us a way of reining in our selfish desires. This vessel must be handled in a way that is true to its ultimate purpose and calling. Yet how we handle it and what we place within it, ultimately determines the true worth of law and legal processes. If we handle it as if it were just another instrument that can bring us monetary value in the open market, then we desecrate its holiness. If we pour into the vessel values of greed, selfishness and indifference, then those who drink from this cup will only taste bitter waters, and will never experience the pure, refreshing and unlimited potential of law to heal and do good in the world. If we examine most, if not all spiritual traditions, we would find that the use of law was a primary instrument through which instruction and guidance were given to the believers. Though the doctrine and laws vary from one tradition to another, the instrument -the vessel- remains the same. The law symbolized what was correct, just and pure. It represented what the believer who codified those values as laws felt was God's desire for their lives. In these religious traditions reverence was given to the process and the substance of law. The manner through which the laws were created, and the laws themselves, were viewed as sacred. It is important that in the secular use of law, we give reverence to the nature and purpose of law, even when we disagree with the substance of a particular law. The possibility for this type of reverence on behalf of individuals in society will be greatly enhanced, and can only be justified and expected, when lawyers and judges can capture the hearts and souls of the society. To do this the public must believe that those who uphold and administer the process are conducting themselves in an honorable, trustworthy and spirit-filled manner. When we see law and our role in it as sacred, then it increases our chances of conducting ourselves in a manner consistent with the public's expectations and demands. This is not an automatic or absolute proposition. It is merely one small step on the long road to credibility, esteem and reverence. It has merit because there is strong evidence that human beings are less likely to trample those things they treasure and revere, than those things they see as mere steppingstones. For too many lawyers, law is viewed as a steppingstone on their road to some other place that they revere and desire.

This spiritual mandate of law is not limited or restricted to those who believe in and follow a particular religious tradition. Lawyers and individuals from various ideological positions share the aspiration for law to serve the highest ideals and meet the greatest needs of people and society. Legal scholars often have made this point as they have struggled to identify and clarify the spiritual foundations of law. One scholar eloquently makes this point in the following statement:

> In other words, my conclusion as to the implicit search for these deepest aspirations has universal and ecumenical applications to all religions. Perhaps they are applicable even to those who have no sense of religion, but who desire to be decent human beings in the practice of law and to escape the present dehumanization of law through materialism, bottom 'lineism,' and the winning/losing phenomenon so common in the profession. The basic thrust of every human being that makes us profoundly human in the first place is a solidarity in the search for these values and aspirations which are spiritual in nature...[93]

The fact that we have numerous examples throughout history of how individuals and societies have used law to pursue other aims does not take away from or destroy this essential nature of law. Water has an essential nature for human beings and society. We cannot live too long without it, and certainly our environment could not be sustained without it. Yet many have chosen, purposefully or unintentionally, to pollute it, drown people in it, and use it to break up legitimate marches for freedom and humanity dignity.[94] Yet this consistent misuse of water does not alter its essential nature, nor does it alter our individual and societal needs for it. The same can be said about law and its essential nature. The spiritual nature of law is there, regardless of how people have used it in the past, and regardless of one's religious belief or lack thereof. When we touch law and agree to embrace and uphold its essential mission, we can be imbued with its sacred power and calling. Yet if we close our eyes to its sacred nature, we can transform the sublime into ordinary mechanical manipulations.

The spiritual nature of law is inherent in its calling. Once we embrace the spiritual nature of law, we should not rationalize it away because we are caught in the daily routine of practice. Even when the matter is small or trivial, the process and outcomes are sacred. If the cases or assignments are routine or obtuse, we must understand that they are pregnant with unrealized possibilities. Part of our quest is to discover the "chances for enlightenment," the opportunities to cultivate and advance the "good," and to always stand in awe of the endless possibilities. Many insightful spiritual writers have echoed this approach to living and working. This is similar to the concept of "radical amazement" coined by Rabbi Abraham Heschel. "What fills us with radical amazement is not the relations in which everything is embedded but the fact that even the minimum of perception is a maximum of enigma. The most incomprehensible fact is the fact that we comprehend at all. The way to faith leads through acts of wonder and radical amazement."[95] Lawyers, inspired by their insatiable curiosity, have discovered small facts that eventually saved someone's life or brought them monetary justice. On the other hand, carelessness on the part of lawyers in regard to small routine matters has cost individuals and institutions large sums of money. Lawyers instinctively understand that amazing results can occur through small revelations. This principle and dynamic is as true in the spiritual realm as it is on the material plane. Every aspect of what we do as lawyers is imbued with ultimate spiritual meaning. A sincerely spoken word, a thoughtful conversation, or a genuine smile, have given depressed and confused clients and colleagues the inspiration to make it through the day and eventually through life. So those of us who are given the privilege of upholding the legal system should understand the inherent power we are given, and the inherent danger in ignoring all of its multiple dimensions.

When we chose to see and treat law only through secular and spirit-less lenses, we corrupt its purpose and overlook the endless possibilities to be amazed by its power and to cultivate good in the world. To pursue the teaching and practice of law is the equivalent of joining the priesthood, or becoming a minister, rabbi or imam. Becoming a lawyer implicitly and explicitly requires that we take a sacred oath of trust, loyalty and service. But the analogy extends beyond the oaths we take. As lawyers we are given a responsibility to care for the needs of those who come to our sanctuaries and, at the same time, are entrusted with the responsibility to preserve and enhance the larger system in which we were inducted. We are the guardians and interpreters of sacred texts which ultimately were designed to create more enlightened human beings and a more harmonious society. People confess to us the deep secrets of their hearts and heads, and they expect us to assist them in their healing. We craft documents that can guide them at every stage of their life. From birth to death, from marriage to divorce, in poverty and riches, we are their counselor, agent and temporary companion on life's journey. We offer people concepts, forms and advice in the same manner that others offer sermons, communion, prayer and tradition, in order to extract more meaning out of life's circumstances and challenges. Lawyers are not mere bystanders in the personal and collective march toward freedom, justice, peace and healing. We are the architects, the designers, the spiritual guides in this sacred procession. Yet the oaths we take seem to give us only a license to earn a living, and not bestow an obligation to earn the respect, reliance and trust that so many place at our altar. We must find ways in which the other implicit values contained in the oaths, are made more explicit. More importantly, we must figure out how to enshrine these commitments in our hearts so that they guide us every day.

Law as Spirit

For those who seek a more meaningful path for their work as lawyers, law professors and law students, it is important to be able to see every aspect of one's work as sacred and special. This can be hard for some because they observe so much

82

manipulation, superficiality and contradictions imbedded in the law and in the practice of law. Even for those who embrace the contradictions and conflicting ideals[96] as a fundamental nature of law, this realization can lead to a sense of cynicism and frustration. It is very easy to get so trapped in details and minutia that we forget to see the essence of what we are being asked to do. Lawyers in their daily work are not just handling cases, opinions, briefs and rules, but are caretakers of spirit. Encased in each rule, each decision, and every argument is an essential part and reflection of life. There is a vital energy or combinations of energies; a therapeutic or anti-therapeutic potential embedded in the rules, policies and procedures, and in our attempt to apply them.[97] If we see these things as inanimate objects, then we treat them in crass and thoughtless manner. We spend time trying to understand the intellectual meaning of a rule or the holding of a case, but very few of us are willing to reflect upon the type of energy or spirit we are promoting and ushering into the universe.[98] For the rule or case not only will have an impact on a person's substantive situation, but also will have an impact upon the person's emotions and spirit. Lawyers and judges should be sensitive to these intangible consequences that flow from their actions and decisions just as they strive to be aware of the material outcomes.

To see law as spirit is a way to get those who handle these delicate forms and processes to be more careful in how they use them. Law as spirit is a way to see life not as a collection of things, but as a way of being. Law as spirit is a way to open up a deeper understanding of those things we think we already comprehend. It is a process of slowing down the practice of law so that it is not a practice, but a celestial procession. Every move we make, every decision we take, affects the state and status of the universe. For if we are all connected and affected through the mediums of air, energy, attitudes and behavior, then our small and large choices and decisions affect endless numbers of people. We never come in contact with all the people our actions and attitudes affect, because our influence is carried through so many others whom we do not touch. If one of us had a contagious disease like SCARS[99] which affected China and Canada in the recent past, and attended a meeting with twenty people and infected only fifty percent of them, could we imagine how many other people could be affected by the end of the day, not to mention the end of a year if nothing were done to protect people from contracting the disease. We understand this "unlimited connectedness" principle in regard to physical diseases, but we overlook or underplay the effects that our attitudes, moods and behavior, and thus spirit, have on the various people we interact with and those we never see. Though we cannot be responsible for the entire condition of the world or even our families, we can be responsible, and thus more thoughtful, for every statement we make and every action we take. If we exercise control and dominion over these things, then we create more possibilities for change in the larger world.

Just as some people see spirit in the trees, in the water and in the wind, we must see spirit in the law. [100] It is not divorced from nature and life, but an important reflection of them. It is not something that is handed down to us, but something that we create and apply. If we are the creators of these life reflections, which we call law, then we encase within them the energy and spirit of life that we possess. If our motives in crafting, passing and interpreting a law are to unnecessarily limit the rights and liberties of others, then we are unleashing that spirit into the universe. Certainly, these are profound value judgments, and depending on one's political orientation, what is oppressive to some appears like appropriate restraint to others. Yet even across these political chasms we can appreciate the fact that sometimes we operate to protect our interests in ways that are insensitive and mean-spirited. Our aim is no longer to protect the rights of those we believe to be vulnerable, but to destroy those who hold the opposite position. When we view law as spirit, we not only must be responsible for the substantive affects that our actions and rulings have on people, but also the emotional and spiritual injuries as well.

Though slavery and segregation were terrible legal processes that had a devastating impact on the educational, economic and political status of African-Americans, the emotional and spiritual harms were just as great. Decades after those rules and processes disappeared we can still see the emotional and spiritual scars on Black people and on this nation. One of the severe attributes of spiritual and emotional harm is its unlimited potential. The harm can last for generations, passed down through culture, stories and internalized oppression. It can spill over into the lives of those who were not the intended victims. Whites in this country have suffered emotionally and spiritually from the creation of white supremacy through the institutions of slavery, segregation and discrimination. Though white privilege has generated enormous material benefits and rewards, it also has contributed to the proliferation of arrogance, insensitivity and guilt- ridden personalities. The collective internal psychological wars of denial and guilt have extracted a toll from the psyche of many White Americans. Having an inflated sense of one's power and self-worth is spiritual damage just as having an inferiority complex is a curse against the divine. Dr. Martin

Luther King once commented in the midst of the civil rights movement that he found himself feeling inadequate to lead the movement because he was stilled trapped by an inferiority complex, which was a product of slavery and segregation. A man as spiritual, intellectually powerful, and gifted as Dr. King was still a spiritual victim of laws passed and enforced decades before he was born. He certainly rose above this feeling and made a tremendous contribution to this nation and the world, yet the spirit encased in those laws created a deep wound in him as it did in so many others. And despite his gallant and historic effort, and the success of the movement he led, we still see the consequences of these spiritual wounds in present generations.

So we must approach our legal work, our cases and certainly our clients with a sense of reverence. For what we do will have numerous and unpredictable consequences, not only on those we know, but also upon those whom we will never see. This should not immobilize us, for we cannot be perfect in all our actions or in our spiritual quest, but we can strive to live in and from an authentic place that nurtures the values of love, humility, forgiveness, service, faith and integrity. We nurture these values by trying to extract and manifest them in all of our encounters with life, and by seeing everything and everyone as spirit. There is nothing but spirit. Physicists have long made us aware that all physical matter is a composite of various forms and levels of energy, packaged in different structures and serving various functions.[101] This principle is not only applicable to our bodies, but also to every aspect of our being.[102] Our true power comes when we can harness the positive spirit within us, and use it to bring about good in the world, in the same way that light and sound were harnessed to

86

improve the quality of life. We must have faith that positive outcomes will flow from our actions. If we try to control the process and the outcomes solely through our intellectual bridle, we may reach results that make us feel as though we have been successful, but we may have diverted energy toward our selfish goal that was needed for even greater good. We also may have won the battle of outcomes, but lost the war of relationship. In many, if not most instances we find more meaning in life out of relationship than we do from outcomes. For example, our material acquisitions are important, but when we have no one to enjoy them with or leave them to, they feel less significant. Many retired lawyers I speak with cherish the people and relationships they created while in practice as much, if not more, than the memory of a large settlement or judgment. Our loyalty to institutions is as much a product of the people who comprise them and embody the values of the place, as the name of the company and the salary we receive. This does not mean that we should not seek the settlement, judgment or salary; it only stands as a sobering reminder that so much of our meaning and joy in life can only be affirmed through our connections with others. When we abuse or take advantage of relationships in pursuit of outcomes, we will eventually pay a high spiritual price. If one does not want to entertain or accept the idea of a spiritual price, there are very clear organizational and societal costs associated with this perspective and behavior.

What I just described could be applied to other disciplines and professions, and to all of life. Law is not in a privileged position when it comes to spirit. The legal profession has a special calling and status in this arena, but it does not stand alone in the midst of the crowd. That is why it is essential to see our path as a partial path. We must see other paths as being just as viable and capable of contributing to the advancement of life or to solving a problem. Too often we believe that a narrow legal solution is the best outcome when, in fact, there may be numerous ways in which to address a problem or situation. Our value as lawyers increases when we are able to direct people to the appropriate resources they need. When we see law as spirit, we also understand that a legal solution might not be the right essential principle or method to offer up into the universe at a particular time. Like precious jewels, it should not be squandered just because someone has asked us for it. Like pure water, it should not be wasted on some clients when others are living on desserts with no oasis in sight.[103] Yet, like love, we should never hoard it, for it does not belong to us. Law is a spirit of the universe, and as lawyers, we are its caretakers. We must care for it as if our lives depended upon it, because so many lives are dependent upon how we use and treat the law. When we see law and the practice of law through this lens, then we are more likely to treasure it instead of trampling others with it.

Chapter Two:
A Search for Sacred Rivers

The Attorney Personality and the Lawyer's Soul[104]

Just as individuals have personalities, so do groups of individuals who are engaged in common experiences or enterprises. General qualities and traits can be unique to a group just as they can be to an individual. Those who are engaged in the study and practice of law embrace and incorporate into their way of being a common set of mental, emotional and behavioral traits. These patterns are instilled within law students through the structure and value systems of legal education, and they are reinforced when the students become lawyers by the structure, customs and patterns of the legal profession. These qualities and traits are directly and subtly offered as the acceptable way to conduct oneself within the profession. Those who embrace these qualities and traits are rewarded, and those who deviate from them can often pay a high price. So embracing and developing an "attorney personality" becomes a constant goal and a consistent defining process for those who want to become lawyers.

The first challenge that new law students face is to learn how to "think like a lawyer." They do not fully understand what this phrase means, and no one fully or accurately describes its constituent parts. Yet they are unequivocally informed that this indescribable state exists, and if they work hard and stay on the path, they will eventually figure out what it is that they are becoming. If they do not, then that is evidence that it was not the path for them. Inherent in the notion of "thinking like a lawyer" is the cardinal rule that you have to give up existing, ineffective norms of thinking and feeling in order to adorn yourself with the more privileged and effective robes for analyzing and resolving problems. This ideal is dramatically captured in the Professor Kingsfield character in the classic movie, "The Paper Chase." Kingsfield states that the role of the law professor is to take a "mind of mush" and turn it into something more useful and valuable to the profession and the society. Most first year law students are informed that their present way of thinking is unacceptable because it does not conform to this archetype. It would be fine if all this meant was that there was a set of ideas, skills and information that students had to know before they could effectively practice this craft. But "thinking like a lawyer" involves more than just understanding the rules and thinking. In fact, it embraces a complete way of being and acting in the world. This pattern of learning and being eventually develops into a personality type that the willing student embraces. This personality type demands that one looks at problems, life and oneself in a different way. Parts of that approach are very healthy and admirable. Thinking like a lawyer demands that one is able to see problems from multiple perspectives and not just from the easy and obvious one. It also suggests that one should be able to feel comfortable with ambiguity. This is important because very few things in life and in law are concrete and fixed. Thus being able to operate comfortably with uncertainty is an important attribute for someone in this profession. In addition, thinking like a lawyer requires one to be very atomistic in the analysis of facts, evidence and rules. The "devil is in the details" is a cardinal principle of the successful practitioner of law. If one is able to master these fundamental traits and attributes then one has acquired the classic tools of an attorney at law that serve lawyers well in many situations.

However, along with these obvious skills come some subtle messages that will eventually take root in the personality of the attorney. To master these traits one is lead to believe that one must detach and remove oneself from the problem and from the individuals being served. Within the domain of the attorney personality is a fundamental belief that emotions get in the way of thinking clearly. It is believed that objectivity comes from emotional distance and will be corrupted or diluted if one becomes too emotionally connected to the client. The burgeoning lawyer is led to believe that mind is the most powerful tool needed to successfully master the discipline and serve the client. These messages result in a personality that is more rigid than flexible, more analytical than caring, more emotionally detached than sympathetic, and more self-centered than altruistic.[105] This does not happen overnight, but becomes the unstated end game of the journey that began on the first day of law school. [106]

There are numerous benefits to this personality type. It serves as a buffer for all of the emotional blood that gets spilled on the lawyer's table. The personality of the attorney is a shield and a sword. It protects the emotional vulnerability that all lawyers need, and it provides a ready rationale for the lawyer when he feels it is necessary to go on the offensive. The "Rambo"[107] style litigator is the archetype of this personality. In the courtroom he stands with the sword of his personality in hand, ready to slay those who stand in the way of his client's victory. In the process, the sword becomes the shield, because in destroying the opponent, the lawyer protects himself from his own insecurities and vulnerabilities. War becomes love. The more this personality goes to war, the more deeply in love he becomes with this pattern of behavior. In essence he begins to define and enjoy the job based on this approach. These traits become calcified and are no longer just blueprints for success, but become hardened, stone-like personality traits that are difficult for the person to break.

Despite the enormous power and appeal of this archetype lawyer personality, experience has demonstrated that it is not always effective, and eventually takes a toll on the person and the profession. Many lawyers have come to realize that to be truly effective, they must bring all of themselves to the enterprise of law. For them, effectiveness is not just measured in status and earnings, but by the degree of real satisfaction that the client obtains. For these lawyers, effectiveness is also measured by the depth of personal satisfaction and meaning they obtain through the work performed. The mind is an indispensable tool for this level of effectiveness, but so is the soul. The soul and spirit of the lawyer is the most overlooked, underdeveloped and underutilized tool of the profession. Its lack of use, development and growth is the source of many of the problems and limitation of lawyers and the profession.

The soul of the lawyer is that part that cares for, and feels for, the clients and the profession in a deep, authentic and genuine manner. It is that boundless energy that allows us to see beyond and through problems. It is that fluid energy that permits us to not only analyze the problem of the client, but also touch their hearts in the process. The soul of the lawyer is different from the personality of the attorney because it has no fixed parameters within which to operate. It permits the lawyer to cry, laugh, hurt, pray, meditate and be in the moment of all her experiences. There is no compartmentalization in the soul. The lawyer's keen analytical mind sits next to her passionate ear. They do not work against each other, but serve as a catalyst for each other's growth for some of our most creative and thoughtful ideas and solutions come when our minds are still, and when our hearts have been stirred. The soul is the repository for our spiritual growth. It is the place where we can see beyond the present day limitations and burdens. It is the place that allows us to see the client not as a person with a problem, but as another soul striving to find its place in the universe. Part of our challenge, the essence of our calling, is to assist them on their journey. This is the spiritual privilege of being a lawyer. People come to us and open up the window to their souls. If we only look with our mind's eye, then we will see only the legal issue. But if we gaze deeply, with the eye of our soul, then we shall see something more precious, and we will be able to help advance something more worthy than the judgment we might secure for them. Life is more than just the accumulation of rights, wealth and material things. It is about the overall advancement and cultivation of the individual and collective human spirit. This work is done with insight and compassion. It is done well when lawyers are able to consistently manifest spiritual values in their lives and work. These are traits and characteristics that cannot be taught, but they can be nurtured and cultivated. They can be lived, and through our living out these values, we impart them to others and we inspire them to follow the path.

"The road to your soul is through your heart." This passage contained in Gary Zukav's, *The Seat of the Soul*, points to one of the side effects of the attorney personality. When some people describe lawyers as heartless, they are trying to describe some unpleasant or disappointing experience that they probably had with one or more members of the legal profession. They know that while in law school the lawyer's heart was not surgically removed, but they sensed an absence of compassion or sincere concern for their situation or for them. This distant method of interaction and cold attitude are direct outgrowths of the lawyer's personality. Most lawyers are trained and nurtured in legal environments that place little value on compassion. Furthermore, lawyers are often advised to remain somewhat detached from the client and the problem. Though there are valid professional reasons for this posture, the side effects can be devastating. Detachment not only cultivates objectivity, but it becomes a breeding ground for coldness, aloofness and cynicism. In the process our hearts become hardened to the very people and problems we were called to serve. If our hearts are calcified because of choice or practice, we cut off the path to our souls. When we cut off that path we cut off an enormous source of internal power to do our jobs and to live our lives to the fullest. The more we care, the more vulnerable we will become, and the more victorious we will be in life. Contrary to the dominant paradigm, creative and effective thinking does not come from detachment, but from immersion.

For every lawyer who operated from a heartless and detached position, there were those who immersed themselves into the problem and the people they represented. Many of them not only won the case, but also won the people as well. They not only secured new rights, but also stirred old souls. Even those who did not prevail in court prevailed in the courtroom of love and life. They stood by and with a soul as it was facing loss of property, prestige, and even life. They stood not only with their analytical minds but also with their pounding hearts. In the process of standing, they allowed another human spirit to stand more erect. These lawyers helped renew someone's faith in the beauty of human beings, and in the process found the opening to their own soul. When lawyers chase their hearts, they find their souls. Chasing one's heart does not mean that we abandon reason, or downplay the importance of mastering doctrine. It does mean that one should not engage in this work from a superficial place. The work the lawyer chooses must be meaningful and fulfilling. The way the lawyer goes about doing that work must be consistent with her values and spiritual quest. This does not necessarily mean that lawyers would never defend the guilty or take a case that stood for principles inconsistent with their political beliefs. It means that our spiritual ways should shape and cover our interactions with the client and everyone else involved. Certain circumstances will challenge those values more than others, but this is the fuel for spiritual growth. Chasing one's heart is placing compassion ahead of detachment. It means treasuring the journey of each case and client, and not just focusing on the end rewards. It may mean foregoing some financial rewards for the sake of internal peace, because the lawyer realizes that more is at stake than a retainer or a fee. The lawyer's soul hangs in the balance.

So when we embrace and surrender completely to the standard attorney personality, we are deciding to forsake the quest for wholeness and to settle for a marginal existence within the profession. But when we can embrace the fundamental skills of the archetype attorney personality and combine it with the lawyer's deep well of compassion and care, then we create a new being. Our ultimate goal in life and in our work should be to reconcile our personality with our soul. The following passage captures this dilemma, tension and reconciliation:

> The personality is interested in itself. It likes thrills, so to speak. It is not necessarily responsible for caring or loving. The soul is the energy of Universal love, wisdom and compassion. It creates with these energies. The personality understands power as external; it perceives in terms of competition, threats, and gains and losses that are measured against those of others. When you align yourself with your personality, you give power to the realm of the five senses, to external circumstances and objects. You disempower yourself. As you grow aware of your spiritual self and origin, your immortalness, and you choose and live according to that first, and the physical second, you close the gap that exist between the personality and the soul. You begin to experience authentic power.[108]

If we continue as a profession to give reverence to the traits of the attorney personality and minimize the importance of emotional and spiritual values, then we are fostering the development of schizophrenic professionals. There will remain a big void between what lawyers think and do, and who they really are. If we are to close this gap at an individual and professional level, then we must not only recognize these other values, but also place them at the head of the line. We must convey the message to both new and experienced lawyers that their ethical and spiritual responsibility is more important than their analytical ability. Otherwise, we will continue to produce lawyers who will use their analytical ability to circumvent their ethical responsibility. We must remind them that their compassion for the client, and their passion for the study and practice of law, are more critical to their satisfaction than the type of law they choose to practice. The more we send these types of messages, embrace and reward these types of values, the more we will assist lawyers in closing the gap that exists between their personality and their soul.

Rivers and Stones

One key for accessing the soul is the use of metaphor. In various religious and spiritual traditions, parables, stories and objects in nature are used to convey insights about life and living. We are instructed through nature and symbols because they contain qualities, attributes and patterns that we admire and desire for ourselves. Through our study, observation and reflection upon concrete and visible aspects of life, we are better able to understand the ethereal characteristics of life. Since it is difficult to describe and comprehend concepts like soul and spirit, we come closer to understanding and appreciating them by other concrete replications of these forces. In Native

American spiritual philosophy this way of knowing is taken to a deeper level, and nature and objects in nature do not just symbolize an insight, they are the insight. The wind, animals and rivers do not just provide meaning to us, they are meaning. [109] Since nature is alive it imbues and influences other aspects of reality with its spirit. The closer we are in contact with a particular aspect of nature, the closer we come to understanding the spirit of the object and, in the process, our own spirit. Through this association we are also able to decipher what this aspect of nature is here to teach us. In African religion and philosophy we find a similar belief. John Mbiti in his classic text, *African Religions and Philosophy,* captures this fundamental point about knowing: "The invisible world presses hard upon the visible: one speaks of the other, and African peoples 'see' that invisible universe when they look at, hear or feel the visible tangible world."[110] As I invoke aspects of nature to assist us on this journey, I am using them to convey both of the above ways of knowing. Nature is used here to symbolize aspects of reality that are hard to pin down, but which we need to better understand. But I am also using it as an embodiment of the ideal being discussed. I am attempting to reach and speak to the analytical and non-analytical aspects of each reader. So not only am I inviting you to compare and contrast the river with law and life, I am also inviting you to feel and to become one with the river.

When I think of soul, I think and feel river. When I think of personality, I feel and think stones. Langston Hughes in one of his most famous poems, "The Negro Speaks of Rivers," compares soul with rivers. He states at various junctures of the poem, "my soul has grown deep like the river." The fluid, natural moving, life-giving force of the river symbolizes the energy of the soul. The river is the repository of those things essential for sustaining life. It provides water, food, travel, reflection and mystery. The river is purposeful, yet changing; simple, yet majestic. It flows through our lives leaving traces of things greater than what we consciously know and experience each day. It overflows at time and fertilizes the area that surrounds it, irrigating those calcified portions of land that one day will produce life-giving food for those who live along its banks. We can bathe our sorrow and ourselves in the river. We travel from one part of our existence to another by following its flow. Our goal in life is not to conquer the river, but to immerse ourselves within its beauty and power. The river appears to have neither a beginning nor an end, and its power comes from a greater source that is even more incomprehensible and immeasurable. So, by staying connected to the river, we are, in essence, connected to and nurtured by that greater source of energy and power. There are times when the waters flow over the rocks and it appears as if the two have become one. At other times the stones create a crystal staircase over which the river glides down its path with a deep sense of familiarity and purpose. Though we could never totally control the river, we can alter its flow by placing stones or building dams within its way. These structures allow us to harness the power of the river, but also expose us to the fury and destructive potential of this seemingly peaceful source. To understand the power and potential of the river, one must spend time gazing at its flow and exploring its unknown reaches. As one river lover once stated, "[a] river is the coziest of friends. You must love it and live with it before you can know it." [111] There is such diversity and differences among the rivers of the earth, yet they all seem to be regulated by a universal pattern of flow. "It has a thousand

colors and a thousand shapes, yet it follows laws so definite that
the tiniest streamlet is an exact replica of a great river."[112] Since
the beginning of time men and women have stood in awe of the
river's beauty, power, diversity and oneness. We have gained
many insights and learned many lessons from gazing upon and
bathing within rivers, yet the greatest gift from the river is when
it leads us to a deeper understanding of ourselves and our soul.

Our soul is similar to the river. The soul is the repository of
our basic sensations and feelings; it is the resting place for our
highest ideals and yearnings. It is the inner life that gives true
meaning to the outer person. Like the river, it is majestic, yet
common to us all, with no beginning or end that we can
detect.[113] The soul nurtures those aspects of our lives that give
us meaning, purpose and joy. As we nurture the highest ideals
of our existence, we increase the flow of our soul's power. As
this energy flows through our lives, it fertilizes the banks of our
personality and irrigates those calcified portions of our external
being. What others perceive and feel from us is a by-product of
the internal flow of our soul, and what they feel, they call our
spirit. In difficult times we wash our sinful clothes on the banks
of this river and it washes our sins away. The energy of the soul
gives us the faith and power to believe in our ability to
overcome the obstacles or dams that we, or others, have placed
in the path of our flow. Some of us believe that our soul, like
the river, connects us with a more powerful source that we refer
to by various names, but is divine, pure and exists for good
purposes. A major goal of our quest in life should be to
diligently seek and draw from this more powerful source which
gives the river - and us - true life. When we are in touch with
this intangible part of ourselves that we call soul, and which
manifests itself as spirit, we are able to do more with our lives

and inspire the lives of those around us. We are able to gain greater insights into ourselves when we take the time to meditate and gaze upon our soul. Like the river, we cannot fully appreciate this immeasurable power unless we spend time gazing upon it and bathing within it.

The souls of lawyers are enhanced when we cultivate and actualize the sacred values in our lives and in the profession. We block the power we have to gain insights and wisdom when we allow the stones to dominate our lives and practice. But lawyers who work from both their heads and their hearts are better able to serve the whole client, and inspire the client to seek and follow his own river. Lawyers that operate primarily within the boundaries of the attorney personality can contribute to the overall goodness of the profession and life, but are restricting their power and potential, and are more likely to obstruct the natural flow of love and justice that resides within them, and within those they serve. When we harness the power of the soul, and combine it with the power of the stones, then we elevate the terrain around us. We create a standard of conduct and being that becomes an attraction to those who want to enter, and who already exist within the profession. The soul, like the river, follows these universal laws and patterns that we cannot fully decipher and comprehend, but which are worthy of our search. In the process of our search, we not only are drawn closer to the river, but also become one with it. We reach a different level of existence and we are better able to help quench the thirst of our clients, for we are not just giving them lifeless legal answers, we are dispensing to them a living water that can help heal conflicts and restore faith. It is written that, "out of his belly shall flow rivers of living water."[114] When we search for and obtain the sacred rivers within us, we become fountains of living water that can help heal conflicts and resolve them. The more we discover about the spiritual power that each of us possesses, the more we create the possibility for the revitalization of the legal profession. It is easy to touch the stones along the riverbank, but it is harder for us to actually become one with the river. It is not the mind of the attorney that has been underdeveloped; it is the soul of the lawyer that for too long we have ignored.

The Beauty of the Stones

It would be easy after reading the metaphorical description of the river to conclude that stones are bad and serve no useful purpose in life. Stones are not bad, and neither is the attorney personality. They help give the river its contour and shape. It is the structure and position of the stones that often increases the flow of the river. The stones along the riverbank provide a sure foundation upon which we can stand to observe the beauty and power of the river. The lawyer personality provides a foundation upon which lawyers can engage in this search for truth, love and justice. Without the concrete skills of analysis, knowledge of cases and laws, and a deep understanding of process and procedures, lawyers would be extremely limited in what they could offer to their clients and to the world. Just as the stones sometimes even protect the shoreline from erosion, the attorney personality can sometimes protect the lawyer from becoming too emotional and too connected with clients and their situations.

One of the dangers with critiquing the dominant legal paradigm is the tendency to overlook or discard the valuable aspects of the prevailing approach. It is easy to conclude that traditional approaches to the practice of law have no, or very little, redeeming value. Therefore, we begin to abandon attributes that, on their surface, may appear to be barriers to progress but, in essence, are fundamental to the viability and success of the profession. The "throwing out the baby with the bathwater" syndrome must be avoided in this quest for wholeness within the legal profession. There is tremendous value to the attorney personality and the attributes that constitute what I call stones. One of those attributes is the ability to dissect problems to their most minute detail. The tendency to analyze the parts of the whole case, contract or situation in such a microscopic manner allows us to understand the complexity that is hidden within every facet of life. Without this approach we tend to gloss over events and information without fully understanding and appreciating what they truly add to life. The statement that "God is in the details," or as some prefer, "the devil is in the details," reminds us that small things, sometimes unobservable at first glance, often make the ultimate difference in critical events and plans. Therefore we should not criticize lawyers for focusing on details, for it is thorough analyzing and understanding the small aspects of a problem that we are empowered in our search for truth and justice. What we should criticize is an approach where lawyers become so obsessed with the details, that they never see the big picture or the whole person. It is not the search for details that trips up lawyers; it is getting so lost in the details that they cannot find themselves or the real meaning behind the work.

Likewise, we should not criticize lawyers for being able to see various sides of an issue or their ability to make arguments to support either side. This is sometimes viewed as evidence that lawyers lack moral fiber and are easily willing to sell their souls to the highest bidder. However, the benefit of this attribute, if understood properly, is that it contributes to our understanding of the illusiveness of truth, and it symbolizes the inherent value that exists in every human being. Standing quietly behind this attribute is a value that reminds us that every person and every perspective needs to be heard and defended. The human tendency to see things in a unilateral way is countered by this fundamental attribute and skill that all good lawyers possess. To see life, events, and people from multiple perspectives is a rare and enduring value. If more of us practiced this in our daily lives and work, we would avoid so many of the limiting and shortsighted decisions we make about people and events. The laws of physics are not just restricted to material matters. Through training a lawyer knows that for every argument there is an equal and opposite argument. The danger with stones is not seeing various sides, but the inability to decide that certain sides are inconsistent with our most sacred values and, thus, should not be embraced on behalf of a client. So it is not the fluidity of thought, but the fluidity of values, or the lack thereof, which contributes to the lawyer's psychological and moral weaknesses.

The attorney personality is also seasoned to probe and push. Lawyers have been trained to understand that facts, events and life are not always as they may appear. Therefore, it is not wise to just accept facts or perspectives according to how they are first presented. The tendency on the part of lawyers to probe behind the facts for more fact or to get underneath a person's skin in order to get at the truth, is often viewed as evidence of our arrogance or stubbornness. Yet, in the scientific world we applaud persons who keep digging, exploring, and probing because we believe that it is the only way to discover a new approach, cure or device that will make life better for all. The lawyer's use of this attribute is the same as the scientist. We believe that the search for truth is hard and long and only achieved after penetrating numerous layers of lies, half-truths and misunderstandings. The search for truth, as illusive as it is, is like the search for a cure to a disease. If we abandon it because it is not easily found, or because others will criticize us for pushing too hard, then we sacrifice truth the same way the scientist sacrifices progress. So it is not the probing that is problematic, but the inability to know when to stop. It is the lawyer's inability to know when it is appropriate, and when it is not, that creates the problem. There are times when the pushing and probing has no other goal other than pushing and probing. The inherent danger in this attribute, more than some of the others is that it can more easily become a part of the lawyer's personality, and thus become as fixed as stone. This attribute, through consistent use, can be transformed into a fundamental and fixed aspect of how some lawyers define and see themselves, instead of remaining just a skill. Lawyers must always keep in mind that these attributes are skills and tools to be used, not things to become. Such skills and attributes of the attorney personality are not the composite of a lawyer; they are only aspects of what lawyers do. Lawyers must bring to the practice of law all of whom they are and the values they possess, so that the stones and the river can work and flow in harmony with each other.

So it is not the presence of the stones that make this profession calcified, it is the absence of the river. The stones are beautiful in themselves and in their rightful place. They provide a foundation for the profession that allows the search for justice and truth to go forth. They give lawyers tools to use that not only contribute to the case before them, but enhance their understanding of life. We must give reverence to the stones as we do the river. But we must make sure that lying next to the stones is always a river, for without the river as representative of our souls, these stones are transformed from foundations of support into weapons of destruction. They no longer search for truth, but crush it if the price is right. They no longer uphold our values; they cover them up if it is necessary to achieve a particular goal. They no longer serve as landmarks that increase the flow of the river; they are obstacles and obstructions that foster stagnation.

Balance is a critical element in any definition or description of wholeness. It is also a key element in the lawyer's quest for wholeness, meaning and purpose. Each aspect of a lawyer's existence must consistently contribute to his overall development, for when we embrace only one part of ourselves at the expense of other parts, we forsake the fullness of the ultimate calling. So those lawyers who have been trained to embrace the attorney personality at the expense of the soul must be reintroduced to the soul of the lawyer. And those lawyers, very few I might add, who have been so immersed in the work of the soul that they totally have abandoned the attorney personality, must rediscover it, and its benefits.

Troubled Waters: Lawyers in Crisis

When a river forcefully overflows its banks and creates destruction, chaos and disruption in the lives of those around it, it is often a sign that there is a deep disturbance somewhere in the universe. This calamity could have been brought about through natural forces like an unceasing rainfall, or by human forces like the construction or malfunction of a dam. Whatever the cause, the river is no longer a place that welcomes us, but is something we want to guard against. We put up barriers in order to minimize the negative effects of the flooding. If possible we try to alter the flow of the river so that the overflow can run into other bodies of water. Whatever we do, our goal is to get the river back to its natural state so that our lives can return to some semblance of order. This same pattern is true with the soul. It can be troubled by events beyond our control, like September 11th and the death of a loved one, or by bad choices we make such as drug and alcohol addictions or unhealthy relationships. These events are not restricted to the intellectual parts of our reality. They affect the way we see ourselves, feel about the world and interface with others. When our souls are troubled, those around us are greatly affected by the overflow. We can pretend that we are fine, but the evidence that our waters are troubled can be observed on our faces, through our attitudes towards others, and certainly in the quality or quantity of our work.

Troubled waters are no stranger to lawyers and the legal profession. Sometimes the disturbance is minor, like an unusually stressful case, or it can be more severe, like a long-term addiction. Instead of seeing such crisis as something that

108

should be covered-up or rationalized away, we must see it as an opening for transformation. Some lawyers are able to adjust their lives and practices because they have thoughtfully decided over time that something needs to change. They observed patterns and practices in their lives which they knew were not consistent with their values and lifestyles, and they purposefully set out to find a better way. However, for some lawyers, like many other human beings, it takes a compelling incident or crisis in order to get their attention. Sometimes that pressure is external, such as the threat of a bar suspension or reprimand, while other times it is internal, such as an illness, the inability to sleep at night, or look at oneself in the mirror. Whatever the reason, these are rare opportunities to dredge the river so that it returns to its natural state and, in the process becomes an even more beautiful and productive body of water. So troubled waters should not frighten away the friends and colleagues of lawyers, nor immobilize the lawyer. If the behavior is extremely violent, then certainly normal precautions should be taken. However, in general, we must view these crises as blessings. Unfortunately many of us have not developed the capacity to change without serious pressure. When we see and understand the pressure through the eyes of the soul, and not through our vision of discomfort, then we realize that these are opportunities to be seized and not people to be judged and labeled. It is certainly painful to lawyers and others in the midst of a crisis, but it is even more painful when these persons do not take advantage of this opportunity for transformation.

Many lawyers find themselves in crisis. Rates of substance abuse, as well as the percentage of divorces and stress-related illnesses are abnormally high among lawyers.[115] This is not only a result of the type of work lawyers do, but also the manner in which they have been trained, given the way in which they see and understand their roles in society. Our waters are troubled because we have not been instructed and encouraged to stay in touch with the natural flow of the river. The profession does not systematically give us permission to pursue those aspects of our lives and work that may provide more meaning. Our internal demons must remain locked behind the bars of formality, long hours, and the external drive for success. Some of our waters are troubled because they were troubled long before we ever became lawyers, and nothing in the process of our education or work provided any new paths of healing. Our waters are troubled because too many of us believe that in the pursuit of excellence, profit or fame, we cannot afford to take the time to dredge our river. There is too much to accomplish and so little time to get it all done. So we keep piling on personal and professional challenges on top of worn out stones. We keep accepting more cases than we can handle, more clients than we can stay in touch with, more memberships in organizations than we can attend. Yet we spend very little time cleaning out the river. We fail to understand all those tasks and challenges that we keep piling upon the banks will eventually find their way into the river. Instead of helping to heal or clean our soul, they end up polluting it. When we choose to allow the volume of work to overrun and replace the sacred practice of "soul gazing," we are creating the perfect scenario for a spiritual flood. As one person who counsels lawyers stated in describing the norms of the legal profession, "what defines success is antithetical to what makes a person healthy."[116] When these waters overflow their banks, they will negatively affect our clients, our family, and eventually, the profession. So a major challenge for members of the profession is to systematically prevent the soul of lawyers from reaching these troubled states. If we were to adopt and embrace a more spiritually-centered way of living and working, this could lead to more balanced and peaceful waters for lawyers. However, this is more easily said than done. Therefore for many lawyers this place will only be reached through a serious crisis. Those who deeply care about the profession and about the flow of the river must be prepared to assist with these precious moments of potential transformation.

A critical question that confronts lawyers who care about their colleagues in crisis, "is how can I assist the person take advantage of this opening for transformation?" We help in the healing process of our colleagues and friends in the same way that we help our clients. We help first by declaring that the waters are troubled. We do them no service by embracing their spirit of denial. We help in their healing by claiming that healing is needed and possible, and by standing with them as they go through the process. Lawyers are not equipped to address every problem that a client possesses, nor are we equipped to handle every problem that our colleagues and friends experience. Part of our goal is to guide them to places and people that will assist in the calming of their waters. Fortunately in many states there are established organizations that specifically address the needs of lawyers in crisis.[117] Some of these organizations, though not directly spiritually- centered, will explore this area as part of their counseling strategy for lawyers. Lawyers Concerned for Lawyers, which has a strong connection to the philosophy of Alcoholic Anonymous, embraces spirituality as a tool for assisting lawyers in crisis.[118] Some clinicians specifically ask questions about spiritual practices because they believe that some lawyers they counsel have abandoned this resource due to the demanding nature of their practice.[119] Other clinicians approach the topic more indirectly by exploring ways in which the lawyer has dealt with adversity in the past.[120] Often spiritual or religious practices are offered as examples of resources used to overcome prior challenges. Still other clinicians only raise the topic if the lawyer raises it.[121] Regardless of the approach taken to utilizing spirituality as a resource for lawyers in crisis, most clinicians would agree that it is "crucial for lawyers to reconnect to their own values, hearts and lives." [122] That is an acceptable definition of spirituality, and an endearing goal of the river.

We also help lawyers in crisis by living a whole and spirited life, and by giving them examples of how lawyers can pursue their craft without corrupting their souls. As a profession we must take seriously the problems that confront our members. Our concerns can no longer be restricted to the confines of nice cocktail party conversations. There are troubled waters all around us, and if we do nothing we will have contributed to the stagnation and demise of this profession. Certainly no change or transformation will occur until the person affected makes the decision to change. This requires that they look through their personality and see their soul, and decide that the two are not in harmony. This is captured eloquently by Gary Zukav, in *Seat of the Soul*, when he states:

> The journey to wholeness requires that you look honestly, openly and with courage into yourself, into the dynamics that lie behind what you feel, what you perceive, what you value, and how you act. It is a journey through your defenses and beyond so that you

112

can experience consciously the nature of your
personality, face what it has produced in your life, and
choose to change that. [123]

Though none of us can make anyone look at themselves, we
can increase the possibility that they take a peek. Rivers always
reflect back that which comes close to them. When our souls,
motives and relationships are pure we create a river that
contributes to the healing of others. Our rivers serve as mirrors
for those who are afraid to look at themselves on their own. If
our souls are in harmony with the divine and constantly seeking
balance and wholeness, then they will serve to reflect back in
striking terms that which is not in harmony. So we keep our
rivers pure and flowing in harmony, not just for ourselves, but
for the sake of other rivers. We can sometimes be there as a
catchment when these other rivers overflow their banks. The
wisdom and insights we have gathered through pure, reflective
life experiences can ease the heavy burdens that others carry
around with them. More importantly, we can be there as a
shining, glimmering symbol of the inherent beauty of the river
and the indescribable peacefulness of its flow.

I have known and heard the stories of various lawyers who
have transformed their lives and practices out of crisis. I did not
know them before the transformation, so it is hard to judge the
distance they have come. But for many of them, the beauty of
their soul, the peacefulness of their demeanor and the depth of
their wisdom all became a compelling example of the power of
transformation. Though I am sure that the process was very
painful for them, their clients and those around them, the end
result makes it all worth the journey and suffering. The
transformative process requires something that serves as a

demarcation line between what was and what one aspires to become. This is often the power of "troubled waters." Usually there is a particular event or a series of events that let the person know that he has reached a crisis state. This line serves as a reminder just how low the person was before he started his ascension. It also stands out as a state that the person never wants to visit again. There is something powerful about creating a vision for how you want your life to be, even though you know you are a long way from that point. This is the place where other lawyers can add value to the process. Without declaring it, or the person claiming it, your mere presence can serve as the catalyst for the creation of a new vision for the person.

From a spiritual standpoint, there has to be a moment of sincere surrender. One must give in to the force of the river. One must trust in the goodness of the river to guide and protect on this journey through life. Lawyers must temporarily abandon the stones. They appear to provide safety and security, but in all honesty, they hold us back from our destinations. The stones will be there after the renewal and rebirth have occurred, but in order to get through the crisis, they must become secondary and the river must be primary. Lawyers moving from crisis to transformation must declare to themselves and eventually to others that they are striving to live a new life, and striving to conduct their practice according to a new set of values. This need not consist of a complete overhaul of the type of practice or the type of clients they represent. However, it does require them to engage the work and connect with people differently. If the change is solely internal and there is no outward manifestation of this new day, then it will gradually disappear.

114

Some lawyers have placed a small sign on their desk that they read before they interact with each client. Others sit quietly and pray at various points throughout the day as a way to remain centered, and as a reminder that the river is in control. Many lawyers have embraced meditation on a regular basis as a way to reduce some of the stress in their lives and to bring a deeper level of peace to their interactions. Others read inspiring and soul stories books on a constant basis as a form of rejuvenation and reflection. Whatever it may be that one does, it must be consistent and manageable. Transformation is a process - it is not an end. It is a process that must be continuous. The crisis may have been the catalyst for change, but the experience in the river must be the force that sustains the lawyer who is on the path to renewal and transformation.

It is vitally important for lawyers in crisis to surround themselves with, or have access to, other lawyers who are attempting to pursue a new direction for their practice that is spiritually grounded. The natural structure and momentum of the profession can easily draw one back into the prior state. There needs to be a counter force that feeds this newly found energy and insight. There are numerous organizations scattered throughout the country today composed of lawyers who are pursuing this path.[124] There are websites[125] and newsletters to which one can subscribe. The spirited legal landscape is not as parch and lonely as it was in the past, but each lawyer must find a place and a path that fits her new specific needs. Despite all the work that has gone into building networks of spirited lawyers and the establishment of alternative practice approaches, there is no fixed formula that anyone is required to follow. This is the beauty and magic of rivers. There are great similarities among rivers around the world, but no two rivers are the same. The same could be said for the soul. Once the decision is made to pursue a new direction for one's life and practice, the unique flow of the river will determine how these changes should occur. Though there are numerous examples to draw upon, the power of transformation rests in the uniqueness it takes in a given life.

There is an old gospel song entitled. "Wade in the Water."[126] There is a line in the song that says, "Wade in the water, God's gonna trouble the water." This song is reflective of various biblical stories of people being healed, redeemed or saved when they placed themselves in the midst of a certain body of water at a time when the water was acted upon by God. There is a strong and consistent spiritual belief that something powerful happens when water is troubled by a divine force. Water has played a critical role in spiritual metaphors of renewal, baptism, sanctification, healing and cleansing. Therefore, troubled waters are not necessarily a bad or unwanted experience. In the midst of the disturbance, change, transformation and healing can occur. Likewise, in the midst of the challenges and crises that lawyers face, there can be transformation and rejuvenation. But as the song suggests, lawyers in crisis must be willing to wade in their troubled waters. They must not run from or avoid the crisis, but use it as an opportunity to reflect deeply about their calling and themselves. If they run from the crisis or attempt to cover it up or deny its existence then nothing will happen but more pain and disappointment. But if they are courageous enough to use this opportunity to be embraced and enveloped by the river, then they can find a healthier and more productive place upon which to rest their practice and their lives.

Temptation and the Ethical Lawyer

One of the most challenging aspects of teaching and practicing law is instilling within lawyers a deep sense of their ethical responsibility on an individual level. Courses are taught on this subject, numerous textbooks and treatises have been written, yet for most legal scholars and many practitioners, this remains an unfulfilling part of their development. The standard approach to addressing this fundamental part of the lawyer's calling is to memorize, and hopefully internalize, the ABA Model Rules of Professional Conduct.[127] For many students in law school this becomes primarily a mental exercise. They remember various sections of the Model Rules in the same manner that they remember other doctrines. They apply the provisions to interesting fact patterns that the professor has created and, if they are able to provide the right answer, then they have crossed the ethical hurdle. This same approach is followed by Bar Examiners when they are deciding if a person is ethically qualified to become a lawyer. Some scholars have argued that ethical responsibility should not be restricted to one course, but should be pervasive throughout the law school curriculum. [128] Though this approach elevates the importance of this ideal when implemented, it still takes a similar mental approach to the issue. Though mastering the rules are critical and indispensable to the success of lawyers, its mastery fails to nurture and develop the type of attitudes and values that will ultimately produce ethical lawyers. Not only do numerous ethical violations occur in every jurisdiction, there are countless unreported violations that lawyers learn to live with on a daily basis. In addition, the rules cannot adequately cover all the ethical challenges and dilemmas that lawyers face. It serves as a central guide to those lawyers who are striving to conduct their

practice in an ethical manner, but it only points to one source
from which they can draw ethical and moral power. That one
source is the mind of the lawyer and her mental mastery of the
rules.

Ethics, like love, emerges from a source within human
beings that is deeper than the mind. A true ethical commitment
to anything comes from the heart and soul of the person. The
mental mastery of the rules is like the stones on the riverbed. It
gives shape and contour to the river, and it provides some limits
and protection, but it does not provide the true internal power
and energy needed to master this aspect of life and lawyering.
Unless the lawyer understands and stays in touch with her soul,
then her ethical commitment is superficial and vulnerable.
When you see ethical responsibility as an external power that
imposes sanctions for improper behavior, then it leaves a gaping
hole for abuses and violations. If the external power is all that
we focus on, then a keen analytical mind will be encouraged to
find ways to circumvent or rationalize away that power. As
difficult as it is to obtain, we must discover ways to nurture and
cultivate the souls of lawyers so that their ethical responsibility
is coming from a deeper and more meaningful place. It must
come from a place that is like the river-deep, sacred and
compelling. It must come from a place that creates some
support and understanding when challenging and tempting
situations arise. Lawyers must develop a perspective about
ethics and tempting situations that permits them to see and
understand what is internally and spiritually at risk.

Since we give lawyers and other professionals so much
discretion in their practice, it is easy for abuses to occur. There

are so many decisions that lawyers make in the secret closet of their minds and offices that it is easy for ethical violations to go unnoticed and unpunished. Some would argue that the answer is to remove some of this discretion and provide more policing of the practice of law. Besides being hard to implement, this approach still views ethics as an external force or power that can control or influence the behavior and choices of lawyers. Yet ethics is fundamentally an internal struggle between the temptations that dwell in the attorney's personality and the energy of the lawyer's soul. Since we cannot completely remove temptation from our practices or our lives, then it is important for us to develop a spiritual understanding of the role of temptation in our lives and in our development as lawyers. Gary Zukav, in *The Seat of the Soul,* describes the role of temptation in the following manner:

> Temptation is the gracious way of introducing each soul to his or her power. When we are seduced or threatened by external circumstances, you lose power. They gain power over you. With each choice that you make to align yourself with the energy of the soul, you empower yourself. This is how authentic power is acquired. It is built up step-by-step, choice-by-choice. It cannot be meditated or prayed into being. It must be earned. [129]

From this perspective, temptation is not something we run from or try to keep away from lawyers.[130] It is something we must first understand and then embrace, because it is inevitable, regardless of how much we try to limit a lawyer's discretion. When a lawyer is tempted to embezzle client funds, it is not the money that is really at stake, but the soul of the lawyer. The presence of the funds under the lawyer's control is a spiritual magnet[131] that is drawing the attorney's awareness to an internal weakness in his personality that must be overcome, and creating an opportunity to strengthen his moral and ethical resolve. Each time the lawyer consciously grapples with the temptation and makes the right choice, it increases his internal power and puts him more in touch with the beauty of his soul. When we make right choices without being conscious of the internal struggle, then we are denying ourselves the opportunity to grow. This does not mean that we should purposely put ourselves in tempting situations, but it does suggest that we must be conscious of the ones that cross our minds and lives everyday. When an attorney has the tendency or practice of withholding documents that should be submitted but could never be discovered, or making false statements which cannot be disputed, this is a physical manifestation of an unresolved fear or addiction that resides in his personality. Even though these practices never come to the attention of others, they come to the attention of his soul. Each time the lawyer chooses to fight against this temptation, to challenge its power, this part of his personality loses some of its power. The energy of the soul is fed and becomes a stronger pull on his subsequent choices and decisions. But when we betray or forsake the river, we eat away at the power of our soul, and we deny ourselves another opportunity to increase our internal and authentic human power. Lawyers who make sound ethical choices in the face of temptation not only have complied with the Model Rules of Professional Conduct, but more importantly, also have learned something about themselves. They have learned that they have the power to make difficult choices which will prepare and empower them to make similar choices in the future. They have experienced a sense of peace and calm similar to that of the river. It is a peace and stillness that is hard to describe and capture; yet those who have experienced or witnessed it are moved by its power and continue to seek it. When we are aligned with our souls, we acquire this majestic quality, like the river, that others will seek and return to because it serves as a reflection of the values they seek for themselves. They will return not just for our skills, but also for the calmness and healing powers of our spirit. More importantly, this will become a place to which we want to consistently return because it provides a reward that no judgment or verdict would ever bring. Therefore, in order for the profession to develop more ethical lawyers, we must spend more time trying to get each other to better understand how we grow ethically. Unlike intellectual mastery, which can occur without directly engaging the personality and soul of the learner, ethical development requires that we enjoin every aspect of the person. Lawyers must better understand that their ethical development resides within the confines of their soul, and their soul grows through an experiential process where temptation is an essential ingredient. "Each temptation is an opportunity through which the soul is able to learn without creating karma, to evolve directly through conscious choice."[132]

From this perspective it is important, as a basic step, for lawyers to understand that there is more at stake than just the external sanction of the Bar. The greater loss to the lawyer who fails the temptation test is the internal erosion of his authentic power as a human actor. It is this internal power that generates sound ethical choices, and is also the source for truly good lawyering. When that power has eroded, we become hollow human beings who can manipulate doctrine and cases but

cannot inspire human confidence and trust. The success of so
many key decisions and actions that lawyers make and take
depends on their ability to get clients, jurors, judges and, even
opposing counsel, to trust them. Our advocacy is more
effective, our negotiation offers are better received, and our
advice is followed more often when people can sense a sincerity
and genuineness in our nature. Trust is not a derivative of our
intellectual power, but is an offspring of the consistency of our
internal power and our external experiences. Therefore the
development of the soul not only leads to better ethical
decisions, it also increases our effectiveness and internal
satisfaction. Yet, this point can be easily rationalized away
since some lawyers are not concerned about their internal
power, but are obsessed with their external prestige and
standing. They are not convinced that one's internal power has
anything to do with one's external success, but our internal
standing cannot be perpetually avoided in this life, whether it
leads to external success or not. At some point in our journey
through life, we will come face - to - face with the reality of our
self worth. During those moments, the external power we have
amassed will not provide us with the peace and security that our
soul requires. In those startling moments of personal crisis or
self-reflection, which are bound to occur, we will need more
than our external plaques, trinkets and wealth. The attorney
personality will not be sharp enough to rationalize away our
shortcomings, loneliness and spiritual emptiness. We prepare
for these moments of personal challenge and crisis by aligning
ourselves with our souls. We do not align ourselves by just
complying with rules or codes, but by consistently living within
the world of values, principles and spirit. When we make sound
ethical decisions in the face of temptation, we are aligning

ourselves with our souls and making deposits in the moral well so that they can be withdrawn in the future, especially during our moments of crisis and self-reflection.

Thus the efforts of law schools and bar associations must be directed as much on matters of the heart, soul and spirit of lawyers, as it is on the Model Rules of Professional Conduct. A profession, like a society, will make very little progress if its efforts for transformation are limited to the laws it adopts. Concurrent with the transformation of laws there must be a transfiguration of people's hearts and spirit. These are matters that law schools and bar associations cannot fully control or accurately measure and predict, but they are matters that they can no longer afford to ignore. The future of professional responsibility in the legal profession will turn on our willingness to venture into these uncharted and unpredictable waters. Though we will encounter rapids that we cannot control, we also will discover new lands that can enrich the lives of those who choose this profession as their calling.

Civility

One of the most distressing parts of the practice of law, especially for those who have been engaged in this craft for a long time, is the declining level of civility among and between lawyers. Historically, civility was a hallmark of the legal profession. Even when attorneys were fierce competitors, they exhibited a high level of courtesy and politeness toward each other. It is not uncommon today to hear judges and lawyers complain about the uncivil behavior of their colleagues.[133] It would be hard to describe exactly when this change occurred and what caused it, but one would have to put some of the blame at the doorstep of the inherent weaknesses in the structure of the attorney personality. Though this personality type was prevalent during periods when lawyers were much more civil towards each other, it was tempered by the intimate and small nature of the practice. When there were a few lawyers in a particular town or city, it was easier to keep the negative attributes of the attorney personality in check. If someone exercised those traits to their logical extension, his reputation could be greatly affected in such a closely knit community of practitioners. In addition, the competition for clients, and thus for profit, was not as fierce in the past. There appeared to be enough business to go around, therefore other lawyers or firms were not viewed as fierce enemies, but as competitive companions. However, as the country and the practice of law grew and expanded, this informal gentlemen's club began to take on the feel of big business. The emergence of large law firms that employed more lawyers than what existed in one town in earlier days, not only made relationships more formal and legal, but also made the financial bottom line much more critical to the definition of success. This increased the competitive nature of the profession and blurred the lines between the rules of practice and the goals of profit.

Uncivil acts, such as withholding documents and witness lists to which the other side is entitled have become commonplace today. Delay tactics, which could be construed as zealous advocacy, are often motivated by mean spiritedness and callous disregard for the interest of opposing counsel and the persons they represent. Even more basic acts of rudeness, character assassination, loudness, and disrespectful comments and conduct contribute to this pervasive sense that lawyers have forsaken one of their most cherished ideals. What is frustrating for so many experienced lawyers who remember the "good old days" is that they cannot understand why those precious values cannot be easily restored. Some presidents of bar associations have argued that law schools should do a better job teaching these values and some of them have been more than willing to visit law schools to impress the importance of this value on the next generation of lawyers. Others believe that stricter sanctions imposed by judges and other disciplinary bodies will correct the problem. However, the problem is much more complex, and the solution will require more than lectures and heavier sanctions.

At the core of the problem is the simple fact that many of the lawyers who complain about this problem "want their cake and want to be able to eat it too." They have to understand that the fundamental way in which they want law schools to teach and evaluate law students contributes to the very problem that frustrates them. The intense competitiveness among law students creates the foundation for the uncivil behavior that will be exhibited once they enter into the intense and competitive practice of law. Law students, because of standard grading systems and class rankings, begin early on to see each other as competitors for the same prized possessions. The same lawyers who complain about uncivil behavior, when they are wearing the hat of employer, want law schools to deliver students to them stacked in neat piles and labeled according to their performance in the grueling competitive race called law school. In order for students to end up with the right label, some of them feel that they have to be self-centered, intensely competitive, and less tolerant of colleagues who may not be mastering the materials as quickly at they. This is not to suggest that law students do not cooperate with each other, for study groups always have been a fundamental way in which student try to collectively master and survive this grueling process. However, when the study group structure becomes a process of inclusion and exclusion it can create artificial barriers among those who are engaged in a collective learning experience. Once this mindset of competitiveness and winner-take-all are sown within the consciousness of law students in an environment that focuses primarily on mental development, then we are encouraging those who already may be inclined toward uncivil behavior to follow their instincts. Those who are more in touch with the internal power of their souls begin to feel that they are at a competitive disadvantage by holding on to the values that have guided them to that place. If the group is not careful, students will abandon their internal power for the illusion of external power. They will easily embrace the old adage, "if you can't beat 'em, join 'em." Thus you have young lawyers engaging in behavior they do not naturally like, but feel is necessary in order to survive in their chosen profession.

I have been fortunate for the last seventeen year to experience a different environment for the nurturing of lawyers. Northeastern University School of Law, where I have served as a professor and dean, has been able to avoid some of the negative competitiveness of legal education by having a grading policy that does not give students letter grades or allow them to be ranked in any ascending or descending order. Though there is no empirical evidence to prove this point, my observation is that students are more cooperative and civil toward each other because of the absence of these unnecessary incentives. Students still strive to achieve academic success and work exceedingly hard; however, they know that they are only competing against themselves and not against the person sitting next to them. Graduates from the law school end up being hired by major firms and prestigious courts in Boston, New York and other cities. Certainly many of our graduates end up doing public interest work, though that is more a product of the school's commitment to social justice than to its grading policies. Despite these benefits and the institution's stellar reputation, as dean I often encountered prominent lawyers and judges who questioned the legitimacy of our grading policy. They wanted something that was similar to what they were seeing at other law schools. Yet these same leaders of the profession would also be concerned about the increasing uncivil behavior among lawyers. It was difficult for them to see a connection between the way lawyers were trained and graded and the way they conducted themselves in the courtroom and in the profession.

The experience at Northeastern demonstrates the point, that if we want to make a real difference in the way lawyers behave, we have to make serious changes in the structures and institutions that provide them with their primary values and insights. The tweaking of the system at the edges by inviting members of bar associations to lecture students about the importance of civility in the profession will not get to the core of the problem. The core of incivility, as it relates to the role of law schools, is similar to the problem of unethical behavior. Too many legal educators have focused too much time molding stones, and not enough time traveling and contemplating rivers. If we want our students to manifest certain values when they are in practice, we must structure the educational process, including its rewards and incentives, in a manner that reinforces and highlights those values. Values of respect, cooperation, sensitivity and honor must be consistently cultivated in the curriculum and in the institution, if we want them to be nurtured in the hearts and minds of our students.

Legal educators do not stand alone in fostering civility among lawyers, and in all frankness, they are not the major contributors to this problem. What happens, or does not happen, in the practice of law is the major source for concern. Lawyers, like law students, are given strong message about which values lead to success and many follow these signs at all cost. If they see their colleagues engage in behavior that appears to intimidate and unnerve opponents, or leads to certain outcomes, they will embrace and model the same behavior. If they see judges overlooking tardiness, rudeness and other uncivil behavior in their courtrooms, then there is a an increased chance that other lawyers will adopt these same patterns. The problem of incivility cannot be solved by tighter controls and harsher punishments. Civility comes from a place of internal peace and harmony, and incivility springs from internal discord and fear. If we do not adequately address the demons within which all of us have, then they will consume us, and we will become the demon. Uncontrollable outbursts, anger, rudeness, and disrespect are minor manifestations of a larger underlying challenge. So many lawyers feel stuck and uninspired. They do not feel as if they are part of a grand tradition that is providing compelling good for the advancement of the society and the world. Many go through the motions of being a lawyer everyday, but are not sure what it means, and how it relates to the other parts of their lives. They see what they do as a job and not as a calling. If it is only a job, a vehicle for earning a living, then there is no reverence for the profession, or for those whom participate within it. When we lose our reverence for a profession then it becomes a dangerous endeavor for ourselves and those who we encounter. "...[B]usiness without reverence, and politics without reverence, and any activity that is done without reverence, reflects the same thing: one soul preying upon another weaker soul." [134] So incivility is souls at war. When lawyers feel powerless in the courtroom, they seek power by taking advantage of others. They have lost touch with their internal authentic power, so they grasp for external power over their opponents, and sometimes over the judge or court officials. The reverence for the profession comes back when more lawyers operate out of a reservoir of internal spiritual power.

Embracing a set of spiritual values and consistently attempting to practice them is a major step toward resolving the internal conflicts that often manifest themselves in uncivil behavior. Unfortunately, the prevailing values and structure of the profession are not conducive to addressing these concerns. The dominant values which govern the profession convey a message to lawyers that long hours, high stress, and the "trap of over activity,"[135] are the pathways to success. Yet the internal peace of the river is always there, waiting for us if we are open to seeking and embracing it. The river reminds us that civility emerges from the twin pillars of self reflection and connectedness. It is something we master by making sure we know our "hot buttons" and learning how to keep them from being pushed, and how to turn them off when they are triggered. It comes also out of a deep appreciation and connectedness to others. When we are alienated from those around us, then they become objects for our abuse and manipulation. The closer we are to other human beings, not just physically and emotionally, but spiritually, the harder it is to use them for our pleasures and earthly goals and desires. Some lawyers feel so disconnected from each other, especially from those who are on the opposite side of the case, that it is very easy for them to engage in uncivil behavior. The dominant pedagogy of legal education probably contributes to the development of this sense of alienation and disconnectedness. To detach oneself from the person in the case you are reading and analyzing can lead to a detachment from the other people who are reading the same case. To go through school with very little, and sometimes no contact, with real clients feeds this sense of alienation and detachment. This process continues into practice when clients are viewed more through a lens of financial necessity than through human service. The attorney personality can lead to a self-centered perspective not only about life, but also about those around you. Thus the profession does not feel like a group of kindred spirits on a similar journey, but like a collection of comparable stones, shaped and molded by a similar experience. So lawyers become disconnected from the very people they work with everyday, and they lose touch with the spiritual cord that binds us all. This disconnectedness, and its consequences, is eloquently captured in the following statement: "Incivility is a love disorder ... (and) imposed obedience cannot rekindle the capacity to love." [136] If the judiciary wants members of the profession to exhibit more civility, it must figure out how the profession can demonstrate and teach each other how to love the profession, and those it serves.

The profession is badly in need of a revival of the spirit of those who participate in the practice of law. This will not come about through lectures, fancy slogans or harsh rules. This will be a slow and deliberate process. The more lawyers who seek the light of their own enlightenment, the more that light will be turned on within others. There are many lawyers seeking the light of their enlightenment, but they are still operating at the margins of this profession.[137] If we want to get to the root problem of incivility, then mainstream legal organizations and institutions must embrace the river and the values which flow from it as fundamental aspects of the practice of law.

Chapter Three:
Practicing From the River

Serving the Whole Client

Traditional lawyers see their role in a client matter as limited to the legal issues and procedures that the facts of the case present. The analysis and resolution of the problem are viewed through a lens of existing structures and legal solutions. The root causes of the problem, the client's role in creating it, the client's motivations for wanting the problem resolved, the emotional attachment of the client to certain solutions, and the spiritual lessons that the problem may be presenting for the client, are generally viewed as outside the bounds of a lawyer's role. Yet many of the problems and challenges that are presented in life do not have neat and narrow legal solutions. Many of the people that lawyers serve are struggling with more than just the narrow legal issue presented. Though the traditional legal solution may temporarily resolve the problem and create a sense of victory for the client, there is a strong likelihood that the problem will reemerge in the future, in the same or different form. If the underlying source of the problem is not put on the table or even acknowledged, then lawyers are not truly serving people, but are the servants of problems. In order to truly serve the client, lawyers must strive to develop a deep understanding of the legal issues and the person. In the time that is spent with clients, lawyers must create a space where clients can share as much about themselves and their surrounding circumstances as is practically feasible. Not only will that information provide for a better solution to the presenting legal problem, but it will also create the possibility for a deeper and more meaningful encounter between lawyers and their clients. Meaningful encounters which touch and embrace the whole person can serve as a catalyst for future human change and transformation.

Serving the whole client goes beyond traditional interviewing and counseling skills. Certainly lawyers must be able to listen effectively and empathetically in order to advise someone who is engaged in a difficult situation. However, many lawyers, who through training or personal attributes are very skilled interviewers, still resort to narrow legal solutions once they obtain the information they were seeking. They see their role through the same tunnel vision that law schools and other lawyers created for them. They are reluctant to step outside the boundaries of the traditional role and envision the client as a person with multiple needs which a lawyer has the ability to address. Sometimes the client needs, in addition to the particular relief they are seeking, a compassionate person who not only will be there with and for them, but also will challenge and encourage them to look at their life, circumstances or business differently. Some clients are locked into deep emotional and psychological patterns and chains that can be changed or broken by a meaningful encounter with someone they trust. There are certainly times when these emotional or psychological challenges exceed the capability of the lawyer, and the best approach is to recommend that the client seek some professional assistance with that aspect of the problem. However, even to assume this level of interest goes beyond the traditional role of most lawyers, and embraces the needs of the whole client. In other situations, clients are seeking revenge in a divorce or family dispute that has more to do with their anger, hurt and sense of betrayal than it does with finding a viable resolution to their legal problems or issues. The lawyer can choose to address only the legal need, but she would serve the client better if those other aspects of the client's motivation and personal entanglement were also addressed.

Even in the criminal defense area a lawyer can choose either to focus solely on matters which will secure an acquittal for the client, or use the opportunity to encourage the client to honestly confront his possible quilt, culpability or emotional pattern that lead to the situation. The attorney client privilege provides a sacred shield for this holistic approach to the lawyer's role. Even if the client is completely innocent there could be other challenges he will face in the future. From a whole client perspective, the lawyer is responsible for helping the client prepare for those future challenges, as she guides them through the present situation. Though these approaches are fraught with danger and subject to abuse, many clients who have had these types of experience with their lawyers have indicated that they gained as much from their interaction with the lawyer as they did from the resolution of the problem.

As lawyers we have more to offer people than just our skills
and legal expertise. When we have spent time in our own river,
and have deepened and widened our souls, there is so much
more insight and guidance we can give to people in need. Life
is as much a product of small, immeasurable, but meaningful
interactions, as it is of major, cataclysmic transformations. We
learn about ourselves and others through the exchange of
minute insights that enable us to discover miniscule treasures
buried in our river. The client comes to our world bringing these
treasures and seeking them from us. We never know when the
learning or insight will occur, but we must always be ready and
available. If we focus too much on the major issues, then we
may overlook the small ones which, in the long run, may be of
greater significance to the client and to us.

John McShane , a very well know attorney in Texas, before
meeting with every client asks himself two questions: What
was this person sent to teach me? How can I serve this person?
[138] Embedded in those questions is the notion that there is more
to the lawyer/client process than just the exchange of legal
expertise for money. "How can I serve the client" is a very
broad and all encompassing question which more lawyers need
to ask. Instead of approaching the relationship with a collection
of pre-packaged solutions based on prior clients and cases, this
question asks the lawyer to try to fashion an approach and
process that can meet the needs of each particular client.
"How" is an extremely broad, and ultimately spiritual,
component of the question. Despite the knowledge, expertise
and experience that the lawyer possesses, the relationship
should begin with a sense of openness and discovery. The
lawyer must be open to discovering the true needs of the person
who has come to be served, and willing to develop a process

and approach that fits his needs. This openness and creative spirit creates the possibility for solutions and approaches that have not been tried before and goes much deeper to the source of the problem, for when flowing rivers intersect, wonderful and unimaginable events and discoveries occur. This natural process of human and spiritual engagement can change or alter the structure of the land, the lives and activities of the people on the land, and can ultimately create new rivers. Lawyers cannot fully predict or determine ahead of time what they may be able to add to a client's life or how they may be able to assist the client's journey. If we see the encounter solely through legal eyes, then we will certainly miss the opportunity to enhance a life, but if we approach the situation through a spiritual lens, then we empower ourselves to see the whole person and provide whatever part of the answer the client's river may be seeking. Most of what we provide may be wrapped in legal rhetoric, but other parts of what we give may be pure, unadulterated emotional, spiritual, educational, cultural and even political gems. We can bring all of whom we are to the experience, and we can empower the client to do the same. We should never impose who we are on the client, but we must be available to go where the river leads us, and be equipped to guide the client when the client is lost in the rapids or feels stuck in the rock of life.

Some legal scholars refer to this approach of serving the whole client as "moral counseling," and argue that it is very consistent with the role of a practicing attorney and supported by the rules of professional conduct.[139] Professor Joseph Allegretti, in *The Lawyer's Calling*, states, "this is the essence of the lawyer's prophetic ministry – to encourage moral reflection." He argues that in lawyer-client interactions, the lawyer must be a "voice calling her client back to their better selves just as the prophets called Israel back to God and neighbor." [140] These scholars point to the Model Rules of Professional Conduct as evidence that the lawyer's counseling terrain is morally broad and not legally narrow.[141] Rule 2.1 indicates that, "[i]n rendering advice, a lawyer may refer not only to law but to other considerations such as moral, economic, social and political factors, that may be relevant to the client's situation." Various comments to the Code support the notion that technical knowledge is not all that a lawyer is empowered to deliver, and that technical legal advice may not be sufficient or worthwhile in a particular situation. [142] There is certainly a danger when lawyers use this broad moral and spiritual power to try to force a decision or perspective upon a client, or try to persuade the client to adopt a particular religious belief. It is for this reason, among others, that some scholars have argued against "moral counseling."[143] Yet this aspect of the lawyer's calling is no different than other forms of discretion that we give lawyers over client funds, communications and technical legal decisions. This privilege must be used with the utmost respect and reverence for the client's autonomy and personhood. This spiritual aspect of the calling does not require the lawyer to preach and condemn, but to comfort, challenge and counsel. We serve clients not only through our legal advice, but also through the words that emanate from our mouths, and the spirit that flows from our being and our actions.

The other question that John McShane asks himself is also compelling and insightful. "What was this person sent here to teach me?" opens up a new avenue of the attorney-client relationship that is rarely explored. Most lawyers, like many other professionals, tend to view their relationship with clients as primarily unilateral. The lawyer is the one who is charged and responsible for ushering in change, imparting knowledge, and pouring wisdom into the empty vessel that the client holds. The lawyer's life, circumstances, and needs are not part of the equation, except for the monetary remuneration for the services provided. The client is supposed to leave the encounter in a different legal place, but the lawyer should remain the same, except for the accumulation of a little more experience. However, from a spiritual perspective, no interaction or relationship is unilateral. We are always giving and receiving, teaching and being taught, and molding and being shaped by life's experiences. There are always numerous lessons in the universe for all of us, if we open ourselves to them and are ready for the teacher to arrive. Each client who walks through our doors may have one of those miniscule or major treasures for us to discover about ourselves. The discovery is not just about how we can do the job better, which is certainly very important, but it may be that our river is blocked, polluted, flowing too fast, or in need of dredging. If we make ourselves available in a complete and authentic way, then we are creating the possibility for this person to add something to the flow of our river. It may be a comment that forces us to think about a person, problem or situation in our own lives that needs addressing. It may be a gesture on the client's part that reminds us of the inherent goodness that we possess. It may be that through the client's personality we are exposed to a weakness in our personality that we need to address and hopefully correct. The client may be providing us with an opportunity to learn to say no, even when there are so many compelling reasons why we want to say yes. Through the life experiences and stories shared with us, the client may expose us to a part of life into which we rarely, if ever venture. Our journey there can teach us something about that world, and also about ourselves.

This type of personal learning on the part of the lawyer can be minimized or dismissed as being very insignificant in the larger scheme of things that most lawyers have to do or understand. Stones have an inherent fear of the river experiences. They know that the force of the water can erode over time their structure and carry away sediment to other places that are unknown and strange. Stones like staying where they are, creating the impression that they are solid, permanent and immoveable. Yet nothing in nature is everlasting - it is all in a constant state of change. The primary question is whether we will remain open to the change or try to resist it in an attempt to hold onto a false sense of security and importance. Each client is creating a new opportunity for us to grow, and that growth becomes more meaningful when we take the time to acknowledge, observe and reflect upon it. We may not have the time to make deep sense out of each encounter, or to process the value of each discovery, but our internal acknowledgment of the constant flow and richness of life deepens our river, and gives more meaning and purpose to our work.

The Search for Truth

One of the most unsettling conversations for lawyers revolves around this ultimate goal of the legal process that we call "the search for truth." Many philosophers have demonstrated the complex and illusive nature of this type of journey.[144] For lawyers this can often be a journey filled with stones of great skepticism. Because lawyers are uniquely aware of the ambiguous nature of facts, rules and policies, they often embrace the notion that truth cannot be the real goal of the adversarial process because the legal system is not equipped to obtain it. Therefore lawyering becomes a battle of process and procedure, a ritualistic dance between rules and facts, a promenade, race or marathon to the finish line of judgments and decrees. Outcomes do not necessarily guarantee us that truth has been obtained or that justice has prevailed, but are merely a representation that the game was played by the rules, and someone had to win and someone had to lose. The lawyer is thus compelled to become a master of process and techniques, an expert in persuasion and presentation. These skills and techniques are more likely to determine the results than the truthfulness or righteousness of the client's claim or position. To participate in and embrace this type of moral reasoning slowly depletes one's moral well. The entire process begins to feel like a game, and the lawyer begins to feel like a gamester. It is at this point that disillusionment, depression and more serious personal disorders begin to set in. Though many lawyers learn to hold their noses before they partake of the legal feast, some are just not able to handle it or reconcile it with their personal values, or their quest for spiritual oneness. So they leave the profession and seek new paths to fulfill their calling in life. But many remain, feeling somewhat depleted of moral fiber and resigning themselves to a life where they may not experience the joy and satisfaction from the practice of law that they once envisioned. So the search for truth has led many to a dead end, after seeing lots of lies and half-truths stacked on law library shelves and scripted on courthouse buildings along the way.

In order to save these individuals and salvage the profession, we must redefine and better explain our search for truth. We must first admit that the adversarial system is not able to guarantee that truth will be at the end of its processes. There is too much ambiguity in facts, laws and policies to make this guarantee. More importantly, too many clients, and some lawyers, have learned to suspend the search for truth in order to secure a favorable judgment or ruling. So the search for truth for the client and for the lawyer cannot be limited to the verdict of the jury or the opinion of the judge. These entities can strive to approximate the truth as best they can, based on the facts that are presented to them. However, many times they will inevitably get it wrong. Also, procedural hurdles and mistakes will sometimes stand in the way of their quest. It is easy to argue that we should abandon these procedural rules when they contribute to a guilty person being set free. However, the answer is not quite that simple. Procedural rules often serve as aids in our search for the truth more than they serve as barriers to the truth. If we focus solely on "truth as outcome," we will trample much truth along the way. Truth must define and give shape to every aspect of our dealings with our clients and our engagement with the legal processes. This is not truth in the narrow sense of whether something conforms with the facts, though this is very important. This is truth in the broadest sense of whether our actions and attitudes spring from a place of sincerity and integrity. Truth is whether we are open to receiving what the river has in store for us. [145] Spiritually we are all being called to fulfill a purpose in life. These things are revealed to us in various ways, sometimes through prayer and meditation, but oft times through conversations and encounters we have with other people. Living and working consistent with the factual reality of our calling is truth.

The search for truth that should govern our conduct as lawyers should embrace the truth that is revealed about us, and the truth that is revealed to our clients about themselves. That which is good for us and allows us to break out of negative and destructive patterns, is also the truth that we seek. This is what is meant by the statement, "ye shall know the truth, and the truth shall make you free."[146] In our interactions with our clients there are so many opportunities for the truth to be revealed and obtained. It can be a revelation about a major psychological barrier, or it could be a minor irritant that keeps the client or the lawyer from being effective. Sometimes having one person believe in you, though the twelve people in the jury box may not, can be the truth that a person is seeking or needs. Being able to tell someone's story to a group of strangers and create a meaningful connection with the person in the process may be the truth that the client needs, even if it was not all that they were seeking. Being consistently respectful to clients is truth. Treating other lawyers with respect and sincerity is part of our search for truth. Conducting our practice and our lives in such a way that they bring honor to the profession and inspire others to pursue this path brings us closer to experiencing the truth about our lives. Loving the practice of law, not just using it as a means of support, is truth. If we hang our hats solely on the "truth of outcomes," we will continue to be disappointed and disillusioned.

The search for truth is too pervasive and profound to place it all in the hands of twelve people or a judge. This is too much for them to handle. When we view the search for truth broadly, then we are not disillusioned when the results do not come out "our way." Since we are generally not there when the crime or incident occurred, we really do not know whether the results we seek are truly consistent with the truth. We believe in our client's innocence or in the righteousness of the client's claim, but we cannot hold ourselves up as gods. Since there is a limit to our ability to know the "truth of outcomes," we should be more willing to embrace the possibility of discovering truths that reveal themselves to us and to our clients right before our eyes as we engage in the process of representing them. While these truths may be illusive, they are no more so than the "truth of outcomes." Revelations that people receive, understandings that they acquire, personal weaknesses that they address, all can be short-lived or quickly disappear, but that does not take away from the value or beauty of that acquisition of truth. Just as clients squander big judgments and return to a life of poverty, just as paroled clients may return to prison, every discovery of truth will not necessarily be permanent. Deep-seated negative patterns are not broken overnight. Yet every opening can ultimately make a contribution to more meaningful and long-term change. This is the redeeming value in our broad search for truth. We do not know exactly where we will find it, and we do not know how much of an impact it will have on the client or us, but if we believe in the value of truth, then we must continue to seek it even in the face of doubt and uncertainty. If lawyers fundamentally live and work out of a deep well of truth, they will not be dismayed when outcomes are different from the facts as they know or understand them. Our calling is not to always be right, but to always strive to live right.

Truth is like mountains which stand majestically in the distance looking God-like. We stand in awe of them, believing that they hold something redeeming and healing for those who seek them and are able to reach the peak. The climb is generally difficult and challenging, and many give up along the way. There are many shapes and contours to the mountains, and there is always the danger that we will get lost. But we keep searching to reach the peak for it represents the height of our experience and exploration. However, we soon discover that there are many peaks, and that there is as much beauty in the climb as there is at the peak. We discover new vistas and viewpoints along the way that enrich our lives and give us a deeper appreciation for the mountains, as well as for the valley below. Like the mountains, truth is not as illusive as we might think. Just as there are numerous peaks to seek and discover, there are numerous truths for us to touch along the way. We must be willing to embrace each discovery. Though we have placed so much emphasis on the "peak truth," we should never overlook the "truth on the trail," especially since we most likely will spend more time on the trail than at the peak. We will spend more time engaging our clients, listening to the stories of their lives and touching their souls, than we will listening to the verdict of the jury or the judgment from the judge. Even if we never reach the peak and never get the outcome we sought, we have cherished the goodness and insights that we have shared with our clients along the way. Mountains should not impress us by how distant they are, but by how close we can bring them to us. Truth should not overwhelm us because of how difficult it is to obtain, but by how all encompassing it is. Truth exists in every fiber of our being and in every aspect of our practice and study of law. It is not just an object that is external to us; it is also a process and a way of life that is internal and constant. It is not just something that others control and hold over us; it is always within our grasp and always discoverable. As long as we remain open to seeking and discovering truth in all of its various forms, then we will be able to make peace with our role as lawyers.

Attorney-Client Privilege

One of the most fundamental aspects of the legal system and the lawyer's role is the attorney-client privilege.[147] This rule gives the client an assurance that conversations she has with her attorney cannot be divulged to another without her consent. There are important exceptions to this rule, such as the prevention of harm or the commission of a crime.[148] Generally, this rule is discussed and considered as a major benefit and protection to the client, and as an albatross around the neck of the lawyer. We have all watched riveting movies where the defendant, after acquittal, confesses his guilt to the lawyer knowing that there is nothing the lawyer can say or do with that newfound information. We also have heard stories of how clients feel free to discuss their lives and secrets with their lawyer because of this privilege. What we do not discuss enough is how the existence of this rule creates a special moral bond between attorney and client that serves to support the vision of "lawyer as healer."[149]

In addition to the practical utility of the rule to encourage the client to be truthful, there is a spiritual thread to it that requires the lawyer to be morally responsible. The mere existence of the rule recognizes that there is something sacred to the relationship between lawyer and client. The types of professions to which this privilege also is extended fall into the category of those which attempt to assist in the emotional and spiritual healing of the client. [150] The law is in a similar situation and under an equivalent moral command. By supporting this arrangement the law is also embracing the sacredness of the relationship and the interchange. If we view this as just a practical rule, then we overlook one of the fundamental aspects of our calling. Inherent in the granting of the privilege is a responsibility to assist the client in understanding and appreciating the information that has been shared. If the rule, except in serious circumstances, precludes us from sharing the information with others, then it should empower us to use it to help serve the whole client. It serves as the moral foundation for engaging the client not just around those things that can be said in court, but those things that were said during the attorney-client relationship. To ignore these things because they have no legal value, suggests that we are just "hired guns," to be used in whatever way the client chooses. We fight against the "hired gun" paradigm when we see our role as encompassing everything that has been shared with us within the relationship. This does not mean that we have an answer, diagnosis or remedy for every problem or challenge that the client reveals, but it does indicate that it is all within our purview of concern and within the boundaries of our calling. What we do with the information and how well we can assist the client, depends on how much we are in touch with the river, and how experienced we are in handling these types of problems. But we should no longer see ourselves as being handcuffed by the rule. The rule empowers us to be true caretakers of the information and of the relationship. Through exercising this power we can sometimes do as much, or more, for the client by engaging her around those privileged statements, than we can through the legal process.

Intentionality

In order to serve the whole client and practice from the river, one must declare one's intention to do so. This declaration can be done publicly, like those who operate out of Holistic Justice Centers,[151] or it can be done privately, like those numerous lawyers who pray, meditate and center themselves before they engage in any aspect of their practice. Spiritual power comes through invocation. One must invite the spirit in and open up to the possibilities of traveling down the river. If we want to practice law from a sincere place of love and compassion, then we must at least declare that to ourselves and continue to do so. Though some of our spiritual growth can occur even when we are not constantly seeking it, our lives, work and life journey can become much more meaningful when we intentionally seek to grow and change. Spiritual intentionality is very similar to the common practice of organizations and individuals who create mission statements that declare their values and define their aspirations. Though one could categorize mission statements as important management tools for individuals and organizations, their value is much greater. When we declare to ourselves and to the world the values we deem important, we are making a conscious decision to embrace certain values and thereby reject others. We also are also setting into motion a spiritual process, which if taken seriously will engage us and the energy around us in a meaningful way. The mere declaration sets in motion a new set of decision-making processes, and creates a different type of reaction by those with whom we interact. If nurtured continuously, the way we spend our time and what we spend our time on changes. We intentionally have set in motion a change process that will lead us down paths that we might not have traveled without the declaration. Spiritual intentionality raises this process to a new level. We are intentionally creating energy pathways for ourselves that will affect not only our attitudes and moods, but also those with whom we interact. By declaring to ourselves that we will try to serve the whole client, we go into the experience looking for ways to achieve this goal, and being available for those opportunities when they present themselves. When we intentionally declare that we want to receive that which we are to learn from a particular client, we increase the possibility that we will embrace the lessons when they arrive and not run from them or rationalize away the experience.

"Every experience, and every change in your experience, reflects an intention. An intention is not only a desire. It is the use of your will." [152] As lawyers we can create the type of practice we desire and the type of profession we know the public deserves if we are willing to use our will to bring this new reality into existence. This will not occur just by passing new bar rules and regulations. It will occur when we intentionally pursue a different understanding of our work and purpose in life, and when we structure our lives and practices in ways that are consistent with our declarations. The qualities and values that we declare, like love, humility, forgiveness, service, faith and integrity, exist within each of us now. For many of us, accessing them in our work is hard because the stones have covered them over, but there is a force, a power, and a will, that can "roll the stones away." These values that lie dormant inside of us will come forth easily, and will become the defining features of our practices and not just marginal aberrations. As lawyers we have used our will primarily to shape and mold the stones of this profession. The treatises and cases we have written, the mega firms we have built, the sophisticated judicial system we have created, and the technological innovations used to do our research, all stand as lasting monuments to the powerful will of lawyers and judges. We must now garner that same energy so that we can nurture the rivers for it is as vital, if not more so, than the monuments of stone we have erected. But if we assume that quality changes to the profession will occur naturally, without any adjustments in our intentions or actions, then we are fooling ourselves. So as individuals and as collectives, we must begin to declare a new path. We can shout it from the mountaintop or we can just whisper it in the closet of our souls. What matters most is whether we have earnestly decided to seek the river. If we have, the river will find us. We may not understand all that it is trying to teach us or know exactly where it is trying to lead us, but if we remain true to our declaration, then we will find ourselves ultimately in a different and better place. The river demands that we change. The river cannot stand still. Its nature will not permit it to stand still. If it ceases to move, to change, to touch, to flow, then it is no longer a river. Once we open our hearts and souls to serving the whole client and engaging in this type of practice, we will become better lawyers who will never be the same tomorrow as we are today.

Faith

I cannot talk about intentionality without next discussing faith. After declaring that we will view and practice law differently, we then must begin this journey. To seek divine guidance in our secular activities, as well as in our sacred life, requires a giant leap of faith. It is written that "faith is the substance of things hoped for, the evidence of things unseen." [153] Lawyers are trained that to prove a claim or defend a position, one must have convincing, verifiable and objective evidence. Without concrete things to point to or enter into evidence, the case appears very weak. Yet, good and experienced lawyers understand that you sometimes must take a case, or make an argument, when the evidence is non-existent or very weak. The lawyer's experience and instincts lead her to believe that there is something to the case or cause, and if she works hard enough the evidence to support the client's position will be discovered or revealed. She believes so deeply in the righteousness of her clients cause or innocence that she is willing to work for years striving to vindicate her client. The lawyer may call what she does something else, but she is really operating on faith. The faith may be in her client, the general principle for which she is advocating, or in ideals like justice or equality. Yet, there is another level of faith that is required to live and practice a spirit-filled life. This faith is in God; in the divine goodness of the universe; in the consistency of the river. This is not a faith rooted in one particular client or cause, but in everything we, as lawyers, do and experience. It is a faith that gives us the comfort and security in knowing that if we fall into the river, we will not drown. It is a faith secure in the knowledge that if we build our practice and life on the values of love, loyalty, humility, forgiveness, service and integrity, then we will not be forsaken.

Faith is critical to those of us who are attempting to transform our practice because everything will not happen in the manner we hope for or predict, and certainly everyone will not respond to us in the way that we think they should. During these moments of doubt, disenchantment or disillusionment, we will need something to serve as our anchor and support. We will need some evidence of those things that are not yet visible in our practice or life. For some of us, the evidence springs from our deep belief in God. For others, it evolves out of a sincere belief in the goodness and correctness of the path they have chosen to follow. Then there are those whose evidence is the joy and peace they feel stitched inside the lining of their hearts, regardless of the circumstances they face. These things cannot be presented to the court, to creditors or to our associates. We cannot take them to the bank, but some lawyers have learned to bank on these intangible, but real beliefs when their sanity and peace of mind are in the balance.

When you practice from the river, faith becomes a constant and necessary companion. You have to be courageous enough to reveal that you are willing to deal with issues that some will label as soft, illogical or fool's gold. You are going against the accepted grain, and thus will encounter losses and setbacks because of who you are and how you approach problems. There will be financial challenges and set backs as well. You may refuse to accept certain cases or engage in certain types of practices because you believe they are inconsistent with where the river is taking you. These decisions could result in temporary reductions in income and access to other resources. During these moments you will be tested externally and internally. Everyone in your immediate circle of colleagues and friends may not agree with your choices or support your journey down this new path. You will have your own doubts about whether you have acted wisely with your life and with your practice. There is no pill you can take, or stone you can stand on, that will get you through these moments of doubt and fear. Your greatest resource will be your faith. If you deeply believe in the divine, or embrace the heaven that exists within you, then you will make it through these rapids and waterfalls, and the river will return to a state of calmness. More importantly, it is through faith that we manifest a new reality for the practice of law. In Hindu the concept of *shraddha* captures the power of faith. It suggests that we will become what exist at the core of our hearts and beliefs. How we see and nurture ourselves will ultimately determine how we interact with and change the world. Thus for lawyers to create alternative approaches to the practice of law, they must first align their hearts and beliefs around this new approach. They must have faith in something that does not yet exist, in order for that reality to one day exist. So lawyers must, in their hearts, value the whole client today so that they can serve the whole client in the future.

It is important for lawyers, who are trained to be very analytical, to become comfortable living in a world of faith, and learning to increase their faith. This can occur through prayer, meditation, reading sacred text, communing with kindred spirits and living what you profess. Over time the rapids will begin to feel like small interferences that are only deepening your faith in the beauty and goodness of the river.

John McShane, the attorney from Texas mentioned earlier, gave me the following poem after I made a presentation to a group of lawyers who were discussing issues of spirituality and law. The note said, "this is your life anthem." I include it under this section of faith because it captures one of the greatest attributes of faith, and explains what sustains me on this river journey.

Dare to Risk
To laugh is to risk appearing the fool
To weep is to risk appearing sentimental
To reach for another is to risk involvement
To expose your ideas, your dreams before a crowd

is to risk their loss
To love is to risk not being loved in return
To live is to risk dying
To believe is to risk failure
But risk must be taken, because the greatest hazard
    in life is to risk nothing
The people who risk nothing, do nothing, have
    nothing, are nothing
They may avoid suffering and sorrow but they
    cannot learn, feel, change, grow, love, live
Chained by their attitude, they are slaves; they have
    forfeited their freedom
Only a person who risks is free.[154]

Our faith frees us to take risks and to live with the consequences of our decisions. It centers us so that we can withstand the storms of life. As lawyers, there are numerous risks that we must be willing to take for our clients and for ourselves. We are generally more comfortable when those risks are defined and somewhat controllable. This is why we feel more comfortable operating from the position of the stones as opposed to flowing with the river. Yet as the poem suggests, there is so much more for us to gain when we venture out. The gains are not always monetary, but they take the form of precious gems that can last us a lifetime. Many retired lawyers bathe in the letters, reflections and comments from former clients who indicated that their heart and soul were touched through the lawyer's work. The joy of living comes through our involvement and connection with people and life, not through sheltering ourselves from them.

The Lawyer As Healer

Healing is not limited to the province of mystics, saints and physicians. All living things have the potential to heal and be healed. Through our interactions with others we either bring people closer to a state of wholeness or we assist in helping them fall apart. Yet for those who enter the lives of people when they are in the midst of trauma, conflict or confusion these interaction becomes even more crucial. Our charge to be each other's keeper runs deeper in these moments, and our rewards and blessings are more divinely ordained. Because of the inherent conflicts that exist in society, lawyers are called onto the stage of human existence to be one of the society's most precious healers.

The grist for the lawyer's mill is conflict. Without it our role and value in society would be greatly diminished. Conflicts between parties, between governmental entities and between various states and countries are our calling cards. Though we benefit enormously from the existence of conflict, our clients suffer immeasurably from our limited understanding of it, and the role it plays in their lives and in society. We believe that our primary responsibility is to resolve conflict, address its consequences, and prevent it from occurring in the future, but we are concerned primarily with only the material and legal aspects of conflict. The traditional legal approach to conflict resolution does not empower us to see inside conflict and observe its emotional and spiritual aspects, the positive consequences which can flow from it, or contemplate what role we play with respect to them. Though the groundbreaking movement toward alternative dispute resolution has brought some of these issues to the surface, it has not become the standard focus for most lawyers. Therefore we need to widen the lens of our understanding of conflict, and understand that we are called to learn from it and be a healing force in the midst of it.

In the midst of all conflicts there is not only disruption and damage to legal relationships, but also to the people involved, and to their individual and collective spiritual wholeness. When marriages fall apart and the parties seek a divorce, their legal connection to each other is disrupted, damaged and ultimately terminated, but their emotional and spiritual connections still exist. This damage or disruption is generally not addressed unless the parties are wise enough to seek counseling or therapy. It is unfortunate that these aspects of the relationship and conflicts are not addressed within the legal arena because they often serve as the fuel for the legal conflict that is brewing in the courtroom or in the lawyer's office. Each party generally suffers from deep emotional feelings of hurt, denial, disappointment, betrayal, and other perplexing feelings. Whether they both want out of the relationship or not, whether one or the other is the primary cause for the disintegration, there is still a critical level of damage that the decree and the proceeding does not generally address.

It is very convenient and efficient for lawyers to disregard these emotions and underlying patterns, and consider them to be outside their domain or area of expertise. However, these seemingly peripheral, and sometimes subtle, aspects of the conflict are generally influencing and affecting the client's and opposing party's legal goals, strategies and actions. Even in business relationships between individuals or corporate parties, there are emotional and spiritual costs that someone pays when existing relationships are negatively disrupted. Though business clients may not reveal or share this aspect of the conflict as readily as clients in the family law arena, the emotional and psychological harm, disruption and concerns still exist. What led to the breach of contract or failure to perform is often a combination of external market realities and internal personal conflicts, perceptions, biases, anxieties, and other emotional forces. Even in the mergers and acquisitions field, there are cultural, emotional and psychological aspects to the arrangements as well as business and legal ones. In this setting, lawyers are facilitating the integration of different value systems, cultures and personalities as well as organizational structures. Understandably, lawyers are very comfortable analyzing and addressing contractual relationships and breaches, but are not as skilled in identifying and addressing the emotional and spiritual relationships that tend to exist with every situation, One could argue that some clients are bringing more emotional discomfort and discord to the table than they are bringing legal issues. Total responsibility for addressing this should not rest on the shoulders of the lawyer who is handling the case, yet the lawyer cannot ignore this critical aspect of the conflict or the client's needs. Lawyers are not only responsible for addressing and healing the legal and material wounds that have been inflicted upon their clients, but also are responsible for addressing and assisting in the healing of the emotional and spiritual wounds that may exist.

The concept of the lawyer as healer is not just a perspective coined or embraced by lawyers striving to practice in a holistic manner. The noted Supreme Court Chief Justice Warren Burger used this label a number of years ago to describe the work of lawyers, [155] and his word has served as a catalyst for the creation of a Centre for Healing and the Law.[156] Lawyers are operating as healers when they draft agreements that create relationships, partnerships and arrangements where none existed before. Through this process, positive and productive businesses, institutions and products can be created. Lawyers are healers when they bring cases that will preserve natural habitats or precious streams that contribute to the balance and wholeness of precious waterways. Certainly lawyers are operating as healers when they facilitate divorces and child custody arrangements that allow individuals to go on with their lives in meaningful and productive ways. I view the lawyers who brought numerous civil rights cases challenging segregation and discrimination as healers, as they attempted to restore human dignity to a society that had abandoned this value. Lawyers who represent average citizens in consumer product cases, landlord tenant disputes and product liability actions, are serving as a healing force for those whose rights, lives and futures have been broken.

Healing also encompasses the restoration and reclamation of one's emotional and spiritual wholeness, an important aspect that is needed not only for individuals, but also for organizations, societies and nations. [157] The perceptive lawyer, who operates from the river, can identify these scars and facilitate their healing as a fundamental part of the legal process. This healing process does not happen quickly or easily, but typically progresses in stages and at different paces. Each person who interacts with a client is in a position to either move him closer to a state of wholeness or move him farther away from his center. The client plays the crucial role in how the responses, interactions, and words of others, will affect him, but the sender of these messages and energy cannot be absolved of responsibility. Thus a lawyer who is central to the resolution of a substantive conflict, and has entered into a special relationship with the client, has a clearer responsibility to be part of the healing process.

As lawyers, we have a responsibility to be sensitive to the underlying sources of our client's problem or conflict. We have a responsibility to see the whole person in front of us, not just a legal situation. We have a responsibility to engage our clients in a manner that suggests there is a caring and sensitive person who is attempting to help them move along the path to wholeness. Clients may not use these words or even understand this is happening, but that will not distract from the power of healing that can occur if we have done our part to create a positive, nurturing and sensitive human environment in which they can unveil their pain. So much of this pain is spilled on a lawyer's table without any probing, but many just ignore it or wipe it away. Unfortunately, it remains, influencing how clients see the problem and limiting their ability to move on with their lives. Many clients place their lives, pain and future in the hands of lawyers, and in the process are expecting and asking them to be their savior. Many lawyers embrace this role and deliver their clients from the legal chains that bind them. However, most lawyers stand a better chance of being healers than saviors. We do not control the final outcome of our client's situation, but we do control every aspect of our interactions with them, and it is during this journey that we can provide enormous value to them and to the future.

Bill van Zyverden, who runs the Holistic Justice Center in Middlebury, Vermont, and is the founder of the International Alliance of Holistic Lawyers, recounts numerous examples of situations when client have come to grips with underlying emotional problems through the process of seeking legal advice. A client charge with DWI, who came to the Center wanting to plead innocent, did not leave with the result he sought, but with the relief he needed. Operating from the perspective of a lawyer as healer, Bill was able to get him to accept the fact that he had a problem, and convinced the client and his family to enter into treatment so that the underlying problem could be addressed. The decision on the client's part to enter a plea of guilty, instead of the innocent plea he initially planned to invoke, was critical to his own recovery. The lawyer as litigator envisions her role in this situation only as being responsible for defending the client based on his wishes. The lawyer as healer believes that defending the client encompasses protecting the client from himself by getting him to look openly and honestly at what brought him to this unfortunate situation. Even in a business conflict, the attorney's insistence that the client meet with the opposing party despite his reluctance to do so, allowed the client to take some responsibility for the conflict, and increased the possibility for future dealings between the parties.[158]

In order for a lawyer to talk to the concerns addressed above and to operate as a healer in any client situation, it is important that the lawyer be centered and whole. The admonition to doctors captured in the phrase, "physician heal thyself," also applies to lawyers. Before we can be the dispenser of healing energies, we must work to be in a place where we have experienced and dealt with those same forces in our own lives. This is not an easy part of our calling. It is certainly not something that all lawyers can provide based on their present training and orientation toward the practice of law. This perspective of the practice of law challenges us to rethink the way in which we train lawyers to assume their role in society, and how bar associations cultivate and promote the profession. There are various practices, perspectives and lifestyles that can contribute to lawyers being at this state, and they are discussed in greater detail in subsequent chapters.[159] Yet what primarily is at stake is whether lawyers embrace this healing goal as part of their role. Some lawyers feel that this is outside of their area of expertise and training, since they are not licensed to be psychotherapists. In addition, they are concerned that this is not something for which they should be billing a client for when there are more qualified individuals who can provide these services and have been trained specifically for this type of situation. These arguments, and many others, serve as legitimate lines that some lawyers draw around their practices and use as a justification for rejecting this role as healer. The difficulty with these positions is that this work and these issues are fundamental to and intertwined with the work the client has asked the lawyers to do. We cannot separate a person's emotional and spiritual state from his legal situation. They are there, staring us in the face, crying out for attention. When we ignore them or pretend that they are a marginal part of the experience, we still are affecting the person and negatively contributing to his unhealthy state. Every person who interfaces with the person during this period of brokenness is either contributing to his healing or contributing to his present state of disequilibrium. We cannot run from this human reality. In effect, we are already billing clients for this work – just not giving them their monies worth. One reason some individuals have negative perceptions of lawyers is because their interaction with them left so much to be desired. Their perceptions are as much a product of the fact that they did not get the results they desired, as their feeling that they or their problem did not get the care they needed.

Being a healer is not about practicing psychotherapy - it is about being a caring, positive and sensitive human being in all our interactions with those we serve. We owe that to them as human beings, and that obligation is increased when people entrust us with their problems and, thus, with their lives. There is no new degree to be earned before we engage clients at this level. There is no new subscript to add to the shingle that hangs outside our offices. This is basic stuff that we have taken for granted and ignored. It is so basic that it has become invisible in the training and practice of law. We must see ourselves as individuals who are in a position to contribute greatly to the healing of people. This does not mean that we have some magic potion that we can dispense. It means that we exist at the eye of the conflict and are positioned to see various aspects of it that others may not be able to see. We also are given access to some of the most private thoughts and feelings of other human beings. We can view these thoughts and feelings as crude stones for our private entertainment, or we can view them as precious gems which, if handled correctly could enrich the lives of those who shared them.

Major adjustments can occur in a person's life, attitude or outlook because of simple, yet insightful comment that someone shares with them. A spiritual wound can be closed because a lawyer authentically stood beside a client and cared for him despite his horrendous crime. Staying in touch with the client during the case, and checking in after it is over, can be extremely reassuring and aid his transformation and healing. Being a healer is about rising above our own limitations and preconceived notions about a person or group, and attempting to understand and appreciate them for whom they are, and affirming the unlimited potential that resides within them. As we counsel our clients, we should not only make them aware of our opinions about what laws cover their situation, but also our insights about what paths they may need to follow in order to get to a better place in their lives. Like our legal advice, it is always up to the client to accept or reject what we have said, but we have at least done our duty of being a counselor in the true sense of that word. However, we cannot counsel without striving to understand the whole person as well as the broken parts. When we see or observe the broken parts, we must be willing to mend them. The broken parts may be lack of trust or low self-esteem; they may be in fear of letting go or losing. If we have healed ourselves, we will have a sense of what the persons struggle really is, and can help guide him to a deeper realization about his healing.

As human beings we are all very fragile. There are so many people, forces, relationships and obligations that can contribute to our internal discord and create a continuing state of unrest. Though this state manifests itself in various material forms, such as the loss of property, rights or privileges, it has its origin in the emotional and spiritual realm. If we have no way of releasing the things that create this discomfort, or no way of protecting ourselves from new ones, then we end up increasing the discomfort for ourselves and for those around us. Many people enter the space of lawyers in this state. If we focus solely on the material manifestation of the discomfort, then we may end up contributing to the person's disquietude instead of helping him release it. To be at a place where we can effectively deal with these external and internal conflicts, difficulties and discomforts that come our way is a major challenge for every lawyer. We must help the client focus on the source of his discomfort as we address the material manifestation of his problem. In a world where so much of our well being and self-esteem are wrapped up in material things, it becomes increasingly important for us to remind our clients of the internal wealth that exists and can provide lasting dividends throughout their lives. The material relationships and arrangements that we carry around with us are more vulnerable to breaches and disturbances than a centered spirit wrapped in God's love. Though our spirits can be disrupted and disturbed, they are much more resilient than the legal and material relationships that we spend so much of our time creating and protecting. In order for lawyers to be truly effective and fulfill their calling as healers, they must be able to help mend broken pieces in both the internal and external worlds.

One of the striking public examples of a lawyer operating as a healer relates to the personal and professional life of singer Natalie Cole. This world renown recording artist, and daughter of the famous singer Nat King Cole, publicly revealed that she had had a drug addiction for numerous years.[160] She described how various individuals around her had tried to get her off drugs, but to no avail. The turning point in this tremendously negative and self-abusive pattern occurred when her lawyer, accountant, and manager approached her one night at her home. They did not come to do business, or to get her to sign a new record deal or touring contract. They came, according to her, because they did not think she was going to make it. The mere presence of these three individuals, dressed in suits and ties, made Natalie look at herself in a way that she had not done before. The fact that these professionals crossed the boundary of their traditional roles and looked inside her soul to share with her what they saw had a profound affect on her decision to seek help. She recalled that her family and friends had had similar conversations with her, but without success. There was something special about these missionaries, and it was the fact that they did not look like missionaries. She had grown accustomed to having her family members raise the unpleasant and difficult issue of drug abuse with her, but she was able to dismiss them because that was their expected role. The attorney and the accountant had limited roles in her life and were expected to fulfill only those narrow responsibilities. When these caring professionals stepped across the traditional boundaries and engaged her from an expanded place, it had a different impact. It was unexpected, but more importantly, carried a level of legitimacy and authority that probably allowed their message to penetrate deeper into her consciousness. As lawyers, our greatest tool in our quest to serve the whole client and assist in that person's healing, is the fact that most people do not expect us to care. When we do, our impact is multiplied.

This story is but one of many examples where lawyers and other professionals believe their responsibilities as human being exceed their professional responsibilities. We are healers not because of our license to perform our craft, but because of our human license to sincerely care for those we serve. In order to express that concern we must sometimes go beyond the limits of the contracts into which we have entered. Within our role comes an unexpected power of persuasion because of what we are and what people expect from us. When we choose to stay behind the professional lines which we have drawn so narrowly, we lose the opportunity to bring healing to the world. Every person will not respond to us in the way that Natalie Cole responded to her lawyer and the other professionals, but that should not stop us from carrying out our moral responsibilities as lawyers. The secrets of healing are buried in our caring hearts, and in our client's expectation that we do not care. When these two forces come together, cataclysmic spiritual eruptions can occur.

Litigators as Healers

One of the most challenging and demanding aspects of the practice of law is litigation, and it is hard to imagine lawyers as healers in this context. There is an enormous amount of pressure placed on those who choose to do this type of work. Not only are their actions under a public microscope, but the consequences of these actions and choices also can have immediate and devastating effects upon the case and the client. Their interactions with the judge and with opposing counsel are often very intense and sometimes very antagonistic. It is hard for some litigators to embrace the notion of a successful litigator as a sensitive and caring person. Metaphors such as "pit bull," "rambo," and "gladiator," which are used to describe litigators, have unfortunately become the dominant paradigm for many who do this type of work. Since this is such a competitive and high stakes environment, it is easy for those entering this type of practice to embrace this dominant approach. The prevailing norms often promote very negative, and sometimes hostile, behavior towards opposing counsel, witnesses and sometimes even the judge. Intimidation is

considered a standard calling card for this type of work.
Humiliating opposing witnesses, talking down to opposing
counsel, and even refusing to share and reveal critical
information have unfortunately become accepted behavior in
this arena. One thus might conclude that it is not appropriate for
litigators to embrace and incorporate the principles of the river
into their practice. Yet it is within the midst of this chaotic,
pressure filled environment that we need the power and spirit of
the river even more. When litigators are able to remain
composed, calm and respectful in the courtroom they are
generally able to be more effective.

Ed Shapiro, a successful corporate litigator in Chicago who
embraces this belief, summarizes his approach to litigation by
invoking the old adage that "the only way to win the battle is
not to be in the battle." [161] Instead of embracing the dominant
paradigm, many litigators are creating a new one. They
earnestly believe that they can be successful without embracing
the standard roles and expectations that some clients, opposing
counsel and judges attempt to impose upon them. One simple
way to litigate from the river is to always remain open for ways
to settle the case so that the parties, and not a third party, end up
making the final decision. The possibility for settlement is
greatly enhanced when lawyers have approached their cases
from a holistic perspective and secured some critical
information that allows them to understand the problem and the
parties. Though traditional litigators, who are wedded to the
stones, negotiate, they do so from the standard of "bargain and
bluff," and not from an authentic and sincere approach. Though
every case and matter cannot be settled, even the most
aggressive litigator should be able to understand the benefits of

collaborative problem-solving approaches. When one is litigating "from within," it makes it much easier to find those places of commonality and compromise.

Even when it is clear that negotiation is not an option and litigation is the only viable path, many practitioners still find a way to approach the litigation from a more humane perspective. Because client expectations are so strong in the attorney-client relationship, it is important to let the client know the plan for approaching and litigating the case. If a lawyer's underlying values and philosophy about litigation and legal practice, in general, are not made explicit, it will create the possibility for enormous frustration in the future. In particular, the client must understand that "matching the behavior of the opposing counsel is not the equivalent of matching their commitment, expertise or excellence." [162] Many clients want their lawyers to be aggressive, mean and a valiant defender of their rights. Any behavior on the part of the lawyer that appears to be giving in to the other side can be viewed as a lack of commitment or experience. To litigate from a humane place requires that the lawyer and the client are comfortable with this approach. It is within the lawyer's power to create this comfort level by fully preparing the client for this different litigation journey.

Litigators who have made this transformation in their own lives and practice have made the deliberate decision not to embrace the standard norm of behavior for litigation, and generally feel more comfortable with themselves and the practice of law. Some have made the conscious decision to "not run down witnesses" during cross-examination. [163] These lawyers believe that they can highlight inconsistencies in a witness story and even demonstrate that the witness is lying, without humiliating or intimidating the person. There are risks associated with these humane practices, especially when opposing counsel is operating out of the dominant paradigm. Members of the jury, through their exposure to lawyers on television or through prior experiences, may have certain expectations about how a lawyer should operate in the courtroom. Often they may read into a quiet and gentle approach some assumptions about competency and veracity. Therefore, as you embrace this transformation, it may be helpful to inform the jury, as you open and close your case, of your intention about how the case should be conducted and how you plan to go about searching for the truth. If you have truly embraced a spirit of sincerity and genuineness, then the jury will know and feel that sincerity. In the process, you are changing their expectations and creating a new model of litigation.

Even opposing counsel can be affected by your attempt to litigate from the river. When stones interact with stones, it increases the possibility that fire will ignite. So if you adopt the negative, humiliating and domineering posture of opposing counsel, then you are feeding into this negative spirit and increasing the possibility that someone will make a mistake, and that someone could be you. Opposing counsel generally feels more comfortable if you engage in the standard "push and push back harder" rhythm of litigation. What is most disconcerting for counsel is when stones meet the river. Generally, though not in every case, there is a calming affect that the river will have upon the stones. While this is not the primary reason for operating from a place of peace and centeredness, it is a consequence that can occur. We operate from the river because it is what we need to be the type of lawyer we were called to be. When we fulfill our mission and purpose in life, we help change and alter the environment around us. So even in the most intense and negative form of practice, there is a place and purpose for the river. Its flow permits lawyers to be healers, even in an arena that has been known for destruction and conquest.

Rituals in Conflicts and Healing

The traditional legal process is filled with important rituals that have been passed down for centuries. The robes that judges wear; the requirement that people stand when judges enter the courtroom; and the opening greetings uttered by lawyers, such as "may it please the court," have become indispensable parts of the fabric of the American judicial system. While none of these things is determinative of the outcome of a case , each serve as a symbol of the seriousness that we should have about the proceeding, and the respect we should give to those who are responsible for overseeing the process. Life without rituals and ceremonies is process without meaning. Cultures create moments and symbols that recognize major and minor transitions in development, relationships and life. These moments and symbols can help imbed the seriousness of the occasion, as well as help broaden one's understanding of oneself and the challenges that lie ahead.

There is a special role for rituals in the process of conflict resolution. Whenever relationships are being created or terminated, the legal system has created rituals that symbolize these transitions. The civil or religious ceremony to consummate a marriage and the court decree that recognizes the dissolution of a marriage are concrete examples of this phenomenon. One could argue that these traditional rituals no longer adequately fulfill the role needed in conflict resolution. Individuals participating in these processes often feel that they are far removed from the significance of the process or ritual. It has meaning only in the fact it brought about the legal creation or dissolution of the relationship. It may not have served as a serious moment of reflection and introspection so that a deeper understanding and purpose could be extracted. The impersonal nature of most of our judicial rituals precludes them from serving as symbols of healing or the opportunity to start anew.

Due to the inadequacies of traditional rituals in the administration of justice, various lawyers have begun to incorporate new rituals as part of their practice. These rituals are not as formal and standard as the ones that have existed for centuries, but can be more personal and meaningful to the individuals involved. Because the traditional court rituals and ceremonies do not provide people with lessons about how to properly end relationships in ways that honor the past and free them to create a new future, some lawyers have taken on this responsibility. Some provide small gifts of potpourri when the person enters their office to recognize the major decision the person has made to terminate an important relationship. [164] Others have prayer or meditation with the client before going to court. This is done not only just to symbolize the importance of the event, but to help the lawyer and client remain emotionally and spiritually ready for the experience. In the divorce arena, for example, this process has evolved to the point where there are "reverse wedding ceremonies" or "divorce closure ceremonies" where both persons participate in a thoughtful and healing process of termination. [165] These ceremonies and this approach to conflict resolution recognize that there is more to the dissolution of a marriage than a legal decree that dictates rights and responsibilities. There are often deep emotional wounds that need an opportunity to be healed. Though complete healing generally cannot occur in one ceremony or ritual, each positive encounter with the river increases the possibility that difficulties in life can be overcome.

In many legal disputes, there is generally a relationship that must continue after the case is decided. This is especially true in divorce matters when children are involved. While the judge can admonish the two parties to place their children's interests first, there still needs to be some clients centered process that brings this point home in a way that is meaningful to them. Rituals conducted by the lawyer or other third parties can better symbolize to the disputants that a new day is dawning in their lives and relationships and that old dysfunctional patterns must be broken and new approaches developed and embraced. The ceremony or process in this instance can include verbal commitments by each party as to how they want to conduct themselves around each other and their children. If appropriate, the children can be present during this ceremony. Children need to see their parents formally make a decision to go in a different direction, but to go with positive attitudes toward each other. This is a powerful way of honoring the children who have been produced through the relationship now ending. Often, in the midst of divorce, children easily internalize the negative aspects of termination and have very few ways through which to visualize or articulate the positive aspects of their parents' decision. Certainly all parties in divorce matters are not at points where they could participate in such a ritual or process. Some cannot stand to be in the same room with each other. In domestic violence situations, it may even be dangerous, psychologically and physically, to encourage a client to go through this type of process. However, this reality does not diminish the role and power of rituals in the healing process.

For some clients in divorce proceedings, the ritual is more personal and focuses on their individual healing. It might be lighting a candle to symbolize a new beginning, or burying an item from the past to symbolize that they are determined not to be haunted by past deeds or abuses. In order to fashion or recommend something that is appropriate for each client requires the lawyer to really know and understand the person she is serving. This comes from being attentive when in their presence, and asking the right questions. These are the same type of questions that a good lawyer would want and need to know in order to provide adequate representation. Yet it is the manner in which they are asked and what is done with the information that allows the lawyer to contribute to the healing process. For lawyers to advise clients about the importance and power of rituals, or to help create and conduct them, is a powerful way in which they operate as healers. When lawyers conduct their practices in this manner, they embrace the whole person and the challenges that such person faces, and not just the need for a legal decree. The lawyer has demonstrated her sensitivity and sophisticated understanding of the complexity of human conflict and her willingness to help the client; the client then can leave the relationship in the strongest emotional and spiritual state possible, under the circumstances. This is the work of the river.

Outside the divorce arena there is a great need for rituals that symbolize the beginning or ending of relationships. In the business arena, for example, there are relationships that have created negative consequences for those involved, and there may be things that the lawyer can do to recognize symbolically the importance of the relationship and the decision to end it.[166] Even courts are beginning to expand their use of rituals. As part of the punishment in a recent drunk driving case, the defendant was ordered to serve a certain period of time in jail, but also was ordered to plant two trees in honor of the victim which she had killed. She was required to plant one tree at her home and another at a place to be designated by the family of the victim. [167] Though this part of the remedy feeds into the notion that some judges are imposing light sentences for serious offenses, there is a powerful meaning behind this decree. The planting of trees cannot bring this victim back to his family, but neither could more time in jail for the defendant. What it can do, that more jail time cannot, is to make defendant personally and publicly acknowledge the life that was taken, and to participate in a symbolic act of commemoration. The tree at the defendant's home will serve as a daily reminder of the dangers and damage that flow from drinking and driving. No ritual can guarantee healing and transformation, but every meaningful ritual has the potential to create dynamics within the human psyche that do not always accompany the mere rendering of a legal decree. These new rituals are in no way intended to replace the existing legal rituals, but to serve as supplementary pathways for healing conflicts, and additional catalysts for nurturing the energy of justice and love.

These rituals, unlike traditional ones, should not be standard or imposed upon a client. There are certainly small things that lawyers can do, such as giving a meaningful and appropriate book, quote, or candle, to a client without seeking the client's input. But other types of rituals, especially those that will require the client's participation, should be discussed first with the client. The goal of these client-centered practices is not to create needless hurdles and uncomfortable moments for the client. These practices are merely tools available to the lawyer that permit her to bring the client into a healing process, rather than having her remain a passive observer of a conflict resolution procedure that will greatly affect her life. When we engage the client in conversation about what the experience or relationship has meant, what it will mean in the future, and how the client would like to symbolize and honor its termination or alteration, then we are helping her place a challenging situation into some functional and meaningful perspective. In a nutshell, that is the definition and practice of healing. When disruptive and disturbing experiences can be understood and utilized for positive future outcomes instead of becoming permanent limitations to a person's ability and psychological health, then healing has occurred. This does not mean that the client forgets the bad experience or dismisses her contribution to its creation. Healing releases the client from feeling haunted, immobilized and imprisoned by events, circumstances and forces that impacted her life. From the perspective of the river, this is an important aspect of the services that lawyers should be providing to their clients. Yet it is equally important for lawyers to remember that in order to assist effectively in healing others, they must be engaged in processes that encourage them to heal themselves.

Thus, another use of rituals in the practice of law is the way in which they are used by lawyers to stay centered and whole. Many lawyers have developed their own rituals which they use before engaging in the work that they are called to do. These rituals of prayer, meditation, candle lighting and other spiritual ceremonies serve as resources that allow the practitioner to stay connected to the flow of the river. These practices have deep meaning for the lawyer who uses them, and that alone is what justifies their usage. Just as the traditional courtroom rituals create a certain vision and understanding of the legal system, these new age rituals create a powerful vision for lawyers who are striving to go against the grain of standard practice and create a new space for themselves, their clients, and all those who are willing to discover something more meaningful. Though it may be easy at first blush to dismiss the importance of these rituals to practicing attorneys, there is sound empirical evidence from other fields that confirm the critical role they play in self-development, and the antidote they serve to some of the stress-producing qualities of professional life. David Hodge, in an article about spiritual assessment, summarized this evidence in the following manner: "Rituals, inherent in essentially every spiritual tradition, have been widely associated with positive outcomes and can serve to ease anxiety and dread, alleviate isolation, promote a sense of security, and establish a sense of being loved and appreciated."[168] Whether these lawyers are aware of all of the benefits that might flow to their clients and to them from their practices, it is clear from the evidence that these rituals are not just "mere rituals."

Lawyers as Leaders

Another way in which lawyers can act as healers is through our leadership roles in the profession and in society. It is often said that lawyers are natural leaders. Members of this profession seem to have an ordained right to wear this label. Because of the critical positions we occupy in society, this label seems to come automatically with the Juris Doctor degree. Not only do our clients see us through a leadership lens, but also the larger society. Despite the long list of lawyer jokes, members of the legal profession are still seen as annointed leaders. Since many lawyers pursue lives in politics, the public becomes even more comfortable pinning this leadership label on us. Even within the profession we are quick to assign this label to those in our ranks who ascend to positions of partner, general counsel, managing attorney, or even law school dean. Yet our legal training only properly prepares us for one aspect of leadership. We frequently end up in leadership positions because of our analytical abilities, status or educational institution we attended. It is important for each of us to critically reflect upon this dynamic, and ask ourselves whether we really have embraced and lived out the values and attributes that constitute true leadership, for there is a major distinction between being in a leadership position, and being a leader.

I would agrue that the culture and values of the legal profession and legal education are not conducive to developing whole, authentic leaders. Some of the fundamental values that create true leaders are some of the very things that we do not reward or promote within the profession. Leadership, in the pure and sacred sense of this word, does not relate to what we

176

do, or the role we occupy in an organization. Leadership
actually relates to the type of person we are, the type of values
we manifest, and the manner by which we go about dealing
with conflicts and differences. Leadership is more about being
than it is about doing. It grows from a deep well of self-
reflection and self-realization as we attempt to transform the
world around us. Leadership is a spirit that emanates from a
source that has the power to see the future and help usher that
future into reality. It is a spiritual is a force that can lift itself
and those around it without even being present. It is not
something you earned based on years in school, grade point
average, hours billed, or rain made. The pure crown of
leadership belongs only to those who have lived their lives in an
authentic and influential way, and have empowered others to do
the same. Unfortunately, these are not the type of values which
are cherished and privelged in the legal profession. The
profession's definition of leadership is more instituionally
focused and relates more to external positions as opposed to
internal power. Yet, sitting at the top of a hierarchical
bureaucratic structure does not make one a leader. It may make
one rich, famous and even despised, but it does not make one a
leader.

True leaders contain and transmit a power that can change
people and circumstances, based not on the authority of the
position, but on the values and talents they have harnessed for
good. So there is a major difference between management and
leadership, and between authority and leadership. Some of the
most effective leaders that I have studied and admired had very
little or any formal authority, but had tremendous human power.
Dr. Martin Luther King's only formal authority was over the
members of a small southern church, yet he used his genuine

leadership ability to alter the laws and hearts of an entire nation. Though Ghandi was a lawyer, his ability to bring an end to British colonialism in India emanated from his spiritual values and authentic leadership ability, not from his professional role. Even those who ushered into existence the American revolution, though men of property and presitige, had very little formal authority in the colonies. Despite this they seized upon a need, articulated a vision that people could understand and embrace, and made personal sacrifices that manifested their sincerity and leadership. None of these individuals were perfect, and some made decisions that were inconsistent with the ideals they professed. But this only indicates that leadership is not a fixed category. It is an ever-evolving process that can elude one's grasp even after it is obtained. Therefore, as lawyers we need some process, some resource that will allow us to stay on track and constantly fine-tune our moral compass. I believe that source can be our spiritual and religious traditions.

If we review the literature on leadership and begin to compile a list of the attributes that many experts suggest are essential for leadership, we will begin to understand that these are fundamentally spiritual values.[169] Though the list varies from author to author, we consistently see attributes such as vision, compassion, creativity, courage, humility, faith, determination, and even love. Though these attributes are related to our intellectual abilities, they do not automatically emerge from an intellectual well. More importantly these attributes are not effective if we can only intellectually identify and recognize them. To be effective, these values must be consistently actualized and manifested in our lives.

Vision, spiritually speaking, is the ability to see that which is not scientifically provable or that presently exists. The bridge between the land of the present and the uncharted territories of progress is made of a small mustard seed called faith. Good managers can figure out the next step that an organization should take or the next professional move to make. But true visionaries are people who are willing to walk where there are no steps. What gives them that ability? Where does this power and ability come from? Though humility is not something that we usually invoke when we are describing CEO's, presidents and generals, it is a value that allows the best of these individuals to succeed. One aspect of humility is the realization on the part of a leader that she doesn't know it all, and therefore must surround herself with people who can bring differing expertise and perspectives to the enterprise. The greatest aspect of humility which connects to another sacred attribute of leadership is that of service. The concept of "servant leadership" was coined by Robert Greenleaf. Greenleaf suggested that "the first and most important choice a leader makes is the choice to serve, without which one's capacity to lead is profoundly limited." That choice, according to him, is not something one does, but is an expression of one's being. [170] Therefore leadership, as it relates to the legal profession, is not measured by how low others bow and give honor to lawyers, but by how low lawyers are willing to go in order to lift someone else up. Creativity emerges when our souls are at peace and we are open to new approaches, not trapped by fear and imprisoned by doubt. So vision, humility, faith and creativity from my perspective are spiritual values which lie dormant inside each of us. But like a fire that is about to go out, they need stoking. These values do not reach their full potential automatically; they must be nurtured in an internal environment that is at peace. Spirituality connotes a process, a practice, a set of consistent rituals and reflections that allow us to actualize the highest values we strive to obtain. There must be a well from whence we can draw the insight, strength and personal fortitude that will set us apart from life's common denominators.

Just as leadership is not determined by the position one occupies, spirituality does not automatically flow from our association with, or leadership within, religious institutions. One can be part of a religious tradition and not be spiritual or able to actualize the highest values of life. We have too many historical and contemporary examples of how individuals in leadership roles within a religious organization inflicted harm and destroyed lives in the name of their religion. But this should not make us abandon this river. We do not reject water because some have chosen to contaminate it. We do not stop breathing air because some have chosen to pollute it. We see our charge as being responsible for purifying that which others have abused. This purification does not occur through speeches, declarations and dogma, but by how we live our lives and how we treat real people in everyday circumstances. We cannot abandon our spiritual quest because some people have abused or polluted this precious source. Spirituality is as essential to our overall growth as are water and air.

So true leadership must consist of those intangible, yet real attributes and values that are essential to this role. We can certainly assume the role of leader without embracing the spirit of leadership and still be effective, but we are limiting our ability and placing a cap on our power. The spirit of leadership will be there even when the position is not. It is the spirit of leadership that allows many of the people whom we admire to leave a mark on this society and our lives. It is not the intellectual power alone of these men and women that leave an impression on our lives; it is the synergistic combination of mind and spirit that allows them to transform not only institutions and their own lives, but also ours. Lawyers are confronted with leadership opportunities and challenges everyday. The way they approach their cases and clients is an act of leadership. Their willingness or unwillingness to go across racial and gender boundaries, and discover and learn from those who are different from them is a challenge of leadership. How lawyers deal with the professional culture which encourages them to act and behave in a certain manner is a challenge to their leadership. Whether lawyers are able to go against the grain when they think the grain is moving in a destructive direction is a question of leadership. If we bathe constantly in the river, it increases our chances of being a leader, whether or not we occupy formal leadership positions. If we are willing to bath in the river, then we will ultimately obtain a more meaningful and successful life. For in the words of Booker T. Washington, "success is to be measured not so much by the position that one has reached in life, as by the obstacles (one) has overcome while trying to succeed." [171]

A critical aspect of leadership is leading through conflict. We tend to think that a healer should be concerned with making conflict disappear and avoiding future conflicts. Yet conflicts are inevitable and pervasive. We will never be able to eliminate them from our lives or our institutions. So instead of focusing so much attention on how to avoid or ignore conflicts, leaders must become comfortable with them, and look forward to using them to enhance and enrich life. Conflicts contain within them the seeds of creativity, growth, and progress. Lawyers as healers must be skilled in harvesting and planting these seeds in the soil of our relationships and the organizations that we serve. If we run from conflict - if we see it as undesirable interference - then we will not be able to harvest the blessings that lie buried inside. Those who are directly engaged in the conflict may not be able to see the benefits from the situation because they are consumed by the emotional or material drama that is unfolding. As healers, lawyers are not only responsible for trying to develop a legal arrangement that will bring a temporary end to conflict, but also must hold up a mirror that will reflect back to the parties the various possibilities, lessons, insights and values that the conflict and the jeopardized relationship contain. If we make no attempt to correct the problem, or if we fail to make those involved aware of the destructive patterns and the potential for change, then we will pass along troubled and destructive relationships to others. As counselors, we should hold up the mirror so they can see these seeds of change, creativity and growth, and decide if they are willing to plant the seeds or ignore them. While they ultimately will be the ones who will harvest the benefits, we certainly can help cultivate this sacred ground.

We cannot overestimate the power of our words and the power of our wisdom on the spirit of the people with whom we interact. We can sometimes remove invisible barriers by our presence, lighten psychological burdens by our words, and even make the sun come out just by our presence, words and the spirit that emanates from us. We can be the "balm in Gilead" to heal sin-sick souls, and make the wounded whole.[172] Helping people to see through conflict and not be consumed and trapped by it is part of our calling as lawyers. It is the tool we bring to the job. So much of the depression, frustration and negativity that swirls around inside people and within relationships is a result of them being locked in emotional, psychological and spiritual patterns that are limiting and stifling. We can be the guides who, in many situations, can lead them out of these dungeons of despair. The circumstances and situations that were creating the despair may not change, but their perspectives about the problem and about themselves can change. Since we are there to serve them and not just the situation or problem, we must do whatever we can to aid in their movement. Many lawyers already instinctively do what is suggested here; however, the benefits can be greatly increased and enhanced if intentionality and reflection are added to this natural power and process.

So the type of leadership that this profession and this country needs in order to fulfill the unfulfilled mandates of the American dream will not be found in administrative positions and handbooks. Instead, it will be found in the hearts and souls of every lawyer, especially those in leadership positions who are willing to go inside themselves and tap into a well of power that can inspire change both within and without. Every lawyer faces this challenge of leadership everyday, and the question before us is whether we face it from our positions of authority, or from our positions of personal power.

Judging From the River

"If we are to engage the viewpoint of the soul, we must cease from judging..."[173]

The above statement from *The Seat of the Soul* seems to suggest that there is a direct conflict between a person's spiritual quest and her judicial responsibility. If interpreted and applied literally, this statement would bring an end to our judicial system. This would be a travesty, given the critical roles in the legal profession and in the administration of justice which judges play. They symbolize, and should embody, the ideals of fairness, impartiality and justice, which are hallmarks of a viable legal system. Unlike the advocates who appear before them, judges have no vested interest in the outcome of a case, except to create a process that is fair to all parties, and reach a result that is consistent with prevailing laws and principles. This is an awesome responsibility that creates numerous challenges, pitfalls and internal struggles for those who serve in these exalted roles. Though most judges intellectually embrace the ideals of fairness and temperance, they find it more challenging to apply them on a daily basis. In the secret chambers of their hearts, many would admit that their personal biases, impatience and stress seep into the process and impact the parties and lawyers who stand before them. They make judgments not only about the issues, but also about the self-worth of the individuals whose lives and futures are in their hands. In doing so, they fall into the spiritual trap that the statement above warns us to avoid.

The admonition that "we must cease from judging" is not a clarion call for the elimination of the judicial process, but rather a sobering reminder of the limitations of the judicial process, and a challenge to judges to approach their work with a renewed sensitivity and purpose. One of the fundamental responsibilities of the judiciary is to make judgments. Yet from a spiritual perspective, one of the most dangerous and damaging process is the internal act of judging people. In the process of rendering decisions about issues, evidence and the law, it is very easy for judges to cross the line and begin to make judgments about the self-worth of the people before them. This can occur in criminal matters where the liberty of a person is at stake, or in civil matters where ideas and issues are being judged and evaluated. Standing behind the judge's assessment of the evidence in both instances is his assessment and valuation of the people who offered that evidence. Despite the principles of fairness and impartiality that are inscribed on courthouse walls, it is very easy for judges to bring their own stereotypes, insensitivities and value judgments to the process. If they are not attempting to purify their river on a systematic basis, then it becomes very easy for them to pollute the streams of justice, and even decide that there is no river worth preserving in the physical temples that stand before them. No judge is equipped to render this type of judgment. No judge can see that deeply into a person or understand all the forces, potential and possibilities that stand before them. All that a judge can do is make a decision or choice based on the evidence, and surrounding circumstances. Yet it is very tempting for judges in these exalted roles to do more than this. It is very easy, especially when presiding over egregious crimes or dealing with belligerent parties, to suspend one's sense of understanding and compassion and to unleash one's negative emotions. The way out of this dilemma for judges and for others who find themselves in similar situations is a concept called non-judgmental justice.

> Non-judgmental justice is a perception that allows you
> to see everything in life, but does not engage your

negative emotions. Non-judgmental justice relieves you of the self-appointed job of judge and jury because you know that everything is being seen—nothing escapes the law of Karma—and this brings forth understanding and compassion. Non-judgmental justice is the freedom of seeing what you see and experiencing what you experience without responding negatively. [174]

In the context of the judge's role in the courtroom, the above perspective is indispensable if the judge wants to maintain fairness, peace and respect in her own life and her courtroom. Non-judgmental justice does not mean that judges cannot render decisions that impose penalties, fines and other forms of punishments, but means they must be rendered with a sense of compassion, serenity and understanding that does not contaminate the process, or view the process as the final arbiter of the worth and value of those involved. When a judge becomes so obsessed with the harm that she becomes the harm, then she has polluted her river, as well as the rivers of those around her. Non-judgmental justice allows judges to seek and implement justice without condemning the person. The passion and understanding that judges must have to do their work cannot be turned on and off, depending on how appealing or unappealing a particular party might be. The values that the judiciary are charged to embody must be there for all, regardless of the crime the person has committed or how unprepared the lawyer may be. The river knows no class or status of people. It flows through and to everyone. All of us have the responsibility, but especially judges, to detect and genuinely respond to those subtle and tumultuous streams of consciousness that come in our direction. This approach does not suggest that judges should be or can be free of negative emotions, or that they are unable to possess deep sympathies for those who have been violated. But it should restrain them from sending negative energy towards the river by increasing penalties and fines, or becoming so emotionally moved by the crime or act that they internalize the experience.

Another important reason why judging from the river is important is the impact that the demeanor and spirit of the judge has on the entire courtroom proceeding. Lawyers, litigants, and other court personnel take their cues from the judge. If there is a genuine respect for all who appear before the judge, then this increases the likelihood that the lawyers, clients or other court personnel will exhibit the same behavior. If parties feel that even in the midst of strong disagreements and difficult moment, the judge maintains a high level of equanimity, it can increase their respect for the judicial process, and in some instances, teach them about how they should conduct themselves in life. Although parties to a lawsuit are very result-oriented and thus less focused on these intangible aspects of the process, the reality is that our legal system is as much about process as it is about substantive results. The manner in which the process is conducted and the people are treated goes to the essence of the administration of justice. If the judge is rude and reckless, then the lawyers may attempt to act in a similar manner. The courtroom becomes an antagonistic battlefield where both sides attempt to intimidate each other through questionable trial tactics and negative attitudes. Certainly, there are lawyers who behave this way regardless of the judge's demeanor and spirit, but that should not define the standards for the court. The judge is required at all times to rise above the negative emotions that both sides would like to use for their benefit, and must not hold these excesses against the parties when making a final decision. This may sound like an awesome and unreasonable standard for judges to meet on a daily basis; however, this is what this special calling requires. This is the spiritual nature of the work they do. This is the search for the sacred; this is the endless quest to obtain, internalize and manifest the highest values that exist within the profession and in life. The salaries that judges are paid may not be commensurate with this high level of centeredness and self-discipline, but the spiritual roots from whence this role emerges requires nothing less.

Therefore, it is extremely important that those selected to serve as judges have internalized and manifested these traits and values. Their intellectual acumen and legal expertise are important, but so are those intangible spiritual traits and values. Unfortunately, this spiritual aspect of a judge's responsibility has been narrowed to a single category called "temperament." What we should seek to discover when selecting and electing judges includes more than whether a judge loses his or her temper during challenging moments. The ultimate test is whether they can see and respect the human dignity that exists in all litigants who come before them. Though this value cannot be easily measured, it is something that can be observed by those who interact with them. The role of judges is an awesome responsibility that should not be undertaken lightly. Not only does it place one in a position to make serious substantive decisions about someone's life or property, it also puts one in the position where he can very easily disrupt the psycho/spiritual equilibrium of each participant in the judicial process. This tendency to go over the line and develop a god-complex based on the power that he has can be very destructive. The destructiveness is not only to others, but also to the judge. Judging from the river is a scared act of striving to bring order to those parts of reality that can be observed and understood, and remain respectful and pay reverence to those parts of reality that are beyond observable powers.

When judges declare to defendants, usually in death penalty cases, "May God have mercy on your soul," there are various ways in which one could interpret this declaration. In the worst light, these words are mere ritual, or worse yet, a statement of contempt for the person and the act. The statement is a throw away line that neither the judge nor the defendant believes. The judge may be so personally offended by the person and the act, that she is not only sentencing the person, but also the person's soul. Though the judge has invoked the concept of mercy, she does not anticipate that God would have mercy for this person or his soul because she certainly does not. Interpreted this way, this statement becomes a classic example of spiritual judging. In the best light, by invoking these words the judge is attempting to recognize the line where her powers cease and where the power of the river ultimately controls. The judge is indicating, whether she is aware of it or not, that despite what she sees on the outside, there is room for a miracle or transformation on the inside. Though done in a perfunctory manner, this is a statement of reverence for that which is always worthy of redemption – the soul.

The mercy that the judge speaks about when she utters the above statement reflects the synergy between God and river. Within the realm of the river, only the Divine can be truly merciful. Since mercy is kind and compassionate treatment of a person under one's power,[175] this restricts what judges can do. Judges have power and control over the circumstances and problems that come before them, but they do not have power over the river. It thus is important for judges to exhibit compassion and mercy for the people and circumstance before them, but it is equally important that they recognize that there is a more powerful source of mercy that they cannot dispense. They cannot redeem the river; therefore, they should not make the river feel unredeemable. They cannot predict the ultimate flow and destination of the river; therefore, they should refrain from putting unnecessary barriers and obstruction in its way. Judging from the river is the only way to reconcile the horrendous task that we ask judges to perform and the sacred mantle that we ask them to uphold. If judges can embrace this position and carry it out with reverence and respect, regardless of how difficult or trivial the decision, then the seeds for the rebirth of a noble profession are continuously planted. With every statement, attitude, emotion and opinion that is offered, comes an opportunity to help revitalize the soul of this profession.

The main point of this section, and a consistent theme through this book, is a reminder that it is extremely difficult for judges to obtain, internalize and manifest these important values that society imposes upon them. These values and ideals are not automatic. They do not emerge merely through the act of putting on a robe. Having been an excellent lawyer does not automatically insulate one from the internal struggles and the continuing challenges of being a fair, compassionate and honorable arbiter. There must be a companion process that reminds judges daily of their awesome responsibility. There must be a vision of the role, a set of values that feed their soul, and a set of practices and processes that keep them centered and balanced. Judges must constantly visit their river and use it as the ultimate source from whence they draw the strength and insights to carry out their responsibilities.

One of the dangers in advocating that judges tap into a spiritual source in order to remain true to the values they strive to uphold is that it appears to open the door for them to interject their religious beliefs into the decision-making process. During this period in history where prayer in schools, gay marriage, abortion and the death penalty are hotly debated public policies that have serious religious overtones, this path seems fraught with danger. Yet judging from the river is not a license for judges to impose their religious beliefs upon others, but is a reminder that they must approach all issues, conflicts and people with a deep reverence, an unyielding sense of fairness, and an unlimited portion of love. Most religious traditions, at their essence and in their purest sense, are mandates of tolerance, understanding and love. Though they may be also filled with very strong mandates about conduct and actions, they inevitably speak to the heart of the hearer, and serve as a mirror for them to watch the flow of their river, and not as a platform for them to condemn the rivers of others. This distinction is a fine and dangerous line that can be abused easily, yet it is a line worth walking if we ever are to reconcile maturely our spiritual commands with our civic responsibilities. None of these decisions are easy or conflict free, but the quality of our lives and our legal processes only can be improved if we allow ourselves to grapple more honestly with these spiritual challenges.

Chapter Four:

Teaching to the River

Instruction for the Soul

> *Every discipline, in its own way, contributes to the noble pursuit of truth and knowledge. As long as a person is directly involved in the discovery, construction and interpretation of meaning around the subject, there is a potential for raising questions of ultimacy. Didactic work can engage the student in a progressive effort of deciphering transcendence, that is, searching beyond the accumulation of data and facts, through the important questions put to the mind by each discipline, and integrating the results into an overall meaning-making process that is both relevant to the individual's life and to forming a connection with the world beyond.* [176]

It is not illogical to assume that, if a deeper sense of values and spiritual insights is needed in order for lawyers to become more ethical and find more meaning and satisfaction in the profession, then law schools should play a critical role in the process. If every discipline has the potential to raise questions of ultimacy and decipher transcendence for their students, then why can't law schools play this role for law students? Despite the possible universal truth to the above quote, law schools and law professors do not systematically engage in this process of searching for ultimate meaning and transformation, and the vast majority are not presently structured or equipped to provide these things. If law professors are not equipped to provide the values and tools that lawyers need, then we need to retool ourselves quickly, or we need to warn students of our inadequacies and indicate to them what they need in order to fulfill their mission properly. There is certainly strong evidence that what we presently are providing students in regard to their ethical development is insufficient. The fact that every lawyer who has been disbarred or who has violated the ethical standards of the profession, passed the Professional Responsibility course in law school and mastered that area on the bar examination, demonstrates that we are not providing students with all that they need.

The immediate response to this indictment would be that ethical responsibility depends on more than just a mastery of the rule. It goes to the character of individuals which is an area law professors neither can measure nor are empowered to correct. If this response is accurate, then law schools should be held to a high standard of "Truth in Advertising." What they are doing to students is analogous to merchants who sell dangerous products to consumers without informing them of the risks or making them aware of the products' limitations. If law professors are not equipped to nurture or otherwise affect the internal value development of future lawyers, then law schools should be required to provide students, boldly and conspicuously with the following warning before accepting their tuition, and continue to reiterate it throughout their legal education:

*In order to operate this machine called law properly
and ethically; and in order to conduct yourself in a
responsible manner, you must frequently lubricate this
machine and yourself with deep values and spiritual
oils that we do not provide. The fact that you pass a
course on Professional Responsibility does not ensure
that you have the values or internal fortitude necessary
to be an ethical lawyer.*

In addition to making students aware of the dangers
associated with the product that we are selling, we also need to
provide them with more consumer information about how to
receive the most satisfaction from the product. Just as
merchants provide consumers with information about "best
usage" and expiration dates, law schools must inform students
that if they "really want to be satisfied with their legal careers,
they must use it along with other disciplines and combine it
with other spiritual insights which we do not provide or even
endorse." Or maybe an analogous prescription warning would
suffice, such as "please do not take what we have given you on
an empty heart." Without providing these disclaimers or
warnings, we are misleading students and hurting the
profession. We know that there are serious limitations to what
we teach, and the manner in which we teach, yet we leave it up
to students to figure out these limitations and dangers without
directing them to other sources. Certainly, no source or path that
they pursue or that we recommend is an absolute guarantee
against ethical intransigencies since as some believe,
"indeterminacy or uncertainty is built into the basic workings of
the Universe."[177] Yet we at least have a moral responsibility to

inform them in clear terms that we have not provided them with all the tools and insights that they will need as attorneys. Though this minimalist approach of just providing warning has some merits, we should at least be willing to explore whether we can impact more directly on the ethical and spiritual development of our students in a positive manner. How to structure our legal curriculum and adjust our teaching methods in order to accomplish this goal is the most challenging part of this enterprise, and what I try to address in this chapter.

Even if one agrees that something more, or different, needs to be done in law school, there is still serious doubt about whether any of it can really make a difference. Susan Daicoff, in her noted article, "Lawyer, Know Thyself: A Review of Empirical Attorney Attributes Bearing on Professionalism,"[178] argues that many of the attributes of lawyers that contribute to the decline of professionalism, the rise of lawyer dissatisfaction and the increase in negative public perceptions of lawyers, existed long before lawyers even enrolled in law school and are irreversible. She reviews and analyzes numerous studies which indicate that law students have a greater need for dominance, [179]a stronger preference for "thinking over feelings," [180]a stronger tendency to be competitive and aggressive, [181] and are overly distressed, [182]but are not overly humanitarian or very concerned about people. [183] These clear and consistent patterns led her to the following conclusion: "Empirical research indicates that some of these attributes are present prior to law school and even as early as childhood, and are thus likely to be extremely difficult to change. Changes in legal education or in the legal profession are thus likely to be ineffective in altering these pre-existing traits."[184] Though many of these traits were acquired or developed before the students were admitted into law school, Professor Daicoff points to studies which indicate that law schools reinforce and exacerbate these pre-existing traits,[185] and do not assist students in the development of emotional and interpersonal skills. [186] She also points out that it may not be in the student's or law school's interest to correct these pre-existing attributes and tendencies since they may be fundamental to the successful practice of law. [187] Thus concerned legal educators not only should throw up their hands, but also should sleep well at night remembering that the evil they know is better than the unknown that they fear.

The difficulty with this approach to the problem is that it overlooks several critical determinants to the present state of the profession. The fact that the legal profession tends to attract people who have a greater tendency to dissect stones instead of following rivers, is not a compelling indicator that we should abandon all hope and dismiss the beauty and power of the river. This pattern is mainly evidence that the profession attracts people according to the dominant messages it sends, the values it projects, and the experiences that people have had with those engaged in the practice of law. In the minds of all potential lawyers is an image or message about the profession which steers certain of them to us and causes others to run away. The three dominant messages of the profession for future law students are: law is potentially a financially lucrative career; law is traditionally an important career that bestows prestige; law is essentially an intellectually challenging career. The evidence is quite compelling that most law students choose law because of one or more of these dominant messages. There are, of course, sub-themes such as serving people, making a difference in the world, and providing a steppingstone to other professional endeavors. Though these sub-themes attract a significant number of students each year, it is the dominant messages that end up attracting students who are more analytical than caring, more externally-oriented than self-reflective, and more affluent than poor. Certainly, admission standards also serve as another screening device that replicates and reinforces these dominant messages. So if we want to attract students with different tendencies, then we need to send, through our actions, policies and programs, some very different messages about what the legal profession stands for, and what it will require of those who choose to follow this path. If we want more caring people, then we must first become a more caring profession. If we want persons who are more inclined to focus on people and seek more holistic solutions, then we must implement, nurture and promote these approaches. If we want law students to be less stressed, depressed and conflicted, then legal education must teach to the heart and souls of its students and not just to their minds.

The other problem with the conclusion reached by Professor Diacoff is its fatalistic tendency. Even if we continued to attract the same type of students, legal education has the power, if it is willing to change, to reverse some of those negative pattern, and create a healthier balance between existing stones and developing rivers. If we open up the curriculum and standard pedagogical approaches so that more questions of ultimacy, meaning and transcendence are discussed and explored, then we increase the possibility for change. We must stop assuming that analytical skills and intuitive insights cannot exist comfortably in the same mind and person. Unless the transformative work done in other fields like psychology and education are bogus, individuals with strong analytical skills can be taught to be more sensitive and intuitive, and gifted intuitive individuals can be taught to be more analytical. What we have come now to understand is that successful and satisfied lawyers need both of these traits. If, as some studies indicate, legal education can alter some students' approaches to morality, then certainly legal education should be able to have an impact in the opposite direction.[188] If, as educators, we are doomed to the existing model which produces serious problems in the profession, then we not only should issue warnings and disclaimers, but also consider whether we are engaged in a process that contributes to our students' development, or whether we are just producing pre-designed, fully packaged individuals who only need our certification, since we cannot add anything that they otherwise could not learn on their own. If this is our lot, we should turn the keys over to our colleagues in computer science, because they can design more efficient software that could teach legal precepts and provide methods for logical analysis.

Yet there is an alternative path for legal educators who do not want to embrace the minimalist or fatalistic approaches described above. If legal educators are to assist in the development of lawyers who are deeply committed to living ethical and value-centered lives, then we must teach to the souls of our students as well as to their minds. This may sound too abstract and unobtainable, but students know when this is occurring. Many of us have had the experience with a class, or a one-on-one encounter with a student, where we knew our impact had exceeded the normal interaction between students and professor. We have been able to reach a part of their psyche that allows them to achieve a more meaningful understanding about themselves or about their role in the legal profession.

These types of interactions must become the norm of our teaching objectives and practices and not just isolated exceptions. Students come to law school and other institutions carrying a multiplicity of ideas, values, emotions and insights. Yet we subtly, and sometimes overtly, let them know that there are only limited parts of their reality that interest us. Law professors are highly skilled at shaping and molding stones through the Socratic method, legal analysis, and tortuous final examinations. At the end of the course we can determine the successful completion of our task if the stone is shaped in a manner that resembles the images that were handed to us by our professors.

Most law professors are comfortable teaching within these historically determined and standard lines of analysis. We are very uncomfortable teaching to the river. It is harder for us to control the river. It is larger than any tools or skill set that our professors gave us. There is no proven way to measure the river at the end of the experience, so it is difficult to know if we had any impact at all. Thus we spend our time primarily breaking and molding rocks, and occasionally dipping our toes in the river. But some legal educators, in the words of Langston Hughes, have "known rivers, deep dusty rivers..."[189] Students come into our classes each year and some of them, despite the barriers we erect, pour out their souls to us and sometimes to the class. They share their deep yearnings and visions for their own life, and for society and the world. They drop their politically correct positions for a moment and share what is really on their minds and in their hearts. Sometimes compelled by past abuses in their own life, or tragedies that they have observed up close or from afar, these students can no longer remain detached from the cases that were assigned. They see themselves and others they know and love in a case. They revisit the pain that they thought they had put behind them. They come out of their shell and resist the limitations of the stone and the molding process. They share their frustrations about their classmates who just "don't get it," no matter how hard they try to explain the situation. Though many times what we get is political posturing, if we have structured the course correctly we will get sincere glimpses at the beauty and the pain of the river. But many professors choose to stare at the river from a distance, afraid that it may offer something that they are not prepared to handle, or that will prevent them from covering all the material they have assigned. Trapped by the pressures of conformity, tenure and acceptance, too many professors have gazed at more rivers than they have touched or known.

To know the river we must be willing to spend time with it. We must listen intently for its movements and rhythms. We must listen, not just for the familiar sounds that we produced, but also for new sounds that we have never heard before, though they were always there. In order to know the river we must be willing to touch it and feel its warm and frigid nature. There are times when we must even be willing to jump in and bathe ourselves in it. We cannot teach to the soul from a distance. We cannot nurture and inspire the ideals within our students if we do not open up the vaults of our own souls. If we are not willing to be vulnerable, then we do not give them access to our humanity. This does not mean that we spend valuable class time telling personal stories about ourselves, but as we discuss concept and cases, we must be willing to share how our own opinions about the subject matter have changed over time. We also must be willing to share our own emotions about the persons in the cases and the outcome. Most importantly, however, we must be willing to demonstrate the connections between the cases and the moral, spiritual and ethical dilemmas that they present for our students and ourselves. We are skilled at giving sterile analyses about the doctrinal aspect of cases, but reluctant to share our emotional and human dilemmas about them and the underlying social conditions from which the case emerges. Many have argued that to show emotions or to share our personal opinions will distract from our ability to create a balanced or open discussion. This artificial posture only reinforces the dehumanizing myth of good lawyering. We must model for our students the art of balancing our personal emotions with our respect for opposing views. If they never see us do that with them or with our colleagues, then we become less useful to them in their quest to become passionate, but sensitive and respectful lawyers.

To teach to the soul we must be willing to create a safe learning environment where students feel comfortable bringing their insights to the discussion, knowing that the process of sharing will be respected, even if people strongly disagree with their conclusions. The professor who teaches to the soul must spend some time preparing the students for the journey and not just launching into the materials. We prepare them for the journey by sharing our expectations for the class and listening to theirs. We prepare our students for the journey in the river by creating ground rules that will govern the quality of discussions that will take place. We prepare them by setting a tone in the beginning of class that indicates that values and emotions are acceptable aspects of the learning process, and exploring these aspects is a clear objective for the course. Though all of these strategies and approaches will consume some valuable class time, they are important investments in the life and quality of the overall success of the class. If professors are only in the classroom to cover a certain amount of cases, concepts and doctrines, then students are paying an extremely high cost for something they can acquire from a bar preparation course in less time and for less money. We are called to do more than just communicate cases and ideas. We are also there to validate that rivers are good and should be allowed to flow through the learning process. We are there to dredge the river when it becomes too polluted and obstructed. We do this because we care about the flow of the learning process, not because we own or control it. So part of our task as professors is to clean, deepen and widen the river.

We clean the river by insisting that statements and comments made in the classroom are shared in a respectful manner. When they are not, we must address the situation in a respectful and timely manner. When we set ground rules at the start of a course, we are anticipating that there will be a need to clean the river of debris at some point during the experience. The ground rules, which hopefully were created collaboratively, serve as the foundation from which this cleanup work can be done. If students are encouraged to participate in this process, it empowers them to create and expect standards of conduct that should guide them in their professional lives.

As professors, we keep the river clean by making sure that we do not dump "stuff" that we are carrying from another situation or experience onto our students when we teach them. The power and privilege we have to stand before students and guide them on their journey should not be taken lightly. We must do whatever it takes to come to the classroom sanctuary not only prepared in regard to the materials, but also emotionally and spiritually grounded; otherwise, we pollute the river and eventually distort or even block its natural flow. As professors, we deepen the river by pushing back, in a nonjudgmental fashion, when students share their emotional and spiritual insights. Just because it comes from the river does not mean that it is as thoughtful as it could be. We cannot create students' values, for that is a personal and internal process, but we can hold up a mirror for them, so that they can better observe what they are saying and feeling, and become more sensitive to the impact it can have on others. Hopefully this helps students deepen some existing values, and reexamine others.

We also can create opportunities for students to test their willingness to go against the grain or challenge existing norms. In my contracts class I would give students supplementary materials that included a compilation of cases from the period of slavery in America. These cases gave students a glimpse of how courts defined and used basic concepts such as fraud, consideration, offer and acceptance, when the focus of the contract and the case was the buying and selling of human beings. This provided them with a glimpse into the values of that period, and the limitations of judges to see beyond doctrine. As one would imagine, there were scathing criticisms by the students of the judges who wrote these opinions. In one class exercise I would do each year where I would ask students to take the facts of one slavery case and decide it using the principles of the Uniform Commercial Code (UCC). I would get various insightful arguments that demonstrated that students had a sound understanding of the UCC, I never had a student who refused to engage in this discussion either for moral reasons (i.e. I cannot discuss the buying and selling human beings), or even strictly legal reasons (i.e., the UCC only applies to the sale of goods, and human beings do not fall within the definition of goods under the UCC.).

Despite the fact that I was teaching a group of very sensitive and mostly progressive students, everyone was willing to suspend their moral judgment because the authority figure had asked them to engage in this classic, but inhumane, law school exercise. This exercise would create an opportunity for me to discuss their reactions, and to show the strong similarities between what they were willing to do and what those judges had done whom they had a few days earlier severely criticized. There were some students who felt that I had "set them up," yet the vast majority appreciated this "moral reality check" to see how easy it was even for caring lawyers to go with the flow and follow the expected path for success. During our discussion I would raise with them how important it is to challenge those you are supposed to respect, even when they have control over something you want, like good grades. If students were not willing to do this in a relatively safe academic environment, it would be even more difficult to do when the stakes were much higher.

The classroom presents numerous "teachable moments" if we are willing to travel the path of the river. Though there was a doctrinal goal to my exercise, there was a broader and deeper goal that related to the emotional and spiritual aspects of the students' lives that are not frequently explored within the context of the classroom. Hopefully, these teaching moments contribute to a deepening and widening of the river by ensuring that multiple perspectives are brought to the classroom discussion. Part of our task, doctrinally and otherwise, is to ensure that our students do not develop tunnel vision. Law professor are very adept at making the counterargument so that students can see the weaknesses in their positions. Though the process is similar when we teach to and from the river, there are some major distinctions. Doctrinal widening takes the form of dualities and competing tensions. Widening the soul takes the form of discovering and recognizing complementarities among various perspectives and insights. This is not intended to gloss over real differences in beliefs, but at this level our job is to show and make connections among various positions and feelings. One of the cardinal axioms of holism is the notion that one cannot really understand reality by analyzing it from just one position or perspective. Therefore, we must caution students about adopting exclusionary perspectives about law or life. Furthermore, holism[190] suggests that within the part there exist the whole. Therefore, part of our task is to demonstrate that within legal doctrines we can discover much of life if we just look close enough.

While teaching consideration in my contracts class, I sometimes encourage students to understand this critical concept from various perspectives. A simple out-of-class assignment that requires students to analyze this legal doctrine from the perspective of their undergraduate major or prior work experiences produces interesting and revealing results. It is very easy to cover this concept purely from a doctrinal perspective of "bargain for exchange." However, with some guidance, students easily can begin to discover the economic, political, social and even spiritual ramifications of this concept. Consideration can open up a dialogue about the economic principles upon which this country was founded, as well as the biblical command of "do unto others as you would have them do unto you." Though these insights are not earth shattering, they cut against the development of tunnel vision. They also subtly remind students that law and legal discussions should not be divorced from other parts of their past and present realities which are important and even sacred. The more we open up the discussion in meaningful ways, the more we create the possibility for students to stay in touch and grapple with important personal values and experiences. A fundamental pedagogical belief for me is that the more the study of law feels like the study of life and values, the greater the possibility that we can produce more humane, sensitive and respectful professionals.

Dredging the river is not a lightweight or menial task. It is a sacred act that should be done with care and reverence. As professors, we are the caretakers of rivers that have been placed temporarily under our guardianship. We can pretend that all we can influence is our students' minds, but the reality is we are affecting their whole being, either negatively or positively. Just as law is not value-neutral, there is not a neutral position for professors when it comes to interacting with rivers. If ignoring the river were the answer, then we would not have the problems we presently have within law schools and the profession. We can teach to our students' souls if we first are willing to recognize that their souls are present in the classroom, with them. We can teach to their souls if we are willing to nurture and cultivate our own. We can teach to the soul if we are willing to take risks. There is no invincible place to stand in this process. We will make mistakes, and if we are truly open to this process, we will learn from those mistakes.

In one of my contracts classes, I attempted to venture into a deep point of the river by trying to raise the consciousness of the class, especially the men in class, about the power of seduction. The textbook I was using included a case about undue influence.[191] There was a passage in the opinion where the judge equated rape with undue influence and compared seduction to persuasion. The judge was trying to make the point that certain acts cross the line, such as rape and undue influence, while other actions are totally permissible even though they may cause a person to change position. I placed this dichotomy on the board and read to the class a definition of seduction. The dictionary defines seduce as "to lead a person away from duty or proper conduct, [to] corrupt."[192] I tried to make the point that in contract formation as in life, there are human activities which we label permissible that end up harming and damaging people. I argued that the date rape that occurs on college campuses is so much a product of men feeling that it is part of their responsibility to "seduce" their companion, that they are unable to interpret "no" as a final answer. My hope was to deepen the river by demonstrating that we, especially men, get messages from the culture and those in positions of authority, that it is permissible to move people away from their preferred position or "proper conduct" as long as it satisfies our needs and does not cross over the line of undue influence or forcible rape. Though this misunderstood social value and practice can sometimes lead to mutually pleasurable experiences, it also can lead to very damaging and destructive behavior and consequences.

I noticed that my presentation did not generate the type of discussion which I had become accustomed in this class, but it was not until after the class that I fully began to understand the problem. I was approached by various women who felt silenced and offended by the mere fact that I had written on the board Undue Influence = Rape. They were not able to embrace the point that I was trying to make because this statement appeared to be trivializing the experience of some who may have been raped. After various discussions they better understood my point, but felt that I should have prepared them more for this discussion. They encouraged me to continue to include this presentation as part of the course, but to "lay a better foundation." These discussions happened solely out of class, so I started the next class apologizing to those students whom I offended, and attempted to make my point again. I had begun some dredging of the river without first letting the river know what I was about to do. I tried to deepen without being sensitive to how every aspect of the presentation might affect those in the class. I certainly was aware that rape is a very sensitive topic to be discussed in any law school class, and certainly in a contracts class where people least expect it. Though I had laid ground rules at the beginning of class and had discussed very sensitive matters before, I still did not get that one right. However, through this experience my river was deepened and I became a more sensitive professor. I have continued to use this case and explore these underlying values, but with more care and foundation building.

So we should not run away from the river because of its force or coldness. We can learn from it as we strive to make it better. When we venture out too far, we should always remember that the stones are usually not too far away. Our discussions, and thus our journeys into the river, should all be related to a fundamental legal concept, perspective or insight that we are striving to convey. If the journey is feeling too unsure for the students or for us, we can always find our way back to the stones, but we must be willing to venture out again when we feel more centered and empowered. Teaching to the soul requires that we be prepared, and that we step with care and with faith. To make this approach a fundamental part of our teaching philosophy, we have to have faith in the ultimate goodness of the river and its ultimate source. If we seriously doubt whether students can be authentic and respectful in their discussion of sensitive and value-laden issues, then we should continue to teach from the stones. An absence of faith in the potential goodness of this process will contribute to destructive consequences. If we embrace the experience from a positive and faithful perspective, then we not only will find more joy in teaching, but our students also will find more joy in learning.

In addition to the approaches we can take in our individual classes that allow us to teach and nurture the whole student, there are broader institutional initiatives that can contribute to this goal. The vision of legal education that is imparted to law students when they first arrive is crucial. If faculty members, and deans in particular, convey a narrow vision of law and its role in society to incoming students, then it will be much harder for them to erase this picture and develop a broader one. Some lawyers argue, in response to my statement that what deans say on the first day of law school is important, that they do not remember what their dean said when they started law school, and therefore those speeches carry very little weight for new students. However, I would argue that the reason many do not remember what was said is because what they heard did not inspire or challenge them to think differently about the study of law. What they heard, for the most part, probably conformed to their basic understanding of law and did not invite them to stretch their minds, hearts and souls as they launched this journey.

Words, images, metaphors and poetry have a more powerful impact upon people than we sometimes realize. Therefore each opportunity to stir the soul and ignite the intellectual engine must be utilized. The mission of the law school must embrace a vision of lawyering that invites students to engage their entire selves in the process, and the spokespersons for the institution must be willing and able to articulate that vision in a compelling manner. This is not a call for more oratory tricks or slick power-point presentations. This is a call for a sincere and inspiring presentation about the full value of law to the development of society and individuals. It also must be a serious reminder of the awesome responsibility that students are about to undertake as they begin their studies to enter into the profession. If we understand and embrace the practice of law as a serious moral and spiritual calling, then anyone entering the profession should be asked to pause and ask themselves whether they are fully ready to take on this awesome responsibility. No speech will transform an immoral person into a saint, yet every opportunity to plant seeds of integrity and challenge the moral fiber of our students should be undertaken.

If law schools are serious about the goal of strengthening the moral, spiritual and ethical fiber of its students, then their commitment must go beyond speeches, a course in Professional

Responsibility, and a few other elective courses. Innovative required courses that expose all students to this aspect of the school's and profession's mission must be instituted. An example of this occurred at Northeastern University School of Law. In order to address concerns raised by students of color that we were not addressing and integrating issues of race into the curriculum in a systematic basis, the faculty created a new required first year course, entitled Law, Culture and Difference. This course at first attempted to expose students to some of the controversial debates around race by inviting noted speakers to campus for lectures. It later evolved into a more substantive course with reading and writing assignments that covered other aspects of difference such as gender, sexuality and class. Over time, those who participated in structuring the course began to see a clear connection between our goal to sensitize students to issues of difference and our goal to develop ethically strong lawyers. Thus exercises were added to the course that asked students to identify conflicts between their values and those of the profession into which they had sought entry, and to describe how they planned to reconcile these differences. In addition, students were given a series of ethical dilemmas which they had to discuss and resolve. Some of the problems involved underlying racial or gender conflicts, so ethical crossroads were not merely limited to narrow, professional ethics situations.

These exercises and this course sent a very strong message to students at the beginning of their legal educational process that values, differences and ethics are fundamental aspects of their growth as lawyers. That message opens a door wherein the institution can better connect the study of law with the study of self, hence the study of spirit. Too often students are subtly taught that the study of law is divorced from them and their ultimate reality as spiritual beings. Traditional legal education leads them to believe that they must immerse themselves in the law, even if it means losing themselves - and their souls - for awhile. This course attempts to let them know that they must immerse themselves in law, life and themselves. They are made aware that certain aspects of life which have stymied the growth of this society will present unique challenges for any lawyer. During the module on torts, students not only debate the legality of hate speech codes, but also are asked to imagine how one creates and maintains an educational environment where respect for human beings and differing opinions and perspectives are fundamental and ingrained. This process sends the message that students are human actors capable of creating the type of environment and world in which they want to live. Though law can play a critical role in this process, their personal and collective values are also extremely important to the achievement of such a sacred goal. The Law, Culture and Difference course is not a panacea. Some students still object to some of the topics and methodology, and it does not adequately address all of the goals that some of us have for it. Yet this course stands as a clear institutional example of how we can teach to the river. The course is structured to get under the skin, soul and spirit of our students by challenging them personally as well as professionally. If we are to revolutionize the study of law, it cannot occur solely through elective courses where students can opt out. Educators are often told to "put your money where your mouth is." To address this change in legal education, deans and faculty members together must put our curriculum where our souls and spirits reside.

A Framework for Teaching to and From the River

One of the most challenging aspect of trying to view teaching law as a spiritual experience is the absence of an established theoretical framework to guide our endeavors. This is a really challenging task for individuals who dwell so heavily in matters of the mind that typically only can be observed, measured and tested. Despite the difficulty of this task, however, it must be done in order to provide the outlines of a path for those who desire to walk in this direction, otherwise these experiences and attempts will degenerate into abstract moralizing. The paradox, though, is that there is no clear, smooth, or chartered path that consistently leads to the same place when we strive to teach to and from the river. Each teacher must find and create the path from an individual and personal search for truth. The mere fact that one is willing to teach from a place inside, as well as from an external text, is what opens the path. Though each of us must bring our own creativity and spiritual insights to process, there are some signposts along the way that can be helpful and instructive. These signposts do not control or guide the flow of the river; they only point us in its direction.

The framework or signposts provided below grew from one of the most innovative and challenging experiences in which I have ever been involved since I became a law professor. The principles and methodology are the result of a project that was undertaken at Northeastern University School of Law in partnership with a major Boston law firm, Hale and Dorr. This joint project on professional fulfillment and leadership eventually grew into a course on values and spiritual growth in the study and practice of law. [193] A casual meeting between John

Hamilton, the then managing partner of the firm, and me resulted in a year long discussion between a few faculty members and partners at the firm about how to teach law in a manner that would inspire students and practicing attorneys to critically and openly reexamine their values and commitment to the practice of law. In developing this upper level course, which included two law professors, twenty students and three partners from the firm, it was important to have some structure to this very innovative and unbounded conversation about law and life. While Jane Scarborough, a professor at Northeastern, gave the course much of its creative structure and pedagogical approach, a set of principles ultimately served as the framework for it. Those principles were Lawyering as a Calling; Value Conflicts and Clarification; Seeking Connections and Embracing Differences; Being vs. Doing; and Human and Institutional Transformation Through Learning.

During the negotiation process with the firm, we also agreed and discovered that there were certain methodologies needed in order to implement and actualize these principles in the educational process. The methodologies were Seizing Life-Changing Opportunities; Encouraging Self-Extension and Risk Taking; Promoting Self-Reflective Practices; Positioning the Teacher as Learner, and Embracing Dialogue as a Healing Force. We are able to create a space that allowed the participants, to varying degrees, to embrace or at least touch and examine these principles through the use of the various methods we employed in designing the overall course structure. Though these principles were developed in the context of designing and implementing a course, I believe they have an even broader relevance to the structure and transformation of an entire institution. In fact, John Hamilton, as the manager of his firm, and I, as dean of the law school, were both committed to participating fully in this course because we wanted to discover some things that could assist us in our efforts to enhance and ultimately transform our respective legal institutions. So these principles and methods are not just guideposts for individual professors, but also are there for administrators and managers of institutions who are striving to lead and be led by the river.

Lawyering as a Calling

When we think of a "calling" we tend to equate it to a religious or maybe artistic endeavor where we recognize that someone possesses something more than just skills. But a calling cannot and should not be restricted to those areas. A calling implies that there is some meaning and purpose to our work that goes beyond our own personal needs and ambitions. It suggests that our motivation derives from sources beyond our intellectual comprehension. Though our personal needs can be satisfied within our calling, our calling transcends our needs. We are there to serve a greater purpose that relates primarily to the needs of others, and to those of society and the world around us. A calling not only relates to the individual choice that someone makes, but also can encompass an entire profession. To teach law from a spiritual perspective requires that we position it as something beyond a mere vocation. Students must be invited to enter into a hallowed place of honor and reverence, even though they and we recognize that law and lawyers have not lived up to this sacred claim. Therefore, those who enter this place must question whether they are prepared and willing to uphold this torch. At the core of this calling is the value of service to others. The greatest joy and the shortest path to self-fulfillment are through unselfish service to others, especially those in need. Law professors and law schools must embody and manifest this value and perspective. They must reposition law as a service profession in the highest sense of that word. In the words of Joseph Allegreti, author of The Lawyer's Calling, "law school is the means to an end – it is the instrument by which we develop the competencies to implement our inner call to service. It is the place where our inner call takes on flesh. Without the public calling of the law school, our private calling would remain ineffectual. Those who serve must learn to serve." [194]

In the Hale and Dorr course, we asked the students and lawyers to develop a mission statement for the legal profession. This was a tedious task, yet we wanted the students and lawyers to put the calling of the profession into their own words, so that they would not accept some externally imposed definition of their work. Original statements from each participant were translated into a composite statement for each group which then was combined into a composite statement for the entire class. While each differed in many respects, the theme of law serving some noble purpose in society was always present. Getting a class to write a mission statement for the legal profession is not the only way, however to internalize the ideal of law as a calling. Professors are presented with numerous opportunities throughout the life of a course to share their understanding and perspective of law. Though we all might describe it differently, if the concept of law as a calling is embedded within our perspective, it will invoke within our students a spiritual notion of their work. The mere invocation of this perspective will invite students to look within themselves. If the course creates additional opportunities for this perspective to be examined and challenged, then this internal glimpse will eventually become a constant, inward reflection which will invite the students to wrestle with their internal conflicts as well as with those that exist between them and their understanding of the profession. This will naturally lead to the next guidepost on this spiritual journey, which is value conflicts and clarification.

Value Conflicts and Clarification

At the heart of most instances of professional dissatisfaction and personal depression are unclear and conflicting values. Values are those beliefs, standards and principles that we hold dear. They derive from our parents, religious traditions, political orientation, life experiences, and self-discovery. Students bring with them varying sets of values, and they embrace them at varying degrees of intensity. The legal profession and the law schools that these students enter also have values that they overtly and subtly cultivate and promote. The values of the profession and the institution are often inconsistent with that of the students. Unfortunately, very little purposeful time is spent in law school voicing, clarifying and reconciling these values. Students are left on their own to wrestle with their values, which may be at odds with their classmates, and to decipher the values of the institution and the profession. Some are able to make it through this maze in good shape, but most are not. Though most students who enter law school graduate with a sound understanding of law and are able to pass the bar exam, they often have paid a heavy personal and psycho-spiritual price in the process, and the institution and the profession have squandered a precious opportunity to assist in the development and growth of those who, in most instances, will remain connected to the institution and profession for the rest of their lives. Some of the personal and professional problems that will manifest later in their careers could have been averted if the students and the institution had had a systematic process for addressing these value conflicts, or at least for making the students more deeply aware of them.

For those who want to teach to and from the river, there must be time devoted to clarifying values and dealing with conflicting ones. We must create within our courses the space where these precious parts of the human and institutional structure can be touched, examined and enhanced. "The space should honor the little stories of the individual and the big stories of the discipline and tradition. A learning space should not be filled with abstractions so bloated that no room remains for the small but soulful realities that grow in our students' lives."[195] Buried within the cases and doctrines we teach are the values of the profession. As we discuss, analyze and search for answers to legal riddles, we not only must discover and articulate the values of the profession, but we must also invite students to share pieces of their internal puzzle. It is not the mastery of legal principles that will determine their ultimate worth as lawyers, but the values that they bring to bear as they use and apply those doctrines. So we must understand that the values that will direct them in the future are with us in the classroom in the present. When we choose to ignore them out of fear, or because of the pressure of time, we are forsaking a fundamental part of our calling as educators. As Parker Palmer notes, "...education is not just the transmission of facts and reasons. It is a process that involves the whole person, and so involves deep feelings as well."[196] Thus our challenge as educators is to understand "the importance of creating classroom space for feelings as well as facts, of establishing an ethos of obedient listening where both facts and feelings can be expressed and responded to."[197]

This can get very messy at times and some blood, and too many tears, will be spilled in the process if these discussions are not handled well by the professor. Our students bring to the classroom values and feelings that are in sharp contrast with those of other students in the class. It is at these intersections and times that true teachers earn their pay on this side of the river, and their crown on the other side. "Holding the tension of paradox so that our students can learn at deeper levels is among the most difficult demands of good teaching...[for] the place where paradoxes are held together is in the teacher's heart, and our inability to hold them is less a failure of technique than a gap in our inner lives."[198] If we have not spent time embracing and clarifying our own values and feelings, we may lose the opportunity to guide others in this process. If we have not felt tested by our own internal paradoxes, then it will be difficult for us to examine the external paradoxes shared by our students.

In the Hale and Dorr course students and lawyers were required to write personal mission statements. Before engaging in this exercise participants were invited to list the values that were important to them. Those values were to serve as the basis for the personal mission statements. The goal behind this exercise was to encourage students to reflect on and clarify their values as it related to the practice of law. We wanted to create the space where students could give themselves a personal compass that could help them stay on track once they entered into the swirling and turbulent waters of the profession. The process of crafting and sharing the statement required everyone to be much more reflective, and revealed the various value conflicts that existed between some of them and the profession. Students also were given a copy of the personal statements written when they were applying to law school. Since all of them were in their second and third year, it was intriguing to hear how the passage of just a brief time had altered their perception of the law and their reason for seeking entry into the profession. The goal of this exercise was to remind them that our glances into the "looking glass of values" should not be restricted to the present. It is through our sincere reflection upon who we were and what we professed in the past that provides us with greater insight into who we are and what we are in the process of becoming.

Our desire for students in the course and the practicing attorneys was that they would turn this exercise of self-reflection into a habitual practice of self-renewal. One of the final assignments for the course required students to write a letter to themselves about how they see themselves as lawyers and what they aspire to be in the future. Those sealed letters were later mailed to the students, unopened, five years after they graduated. Through this small act the law school was institutionalizing the act of self- reflection and self-renewal. One of the most compelling experiences was to see how students were able to clarify and expand their values over time. Some students who saw big firm practice as inconsistent with their professional values developed a healthier appreciation for the worthiness of this type of work by spending serious time and having candid discussions with attorneys in the course who were from a large firm. Our values are rarely clarified in a vacuum. They demand the refining pressures of real people and real circumstances. If they can withstand the test of internal and external probing, without causing us serious pain or alienation, then we have grown in our understanding of self and others. These clarified values will serve as true anchors that can sustain us as we navigate through difficult waters of our calling. Yet they must be revisited over time because as we grow our understanding of our values may change as they, too, evolve.

The legal profession is not a value-neutral enterprise. Some of the values of honesty, integrity, service, fairness and justice need to be awakened and cultivated within lawyers and legal institutions in a more purposeful and meaningful manner. Other values that have grown up along side the ones above, like greed, selfishness, dishonesty, manipulation and an amoral perspective to our work need to be weeded out. Neither of these goals will be achieved if law schools and the profession do not create the time and space for its members to recognize, clarify and reconcile values.

Seeking Connections and Embracing Differences

As students clarify and reconcile their values, they also must feel connected to the learning process. Since many law students have been forced to do value clarification work on their own, there are many lawyers who graduated with their values in tack, but who feel very isolated and alienated from their law school and the legal profession. Incivility, dissatisfaction and personal abuses often increase when lawyers feel disconnected from themselves, the learning process and the profession. Much of this disconnection begins in law school. Students often feel as if they are going through a process, but are not feeling as if that process is flowing through them and gathering parts of their selves to enrich the flow or the land around them. Though they master the process, they begin to feel alienated from it. If this continues into their practice of law, then these lawyers become prime candidates for periods of depression, professional dissatisfaction, or personal abuse. As professors, we must ensure that there is a connectedness between our students and the learning process regardless of the size of our classes. Parker Palmer, a noted leader in the field of spirituality and education, eloquently captured this goal in the following quote:

> Good teachers possess a capacity for connectedness. They are able to weave a complex web of connections among themselves, their subjects, and their students so that students can learn to weave a world for themselves. The methods used by these weavers vary widely: lectures, Socratic dialogues, laboratory experiments, collaborative problem solving, and creative chaos. The connections made by good teachers are held not in their methods but in their hearts – meaning heart in its ancient sense, as the place where intellect and emotions and spirit will converge in the human self.[199]

In order to hold the teaching and learning process in our hearts, we must constantly invite students to feel that they are part of the learning process, and help them to see themselves reflected in what we teach. This can range from simple acts of kindness, such as remembering their names, special things about them and their values, to more profound acts such as allowing them to help shape the contours of the learning process. I approach all of my courses with a plan and syllabus, but I always view them as starting points and never as roadmaps carved in stone. I try to make it a standard practice to check in with the students and have heart-to-heart conversations about how the course is going. Sometimes no major adjustments are needed, yet at other times I learn that my assumptions about how the course is going and how connected the students are to what I am teaching are inconsistent with their reality. We made major adjustments along the way in the Hale and Dorr course in order to address the developing needs of the students. This is certainly harder to do in substantive courses when we feel we have a finite amount of material to cover; however, even in those settings we must make time for the evolving needs and yearnings of our students.

One of the dangers in our quest for connectedness is to assume that all students connect to our class, the institution and the profession in the same manner. With the inclusion of so many new entrants into the profession, like women and persons of color, it is critical that we expand our methods and approaches to connectedness.

There is often an assumption that since one is pursuing a spiritual connection with students, the same paths and methods can be used because spirit is the same. Yet we all access that part of ourselves, and see that part in others through different pathways and lens. The teacher must know herself and feel connected to the profession in her own special way, but she also must begin to appreciate how others connect to the profession, and realize that harnessing the power of difference is much more rewarding than coordinating the strengths of sameness.

Being vs. Doing

Lawyers, more so than other professionals, are obsessed with "doing." Even doctors are made aware of the fact that their "bedside" manner is an important part of their practice as physicians. Bedside manner embodies the ideal that doctors must be able to "be" with their patient during the time physically spent with them, as well as prescribe technical treatment. The medical profession, though some would argue it has also lost its way, instinctively realized that one's presence, touch, kindness and time can contribute to healing as well as medicine and surgery. Likewise, the emotional, spiritual and social healing that lawyers are called to perform are also aided by our ability to connect with our inner selves and enter "into faithful relationship with all of life." [200] As teachers and guides to future lawyers, we are partly responsible for their obsession with "doing." We cram their lives with numerous courses that require them to read voluminous cases and other materials, and complete circuitous research and writing assignments. We end each act of the drama with a final exam that requires them to remember and apply all the materials which they learned during the course. They must never lose sight of the fact that at the end of their formal legal education, they must remember and apply everything which they have learned over the last three years. Most of them must go through this process while simultaneously wrestling with how they will pay for this tortuous experience. Personal relationships, family responsibilities, health care and fun must be tightly squeezed within the few open spaces in their lives. The competitive nature of most law schools, and the high stakes that derive from grades and class rank, makes it dangerous and costly if they reject or disclaim the "doing obsession." Our students enter the profession already living off the adrenalin of "doing," and intoxicated by the allure of the prestige, status, and, for some, financial rewards that the profession offers. The pace and culture of the practice of law only reinforces the value of "doing" over "being."

If legal educators are to reverse this obsession with doing over being, then we must reexamine the content, pace and ethos of our courses and classrooms. The principle of "being" requires that we slow down the learning process and find the space and time to allow our students to reflect critically upon how they are internalizing the values of the profession. We must have exercises and opportunities that invite them to sit with us and share their feelings about the things they are learning. We also must emphasize the importance of character, sensitivity and emotions in their development as lawyers. "Being" suggests that emotional intelligence is just as important as intellectual and analytical rigor. To enhance the quality of what lawyers produce, we must enhance the inner qualities of lawyers. The Hale and Door project required a significant investment of resources into the development and delivery of just one course, but it is an extraordinary example of the shift that we must begin to make within the academy and the legal profession. To enhance the quality of lawyers, a law school and a law firm were willing to invest in the souls and spirits of future and present lawyers. In the midst of numerous new areas of law to discover and master, we chose to find and make the time for lawyers to be reflective, thoughtful, and quiet. There were no doctrines to remember, no predetermined pattern that everyone had to fit into, and no rush to get it all covered at the end. The people in the room were the objects and subjects of the course. The readings, cases, legal culture and paradoxes that we explored were merely means to get each of us to more deep, thoughtful and quiet place within ourselves. The places we were exploring within and around us aided us on our journey into doing. For being and doing are not in contradiction to each other if we create the space for both. The dividends from our internal explorations will manifest themselves in the quality of the work we do, and in the quality of the life we live.

Creating the space in the learning environment of law schools so that our students can experience and comprehend the concept of "being" is not limited to a Hale and Dorr type of course. In traditional courses we can find and make the time so that this aspect of human and professional development can occur, but we first must see the value of this concept in our own lives and in the educational experience. In my twenty-two years of teaching law, I have been amazed at how we make space within our courses and curriculum for those things we determine are valuable. My contracts course has gone though various iterations as I have grown in my understanding of law, and as institutional priorities have shifted and changed. Curriculum innovation is not an issue of time or space, but a challenge of will. Our individual and collective will can transform this fast- pace, externally focused learning experience into a more balanced and insightful exploration of law and life. The only question is whether we will let it happen and support it when it does.

Human and Institutional Transformation Through Learning
The most sacred principle and guidepost is our unyielding belief in the possibility of human and institutional change. This belief is anchored in a broad and cosmic understanding of the power of learning. No matter what type of situation human beings and institutions face, there is always the possibility for change and transformation if we open ourselves up to

instruction and guidance. "The teacher will appear when the student is ready."[201] Yet transformation will occur only if the student and the teacher deeply believe not only in the possibility of change, but also in its inevitability.

As legal scholars and teachers we all embrace the power of learning. Too often we limit this sacred process to the mastery of rules, doctrine and process. We do not see the learning process as a means for transforming people and institutions. Even when we see changes in our students outside the narrow confines of analysis and writing, we are not able to connect this change to the learning process in which they were engaged. We do not have course or institutional learning objectives that focus on the emotional development of our students. Their maturation is someone else's responsibility, though during the three years of law school, they spend collectively more time with us and our ideas, than with anyone else in their lives. If we are to reclaim this profession and produce lawyers who are grounded, mature and sensitive human beings, then we must expand our learning goals and create exercises, reading materials, and pedagogy that helps us to achieve these objectives

One of those learning objectives must be to develop within our students a deep appreciation of the power of change, and instruct them on how to facilitate transformation in their lives and in the lives of those they will serve. Change is not a process limited to intellectual mastery. In order to assist people in transforming their present situation, they need more than just an analytical summary of the facts and options. They need the support of someone who understands at a very deep level that change comes from a deep reservoir of human will and power. If our students can only counsel their clients on the pros and cons of their situation, but cannot look inward to find spiritual insight to help these clients create a more meaningful life for themselves, then our students have underserved their clients. They have done what the stones of law require, but they have not answered the call of the river. The river demands that they embrace the possibility of true transformation in every situation. Change should not frighten or immobilize the lawyers we produce, for it is the basis of their work and the goal of their calling. They should understand that positive change comes through learning opportunities. Each encounter they have with a client creates a possibility for that person to learn something not only about the law, but also about life, and themselves. The attorney must approach each situation prepared to invoke the transformative powers that lie dormant in us all. Therefore, the teacher must embrace each teaching encounter with the same expectation and faith, for once students see this in their own lives and in the lives of others, they will embrace it as a fundamental part of what lawyers strive to bring about in the world.

This same process of change must be applied to institutions as well as human beings. John Hamilton and I approached the Hale and Dorr course with a profound belief that we would learn something special which we could use to transform the institutions we were responsible for leading. We felt that if members of our respective organizations could be exposed to a different pedagogical approach to law and life, it would plant seeds in the institution for greater change. Though each of us had authority through our positions to mandate change through new policies or incentives, we knew that true transformation would occur only through enlightened souls. We both participated in the course because we wanted to enlighten our souls first. Each of us gained insight and ideas that we attempted to weave into the framework of our respective institutions. But organizational transformation is a long and slow process that is often fraught with other unanticipated challenges and changes. So the seeds we planted are still germinating, but we both know that it was the process of planting that gave our leadership more meaning. Where and when those seeds finally take root will be guided more by divine inspiration than planned events.

Change and transformation occur more readily through learning than through force and policies, but learning is not just a process of the mind. It is a process that must engage the whole person. Our classrooms must reflect the wholeness of learning, and the beauty that lies within the possibility of change. We must symbolize this beauty for our students, and we must use whatever tools at our disposal to demonstrate this principle. To handle the depressing, seemingly intractable, and sometimes gruesome situations that lawyers must face, our students must have a deep faith in the power of human and institutional transformation. One of the greatest spiritual gifts that anyone can have is the power to see beyond present situations and circumstances. The spiritual lawyer sees suffering, but knows that "joy cometh in the morning." The spiritual lawyer also understands that joy is not always a product of a favorable judgment, but may emerge from the peace and solitude the client finds within. Intransigence does not always signal an end for advocacy, but maybe the beginning of prayer, for -

> [p]rayer is the way of paradox – a way of entering into silence so deeply that we can hear the whole world's

speech, a way of entering into solitude so deeply that we can feel the whole world's connection. In prayer we touch that transcendent Spirit from whom all things arise and to whom all things return, who makes all things kindred as they go.[202]

That transcendent Spirit is our greatest hope for personal and institutional transformation. When we stay connected to that source, we gain a deeper ability to change our lives, and tap into the unlimited possibilities for change. If we can make our students aware of this universal and personal power, without imposing our particular spiritual beliefs, we would have given them a gift of a lifetime.

Methodologies

In order for students and professors to internalize and actualize the above principles, there must be some concrete processes employed during the learning experience. We employed various exercises, techniques and structures that fell within one of the broad categories previously discussed; namely, Creating Life Changing Experiences, Encouraging Risk Taking and Self Extension, Self Reflection, Role Reversal, and Healing Dialogues. Many of the exercises under these categories I have already covered, so I will mention only those that have not been touched on previously.

Often lawyers seek to change their lives for the better and find more meaning in their work after they have encountered some crisis in their personal and professional life. When the secure patterns and predictable comforts begin to fall away and we cannot easily cover up our vulnerabilities, we tend to search for something more meaningful and genuine inside. Since educators cannot predict life crises, it would be difficult to build a course around personal crisis, but we can create a learning environment where self-revelation and growth are likely to occur. The normal four walls and predictable patterns of the classroom can create a sense of artificiality that privileges the mind over other aspects of human development. It is useful to change the dynamic at times in order to broaden the lens of the learning process. A fundamental requirement of the Hale and Dorr course was a weekend retreat that all participants were obligated to attend. This setting, nestled in the woods of Ashland, Massachusetts, created a framework for deeper self-reflection and group exploration.

We had two instructors who guided us through a low and high ropes course. The retreat, in general, and the ropes course, in particular, created the foundation and stimulus that are similar to other life challenges which foster personal growth. There was a sense of vulnerability that each of us experienced, at varying degrees, especially when we were on the high ropes. This rope experience created a "leveling affect" that stripped us of our titles of dean, managing partner, professor, partner, or bright student. The laws of nature had no respect for titles, color or gender. We were each dependent upon one another in ways that a classroom setting does not engender. We were asked to take a physical risk which, through reflection and dialogue, we analogized and translated into personal and professional risk. One student declined to go on the high ropes, and dramatically stated, "I live up there everyday." Her statement and the sincere passion in her voice gave me a deeper insight into her personal and professional struggles more than any of the conversations in which we had engaged during her numerous visits to my office.

So experiential learning is more than just students practicing their discipline in appropriate work settings. To learn through experience requires that we put ourselves in different settings, and under different challenges, so that we can open ourselves to deeper levels of self-understanding. The life lessons that help us develop meaningful relationships and enhance our internal capacity to empathize and "see with the heart," cannot be easily captured in casebooks. They must be experienced through ordinary and extraordinary circumstances and situations. By placing ourselves in an extraordinary setting, we were increasing the likelihood that we would respond to each other differently. New "learning symbols," like the ropes, were invoked so that we could explore old and new topics from different perspectives. The ropes became a symbol of how vulnerable we all were, and how we could draw strength and confidence from those around us. For lawyers and law students who are subtly and sometimes directly trained to appear invincible and independent, this became a powerful, alternative vision to invoke in the learning process. The ropes also symbolized the importance of taking risks and extending ourselves beyond our safe comfort zone. Though some embrace a vision of law and lawyers as risk-takers, there is a prevailing conservative nature to this profession. Lawyers are creatures of habit and form. We draft documents the way the firm has always drafted them, with some minor revisions around the edges. We dress, act and conduct our practices in the same manner and tradition that was handled down to us. Law professors teach their courses in a manner that is very similar to the approach that existed when Christopher Columbus Langdell invented the casebook method in 1871.[203]

We must develop and implement new "learning symbols" and experiences in our traditional teaching environment that encourage risk-taking and self-extension. It is up to each professor and student to interpret and internalize the meaning of these symbols in ways that make sense to them and to the profession. The greatest barriers standing between a revitalized profession and us are those that trap our feelings, imprison our emotions, and stifle our creativity, natural instincts and wisdom. Walking on ropes suspended between two trees and twenty feet above the ground made us ripe for deeper self-reflection once it was time for us to write in our journals. Since pure teaching comes from a place of authenticity and integrity, the more professors are in touch with their own fears, desires, motivations and yearnings, the better they can inspire others toward self- and life discovery.

During the retreat we engaged in other exercises that were "learning symbols" of trust. Guided blind walks and other activities reminded me that trust is one of the most precious tools in the teaching and practice of law. But it is not just the trust we must have in our colleagues and in the system that is so critical - it is also the trust that we must have in our own instincts and divine goodness. Many of the ethical mistakes and unprofessional behavior in which lawyers engage grow out of a sense of distrust. Part of that distrust grows not just out of a deep fear of losing external power, such a finances, status and job security, but ultimately grows out of a mistrust of our internal power to meet successfully the challenges in our personal and professional lives. Just as the blind walk serves as a symbol and reminder that trust is earned and learned, so must lawyers be provided with educational opportunities to learn how to trust themselves and others.

Journal writing has become a common part of various academic experiences. We employed this methodology in the Hale and Dorr course as a "learning symbol" of the sacredness and importance of self-reflection. The journals were personal and not required to be submitted at any time during the course. We created designated journal writing time during the retreat so that we could reflect on an experience, but left it up to each person to decide when to write. Though we later felt that perhaps we should have reinforced this symbol more often, the real gift was the symbolic nature of journal writing. We were asking students to trust and believe in their feelings. We were suggesting that learning occurs in quiet moments of self-reflection just as it does in the lecture hall. We were striving to point the students inward as they tried to transverse an external learning environment. These journals were a reminder that a lawyer's real strength emerges from the lawyer's internal thoughts and reflections. In quiet moments between cases and clients often comes the revelation that makes a difference for the client and the lawyer. But these revelations, insights and communiqués from the river must not be left to chance. We must seek these internal pearls of wisdom just as we research cases and statutes. It is what each person brings to the law that really gives it life and meaning. The more we engage in self-reflection, either through journal writing, meditation or prayer, the more we have to bring to the teaching and practice of law. As educators we must insert within the classroom experiences more symbols and exercises that provide opportunities for students to internalize these valuable lessons.

The lawyers, who were all partners in the firm, were asked to assume the role of teacher/learner. Though they were helping the professors guide and structure the course, it was important for them and the students to embrace this experience from the standpoint of a student. Their inclusion in the course was aimed purposefully at assisting the students in taking a deeper reexamination of their values and motivation with respect to the practice of law. The partners were powerful "learning symbols" for the students. They were sometimes symbols of what the students wanted to become and sometimes of what they wanted to avoid at all costs, but when the students began to engage with them on a personal level and not as the symbol a different type of learning occurred. Within the context of a course like this, they were not only learning from the expertise and experience that the lawyers possessed, but they were also learning about, and challenging, the values, motivation and insights of these seasoned practitioners.

Something powerful occurs in an educational environment when those things that are abstract learning symbols become real and present. It is easy for law professors and students to create arch-types for lawyering and never explore the flesh and blood reality of the challenge of being a practicing attorney. It is also easy for lawyers to enter the learning environment in the role of as teacher/practitioner and assume that they are the ultimate repositories of wisdom and insight. It is much more enlightening for the students and lawyers, upon entering the process, to be open to being taught as much as they are conveying. During the course of this journey, both sides gained a deeper understanding of what it means to be a lawyer. Touching and seeing the fresh, uncorrupted aspirations of the students permitted the lawyers to revisit that place within themselves. Having had lawyers reflect candidly about their love and aspirations for the profession, despite its glaring weaknesses, provided students with a vision of hope.

Dialogue is a fundamental part of the traditional classroom experience. Yet in our traditional classroom settings we rarely employ it as a healing force. We structure discussions primarily as if words were weapons used to destroy the weaknesses in other people's arguments, or to demonstrate that we are well read. The energy that travels with these words sometimes can be oppressive, antagonistic, and certainly, impersonal. Our conversations can bring about a deeper understanding of a complex and difficult legal concept, but they also can promote a very shallow understanding of those around us and our interconnectedness with each other. Though mastering the law and legal concepts is a worthy and laudable goal of human interchanges, there is so much more power hidden within this standard teaching tool. To see dialogue as a healing force in the classroom requires the teacher to embrace the learning experience with heart and head. It requires that we are not just to probe for the logical weaknesses that exist within a statement, but to explore the openings in the statement that create a passageway to understanding the person who made it. Hidden behind many of our comments are our fears, values and aspirations. When we can demonstrate connections between those fears, values and aspirations in a professional and sensitive way then we are on the path of not just teaching, but healing.

Dr. Rachael Remen, who teaches courses for medical students at the University of California at San Francisco School of Medicine called "The Care of the Soul and Relationship-Centered Care", argues that "...there is a place where 'to educate' and 'to heal' mean the same thing. Educators are healers. Educators and healers both trust in the wholeness of life and in the wholeness of people."[204] In her course she attempts, through the use of thoughtful dialogue and silence, to get medical students and practicing physicians to touch their fears and those values that they want to preserve throughout their studies and practice. She also challenges them to appreciate the connections that exist between each student. Through this structured process as she asks a series of simple, but probing questions, the "masks of control and professionalism fall away, and the students find an acceptance for personal aspects and concerns they have hidden because the dominant culture disavows them. The groups then develop and discuss ways to feed and nurture these parts of themselves. Very specific approaches – which may involve rituals, imagery, journal writing, poetry, music, and meditation – are designed by the students, shared with the small group, and validated."[205] This process is not just a break from the agony of professional training - it is a fundamental part of the students' professional development. The overarching goal of the course is to develop physicians who possess compassion for their patients. Certainly, compassion is not something that can be taught, but it is something that effective professionals must possess. Thus effective educators must create learning environments where these same values can be exposed, nurtured and celebrated. When we structure our courses and our educational institutions in ways that isolate the inner feelings of our students from themselves and each other, then we are sowing the seeds for dispassionate professionals. When we fail to use dialogue as a means of connecting students to themselves and to the world around them, then we are draining our professional well of one of its most precious resources -compassion. Dr. Remen's description of compassion, found in the following quote, demonstrates why this attribute is so essential to the study and practice of law:

> Compassion emerges from a sense of belonging: the experience that all suffering is like our suffering and all joy is like our joy. When we know ourselves to be connected to all others, acting compassionately is simply the natural thing to do. True compassion requires us to attend to our own humanity, to come to a deep acceptance of our own life as it is. It requires us to come into right relationship with that which is most human in ourselves, that which is most capable of suffering. By recognizing and attending to that basic humanness, our basic integrity, we find the place of profound connection to all life.[206]

Our clients and students need to feel our concern for their problems and situation, and we must be able to access that reservoir of feelings that exist inside us so that we can provide them with service that flows from our hearts as well as from our heads. In the Hale and Dorr course we attempted to use dialogue as a healing force by respecting the unique voice of every student in the course. Each session began with a "healing circle" where any thoughts, comments or reflections on what transpired at the last class, or between classes, could be shared. Through the use of special prose and metaphors that individuals read or shared at the retreat, we created a learning environment where everyone could better connect with their own humanity, and with the world around them. By having the lawyers in the course share their fears, anxieties and doubts, students were given the opportunity to connect with the humanity that exists within the profession, instead of just embracing the "rules of the game." Based on the evaluations we received at the end of the course, this experience allowed students to connect with their humanity and that of the profession in ways that they had not experienced before. These healing exchanges would not have occurred unless those who guided the discussions were willing to reveal their own humanity, as well as respect the array of humanity of those who participated in the course, even though clothed in various genders, races, sexualities and ages.

The methodologies described above are not restricted to special courses like the one I just described, since every course cannot be taught using ropes as the primary learning symbol. However, there are learning symbols hidden in the traditional classroom, but we must make them more apparent. All students bring various symbols of their journey through life. It may be the fears or joy they express about a case or it could be a heated exchange they have with a classmate. It may be hidden in the type of questions they consistently ask of us or in the lack of preparation that is exposed when we ask them a question. All of these occurrences, which we traditionally view as minor additions to, or interferences with, the learning process, are symbols or indicators that convey something important to us about the students in the room and the educational challenge that we confront. There are times when we can create the symbol through various things we bring to the classroom. The symbol could be a provocative movie about the legal profession or the subject we are teaching that gives a common language and experience from whence we can critically view the profession. It could be a metaphor or story that we invoke and weave throughout the course as a way to get the students to go beyond the normal classroom boundaries. What matters most is whether it is a true and authentic expression of the goals that we have for the course that can be utilized to achieve those learning objectives. If we truly see ourselves as those who educate, meaning those who "lead forth the hidden wholeness," [207] then we must be concerned with creating an environment where students can bring forth the fractured gems that lie within them. Through the educational process, we not only give them new tools, but also assist them in mending these precious parts of themselves into a whole stone that can reinforce and draw strength from the river.

Diversity: Educating the Whole Student for the Whole World

There has been an enormous amount written about affirmative action and diversity in higher education. The Supreme Court ruled that race is a permissible factor to be considered in the admissions of students in the University of Michigan Law School and undergraduate cases.[208] This affirmation of the Bakke decision gives new life to legal educators' quest to create a diversified legal profession. As the country continues to debate and discuss the legal, political, and educational aspects of affirmative action, hence diversity, it is important that we explore the spiritual dimensions of diversity in higher education, especially in law schools.

From a holistic educational perspective, educators are more than incidental characters in the life stories of young men and women. They are key players and actors in the unfolding of a great human drama. How this drama unfolds can be influenced greatly by the type of teachers and classmates they encounter during the scripting of their lives. The values that the educational environment reflects become critical markers in students' development. Even traditional educators recognize that they are not just called to teach students how to remember and regurgitate facts, dates and places. There is more to legal educational than the ability to comprehend, analyze and research cases. Educators, from a spiritual perspective, are called upon to educate the whole student and to touch and inspire every facet of their being. If we are to develop and help nurture those who sit in front of us each day, then we must be able not only to teach their minds, but also to inspire their hearts and souls. We must not only be able to give them a deep understanding of the past, but also prepare them for the complex and diverse future that awaits them. Our journey into the past must not be narrow and sterile. Our travels must capture the nuances of history, the blessings and sins of a nation, and must recognize the unsung heroes and heroines that created and wove this historical tapestry. This process of reflection must instill within them values of pride and humility which permits them to assess earnestly the place they occupy in the world, and to develop a deep appreciation for the various ways in which they are linked inextricably to others in the world. We are preparing them to be leaders and positive contributors to a very complex, diverse and changing universe. Many of the cases and rulings that we are teaching will be overturned or outdated by the time they are called upon to use them. Therefore, we must ensure that we impart to them, and extract from them, values that can withstand the test of time and the winds of change.

So it is within this broad educational context that we must discuss, understand and embrace the concept of diversity. First, we must understand that diversity is not an add-on to an already existing and well-formed curriculum and educational mission. Developing a deep appreciation and respect for others and their life circumstances is a core spiritual tenet, and thus a critical educational objective. Creating and nurturing a diverse educational environment gives more integrity, meaning and relevance to the very things that we are called upon to do. If we give our students a narrow, one-sided and sanitized version of history and reality, then we have not educated them; we have participated in a process that stifles their minds, hearts and imagination. We are called to unleash their spirits, not corral them. We are called to ignite a flame of curiosity and creativity, not to pour water on their emerging fires. We not only must entice them to explore the world around them, but also must bring the world to them by reflecting it in the values we embrace, the pedagogy we adopt, and the people we hire to teach them.

Since the life stories we are teaching contain varying degrees of injustice, cruelty and unfairness, we must demonstrate to students how we, as educators and educational institutions are attempting spiritually to grapple with and repair these spiritual rifts in our social fabric. If their personal history and that of others like them are the only histories to which they are exposed then we have failed to prepare them for life. Our individual paths are precious and sacred, but they are not a reflection of the whole and do not always capture the inextricable ways in which our personal realities are so interwoven with the personal triumphs and tragedies of others. We begin the journey of wholeness by traveling the paths of others and by attempting to understand reality from the perspective of other parts of the whole. Diversity emerges from a spirit of humility and a curious mind which does not assume that the knowledge one possess about people and places is enough to form concrete and fixed conclusions about them, and certainly not about their self-worth. Diversity begins when professors understand that the students who sit before them have as much to offer about life as they have to offer about a particular subject. Thus the more diverse the students are, the more everyone around them learns about life and about what it demands both intellectually and spiritually.

I never sat in class with white students until my freshman year in college. My knowledge of them and my understanding of how I would live in an integrated environment were drastically changed because of this experience. The intellectual and spiritual walls which society and I had erected were tested and eventually cracked. The sincere appreciation and deep friendships which I have developed over the years for and with individuals who are different from me, were born out of those early educational experiences when new worlds were laid at my mental, emotional and spiritual doorsteps. Both negative and positive aspects of these experiences reshaped my world and made me a better person. Struggling against racist and insensitive attitudes, as well as witnessing white students and professors embrace the quest for racial justice, has contributed to enlightening my world and expanding the horizons of my beliefs. I could no longer hold onto feelings of hate, and I gladly also had to let go of presumptions about superiority that years of internalized oppression had created. Some beliefs and stereotypes were confirmed, and others were shattered. This transformation occurred not just through courses I took, but through the values, people and experiences that my educational journey provided. All of this could have occurred sooner and at a deeper level if the educational institutions which I attended had valued and systematically cultivated a diverse learning environment.

Diversity grows and flourishes by creating an institution and a curriculum that has at its core a deep respect for human existence. It must be reflected in the way people are treated in an institution, and in the way the institution serves the needs of those who enter, especially those in need. It is at this point that diversity and spirituality dynamically converge. Despite one's political perspective on affirmative action, spiritually, it is hard to ignore that at its core, affirmative action is attempting to address the social guilt of this nation. Racism created gaping holes that fostered generations of systemic inequalities. These were not just random acts done by private individuals, but were government-endorsed laws, policies and customs that stifled and hindered the progress of some, while benefiting and enhancing the progress of others. This history and dynamic created a spiritual challenge for those on both sides of this moral pendulum. For those who directly and indirectly benefited, there is the challenge to see and accept the moral frailty in the privileges and power one may possess. It is a compelling lesson in humility to understand that one's status and achievement is colored or influenced by the suffering of others. This does not take away from the hard work and talents that one possesses, but it gives the moral actor an opportunity to place that work and those talents in a broader and more challenging life perspective. Those who stand on this side of the moral pendulum are also faced with the spiritual challenge of trying to balance the moral scales. Those who suffer from social ills, injustices or indifference have been the traditional focal point for spiritual growth. Service to them always has been the train that spiritual leaders and believers have ridden to paradise. Failure to address their needs and make appropriate sacrifices has been considered by some sacred texts to be a justification for exclusion from heaven. So the history of racism in this country and its consequences, have generated a spiritual dilemma for believers as well as legal and political challenges.

This spiritual challenge is not removed because one was not directly responsible for creating the problem. Those spiritualists who embraced the challenge of serving those in need were not responsible for their suffering or condition, but felt responsible for their healing, salvation and liberation. They did not become concerned with the inability of the needy to change their own condition, as many who oppose social justice approaches and remedies do today. Our spiritual calling is not to judge, but to serve. Many today oppose affirmative action because they believe that if people of color had worked harder, they would have overcome obstacles such as slavery, institutionalized racism and court approved discrimination that were placed in their path. This may be a worthy and viable sociological inquiry, but it is an incredibly weak spiritual argument. We do not meet and pass our spiritual test by judging the worthiness of those in need. The spiritual challenge for those who stand on this side of the moral pendulum is to ensure that they have done everything within their present power to address the suffering.

Sometimes a decision to do nothing benefits those in need because it forces them to tap into unused internal powers, but it is never the best spiritual answer for those who are challenged to serve. It is only through service that we release the chains that bind us to our earthly limitations.

Those on the other side of the moral pendulum have spiritual challenges as well. The greatest challenge is forgiveness. When an injustice has occurred in our life or in the lives of those who are part of our family, group or nationality, there is an instinctive reaction that makes us want to hate or deeply dislike the persons who were responsible for the injustice, including those who identified with them. Though this is a natural feeling, it only serves to imprison us in the wrong and in ourselves. We free our spirit when we let go of the hate, contempt, or feelings of revenge that we have for those on the other side of the moral pendulum. Forgiveness does not mean that we accept social and political realities, or that we refrain from engaging in a critical analysis of past and present policies and decisions that perpetuate the injustice. It primarily means that we engage in such activities from a place of love for those who suffered and continue to suffer, and not from a place of hate for those who created or benefited from these wrongs. There is also a spiritual challenge of dependency for those who have been the victims of injustice. Injustice creates a psychology of dependency and vulnerability that leads to a belief that only some external solution or policy can make us whole. Therefore, they wait patiently for an apology, remedy or judgment in order to go on with their lives. While an appropriate ruling can make a major difference in the material conditions of those who suffer, it is but a spiritual placebo for

246

them, because emotionally and psychologically they can still remain in bondage. Spiritually, the oppressed always hold the key to their own salvation and liberation. Though those on the other side have an obligation to serve them and to work for social justice, regardless of whether they created the wrong or not, those who have suffered cannot spiritually hold others accountable for their bondage. This gives too much power to those who have authority and privilege, and depletes the internal power of those who suffer.

From the perspective of the river, our spiritual freedom is always in our hands. Thus our quest for social and political freedom must emerge from a purified well that is not tainted with hate, dependency or retaliation. Otherwise, in our pursuit of justice, we will pollute our rivers and create more injustice within ourselves and our social and political structures. So affirmative action, like reparations for the nation,[209] is as much a spiritual test of our educational institutions, as it is an educational policy. Diversity and affirmative action are not mere legal issues to be debated by lawyers and interpreted by judges; they contain deep spiritual messages and lessons that are fashioned for this present age. If all we see are the legal issues, then we will miss an opportunity to educate the whole student and heal the whole nation.

I believe all educators, including legal educators, have a special mission which should allow us to embrace and comprehend diversity in ways that other institutions might not. A major part of our mission, though often overlooked, is to serve those students whom the society has labeled or dismissed. Though as legal educators we depend on other educational institutions to screen out those who have struggled educationally, we still cannot ignore this fundamental educational imperative. Without an institutional commitment to racial and economic diversity, we will end up teaching primarily to privileged students who represent a limited aspect of reality. If we can only be educators for those students who look like us and enter our institutions with stellar scores, then we do not understand or embrace the fullness of our calling. To be educators, in the broadest and most spiritual sense of this ideal, requires us to assist in extracting the wholeness that exists within all of those who sit in front of us. That wholeness will never come forth if we cannot see, accept and embrace the differences that exist among our students, and, ultimately, see beyond the statistical indicators that we value so much. To fulfill this spiritual educational mission of transformation, we must go beyond our own experience to inspire students who faced different educational obstacles. We must understand that from a spiritual perspective the type of obstacle one faces is not the measure of one's self worth. In this society, race, class, gender, sexuality and disabilities are educational obstacles for many people. The society through its laws, customs and policies has made them so. They are not only obstacles for those whom society has labeled, but also for those who imposed and condoned the negative connotations of these labels. Race, in particular, has been used as a way of questioning the worthiness of an entire group of people. It became an impenetrable barrier that was used to create and separate the "haves" from the "have-nots." It was a stamp of inferiority used to relegate individuals to the back of buses, and hinder their access to restaurants, classrooms, and even life itself.

But there were always those, on both sides of the racial line, who would not allow this societal generated challenge to condemn them to self-destruction or hate. They chose to turn the challenge into an opportunity. Dr. Martin Luther King is a classic example of someone who tried to turn America's challenging nightmare into a promising dream. Many others threw off the shackles of oppression by seeing beyond artificially constructed horizons and embracing potential blessings of the unknown. This is the essence of our educational challenge. Each day we are asked to teach and nurture students who have various challenges, even though many of those challenges are invisible and unarticulated. The caring educator strives to find ways to inspire and motivate those students through the use of various teaching methods and strategies. In the process we experience the joy of educational breakthroughs that occur when students master difficult and complex concepts and ideas because of these challenges. We become better teachers and they become better students.

Diversity demands the same intellectual curiosity and innovation from all educational institutions and society. These students, people, cultures and traditions that challenge society will become the means through which we gain a deeper understanding of our educational mission as well as life itself. Lying on the other side of our present educational reality are much richer and deeper institutions. Lying on the other side of the status quo is a bridge that can lead us to a place and process where we become more enlightened educators. There are future students from various parts of this nation and with different backgrounds who must be the beneficiaries of our insight and resources. There are teachers who are not in the academy, but should be there, who can help unlock doors of learning that we may have failed to investigate. But we will never benefit from these experiences, and we will never have the opportunity to learn these precious lessons, if we don't figure out how to open the gates of our educational institutions more widely. No, it is not the physical barriers around our law schools and universities that keep out diversity, but the barriers that inhabit cerebral places and serve as obstructions in our spirits. The dramatic entry of people of color and women into the legal academy over the last two decades has spurned new theories and perspectives that were not available two decades ago. Critical Race Theory, Critical Feminist Theory, LatCrit Theory, Intersectionality, and other race and gender sensitive perspectives would not have emerged, but for the opening of our legal doors, minds and spirits. Our students, and thus society are the beneficiaries of these creative and provocative ideas. These movements brought vitality into the legal academy, the growth of which effectively had been stifled by its previously held constricted view of law and life.

Of course, it is virtually impossible to have a racially diverse institution if the faculty and students are exclusively or almost exclusively one race. On the other hand, an institution can be racially mixed, yet still not be diverse. Diversity stands for more than just numbers, though numbers are critically important. Diversity is a value - a spiritual value. It is an offspring of the underlying principles of respect, love and humility, which should reside in the heart and soul of an institution. Educational institutions not only must attempt to be reflective of the world around them, but also must be reflective of the ideals that can help transform the world around them. The problems in the world that plague us the most are not products of the fact that people have been physically isolated from each other, though that has contributed greatly to the problem. The most significant cause of the world's problems is the alienation and isolation of our hearts from the values of love, humility, compassion and truth.

Whether one agrees with the war in Iraq or not, it should be clear that we are not involved in this serious loss of lives because we do not have enough information about each other, or because we lack the opportunity to interact with each other. We are engaged in this human tragedy because of the hardness of hearts; because of the yearning for absolute power and control; and because of the utter failure of all our systems and institutions to transform our deeply held beliefs about each other. So sitting next to each other at the table of brotherhood and sisterhood is an important first step, but we must bring to that table a bread of life that can nourish and heal our souls. Educators thus cannot accept a narrow definition of diversity that only focuses on numbers, for we are not teaching to numbers. We are teaching whole human beings who need to see both inside and beyond themselves when they look in the institutional mirror. They also need to know that there is an institutional well from which they can drink to nourish the essence of their souls. Professor and educational administrators are the creators of that mirror and the keepers of that well. We will see nothing more beautiful than what we create, and we will find nothing more precious to drink than those values and experiences which we pour into the well.

Though diversity is a critical value for every discipline and profession, it is extremely so to the legal profession. This view was reflected in numerous briefs filed in the University of

Michigan Law School affirmative action case. Diversity is no longer an article of faith in America - It has become a preamble of fact. Institutions and businesses have seen its benefits and concluded that they far outweigh the downside. Diversity is a spiritual value because it provides the legal profession with the precious talent that it needs, but that it otherwise would ignore. We lose this precious talent not because we cannot find it, but because traditional criteria and methods oft times conceal it. Diversity is a spiritual value because the legal profession owes a deep responsibility to society to ensure that the image of justice is not just white and male. In an ABA[210] study entitled, "Perceptions of the U.S. Justice System," almost 50% of those polled felt that courts did not treat persons of color the same as they did whites, "and persons of color significantly outnumbered whites in expressing these perceptions of bias."[211] When people cannot see themselves in the administration of justice, they begin to distance themselves and lose faith in that system. When people distance themselves from the administration of justice, some resort to other, less desirable means of resolving disputes and redressing wrongs. When this occurs perhaps the most fundamental role of law in our society is subverted to our detriment.

Diversity is a value because this society, with the legal profession at the helm, created the very disparity and inequality that our efforts in this area are now trying to correct. For lawyers to sit at the sidelines while others try to run interference and correct the consequences from this horrendous crime against humanity, means that law is not a calling, but just a business which does not demand of them any responsibility other than the maximization of profit. Our effort to diversify the legal profession is another reminder of our sacred calling as a profession. We are called not only to understand and comprehend the law; we are called to use the law to eradicate great social ills. We are called to use law to undo what others have done to subjugate and destroy human beings. We are called to bring sunlight into dark places, and to tear down invisible walls that separate us from others and from ourselves. Some recoil at this grand calling because it appears too overwhelming, and thus impossible. Some may ask "how" or "why" regarding the involvement of their organization in undoing centuries of wrongs which it had no responsibility for creating. The answer is that while no one institution can erase all of these sins, each of us has a responsibility to make a difference whenever we can. We cannot save the entire world, but we can try to save that part of the world in which we reside. Such responsibility does not derive from direct culpability, but from a deeper spiritual well out of which we must drink if we are to realize our full human potential.

America still suffers from a reputation that is lined with negative racial images. Though much of this is rooted in a past that is behind us, mountains still remain which this nation must ascend in order to reach a place that is free of obstructions for all its citizens. The legal community must be in the vanguard of this transformation process. Lawyers must contribute their time and resources to create a place that truly reflects the best ideals of this nation. The future vision of diversity in this America must be embraced in good and bad economic times. It must be a vision that affects the culture of our legal and business organizations. The inclusion of people of color and women in them must not just be a token presence, but rather an indication of a true shift in values of the organizations. That brings a new spirit and life to them. These individuals are there to open the door to a new understanding about our calling and how we conduct our lives and businesses. They are there to give us a different perspective on the bridges we must build between family and work, between profit and service, between institution and community, and between love and social justice. But if we include them at the table, and the revolving doors of our standard operating procedures and narrow policies quickly usher them out, then we will lose the benefit of their excellence and creativity. If we allow them to stay, but diminish their relevance, minimize their contributions and their insights, and quiet their voices, then we will not hear the sacred messages that were sent to us, and only will continue to hear our echoes, as we continue to repeat the same old mistakes.

Though the diversity ideal seems illusive, educational and professional organizations must continue to pursue this spiritual value. The leaders of these organizations, as well as those they lead, must seek it with their heads and hearts as if their lives depended upon it, because they do. Our lives ultimately will be measured by the good we do in the world and by the love and service that we give, especially to those in need. We must seek this ideal not only in our courtrooms and law offices, but also in every aspect of our lives, every waking hour. We must even seek it in our dreams. If we do that, then when we awaken, we will no longer be pursuing an ideal, but will be living that reality. We will have come to understand that the ideal sought was first born in us, and then took wing and changed the course of our educational institutions. This search will have taught us that our institutions, like law, are precious vessels that can dispense nothing better than what we pour into them. If lawyers and legal educators pour more of their spiritual values into this vessel we call law, then we will create a legal profession that reflects the human diversity which exists around us and which we are called to serve.

Chapter Five:

The Social Justice River

Social Justice as Spiritual Behavior

Many progressive and socially enlightened lawyers shy away from discussions of spirituality because they fear that it will be used as a modern "opiate of the people," and distract us from addressing the real, concrete problems that confront human beings every day. Religion and spirituality can be positioned easily as concepts that are only concerned with the internal peace and well-being of an individual. Yet the ideals of justice and social justice are fundamental precepts and commands to most, if not all religious traditions. Judaism is, in part, rooted in the notion of service to others. A devout Jew sees social justice as one of the highest commands of the prophets, and as part of one's daily calling and responsibility. According to some theologians, "The Old Testament doctrine of God is based on the idea of justice. The relationship between God and persons was based on the idea of justice. God is the author of justice...It is the common denominator that gives religious unity to Israel."[212]   In the Christian tradition, a consistent theme in Jesus' messages to his followers was the commitment to serving the poor, defending the defenseless, and healing the sick. The New Testament indicates that one's entrance into the kingdom of heaven is dependent upon how one treats those who are hungry, homeless and imprisoned. Likewise, Islam is embedded with notions of service to the poor and care for widows and the distressed. Even Buddhism, which focuses more on the internal dimensions of its followers and embraces suffering as a fundamental way of life, still recognizes that it is through one's attempts to change external conditions that internal peace emerges. Though all major religions have, at various times, condoned, supported and rationalized social injustice, buried within the philosophy of each is a strong social justice mandate. The history books are filled with examples of religiously inspired individuals who worked tirelessly to end oppressive conditions including slavery, segregation, gender discrimination, poverty, fascism, homophobia, and other forms of human suffering.

Drawing from the wells of Liberation Theology, in general, and Black Liberation Theology, in particular, the intersection between spirituality and social justice becomes even clearer and more compelling. Liberation theology strongly suggests that there is no separation between the profane and the sacred because one's spiritual command permeates every aspect of one's life and social reality. Furthermore, it transforms the notion of charity for the poor into an active command to create a just social order so that the poor can experience heaven on earth. Finally, it serves to remind believers that morality is not neutral, but gives primacy to social concerns over individual pleasures and spiritual fulfillment.[213] From this perspective the poor have a favored status in the eyes of the divine. Thus one's service and commitment to the poor create favor in the sight of the divine and become prerequisites for filling the moral and spiritual commands of one's faith. Though this concept of "preferential option for the poor"[214] has been criticized by many theologians,[215] it appears to have support in various sacred texts, especially in the New Testament. God's partisanship for the poor is based on a sense of spiritual justice that sends the message to those oppressed that "despite your conditions and surrounding circumstances you are still loved and not forgotten." This spiritual message is available to all, but takes on a greater meaning for those in need. In addition, God's partisanship for the poor is based on the seeming reality that those who suffer from material deprivation often have a deeper yearning and appreciation for the divine, and a deeper connection with concepts of grace and salvation. Yet this partisanship is not unilateral. Those who have been blessed with relative security as to their external material needs are expected to satisfy their internal quest for closeness with God through serving the poor. Yet Liberation theologians suggest that this service should not be random acts of charity, propelled by momentary feelings of guilt, but should be derived from a deeper spiritual commitment to eradicating social conditions which entrap the lives and spirit of the poor. The religious activist goal is to create a just social order, such that "by uprooting the structural causes of poverty, preferential action ultimately benefits the universal good." [216]

From this spiritual perspective, lawyers are called to manifest their love and pursuit of justice on the social plane. "Justice on this level is primarily social, which calls for the transformation of structures that fail to respect human dignity and which enable the poor to participate in the workplace and to

258

have a political voice." [217] Black Liberation theology expands this command to social structures that oppress and subjugate people based on race, and feminist liberation theologians apply the same command to structures based on gender. Religion becomes more than a shield to protect one from the evils of the world - it becomes a sword that propels one to change the conditions of God's beloved people. Though these types of religious metaphors certainly have been used to uphold corrupt and oppressive political regimes, at the essence of their core, they provide a platform upon which spiritual work becomes an external pull for good, and the worship of God is translated into service to God's people.

Even within secular spiritualist traditions there is a strong belief that working to change social conditions is what gives spiritual meaning and purpose to life. Some have argued that democracy and equality are spiritual mandates, and that the transformation of oppressive social policies and hierarchies unleashes the collective spiritual power of those oppressed. [218] In describing the social justice philosophy and work of W.E.B. Dubois, one scholar described his spiritual philosophy in the following manner:

> If a disenfranchised entity or stigmatized soul suffered, then an adverse spiritual presence was gripping humanity and preventing all people from attaining maximum potentiality. Holistic spirituality demanded promoting the spread of democracy and equality, and that spreading was the actual flooding of the entire society with an empowered and reconfigured set of human relationships — a bottom-up, decentralized norm. For Du Bois, ultimate spirituality fostered the

259

enhanced vitality of the poor to exercise decisive power. Social justice was spiritual behavior.[219]

If social justice is spiritual behavior, whether from a religious or secular spiritualist perspective, then lawyers and judges, as the guardians of our ideals of justice, should have a special connection to this type of behavior. Yet too often members of this profession separate out their spiritual commands from their legal obligations. Our professional pro bono and public service ideals often are viewed as impositions, and not as professionally inspired spiritual obligations. When we ensure that all people, regardless of their income or status, have access to the legal system, we are trying to bathe the society with ideals of equality, which are so fundamental to the integrity of the legal system. When we go beyond this point and try to ensure that social, political and economic barriers which marginalize human beings are altered or destroyed, we are trying to ensure that a "liberating spirit inhabit these places where forgotten people live."[220]

While there are lawyers who embrace spirituality as a fundamental view of their professional role, many still have a hard time connecting to a social justice mandate. They believe and argue that love is the fundamental spiritual command and, if they get that right, then prior and existing social inequities really do not matter. These lawyers become so concerned with their internal peace and wholeness, they forget about the external world around them. Love from this perspective becomes a narcotic. It puts the lawyer in a state of euphoria that can be counterproductive to the true calling of this profession. I recall a lawyer at a holistic conference once stating that he was

260

offended by the slogan, "No Justice, No Peace," which some protestors had used at various times. From his perspective, to link justice with peace was a threat that ran counter to the principle of love, and he was unable to see the slogan as a mere spiritual and philosophical truism. Nonetheless, love and justice are inextricably linked, and are twin pillars of our calling as lawyers. Dr. King captured this connection so eloquently when he stated, "love is one of the principal parts of the Christian faith. There is another side called justice...Justice is love correcting that which would work against love...Standing beside love is always justice." [221] From Dr. King's perspective, love without justice was hollow love. Love must have a substantive basis to it, especially since we are operating through it to connect with others. It is very easy for new age, holistic lawyers, and others, to wrap themselves in the blanket of love, and forget that there are people suffering all around them.

Love does not insulate us from poverty, racism, sexism, homophobia or any other barrier to human fulfillment. To the contrary, it propels us to be agents for change, for injustice eats away at our internal sense of peace and pollutes and obstructs the natural flow of the rivers. The long history of racism in this society has created conditions that not only affect the life and safety of Black people and other persons of color, but also spills over into the larger society and adversely affects the safety and well-being of everyone. Domestic violence has imprisoned the souls of women, as well as the souls of men. The lives that this spiritual sickness has taken can never be replaced. The impact it has had, not only on the victims, but also on their children, family and friends, is immeasurable. It has polluted the way men and women flow together in relationship to each other. So when we clean the river of these things, we not only make it better for those who are directly affected, but also make it better for all of us. In this respect social justice should be viewed naturally as a powerful and indispensable agent in our quest for love and for a better world. J Deotis Roberts makes this point eloquently when he states the following:

> Justice, in fact becomes an indispensable expression and instrument of love. The distinction between the ideal of justice and love is simply that justice establishes the general conditions for the good life of a group and represents the demands of love for all persons of the group. Love at the same time seeks to fulfill the special needs of persons, individually and in relation to other persons. Love requires the criticism and transformation of actual justice according to the goals of ideal justice.[222]

The neglect of justice has been a common mistake of many spiritual movements in the past. The quest for love became such an inward journey that social responsibility was rationalized away. The fact that various religious organizations supported the existence of racism and sexism within their policies and practices is an important reminder that spirituality without the practice of justice is like faith without works - dead.

Though there are compelling reasons for religious leaders not to ignore their social justice responsibilities, there are more compelling reasons why lawyers cannot ignore this mandate. Justice becomes a fundamental tenet of the system we are sworn to uphold. It is the pursuit of justice and the possibility of obtaining it that gives meaning, purpose and legitimacy to the legal system. It is very easy for us to embrace this mandate as it relates to our individual clients, but this mandate extends far beyond them. It goes to underlying conditions in society that harm, stigmatize, and oppress the people within. The legal system can neither operate effectively nor dispense justice fairly, if there are major social barriers and impediments to people's access to the justice system, or if there are underlying social inequities that make justice an illusion. Thus love and justice for lawyers must go hand and hand. We should not pursue one without pursuing the other. The search for each fuels our spirits. Love and justice work together to create our internal peace and change our external realities. Social justice is the enlightened lawyers' way of putting love, and thus spirituality, into practice, and thus into the world.

Serving and Defending the Poor

Though all lawyers are responsible for obeying this spiritually inspired social justice mandate, this burden unfortunately is often carried by only a small segment of the profession. Since this responsibility has not been embraced widely across the profession, there are special spiritual challenges for those who choose to serve and represent the poor in this society.[223] It is very easy for those who do this work to downplay the spiritual dimensions of their work. If social justice is spiritual behavior then some feel that their work is their spiritual salvation. Each day they see and serve those whom society has rejected or would like to imprison. Each day they make a sacrifice with respect to money, prestige and lifestyle in order to practice this type of law. Many have the skills and experience to move to better paying positions and less stress-filled environments, but still they remain on the battlefield. In doing so they make a statement about their souls, and sometimes, about their hearts. They believe in their work, and many love the people whom they serve.

However, there is a danger for the social justice crusaders who ignore the river because they believe they already are doing divine work. Even when our work is totally compatible with our spiritual values, it is imperative that we continue to nurture our souls, for the work of serving the poor does not give us a spiritual pass - it only gives us a more direct path to the river. If we do not approach our work from a centered and whole place, then we can become part of the problem. Just doing our work is not a spiritual act. It is only when we advocate for the poor with our hearts and soul that we give them the spiritual medicine – respect and love - which society often denies them.

Another challenge that those who serve the poor confront is the high level of stress, frustration and burnout which plague them. There are too many clients with too many problems for one person to reasonably handle. There are constant political battles to defend and fund the type of work that is done, and there are internal organizational struggles that never seem to end. I often have argued that legal service lawyers and public defenders represent the soul of the legal profession. If the people they represent were not able to secure legal help, then the integrity of our entire legal system would be called into question. A legal system cannot be judged by how it treats the rich and powerful, but by how it treats the poor and powerless. Yet if those who symbolize the soul of the profession are not keeping their souls intact then we are in danger of becoming a calcified system of justice.

The river calls these servants of the poor. It asks them to provide their legal services with a kindness and tenderness that their clients may have never experienced before. It reminds these lawyers that those who have been rejected are in great need of sensitive hands to hold them; those who have been despised need genuine hearts to love them. Clients who may have committed heinous acts of destruction need a lawyer who not only will defend them, but also help them heal their souls, and inspire them to mend the social, personal and emotional wounds which they have created. The spirit of the river expects them to visit the river daily. Their work is so sacred that they must find the internal power not only to understand legal concepts and remedies, but also to be a healer of broken wings. For those clients who are trapped by poverty, racism, crime and despair want to take flight to a different reality, but feel as if there are no wings upon which they can soar. They sometimes are unable to see the spiritual and mental wings which they do possess, and sometimes those wings are broken. It is hard to stop the vicious attacks of a domestic partner when your spiritual wings are broken. It is hard to inspire your children to take flight and escape the clutches of drugs and dependency when you are still within the embrace of these demons. When you have lived in generational poverty all your life, it is hard to believe that there is no another way to exist except through support and hand-outs. Some clients cannot envision a knight in shining armor coming to rescue them, but they do have the capacity and desire to be healed. They can discover the power that still exists in their broken wings because the lawyers who work at the margins of their lives have the power to be a catalyst for the healing of broken wings. But lawyers cannot be a stimulus for healing when they are detached, depleted and spiritually broken themselves. So the river calls those who are lawyers for the poor because their work is the most cherished work of the river. If this work is not done from a pure and enlightened place, then the work is in vain, and the river mourns the lost of another precious opportunity to bring healing to the earth.

It is written that for some of us our entry into the kingdom of heaven will be determined by how we treat the "least of these."[224] Attorneys who represent the poor find themselves in a special, yet challenging spiritual place. In their hands is the opportunity to do great legal and spiritual work. They can utilize this sacred space to fulfill this divine calling, or they can abuse this privilege by just going through the motions. The pledge to be a public defender or to serve the poor comes with a high spiritual cost. If done correctly, it brings much joy to the client and great meaning to the lawyer; if it is not, it pollutes the great river of this profession. Though spiritually all lawyers occupy roles that are analogous to priests, pastors, imams and rabbis, those who serve the poor have an extra special spiritual vulnerability and responsibility. When this sacred mantle is ignored, it is analogous to a priest that sexually abuses small children who have been placed in his care. Though we should be concerned about abuse regardless of the victim, there is something troubling to us when those who have accepted the call to serve the most vulnerable in our society choose to take advantage of their vulnerability. The abuse that the detached legal services lawyer or public defender commits is not physical or financial. It is an abuse of the spirit - an abuse of the hallowed privilege to serve someone in need who cannot effectively defend or advocate for herself.

So it becomes critically important that legal service lawyers and public defenders not ignore or pollute the river. In some ways it is more difficult for these committed individuals to find the support they need to stay centered and whole. There are more clients than they can possibly handle, and fewer resources within their organizations to draw upon for help, support or release time. Yet it is vitally important for these attorneys, and those who manage these organizations, to create the space, culture and time for self- healing, otherwise the burn out rate will continue to grow. Even though many continue to do this work for life, many others leave sooner than they otherwise want because neither they, nor their organization, have found a way to counter the overwhelming frustration and stress that comes with this type of work. Individual and organizational changes must occur if these patterns are to be reversed and more meaningful work conducted. Even if it means that fewer clients are served, it is worth it if those who are served are served well. Though the legal problems outstrip the allocated resources, this does not justify a frantic, soulless legal chase. Lawyers are in the business of healing clients, not counting how many widgets are produced. Therefore, one must find the time and space to stay centered, focused and present. As one lawyer who embraced meditation as a daily ritual within his practice stated,

> One of the biggest challenges during our work day is
> to remember to pay attention, to actually be present in
> the moment. We frequently find ourselves in difficult
> situations at work because we have failed to exercise
> care and attention – to simply be conscious and aware

of what we are doing.... Professional errors and misjudgments are a symptom of divided concentration and a lack of inner balance.[225]

When these types of errors continue on a regular basis they not only hurt the clients but also lead to a situation of termination or burn out. Though some mistakes in practice are unavoidable, these mistakes are a direct result of the frantic pace and unreasonable burdens that we impose upon lawyers who serve the poor.

When one feels burnout, it may be a spiritual signal that it is time to pursue a different path of service, yet it may be a sign that one is not understanding and approaching work from the perspective of the river. Burnout in its classic definition means that there is excessive heat and friction that is occurring within a device so that it cannot function properly.[226] We have applied this definition to human situations because excessive activity and conflict within the person or organization can create so much stress and heat that the individual is not able to function effectively. Burnout has a physical, mental and spiritual dimension. Lawyers sometimes reach this point when they have physically overworked themselves due to the intensity or volume of their work. It also can occur because the work is no longer intellectually challenging or emotionally satisfying, but feels like an empty routine which a well-oiled machine could do. Both of these dimensions can be corrected by simple, though often unrealistic, adjustments in work habits and patterns. A reduction of cases or reassignment to different and more challenging cases are obvious answers.

Spiritual burnout is harder to understand and discuss. When we lose touch with our calling, purpose and meaning in the work we do, then this is a more serious problem to correct. When lawyers who chose to serve the poor for the right purpose cannot touch that place that made them want to get up each day and do this often thankless work, then a serious challenge has emerged. The two obvious choices for lawyers who find themselves in this position are either to find another type of law practice or find their way back to the river. Meaning and purpose are lost when we stray from the source that gives us that meaning and purpose. Most lawyers who choose to work for the poor do so because they have a deep desire to serve those in need. It is a direct and sincere way for them to reconcile the differences which they believe exists between their personal values and the practice of law. These are generally not jobs of necessity but jobs of choice, which for most people are a labor of love. Spiritual burnout can occur at various stages in a lawyer's career, and it raises different and deeper questions than do physical burnout.

For young attorneys who do this work, the spiritual burnout sets in because they feel as if they are not making a difference in the lives of their clients or in their area of specialty. They see recurring problems and repeat clients. Their victories appear to vanish as quickly as they were secured. Federal and state budget reductions send the message that society does not really support their work, yet they are undergoing personal sacrifices to do it. Friends and family begin to question whether the sacrifice is worth it by pointing to other lawyers who are living well. Their student loan bill cuts into so much of their monthly salary that even those who are fortunate enough to have graduated from a law school which has a loan deferral or forgiveness program realize that the amounts provided do not fully cover their loan obligation. The young poverty lawyer reaches this fork in the road and must decide if the work is worth all the sacrifices, stress and disappointment that come with the role.

For more experienced lawyers the spiritual burn out is often the product of having done the work for decades and finally reached that point where it is necessary to take stock of their life and future. The work was meaningful but their personal and professional sacrifices have taken a great toll on them. Their peers are sending their children to schools and camps which these legal service lawyers cannot afford, and their retirement nest egg, even before the bottom fell out of the market, was in another world when compared to their colleagues who took the downtown law firm path. The poor begin to feel like a heavy burden around their neck instead of a symbol of why they chose to study law. So for both the young and the experienced attorney, this glorious path of service now has led to a critical crossroad. Yet spiritual burnout is not a product of the fact that many lawyers find themselves at the crossroad; rather it is a product of the fact that they choose to remain at the crossroads. They neither definitively resolve the dilemma nor fully understand the messages that the journey is sending to them. Thus they continue to go through the motions of feeling fulfilled without having a fulfilling moment. Client cases are handled, some victories are secured but their souls are not found in their work, and those they served felt as if they had encountered a computerized message that gave them the information they desired, but not the spirit they needed.

If lawyers at the crossroads would earnestly, consistently and honestly seek the river, it would remind them that it is their heart, not their skills, that is absent and needed in the lives of those they serve. The river would let them touch again that place inside that gave birth to a genuine feeling of service. In touching that place, they would become clear that "being" is as important as "doing." The river measures their contribution by the size of their hearts and not by the number of victorious judgments. The river will remind them that many of their victories and successes they will never see, for their eyes cannot always detect movements of the soul and spirit. For the work of spirited and soulful lawyers has rippling effects upon the consciousness and spirit of their client and people they serve. The river flows for generations and the work they are called to do is generational work. So they cannot measure their worth or success by what happens in their present generation. If they abandon the work before their calling to do it is complete, then we unnecessarily delay the transformation process.

Lawyers are engaged in a battle that we cannot see. It is a spiritual war of values: a war of love against hate, of compassion against indifference, of cultural exploration against ethnocentric hegemony. This war of values in the legal arena cannot be waged by doctrines, depositions and decrees alone. It must be fought from and with our hearts. Enlightened public legal servants who bathe daily in the river must wage this war. We cannot reverse centuries of neglect, denial and discrimination by just flashing legal tools. Those who fight each day in the trenches of poverty, and in the foxholes of despair, must "put on the whole armor of God."[227] This is not an appeal to religious doctrine or a criticism of those who choose not to embrace a religious tradition. It is a reminder to those of us who do follow a religious path that we cannot afford to do this work with our souls and spirits tied behind our backs. We must bring all of who we are to the task of serving those in need. We must tap deep into the reservoir of our mind, spirit and hearts in order to secure the strength, determination and compassion necessary to do this work.

Spiritual burnout, unlike physical or mental burnout cannot be cured or reversed by external forces such as office managers and supervisors. This is an internal process that each individual must undertake personally. This is a journey of those who want to know themselves, their calling and their work at a deeper level. It requires a decision to do those things that bring about peace and reflection, and helps one make sense out of tragedy and disappointment. It requires finding constant ways to stay in touch with oneself, and with the essence and source of one's strength. A person cannot stray away from the river and expect to be nurtured by it. The lawyer for the poor cannot stand on the stones and expect their clients to be healed by the river. There must be a deep personal commitment to live there yourself. The spiritual petitions for justice must be made on behalf of the client and the lawyer. Thus the healer must regularly travel the pathway to wholeness if she is to lead others to this place.

Partnering for Justice

Another aspect of the social justice river relates to the responsibility of lawyers to look beyond their legal training and expertise for assistance in their pursuit of justice. All lawyers, especially those who serve the poor and other vulnerable segments of society, must examine their clients' situations from a broad perspective. It is critical to partner with other groups, organizations and agencies that can assist in the change and transformation process. For many clients, the only way their lawyers can secure justice is through the creation of dynamic and compelling partnerships that can transform the conditions that the clients confront. Justice is not just hidden behind the curtains of law. The justice that some clients and their communities need is concealed by centuries of inequality, hatred and indifference that have produced physical, psychological, political, educational and economic barriers and burdens. If we think law alone can destroy these mountains of inequity and resistance, then we are deluding ourselves and practicing a very narrow and sterile form of law.

If lawyers come into the lives of certain client bearing only the tools of the legal trade, then they will not be their healers; they will be their wizards. They will lead clients to believe that they have answers, when at times all they can do for them is tell them what they and the law can't do for them. But when we partner with other agencies, organizations and individuals we greatly increase our chances of not only meeting their needs, but also assisting in the transformation of their lives. Though many lawyers will never embrace this label, we must all become holistic practitioners so that we can address the needs of the whole client. We must see our clients as individuals who have multiple needs that are so intertwined that it is impossible to tease them apart, and often meaningless to address only one part.

Legal services lawyers, for example, cannot combat problems of homelessness without working with those who understand the various challenges that confront people who are homeless. As lawyers, they may restore benefits to a homeless person, but may overlook the devastating impact this temporary state has on the client's pride and self-esteem, and thus fail to offer a strategy that can break this vicious cycle of despair. Agencies and organizations that work with and study the homeless can enhance and augment legal approaches, and serve to remind lawyers of the deep psychological aspects of this problem. Long term solutions to this problem will require the development of innovative social policies and political interventions in which lawyers can and must play a role. Domestic violence is more than just a criminal act that justifies a restraining order. It represents deep emotional, economic, medical and power-laden dynamics that require lawyers to work closely with shelters, hospitals, community health clinics, law enforcement agencies, and various community groups who also are engaged in preventing and correcting this human tragedy. Without the perspective and insight of these other partners, lawyers can only provide temporary, band-aid solutions that will inevitably send a client back into the same destructive situation. A partnership must exist between those who serve the victims and those who attempt to serve, punish and transform the abuser. Justice in a domestic violence context not only entails punishing the abuser and protecting the victim, but also must include a transformation of both individuals and the power dynamics and imbalances which contribute to this human and social tragedy.

These partnerships and arrangements cannot be temporary, ad hoc solutions to intractable problems. Lawyers and legal organizations must invest the time, energy and creativity into establishing long-term and substantive connections with those who have a similar mission or goal. Partnering for justice requires that we re-examine traditional barriers and boundaries that separate us from those who can help. We must be willing to relinquish control where they are not needed, and dismantle hierarchical structures that unnecessarily separate lawyers from paralegals, pro bono coordinators and other legal professionals who can make a difference in the lives of clients. These partnerships and arrangements should not be limited to mainstream agencies. Lawyers who serve the poor, for example, must know the grass-root organizations, churches, community leaders, civil rights organizations, and other caring and committed individuals who can assist them in bringing justice to the people they serve.

In addition to the holistic perspective that we must bring to individual cases, we also must bring a broad perspective to the collective, systemic problems that certain clients confront. The education of children in urban, and sometimes rural, areas may not raise concrete legal issues that can give rise to a lawsuit, but legal services lawyers must directly and indirectly work with those who are striving to improve the quality of education for all children. Unless we can strengthen the education of the poor, we will never break the chains of generational poverty that still abound. Though economic development is a challenging issue for some lawyers who practice outside of the commercial law area, they must partner with lawyers who deal with these issues everyday, and they must work with those individuals in and outside the community who can bring economic justice to those who have been relegated to the sidelines of this economy. Certainly, there are serious structural barriers that will make this work seem like a utopian dream, but while some sit idly by waiting for massive redistribution of wealth and values, others will strive to create a small oasis of economic prosperity in places where deprivation and doom once ruled.

When lawyers see their role through these lenses, they will understand that there is an enormous power in partnerships. "The Power of Partnerships,"[228] is more than just working with others to form new, temporary arrangements for the benefit of our clients. The real power of partnerships is that they can serve as a catalyst to help us explore a different conception of the role and practice of law in society. When we see law in partnerships for social justice then we are giving new life to the law. When we do this we are taking law off its pedestal, lowering it so that more people can touch it and find meaning in it. In effect, by lowering the law we are elevating it. We are spreading the law so that others can come under its umbrella to serve and be served. When we do this we also are putting law in its proper place and recognizing that there is room at this table of social justice for other disciplines, organizations and individuals.

The practice of law must be recast so that it can communicate with the powerful, commune with the powerless, and in the process, redefine the meaning of power. When we approach and discuss law from this perspective lawyers are in essence taking off our capes, removing the "S" from our chest, and realizing that we are not superheroes. Lawyers can do great things, but we cannot do them alone. Our license does not empower us to perform magic, but it does empower us to heal. Healing is a collective process that first involves those we serve, and then those who can directly and indirectly impact our clients' situations and lives. So the power of partnerships is not just the enhanced power and possibility to transform the lives and conditions of our clients, but is rather an enhanced power and possibility to transform the practice of law and ourselves as lawyers.

So partnering for social justice is more than an organizational, political or economic strategy - it is a spiritual command. This does not mean that it is a call for us to abandon our legal expertise in exchange for meditation, prayer and healing circles. Rather it is a serious recognition that there is a limitation to law, but there is no limitation to the power of divinely inspired human beings to change hearts, social structures and reality. We celebrate Dr. Martin Luther King's birthday, but often ignore the fact that it was his deeply held spiritual beliefs that empowered him and so many others to transform segregated cities of hate into integrated hamlets where love could be born. Some of us honor Malcolm X, but forget that his faith allowed him to speak truth to power and transform himself in the process. We revere Ghandi, a lawyer by training, but downplay the fact that his deep spiritual power propelled him to dismantle British colonialism through non-violence and love. The list of lawyers and non-lawyers who mounted spiritual wings in their pursuit of social justice is endless.

So if in the years to come you see groups of lawyers meditating or praying, do not be alarmed. If you see them performing miracles in the courtroom with their heads and with their hearts, do not object. If you see them mounting wings to transform communities as they serve their clients, know that they are not leaning on their legal expertise alone. They will be resting on the majestic and divine wings of justice, being propelled by the power of true partnerships and the winds of a loving, healed and whole client community. When we combine our deep spiritual insights with the resources and expertise of those in other disciplines and professions, there is no limit to the progress that law and lawyers can usher upon the human stage. This is the pure vision of social justice as spiritual behavior.

Chapter Six:

New Streams and Old Dams

Holistic Forms of Practice

For generations lawyers have been seeking different paths for the fulfillment of their aspirations to serve people through the law. Many have been on individual journeys that at times felt lonely and disconnected. These were pioneers who knew that something was missing from the traditional study and practice of law, and they attempted to find the missing pieces. Some sought the promised land through intellectual discourse, and thus created new theories of law that called into question some of the fundamental precepts of traditional law and legal processes. [229] Others tried to create organizational structures, such as legal cooperatives, that created different business relationships among lawyers in practice. For a select group of the discontent however, what was missing was a stronger connection between the practice of law and their personal values or spiritual tradition. For various reasons these individuals marched to the beat of a different drummer. Many of them grew up in a period in this country where many traditional values were being questioned and challenged. They had pursued alternative life styles before they became lawyers, and it left a sweet taste in their mouths, even though they had chosen a very traditional and rigid profession. They were often criticized or marginalized by the mainstream establishment, but continued to answer the call of the river. They weren't always able to articulate what they were seeking in ways that were convincing to other lawyers, but they continued to try to teach, study and practice law in a way that was more consistent with their values and philosophy of life.

In the last few decades many of these individual travelers came together and developed organized patterns and approaches to the study and practice of law. There is no agreed upon banner under which all of these approaches rest. One source[230] that tries to track all of these approaches labels them as Transformational Law, yet recognizes that this movement is referred to by other labels such as Visionary Law, Integral Law, Comprehensive Law and Holistic Law. They list about twenty-five different approaches that fall under these broad banners. Professor Susan Daicoff[231] refers to the different approaches as vectors, and attempts to identify and explain the principles that unify these approaches. Though there is a strong appeal to the unifying theme of Transformational Law, I prefer to label these various approaches as varying forms of Holistic Legal Practices.

The concept of holism, by its nature, captures much of what many of these lawyers are seeking. Transformation addresses the end product and goal of these approaches, but it does not capture the underlying philosophy that gives these forms of practice meaning. Holism is a way of being, and a way of understanding and relating to the world around us. It focuses on more than what we hope to do to existing legal structures and processes, which is to transform them. It speaks to how we must be, and how we must see the practice of law and ourselves in order to usher in this transformation. The concept of holism has deep intellectual and spiritual roots that make it an ideal canvas upon which to lay these colorful and diverse strokes of legal practices. Holism rejects the departmentalization of life. It grows out of the belief that the whole is greater than the sum of its parts; therefore one cannot understand life or anything else by just focusing on its constituent parts.

Those lawyers who have been thirsting for something different in their practice intuitively know that they will not find it by divorcing their practice from the rest of their lives. They instinctively understand that their spiritual lives provide energy and sustenance for the work they do. They also know that the problems their clients present encompass more than just the obvious legal issues. They seek a perspective that allows them to embrace their total being and all of what they know about themselves and their client, as they "seek to do good as they do well." Holism suggests that all problems and conflicts grow out of a multi-faceted context, which must be embraced and understood in order to understand and resolve the conflict. The spiritual dimensions of holism suggest that each person and situation in our lives is there to teach us something, and thus we should be reluctant to view life through the prism of win/lose. Lawyers who embrace this perspective are looking for ways that their clients, and sometimes all parties, can leave the dispute process with more than what they brought, regardless of the outcome. Holistic practices are those that seek some form of healing, and not just the imposition of guilt and blame.

Another reason many lawyers who embrace the above values also embrace the label of holism is due to the organizational efforts of some of their colleagues. The International Alliance of Holistic Lawyers, under the leadership of its founder Bill van Zyverden brings together various lawyers from around the country and world on an annual basis, to share their insights about their practices. These conferences and workshops not only have given legitimacy and prominence to this approach to the practice of law, but also have enriched our understanding of similar forms of practice that continue to emerge. Since the river cannot be fully contained or completely described, under this banner of holism numerous tributaries, streams and other minor bodies of water are found. They come together, feed into each other, and ultimately go their own way. These smaller bodies of water create their own patterns and rhythms that are worthy of independent study and observation. They have their own operating principles and guides, and a core group of lawyers who are deeply committed to nurturing and developing these novel forms of practice. This has brought about an important change in the legal profession within the last twenty years. Presently there are various well thought-out approaches to the practice of law that both new and seasoned lawyers seeking a new approach can adopt. Instead of drifting at sea, trying to create a new path that embraces their values and vision of law and life, lawyers can choose to follow various well developed new streams of practice. However, since so many of these approaches are in varying stages of development, the new lawyer will find room for innovation and creativity. What each of these approaches contains is a fresh hope for a profession that needs revitalization. They embrace and thus reflect a level of creativity that is too often missing from the standard practice of law, and they have the potential to guide the entire profession toward its spiritual center. I will not endeavor to describe all of the forms of legal practice that could fall under this banner of holistic law, but there are four major ones that I do describe: Collaborative law, Therapeutic Jurisprudence, Contemplative Law Practice, and Restorative Justice. Each of these movements has made a unique contribution to the revitalization of the profession, and each has a direct connection to the work of the river.

Collaborative Law

This movement within the profession is similar to alternative dispute resolution; however, it structurally and theoretically takes negotiation and mediation to a new level. It was founded by Stu Webb, a family law practitioner in Minneapolis, Minnesota who became frustrated with the negative effects that the adversarial model had on him and his clients.[232] After a less than favorable first encounter, Webb and three other lawyers launched this new innovative approach in 1990. Fundamentally, lawyers who practice collaborative law agree with their clients that they not will pursue litigation as a way to resolve the conflict or dispute. The other party to the matter must hire an attorney who is a trained collaborative lawyer and agrees to the same stipulations. This entire arrangement is governed by what is called in this area, a Participation Agreement. The parties do not waive their rights to litigation or give up any claims they may have, but they will not be able to pursue those claims in court with the lawyers that have been hired to reach a settlement. The power of this agreement is that it removes the threat of litigation from the negotiation process. This threat has often stood as a barrier to lawyers being willing to work creatively and sincerely to reach settlements. In traditional attempts at settlement, attorneys often go through the motions, playing hardball because they have the threat of litigation hanging over the heads of the other party, or can use it to persuade their clients not to accept a reasonable settlement offer because they might get more in court. When this weapon is taken away from both attorneys, they are more likely to work in earnest to resolve the matter and protect the respective interest of their clients.

However, collaborative law is more than a structural tool, it is a philosophy and method of lawyering that springs from a deeper well. Collaborative lawyers and their clients deeply believe that better resolutions of disputes occur when individuals approach the negotiation process with a sincere and deep belief that cooperation is better than an adversarial stance. They genuinely see the work as something that does not have a concrete answer, but involves a process as well as a solution. The process embraces not only the legal issues at hand, but also the relationship between the parties. The lawyers must strive to be as sensitive to the broader emotional, spiritual and even political issues which are present, as they are to the legal ones. They must employ a set of tools different than the standard ones designed primarily for litigation. As one collaborative lawyer stated, "aggressive arguments will be less effective than attentive listening."[233]

Collaborative lawyers also have to adopt a broader understanding of their role in this novel dispute resolution process. "Although the collaborative lawyer is not actually a neutral, his responsibilities shift away from those associated with 'pure' advocacy and toward the creative, flexible representation that characterizes neutrality. A lawyer can become so comfortable with pushing the very specific agenda of his client, and only his client, that it can be difficult for him to shift perspectives toward a truly creative and truly collaborative mindset."[234] Though the client's interest remains the lawyer's first and foremost responsibility, the lawyer must be willing to understand and embrace the concerns of the other side; otherwise she may find herself engaged in the spirit of litigation in the midst of a collaborative law process. The process creates a multi-dimensional dialogue between and among the clients and their collaborative law attorneys. Unlike most litigation patterns, it provides the lawyers with an opportunity to meet and engage the other party at an early stage in the process.[235] Therefore the lawyer's insights and ability to seek a solution are not limited to the perceptions and biases of the client they represent. The process also forces the lawyers to work collaboratively and cooperatively in order to create an environment where their clients can achieve their goals. This requires the lawyers to collectively plan a tentative agenda for the meeting, brainstorm between meetings, and try to strategize about how to move the conflict resolution and healing aspects of the process forward. During the process the attorneys can look to each other to help them sacredly "hold the emotions," identify common ground and themes, share responsibility for success and setbacks, and serve as guides through the movement of the river. There are various organizations[236] around the country that provide training for lawyers who do this type of work, and they require that the lawyers go through the training before they can be certified as a collaborative lawyer.

There is even a Collaborative Law Standards of Conduct, adopted by the International Association of Collaborative Professionals that sets out very clearly what is permissible and expected of those who participate in this process.

Those who embrace this approach to the practice of law must make sure their clients fully understand the process before it begins. For these attorneys this is not a preliminary step in the litigation process - it is the only step. Clients must understand this limitation or they will become very frustrated with the approach and with their lawyer. They have to accept the underlying philosophy and goals, and be willing to forego what they may perceive as a quick and easy solution. It is also essential that the lawyers involved fully embrace this approach. Collaborative law works only when both lawyers enter into the same type of agreement with their respective clients, and both lawyers fully embrace the approach. There are some lawyers who generally structure their entire practice around this method, while others do it only on occasions. Though some still engage in litigation in other matters, the true collaborative lawyer does only this. They have embraced this approach because of their frustration with the adversariness of the litigation model. They grew tired of the limited results that were reached through that traditional approach and wanted something more meaningful and compatible with their values that could address the true needs of their clients.

Though litigation, and negotiation with litigation hanging in the background, can produce excellent results in some situations, in most they leave much to be desired. Even the victorious parties do not always feel as if they were made whole by the process. They may have a judgment which represents that they are monetarily whole, but they have a hole in their hearts and spirits which the process did not mend or heal. As one psychologist noted after reflecting on her experience of securing a divorce through the traditional legal process, "neither Canadian civil law nor counseling had provided a format to bring psychological closure to my pain."[237] The focus of collaborative law is to create a forum where the psychological pain of the conflict and dispute can be addressed along with the legal issues. The goal is to move the parties away from "blaming" and towards a forward- looking problem solving approach. [238] Another limitation of the traditional adversarial model is that the losing parties generally do not emerge from the process in a better space for having dealt with the real challenges that they faced and the real opportunities that the experience provided. They often have a decree which orders them to do something which they still have not internally accepted. Even when a party has contributed greatly to the destruction of the relationship, having a judge declare that they are responsible does not necessarily mean that the process allowed them to come to grips with their deficiencies and limitations. Because the adversarial process requires that litigants "put their best foot forward," and sometimes even exaggerate the size of their foot, there is rarely the opportunity to internalize and reflect on the dynamic that brought them to that place.

Since most lawyers in the adversarial process feel that they must prepare their clients to "go to battle," it is difficult for them to also prepare the clients to make peace with themselves and the other party, or even to see the matter from the perspective of the other person. Therefore losing is just that – a lost opportunity. Growth and self-reflection rarely occur, because all the individuals working with the litigants are trying to demonstrate why they should not be punished, fined or have a judgment rendered against them. There is no part of the process that is systematically directed towards the river. The stones are where most traditional litigators focus their attention. Yet swirling all around the stones, beating against their sides is a subtle, but powerful motion that possibly could lead to a better result, including the healing of those involved in the conflict. Collaborative lawyers have made the conscious decision to work from the river, and to use the stones to guide them to shore. Some report examples of what one calls "moments of spontaneous generosity,"[239] where in the midst of a collaborative dispute resolution process one party agrees to address the real needs of the other and goes beyond what traditionally would be required, because for the first time that party listened to, touched and accepted responsibility for the pain that had been inflicted on the other person. Collaborative law allows the parties to "come to a fuller comprehension of the impact of their deeds and acts."[240] This does not occur automatically, and it is important for the lawyers to set collectively a tone of dignity, respect and trust as governing principles and practices for the process. When it is done right, the process can empower clients to construct their future instead of having it imposed upon them by a third party. It also provides them with a sense of privacy as they confront and reveal some of the most intimate and troubling aspects of their lives.

Like mediation and other forms of alternative dispute resolution techniques, collaborative lawyering is not for everyone or every type of case. This practice is restricted to civil matters since they are the ones where clients can make the decision to forego litigation. In criminal matters that decision does not rest with the parties, but with the state. One could imagine that in some minor misdemeanor situations a state could develop a process where the prosecutor had the discretion to pursue a settlement or alternative remedy rather than engage in trail proceedings. This might be cumbersome and resource intensive, but the amount of money and time now that is wasted in courts on minor violations surely could be devoted to this type of process. Drug Courts and other restorative justice approaches consistent with this approach have already been adopted by various state and local authorities, and are very successful.

Alternative dispute resolution approaches have been viewed traditionally as inappropriate for situations where there is a serious imbalance of power. When one party to the dispute has a tremendous amount of economic, psychological, or even physical power over the other party, there is concern that the result reached, though ostensibly through consensus, is blatantly unfair to one of the parties. This power imbalance can also dilute the natural benefits this process provides because it can distort the open exchange of ideas and emotions. Though these are real concerns that must not be minimized, they do not preclude every power imbalance case from being handled through collaborative law. The attorneys handling the matter are the key to the fairness of the process in such instances. Part of their role is to restore or create some balance between the parties. Unlike mediation where the mediator is there primarily to assist the parties reach a resolution, collaborative lawyers are there to protect and defend their party's interest. If they detect that the process is moving in a direction that takes advantage of their party's weakness, not only must they strive to prevent that from happening, but also must make that issue part of the process. This creates an opportunity for the powerful party to come face - to - face with how that power has been used in the past to disadvantage the other party, and how the same thing is happening in the collaborative law process. This must be done in a skillful manner so that the powerful party can see and deal with it as an acceptable part of the process.

Likewise the less powerful party must also deal with how they may have contributed to this imbalance in the relationship. The goal is not to force either party through a therapy session, but to make it obvious to both that the resolution to their problem involves more than just reaching a number with which they can live. What allows this form of legal practice to be more meaningful is that the parties leave the process feeling as if they reached an agreement without the trauma and artificiality of the litigation process, but with a deeper understanding of the other person to the dispute as well as of themselves and the relationship. These are particularly valuable outcomes in disputes where the relationship will continue after the disputes are resolved, such as in divorces where children are involved, and business relationships where future transactions will occur.

Of course, collaborative law does not always work. There are times when the parties are unable to reach a resolution, or the attorneys conclude that the parties are not truly committed to the process. Unfortunately, there also are examples where one of the attorneys does not fully understand the process, even though they may have attended a collaborative law training program. The arrangement is terminated at that time and the parties are free to pursue some other form of dispute resolution, including litigation. They must do so, however, with other attorneys. The attorney-client privilege, coupled with a standard confidentiality agreement among all of the parties, covers communications during the collaborative process and prevents these communications from being used in subsequent litigation. Even though most of these issues have not been litigated in court, the experience of most attorneys in this area is that very few of their client relationships are being terminated prior to reaching a resolution. There are great incentives for the attorneys and their clients to reach a fair and meaningful settlement. The lawyers cannot easily back out because litigation is not a path they can pursue, and the clients by adopting the approach, are generally predisposed toward finding a way to resolve the matter.

However, there are some ethical issues of which collaborative lawyers should be aware before plunging into the river. They should understand that there is not a direct conflict between the collaborative process and their ethical commitment of "zealous representation."[241] Since the parties have agreed to go through a collaborative process in order to solve a problem, they have, in essence, assented to this approach as the most "zealous" representation that they want at this time. However, the lawyers must be careful, even within the confines of the participation agreement, to ensure that they do not unwittingly give away the rights of their client, nor suggest solutions that unduly compromise the client's interest. On the other hand, a client may forego resources, rights and privileges to which they are entitled because they are more concerned about investing in the long term health of the relationship.[242] In addition, if the collaborative process is unsuccessful, these lawyers will have to consider how they will assist the client in making a transition to a litigation attorney. Professional rules of conduct require lawyers to pass on materials to new counsel and even assist the client in securing new counsel. However the confidentiality agreement, which is a part of the Participation Agreement, puts some limits on what lawyers can share with the litigation attorney. How to balance the needs of the client going forward and respecting the process that just ended, albeit unsuccessfully, will be a unique challenge for the lawyers who confront this problem. Having these discussions ahead of time and agreeing more specifically about what can be shared and what cannot, would minimize this ethical dilemma for lawyers in the future. Lastly, though there is language in most Participation Agreements that requires each side to "make full and fair disclosures to their attorneys and the other party of all facts pertinent to their legal matter,"[243] this can be interpreted to apply to requested information only.[244] It thus can curtail the ability of the parties to reach a creative and fair solution as well as jeopardize the emotional and spiritual benefits to be derived from the process.

As this movement evolves, there will be more ethical challenges for those who choose to participate in this type of process. The collaborative and consensual nature of this practice may make it easier for lawyers and clients to find acceptable solutions to these dilemmas. Lawyers, by their calling are really problem solvers, and once they embrace this calling the hurdles become much lower. Unfortunately, too many lawyers have been trained to be problem creators, and use the acquired skills masterfully to sustain and prolong litigation, and to intimidate opposing counsel. Collaborative law stands as a powerful alternative for lawyers and clients who are seeking a different path. It can bring order to a chaotic legal process that often leaves much emotional blood on the floor. It can serve as a tool and an arena in which lawyers can be healers in a dramatic and systemic manner. It can serve as a consumer protection device that holds down the cost of lengthy litigation. It also has served as a magnet to keep brilliant and dedicated people in the profession who otherwise would have abandoned it long ago because they could not reconcile their traditional practices with their values and beliefs. Collaborative law has become their home, their access to the river. From the river these lawyers are able to provide better results for their clients which allowed the client to feel good about taking control over their situation and challenge, instead of turning over their lives and future to a strange judge and jury that may never fully understand them or their problem. This is not a limitation inherent to judges or juries, but a limitation built into the structure of our traditional approaches to law and the legal process. Collaborative law not only breaks through those limitations, but also fosters a new spirit for the resolution of disputes. This is a spiritual and holistic perspective that lives and thrives in the river.

Though every lawyer who gravitated toward this approach may not have done so for spiritual purposes, collaborative law has allowed many lawyers to more closely reconcile their spiritual or religious beliefs with their chosen profession. This connection and the motivation for seeking it are captured in the story of Rita Pollak, a divorce lawyer who practices in Boston. In discussing her reasons for abandoning the traditional form of divorce practice, she shared this reflection:

Early in my career, I used to become physically sick, especially before going to court on particular cases or dealing with particular attorneys. I'd lie awake at night, night after night, rehearsing arguments, persuading, cajoling, pleading, demanding, and trying to "force" a result. I'd have diarrhea; I'd throw up: my back and neck would spasm (that's how hard I was working to make "my" result prevail.) On at least an annual basis, I'd end up in bed with my back "out" for a week to 10 days.[245]

In addition to the physical pain, there was a spiritual and emotional disjunction for Rita as well. She felt that the practice of law created a struggle between the connectedness she sought on her spiritual path and the profound disconnectedness exemplified by some of her work.[246] As she began to study and reflect more on her religious tradition of Judaism, collaborative law became a viable bridge between her faith and her work as a divorce lawyer. She found support for what she now does in the sacred scriptures and text of her religion. The following creation story contained in the *Kabbalah* served as a basis for a deeper understanding of her calling as a lawyer:

God is pure light. God's light exceeded the vessels that were supposed to contain them. The light pouring into the vessels shattered them, and bits of light were scattered to the lowest depths, to what became our place of existence. These pinpoints of light rest within each one of us. We hold sparks of Divinity in the essence of our beings.[247]

So instead of conceptualizing law and her participation within it as a destructive process of "shattering the vessels," Rita now sees her role as a divorce lawyer through an empowering spiritual lens. This is eloquently captured in the following statement:

> According to Jewish tradition, our task here in life, in this place, is to gather up all the scattered sparks of light and repair the vessel that shattered at the time of creation, pour light into the made-whole vessel and in this way join God in the act of creation. So the task of Tikkun is to heal or repair that which is broken in the world, beginning with that which is broken in us. ...I do see my path as a gatherer of sparks....[248]

For many who have practiced law for a lot of years in the traditional manner, the discovery of collaborative law is often described as analogous to the religious experience of "being born again."[249] It was for some the last hope before they abandoned the profession. They found a middle path where they could place their values and their work, their minds and their hearts, their joys and their frustrations, all in the same circle and call it home. This does not mean that collaborative law is a panacea. There are numerous ethical dilemmas that this type of practice presents, and there are varying client expectations about the process that must be managed and better understood. The work can be very stressful and emotionally challenging for both clients and lawyers, and there is a tendency by some to sanitize the process. A lawyer's values can creep into the process in ways that reaffirm relational hierarchies instead of dismantling or rearranging them. Yet despite these challenges and growing pains, this approach offers a wonderful way for lawyers and clients to find more meaning, wholeness and dignity in the midst of difficult and perplexing situations.

Therapeutic Jurisprudence

This perspective of the law finds its roots more in the academy than in the practice of law, and leading legal scholars around the country have written a great deal about it. [250] Therapeutic Jurisprudence is a systematic examination of the "extent to which substantive rules, legal procedures and the roles of lawyers and judges produce therapeutic or anti-therapeutic consequences." [251] Ideally law should be embracing those rules and practices that promote therapeutic goals that are consistent with our notions of justice. Though it has it roots in mental health law, it has wider application and implications for the study and practice of law. David Wexler introduced the term in 1987 and it has been refined, expanded and applied by numerous scholars to a host of legal problems. Since law is a "therapeutic agent" which can heal or destroy, lawyers, judges and legislators must be very sensitive to the non-legal effects of law and legal processes when conducting their respective work. This approach at its highest level implicates an understanding of other disciplines such as psychology and psychotherapy. Wexler cautions us against embracing this approach in a superficial manner:

> Identifying areas of the law ripe for a therapeutic jurisprudence analysis requires a reasonable degree of psychological sophistication. For example, an analysis must be able to determine which sector of the population a given law is most likely to affect; to explore the psychological dynamics of that sector; and

given these dynamics, to examine what effect the law is likely to have. Without all three components the analysis will be incomplete.[252]

This warning should not prevent us from embracing this perspective, but should encourage us not to view law as an isolated entity that can serve justice without the insights and sensitivities from other disciplines.

Wexler argues that law has three different dimensions which are the objects of the therapeutic jurisprudence inquiry. The three dimensions are legal rules, legal procedures, and legal actors. [253] Each of these dimensions can produce actions, reactions and dysfunctional behavior that can have negative impacts on those involved in the legal process as well as society in general. It is the last of these three components, legal actors, that is the most germane to this work, but I will briefly discuss the first two. Take, for example, the "Don't Ask, Don't Tell" rule which appears on its face to protect the privacy of gay persons in the military by precluding military official from inquiring about a person's sexual orientation, but which in effect, may create negative psychological effects of isolation, marginalization and alienation.[254] These unintended consequences must be considered with the constitutional issues that are on the table. Law is a reflection of the values of society; therefore, the norms, biases, and subliminal messages that are ingrained within society are also reflected in the law. Thus, the application of rules in the arena of human actors invariably means that legal decisions and processes will have a powerful impact on the psychological make-up of individuals.

Therapeutic Jurisprudence recognizes that one cannot ignore the psychological impacts without paying a cost. As we analyze existing laws and certainly as we consider implementing new ones, we must contemplate whether such laws "foster psychopathology and dysfunctional behavior."[255] This raises extremely important research questions which will require lawyers to seek the assistance of empirical researchers from the fields of psychology and social sciences in general. This multidisciplinary approach has not distracted from the importance of legal analysis, but rather enhanced its value. The type of questions it raises, and the human sensitivity it encourages, are not limited to rules in the mental health field. This approach has been embraced by those who are striving to bring a more therapeutic approach to "criminal law... juvenile law, family law, disability and employment law, torts law, workers compensation ...contracts,"[256] and numerous other substantive areas.

The second dimension that Wexler identifies relates to legal processes that can have anti-therapeutic effects. Take the example of child custody proceedings in which the structure of the adversarial process encourages each side to vilify the other. Since very emotionally charged issues are raised in a public setting, this may have extremely negative effects on the child involved and on the individuals who will be responsible for jointly raising the child in the future.[257]This perspective offers a systematic lens through which the entire legal processes, or specific procedures, can be analyzed. This example does not necessarily mean that we abandon the adversarial system altogether, but it does challenge us not to limit our analysis to just the fairness of a procedure, but to weigh the negative and traumatic behavior the procedure may be encouraging and supporting. Though the procedure may be fair on its face and lead to a result, the psychological and spiritual costs of that result may be higher than calculated. This approach reminds us that those costs to the people served, and to the lawyers and judges involved, are just as critical as the procedure or the rule it upholds. Through the lens of therapeutic jurisprudence we are able to appreciate better alternative legal procedures and processes such as mediation and collaborative law. This approach can provide a scientific basis for the concerns we have about the adversarial process in some cases. One reasons collaborative law is so appealing to certain clients and practitioners is its therapeutic effect which is not usually present in the traditional adversarial structure.

The third dimension of Wexler's taxonomy relates to the behavior of lawyers and judges as they interact with the client and each other. It is this dimension that has the greatest relevance to this inquiry. What judges and lawyers say to clients, and how they say it, is as relevant to the legal process as are rules and decisions. Therapeutic jurisprudence ask the major actors in the legal drama to hold up a mirror in order to see more clearly the legal issues before them and their impact on the parties as well as their roles as the major inhibitors or facilitators of justice and healing. As one author in this field indicates:

> We serve our clients best if we have emotional intelligence, if we are able to understand their fears, hopes and dreams. In fact, whether we undertake the task consciously or otherwise, when we counsel our

> clients we are dealing with their psyches. The Good
> Lawyer must be accountable for this responsibility.[258]

When our clients enter the legal arena, they bring with them all of the sensitivities and vulnerabilities that they possess. Woven into their legal disputes and problems are emotional, spiritual and psychological struggles. The attorney who only sees and deals with the legal problem only brings a limited approach to solving the problem and will miss a sacred and special opportunity to assist in the client's healing. There is an old adage which says that, "if the only thing you have is a hammer, then everything looks like a nail." [259] Too many lawyers and judges approach the practice of law with a finely carved assortment of hammers which they call rules and procedures. They spend their professional lives looking for nails, which they call legal issues that can be driven into the fabric of society and into the lives of the people who stand before them. Too often they end up hitting their clients over the head with solutions that do not fit their lives, circumstances or psychological or spiritual needs. Lawyers often feel compelled to use a hammer because it is the only tool they have been taught to use.

Therapeutic jurisprudence attempts to offer to lawyers and judges different tools, and to remind them that their attitudes, actions and insights are very valuable and useful ones in the service of justice and their clients. While these new psychological and spiritual tools may not be appropriate in every situation, they must always be included in the tool kit. Not all of the instruments which an Emergency Medical Service professional brings to the scene of an accident are needed, yet it would be unprofessional for them to only bring a band-aid. It is also part of their professional duty to recognize when the problems exceeds their capabilities. Likewise, lawyers must bring all of who they are to the problems of their clients, even though each skill, insight or value is not needed in every situation. Developing literature and practices concerning the identification of "psychological soft spots" are available to assist lawyers in recognizing the emotional consequences of various forms of legal interventions.[260] Lawyers must also be aware that these emotional connections and tools can create traps that should be avoided. As professionals they must be aware of the dangers of transference and counter-transference of emotional feelings which can result in inappropriate relationships between them and their clients. Yet these dangers should not make the emotional and spiritual aspect of the lawyer-client relationship disappear. To the contrary, it is only through these tools that lawyers can cope effectively with this challenge. As one scholar states:

> [T]o avoid boundary violations, lawyers must acknowledge that emotional responses are triggered in virtually every human encounter. The goal need not be - indeed could not be - to eradicate these responses. Rather the goal should be to recognize them, analyze how, if at all, they may affect the lawyer/client relationship, and resolve them appropriately.[261]

This cannot be done effectively if lawyers operate in a state of emotional denial, where they refuse to grapple with the emotional reactions and responses of their clients as well as their own. Nor can it be done if lawyers chose to ignore the significant historical and contemporary legal literature on this topic.[262] In addition, lawyers must be willing and able to recognize situations in which the psychological problems of their clients require referrals to a trained professional who can address them appropriately. Therapeutic jurisprudence does not encourage lawyers to practice psychotherapy. It very clearly recommends that attorneys refer their clients to a licensed psychotherapist when necessary. When clients are suffering from very deep mental and emotional problems it is in everyone's interest to get them to an experienced mental health practitioner who knows what to do. However, many of the challenges that clients are facing do not require that level of help. Their healing can be encouraged, fostered, and facilitated by a caring and sensitive person who is able to see them for the person they are and not merely as a source of income. Some of the basic things in life such as a gentle disposition, a listening ear, a caring spirit, a strong but passionate no, and a genuine smile can make all the difference to a person who is facing a difficult and challenging situation. Lawyers who refuse to live behind stonewalls, and are willing to reveal parts of themselves and their humanity can open a path to help clients break through an emotional barrier they have created or someone has placed in their way. The relationship created between the client and the attorney is bilateral. It cannot work effectively if one is human and the other is mechanical. However, there is more to this approach than just smiling and being nice. It requires lawyers to become more sophisticated in their understanding of the human makeup.

Developing collaborative relationships and friendships with trained therapists is a good way to develop these insights. Some lawyers who adopt this approach are former therapists who decided to pursue a law degree in order to better serve the causes and people they were drawn to for a long time. Reading books in this area to become more conversant in the language of therapists and more sensitive to identifying more deep-seated problems are important investments for those who choose to follow this path. Certainly, there may appear to be a threat to other professions when lawyers begin to embrace perspectives and utilize skills which they were not traditionally trained to provide. There have been many discussions and meetings between those who practice law from this perspective and those who are licensed therapists. For many there is a common and comfortable ground that has been staked out. Enlightened therapists agree that some of the problems they end up having to deal with are products of minor, yet recurring incidents and encounters that were not addressed at earlier stages. They believe that lawyers and other professionals have the power to assist in the healing of others. They recognize that while there is a danger in amateurs handling issues that can end up exploding in their faces, they also recognize that denial and avoidance by those who encounter people everyday may be an even greater danger. Therefore everyone in a person's life, through their actions and attitudes, can have a therapeutic or anti-therapeutic effect on the person.

But lawyers are in a different category than friends, co-workers and family members who encounter people on a daily basis. Individuals specifically turn to lawyers because they seek resolution to a problem. When they reveal the problem they are simultaneously revealing themselves. As lawyers, we do not have a license to engage in therapy, but we do have a calling to serve them. That calling empowers us to see not only the problem, but also its possible causes and sources. We may not be able to provide easy, packaged answers, but it is our responsibility to engage the client about possible solutions or paths that can be pursued to reach a resolution. As we work with them over time, we are in such a unique position to be a constant, positive reinforcing spirit in their lives. We can pretend that it is only the legal problem that we are called to serve, but when we embrace that narrow perspective, we have contributed to turning the profession into a sterile, mechanical process that could be better performed by high-powered computers. If we want to preserve and restore the soul of this profession, we must conduct our practices in a manner that reflects our soul and cherishes the souls of those who come through our doors. Some have recognized that therapeutic jurisprudence is a tool that lawyers can use in the search to become healers, and in their search to heal themselves. Michael Perlin wrote, "[f]or I believe that a law of healing is possible, that the phrase should not make anyone's list of favorite oxymorons, and that therapeutic jurisprudence is one of the key paths that we must take if we are to create such a body of law."[263] And I would add that it is also one of the key paths we must take if we are to create a body of lawyers and judges who operate as healers.

This approach also has tremendous potential for the education of future lawyers. In addition to the legal scholars who write extensively about this topic, some legal educators have attempted to incorporate therapeutic jurisprudence into the actual teaching of law. Though much of this activity has occurred in the clinical arena, these insights are applicable to the whole of legal education. Various scholars have argued that some of the essential aspects of the practice of law and legal education (i.e., problem solving, client counseling, self reflection, and professional responsibility) are enhanced by adopting a therapeutic jurisprudence approach. [264] In addition, it has been suggested that therapeutic jurisprudence "improves our teaching skills, gives us a better understanding of the dynamics of clinical relationships, investigates ethical concerns and the effects on lawyering roles, and invigorates the way we as teachers and students question accepted legal practices."[265] Though clinics provide a more appropriate venue for the development of these skills and values, it is critical that all law professors become sensitive to these aspects of the teaching and learning process. The therapeutic jurisprudence framework may serve as a catalyst for the reexamination of the learning goals for law courses and an upgrading of the skills necessary to teach.

Even in the traditional substantive courses we should be teaching students to be creative problem solvers. Though the materials that we give them are generally appellate cases, there are numerous problems buried within the doctrines and language of each case. Rarely do we use this opportunity to critique the choices and behavior of the parties to the litigation, especially with an eye towards developing different solutions than the one rendered by the court. Certainly there are limitations with respect to the amount of real facts about the parties and the surrounding circumstances, but that should not preclude us from creating hypothetical situations to explore alternative solutions. If we want to develop more humane and creative lawyers, we should encourage students to explore some of the non-legal solutions that may be present in each case. This does not mean that we disregard the essential doctrines and rules which students must know, but it highlights for them at an early stage in their development that though law rules, it does not govern all of human reality or emotions.

Client counseling is certainly a skill that can be more appropriately developed in a clinic or legal practice setting, yet we can raise students' sensitivity toward being client-centered attorneys even in the traditional classroom. In discussing any case there are certain options that the client had before the case was filed and even during the course of the litigation. It is important for students not only to consider the various options from the client's perspective, but also to consider the "psychological or therapeutic value" of a particular path. [266] Certainly this process becomes somewhat artificial since the real client is not present, but it is no more artificial than the normal discussions of cases where the parties to the litigation and the judge are not present to react to our critiques, assumptions or innuendoes. Through role-playing in and outside class students have the opportunity to explore client reactions to the litigation process and begin to develop an appreciation for the anxiety, stress and depression that sometimes can be an outgrowth of this process. There is no easy cost-benefit formula that lawyers can offer clients to measures the psychological cost of litigation in comparison to various outcomes, but at least students should be aware of these costs and begin to develop strategies for recognizing and explaining them to their future clients. These theories and ideas can be incorporated into the reading materials for substantive and clinical courses.

One of the greatest weaknesses of the traditional legal educational approach is its failure to develop "self-reflective" learners. Though we argue that we are teaching students a process of analysis as opposed to teaching them the law, that virtue is directed almost exclusively to the external world. Other than in clinics and other experiential settings, there is very little opportunity for students to reflect upon the learning process through which they are going or, more importantly, to reflect upon their own internal development. The cases and rules become the concern of most students during much of their waking hours. It is certainly common for students to vent about the horrors of law school, but this only leads to the development of a negative "love-hate" orientation toward their chosen profession. Therapeutic Jurisprudence implicitly suggests that legal educators should incorporate within the learning process a method through which students systematically reflect upon the learning process. It is common for dedicated faculty members to pause and provide review sessions as students prepare for final examinations, but it is rare for them to pause and have students reflect on the methods, culture and values that they are encountering during the learning process. More importantly, students need to constructively engage in dialogues with professors about how the materials and learning process are impacting their personal values and perspectives. The discussion of emotionally charged subjects in substantive courses like torts, constitutional and criminal law creates a precious human laboratory for the exploration of biases and blinders that students are shedding and putting on as they don the garments of this profession. A Therapeutic Jurisprudence approach would encourage faculty members to create a learning environment where students would ask themselves questions about their values, perspectives on the practice of law, and other questions of self discovery that often go unasked and unanswered. The goal of these processes is to develop self-reflective practitioners. If students get the message early on that

308

it is appropriate to explore the psychological, emotional and spiritual aspect of a lawyer-client relationship, they will be more likely to continue this practice once they become lawyers. If they are lead to believe that these areas are off-limits to the study and practice of law, then they will bury their feelings and discontent with expensive bottles of intoxicating beverages and cheap thrills that can cause them and the profession so much grief.

If, as law professors, we saw ourselves as "therapeutic agents" in the classroom, we would be more sensitive to the serious impact that our teaching styles, comments, and feedback have on the development of our students. This realization should not serve as a silencer to prolific and charismatic teachers, but it should serve as a reminder and a warning that we are not just "teaching law, but teaching people."[267] The people we are teaching will carry with them either the therapeutic and spiritual gifs of enlightenment we model and convey, or they will carry the psychological baggage of insensitivity that we dump on them. Whatever we give them, they more than likely will convey it to their clients and those who interact with them in the profession. So in our quest to create a learning environment that is more student-centered than doctrine-focused, we increase the chances that they will be more client-focused. In our quest to teach our courses in a manner that explores all aspects of human reality, we increase the possibility that our students will practice law in a holistic manner that seeks the best outcome for their clients even if it is accomplished outside the traditional legal arena. In our quest to plant emotional integrity and a genuine spirit of service into the legal educational process, we are giving honorable seeds to future lawyers who can plant them in the future fertile grounds of this profession. Only then will the public begin to believe that we "practice from an ethic of care,"[268] and not from an ethos of greed.

It is unrealistic to expect that all of the above objectives and techniques can be explored with respect to every case and topic that is covered in a substantive course. Time does not permit this luxury. However, even within its constraints, we can achieve some of these objectives if we are thoughtful and selective about the process. Using one topic to explore issues of client-centeredness may be enough to raise the awareness of students to the critical nature of this virtue. Using another chapter to explore creative problem solving techniques will, at least, plant the seeds in students that litigation and law are not the only tools in their hands and hearts. We should strive to create a learning environment that always encourages self-reflection even though the classroom may not be the only venue in which this is expressed or explored. The use of technology can greatly facilitate constructive chat room discussion between students and faculty about this aspect of their learning. Of course, all of this involves time which most professors would argue they have very little of these days. Yet if we do not take time for these things, then ultimately we will lose the opportunity to transform this profession into one that we can all be proud to call our own.

Therapeutic Jurisprudence is holistic in nature, and unlike other interdisciplinary approaches to law, does not suggest that the therapeutic consequences of a particular rule or legal procedure should always prevail over other factors and perspectives. It does not attempt to place the psychological well-being of a person on a pedestal only to sacrifice other parts of that person's reality or other goals of the law. It does, from a holistic perspective, seek to bring the psychological variables to the legal table in a more direct and consequential manner. The heart and soul of this approach embraces an expanded notion of legal practice. Those academics and practitioners who embrace this approach take the position that emotional and psychological challenges comprise much of the problems with which clients deal in legal situations. Therefore, if lawyers are not able to effectively identify and address those aspects of the problem, they are not effectively serving their clients.

Therapeutic Jurisprudence is also holistic because it invites inquiry into the spiritual dimensions of the client and lawyer. Though this is not an explicit tenet of therapeutic jurisprudence, one cannot dance with the psychological impacts of law without flirting with its spiritual dimensions. Spirituality embraces the notion that "there is far more to reality than merely that which can be seen, heard, touched, and tasted."[269] Though psychology finds its roots in the study of the mind and emotions, it often finds itself trying to describe and capture those aspects of human reality that are not always visible to the naked eye. So much of human emotions and mental states are influenced by one's search for the sacred or one's denial of this aspect of reality. The study of psychology has numerous inter-linkages with spirituality and religion. Some psychologists argue that spirituality and religion "are inherently social-psychological phenomena."[270] Few aspects of human reality "may be as integral across life span development as religious and spiritual concerns."[271] Spirituality and religion are "related to affect and emotion,"[272] are connected to one's mental health,[273] are effective coping mechanisms, and are at the heart of human makeup. We cannot open the door to the emotional inner world of our clients without also walking into the inner chambers of their search for the sacred. Therapeutic Jurisprudence has become a legitimate intellectual pathway to the inward dimensions of human reality and law.

This movement is different from other "law and..." movements that have existed within the academy in the last half of the 20th century. Therapeutic Jurisprudence is not just suggesting that lawyers should be able to interject and use the knowledge and expertise of psychology and psychologists in their briefs and trials. They are advocating for a merging of these two fields in a very practical and symbolic manner. As two major proponents of this approach confirm, Therapeutic Jurisprudence is seeking a different type of partnership between law and psychology. "Our aim is to suggest that legal decision makers explicitly take account of this impact [law on therapeutic values], that they become more sophisticated about and make better use of the insights and methods of the behavioral sciences, and that behavioral sciences audit law's success or failure in this regard."[274] This merging of two disciplines is not intended to subordinate one to the other, but to create a fresh perspective for each one as they go about fulfilling their mission of serving humanity. The benefits of this approach are aimed at the clients and the profession, and its underlying philosophy may attract a different type of person to the practice of law, and better care for those who are already here. This aspiration is captured in the following quote by one of the founders of this movement:

The hope, of course, is that bringing an explicit ethic of care into law practice will better serve clients, humanize law practice for clients and lawyers, contribute to lawyer satisfaction and decrease lawyer distress, and begin to attract to the legal profession many who have opted out of practicing in a culture of critique. [275]

There are other movements, such as Preventative Law, Lawyers as Creative Problem Solvers, and Humanizing Legal Education, that are very much related to Therapeutic Jurisprudence. Preventative Law and Lawyers as Creative Problem Solvers rest on the premise that a broader and more sensitive approach must be developed for the practice of law. California Western School of Law is a leader in this area and describes the premise of their Center in the following manner:

The premise of preventative law is that the legal profession can better serve clients by investing resources in consultation and planning rather than relying on litigation as the primary means of addressing legal problems. This theory recognizes that while litigation is sometimes necessary to address past wrongs, the fact that one ends up in an adversarial proceeding may be evidence of a lack of planning or communication. By applying foresight, lawyers may limit the frequency and scope of future legal problems. Preventive law techniques are currently being practiced in the design of sexual harassment policies, in environmental law, in family law (especially estate planning) and in computer law. Virtually any forum setting with avoidable legal problems has room for the practice of preventive law.[276]

Humanizing Legal Education is a movement of legal educators who are deeply concerned about the anti-therapeutic effects of law schools on the students who attend these institutions. Through scholarship, empirical research and conferences, various legal educators have been able to persuasively argue that much of the stress, depression, substance abuse and other negative behavior among law students are, in part, a product of the structure and practices of legal education. This approach attempts to systematically sensitize students and faculty members to the various ways these negative consequences can be prevented and addressed. Florida State University School of Law is the center for much of this scholarly activity.[277]

What all of these movements have in common, and what separates them from the traditional approaches to law, is a deep realization that the practice of law does not exist in a vacuum. It is influenced greatly by various forces and trends. Some of those forces are structural such as economic trends, emerging technologies and climate shifts. But many of those forces are personal, and are found within the individuals who participate in the legal process. To fully address the impact of law on people, we must have a sophisticated understanding of these emotional and spiritual variables. If we ignore them for too long, then law, and the society it serves will suffer.

314

Contemplative Law Practice (Mindfulness Awareness)[278]

One of the most recent movements within the profession is Contemplative Law practice. Unlike Collaborative law and Therapeutic Jurisprudence, Contemplative practices are not forms of legal practice or principles, but a meditative process that assists those who are engaged in the practice and study of law to remain balanced, thoughtful and reflective. There is widespread evidence that those who engage in systematic mindful meditation are better able to cope with stress in their lives and work, and are able to bring a more cooperative style and a less self-centered approach to whatever they do. Contemplative practice is a process of "disciplining the mind by focusing on a specific object or thought or by completely letting go of all thoughts and emotions, and just simply watching or witnessing whatever arises in consciousness. Mindfulness meditation is just one form of meditation, but it, along with yoga, has been the primary technique used in the Contemplative Law movement. Such practice usually results in a growing awareness of non-attachment to our mind, with an increasing ability to exercise choice in how we use our mind. In practical terms, this usually brings about a greater sense of self-mastery, well being, equanimity and reduced stress."[279]

These contemplative practices have been used by various individuals and groups for centuries, and have been applied to various professions, including professional basketball, and finally have seeped into one of the most rigid and closed clubs – the legal profession. Contemplative practices are finding a home within the profession because many lawyers are not finding in their legal work those things that fulfill them or give them something back so that they can remain balance and centered. Lawyers across the spectrum of the profession, from corporate attorneys to legal service and public defenders, have embraced these practices. There have been numerous gatherings of lawyers around the country who have participated in meditation retreats as a way of restoring balance and peace in their lives, practice, study, teaching and scholarship. Retreats have been held for students at prestigious institutions, such as, Yale and Columbia Law Schools, and large and prestigious law firms, such as Hale and Dorr in Boston, have been sending their attorneys to attend. This renaissance has been orchestrated by the efforts of the Center for Contemplative Mind in Society, which promotes and cultivates the use of meditation in various professions and aspects of life. It initiated a Law Program which held its first retreat for lawyers and law students in 1999. The Center defines contemplative practices as a way to "quiet the mind in the midst of the stress and distraction of everyday life in order to cultivate a personal capacity for deep concentration and insight."[280] The Center has a very comprehensive understanding of how contemplative practices can take place in everyday life. "Although usually practiced in silence, examples of contemplative practice include not only sitting in silence but also many forms of single-minded concentration, including meditation, contemplative prayer, mindful walking, focused experiences in nature, yoga and other contemplative physical or artistic practices."[281] Although these practices have strong roots in the Buddhist spiritual tradition, the Center is not a religious organization, and lawyers from various faith traditions have participated in the retreats and embraced the insights and wisdom of contemplative practices. Many see strong correlations between their faith traditions and these practices.

Other pioneers in this area include the Harvard Negotiation Insight Initiative,[282] which is dedicated to examining how contemplative practices can be beneficial in regards to negotiations and other alternative dispute resolution processes. Professor Len Riskin at the University of Missouri School of Law also has launched an Initiative on Mindfulness in Law and Dispute Resolution,[283] which focuses on the use of mindfulness in the legal educational arena. The project conducts training for lawyers, law students and mediators who are attempting to bring a different perspective to their work. Professor Riskin has also introduced mindfulness into law school courses with very positive results.

Lawyers have been engaging in various forms of meditation for quite sometime. What distinguishes this movement today is the fact that it is not being viewed as the mere individual efforts of a few lawyers, but is being supported and promoted by legal institutions as a legitimate and important part of their culture. There also has been important groundbreaking scholarship that attempts to demonstrate the benefits that lawyers and the legal profession derive from contemplative practices. Leonard Riskin in his seminal article, "The Contemplative Lawyer: On the Potential Contributions of Mindfulness Meditation to Law Students, Lawyers, and their Clients,"[284] provides a thorough overview of this movement within the profession and the legal academy. He also identifies various benefits that can be derived from mindfulness meditation. Riskin argues that these practices can help lawyers feel better about themselves and perform their various tasks at a higher level. When lawyers can reduce the enormous stress in their lives, they can concentrate on their work in more meaningful ways. In addition, he argues that the emotional intelligence of lawyers is improved, thus allowing them to enhance their "self awareness, self regulation, motivation, empathy, and social skills."[285] Riskin believes that there are numerous opportunities which are overlooked because lawyers are locked into a particular mindset. He then demonstrates how contemplative practices could improve ones ability to listen, react, respond and negotiate in a more meaningful manner. Having more control over their minds, cravings and auto-responses can put lawyers in better control of their "ego needs," thus enabling them to make better choices and decisions for themselves and their clients. Especially in the area of negotiation, where it is vital for lawyers to see the problem from multiple perspectives and to develop creative solutions to complex problems, it is critical that they "understand and deal with the emotions that affect all participants."[286] In the field of negotiation there has been important empirical research that supports the conclusion that Professor Riskin offers.[287]

Contemplative practice is more than an exercise for lawyers to engage in during their spare time. It is a comprehensive spiritual way for lawyers to view their role in society and to develop a deeper understanding about how to conduct their practice of law. Those who subscribe to a mindfulness practice believe that it produces a better and more meaningful analysis of legal and human issues. They argue that it allows them to bring more to the negotiation[288] and litigation process. Having placed themselves on a routine where this is a standard part of their lives, they are able to access this power and insight throughout the course of their work. Though some embrace this practice by engaging in meditation at the beginning of their day, this approach can permeate much of what lawyers do throughout the day. Lawyers can engage in mindfulness as they walk to meetings, eat a meal, write a brief, or contemplate the next court appearance. It should not be relegated to a state of being entered in the morning but lost as the hectic day develops. This contemplative state must be the place that is entered on a regular and consistent basis throughout the day. As with religious beliefs, the ultimate goal is not to apply a specific faith to the practice of law, but to practice law from a spiritual place. Likewise, with contemplative practices, the goal is not to "apply mindfulness meditation as another skill or ability, the goal is to fundamentally establish oneself in mindful awareness and then practice law from that place." [289]

Contemplative mind, or mindfulness, is both an intellectual and spiritual approach to life and to the practice of law. There are those who argue that mindfulness meditation is very consistent with legal reasoning.[290] Professor Douglas Codiga argues that one of the powerful benefits of meditation is the sharpening of the mind's ability to concentrate, analyze, and evaluate reality. This is not a tradition that casts dispersion on intellectual prowess. It merely suggests that one must be able to harness this powerful mental engine, or else it will harness or destroy one's creative and spiritual dimensions. Professor Codiga suggest that lawyers who have not tried mindfulness meditation should not fall into the trap of believing that it is an anti-intellectual, otherworldly experience that will take them away from their daily tasks and livelihood. Contemplative practices can give them more control over how they see those daily activities and, more importantly, how they react to the various emotions that are embedded in those activities. Contemplative practices, like some faith traditions, can serve to remind those who are caught in the throes of minutiae each day that the sacred is not in some other world far beyond their reach. The sacred is imminent, present, and buried within the numerous details and people they encounter each day.

Only when we are mindful enough to uncover the "divine in the details," will we, as lawyers, be able to find more meaning and satisfaction in our work. Every emotion that we are better able to identify and re-channel permits us to treat our clients and colleagues in a more divine manner. Every time we are able to think creatively, unrestricted by traditional mindsets and habits, we are more likely to reach better results for our clients and others involved, and thus bring more joy to the earth. Every time we can see beyond someone's present condition and circumstances and gaze upon their true needs, we have opened ourselves up to the possibility of participating in their healing. When we are able to treat them with the respect, dignity and kindness they deserve, then we have become potential instruments of God's healing power. Though the intellectual and psychological benefits of contemplative practices are critical to contemporary lawyers, those who practice it believe that "[m]editation is no mere self-improvement tool; it is a spiritual practice. It does more than generate good feelings or superior performance; it transforms our sense of self and the world. Thus understood, meditation offers an antidote to what ails the profession..."[291]

An increasing number of lawyers have tapped into this ancient wisdom system in order to address some of the critical personal and professional challenges that many of them face on a daily basis. Their gravitation toward this part of the river suggests that how we "think" about problems depend greatly on our spirits and emotions. So as we strive to harness and refine our intellectual powers so that we can solve legal challenges, it is important to harness and utilize our spiritual powers as well. The two together, working and flowing in unison and not in opposition, provide a powerful way for addressing our work. This approach has called directly into question the traditional notion of "thinking like a lawyer." What once was believed to be a sterile, sharp analytical process is now being recast to contain different contours, flexibility and sensitivities. It demonstrates that the traditional approach was lacking some very key ingredients. Instead of asking people to abandon themselves and focus only on the external, this approach is asking just the opposite. It is applauding and promoting the internal journey as a prerequisite to facilitating and producing more meaningful external solutions.

Restorative Justice

Within the criminal law community, a movement called Restorative Justice has existed for some time now. It finds its roots in the justice systems of various indigenous cultures, such as the Native American and aboriginal nations where violations of social norms are seen through a collective lens, and one's connection to community is essential in trying to make a decision about punishment, restoration and healing. It has gained more acceptance in modern legal systems as more people recognize the numerous limitations of the traditional criminal justice processes. The classic philosophical foundations for the criminal justice system - retribution, deterrence and rehabilitation, have all proven to be very atomistic and somewhat incomplete. Though each has its own spiritual roots and social justification, they all focus on just one side of the problem. According to Michael Hadley, "all three of these theories of punishment...focus primarily upon what should be done to the offender. The retributivists want to give them their just desserts, the [deterrents] want to deter them (and other potential offenders) from offending, and the rehabilitationist want to cure them. None of them have much, if anything, to say about how criminal justice should take into account the injustice done to the actual victim of an offense."[292] Even when defendants are held responsible for the crimes they have committed, the victims often do not feel whole and complete. As importantly, the defendants may never fully understand and appreciate the depth of the harm they have created because they have not dealt directly with the victim, but have only told their story to the police, lawyers, and other court personnel. The emphasis under traditional approaches is on the "centrality of State authority," [293] and even the harm is viewed as having been perpetrated against a set of laws created by a collective body called the State. Restorative Justice is a holistic approach to addressing the various consequences of crime and trying to rebuild or restore the underlying relationships that have been affected. It focuses on the victim, the offender and the community. Though it recognizes the existence and importance of state laws and interest, its emphasis is more on the parties directly involved, members of the community who are indirectly involved, and the process that will help all of them "resolve how to deal with the offence, its consequences and its implications for the future."[294]

In order for this approach to work, the defendant and the victim must be open to an approach that requires each of them to interact with each other in ways that the traditional criminal justice process did not provide. The goal of this process is not to determine a winner or loser, but to try to make the victim whole and allow the defendant to accept responsibility for the injury or harm suffered by the victim. There are three primary components to an effective restorative justice outcome. First, there must be an acknowledgement of the wrong by the defendant. This process will not work if the defendant is still trying to avoid responsibility or is not dealing openly and honestly with the situation or with himself. One of the critical weaknesses in the present criminal justice system, especially for the victim, is the lack of acknowledgement of the crime or harm on the part of the defendant. Even when individuals are found guilty of an offense, they are reluctant to acknowledge their responsibility because of the consequences of such behavior in the traditional criminal justice process. The victim feels cheated when they never hear a sincere, "I'm sorry for what I've done," from the defendant. Therefore the sincerity and depth of the acknowledgement of the crime is a fundamental part of a restorative justice process. The other steps become meaningless if this first step is not taken. Even in serious criminal matters such as murder and rape, there is a deep need on the part of the victim, or the victim's relatives, for the defendant to take responsibility for the crime. For some victims or relatives this does not reduce their pain or support their healing, but for others it is indispensable.

Second, there must be an agreement to restore that which was damaged, or taken away from the victim. Some form of compensation or restoration is necessary, or else we have not achieved the goal of justice. The compensation can take various forms (including a prison sentence),[295] and is not limited to the payment of money. Many times it is the non-monetary acts that are of greatest importance to the victim. Third, there must be some focus on trying to make sure this type of violation does not occur in the future. It is at this stage that the relationship between the parties becomes very important. This is especially true when there is an ongoing relationship between them. If the individuals are related or live in the same neighborhood, then this is a critical component. There must be some restrictions on how the future interactions with each other will occur in the future. This is an opportunity for the defendants not only to try to correct the problems of the past, but also improve the possibility of creating a better future. From my perspective, it is this final component of the restorative justice process that truly sets it apart from the traditional criminal justice process. Besides incarcerating the defendant in order to prevent more victimization, there is very little the traditional process can do to insure that there is a change in the heart, behavior and activities of the defendant. A critical element of the restorative justice process is the understanding that the past problem not only must be corrected, but never repeated in the future.

Restoration is a fundamental principle of law that has deep historical roots. In contracts law it is the appropriate remedy for claims of unjust enrichment. The goal of this historical remedy was to put the parties back into the position they were in prior to the breach, yet in this criminal law context the goal is much broader and deeper. The compensation component of restorative justice accomplishes this traditional goal of restitution. The other prongs attempt to put both parties in a better position than the one they were in prior to the violation. By requiring an acknowledgement of the harm, the victim may be healed of past injuries as well. The victim may have had a history of people violating them and never accepting responsibility for the harm they inflicted. This accumulated sense of denial, abuse and rejection can sometimes be washed away when the victim experiences something very different from past patterns. The same can be true for the defendant. The offender may have a pattern of denial of responsibility that needs to be broken. The process generally requires the offender to come face-to-face with the person he has injured, so that he can personalize the harm. Getting him to authentically accept responsibility for his actions can be a powerful lesson about how to accept responsibility in life in general. The healing of emotional harms and the destruction of negative patterns can occur in ways that are not always predictable. Therefore, it is necessary to approach each situation with a deep and sincere level of sensitivity because more can occur than just the resolution of the present dispute. The third component of restorative justice, which is directed towards the future, is another way in which this traditional legal concept is expanded. When both parties, but especially the defendant, work on the underlying problem or relationship, they have an opportunity to enhance their overall ability to succeed in life. The process can sometimes end up as a mere statement on paper that is never acted upon, but in those instances where it is truly taken seriously, it can enhance not only the quality of dispute resolution, but also the quality of life for the people involved.

A restorative justice process can take different forms and can occur in different settings and places. Some of them have become part of standard court proceedings,[296] while others operate outside the regular criminal justice process.[297] They all require a skilled facilitator who is not only trained in the law, but also understands the complex dynamics of human conflict and resolution. Sometimes, another individual can support each party during the process, and in special power imbalance situations, a representative supports only one party during the proceedings.[298] Regardless of the structure, the hope and goal is to "create an environment in which participants feel comfortable and able to speak for themselves and in which the heart and minds of offender and victim might be touched, perhaps changed."[299] In order for this goal to be realized, everyone involved must understand the deep spiritual nature of this process. If restorative justice is viewed as just another alternative dispute resolution procedure involving mechanical processes that can be manipulated and twisted to achieve a desired end, then it will not produce any better results than the traditional criminal justice system.

The roots of the present day restorative justice movement can be found in various religious and spiritual traditions. In a masterful text edited by Michael L. Hadley, entitled *The Spiritual Roots of Restorative Justice*,[300] many of these connections are persuasively explored. In this text various writers demonstrate that different religious and spiritual traditions, such as Islam, Judaism, Christianity, Buddhism, Sikhism and Aboriginal Spiritual beliefs systems, all embrace sacred notions of restorative justice. A common theme emerges which demonstrates that when these sacred traditions are embraced or adopted by political structures and systems, the restorative aspects of the religious beliefs systems are often minimized or ignored, and the retributive aspects of the faith are highlighted and promoted. Despite the fact that "Jesus preached the revolutionary ethic of forgiveness, nonviolence, reconciliation, and love for each human individual," [301] Christian politicians and believers are often the lead advocates for the death penalty, and for other harsh forms of retributive judgments. Though the Qur'an describes Allah with such attributes as "the Beneficent, the Merciful, the Compassionate," and is filled with various passages about forgiveness, various Islamic countries embrace harsh, final and unforgiving forms of punishment for criminal acts. Though punishment is certainly not inconsistent with restorative forms of justice, buried within each tradition are tenets or precepts that have been interpreted to justify vengeful forms of punishment that exceed the needs for social order.

Often overlooked and rarely embraced in the administration of justice is the human worth, value, and interconnectedness which serve as the foundation of these religious and spiritual beliefs, and as the source of insight for Restorative Justice. Aboriginal cosmology recognizes the interrelationship between all human beings and all things in the universe. From this spiritual perspective, "all events, including crime, are a responsibility because they arise out of relationships. When misfortune occurs, people are responsible for determining the cause of the breach and for correcting it."[302] This responsibility does not reside with the State, but with every person connected or affected by the harm. One's responsibility in this belief system is not to just sit as a spectator who watches the unfolding of a drama between the victors and vanquished, but to engage in a "healing process" that can restore the victim, transform the offender, and reaffirm the power and importance of community and family. Some legal and religious writers argue that Jewish law is more than biblical law. "Judaism speaks of the sanctity of people in a universe where God places upon each individual the responsibility for working toward the completion of His Creation. Judaism sees a world in which no human being is a 'throw-away' person."[303]This ideal sets the tone for a Restorative Justice approach and process.

The reason Restorative Justice focuses on restoring the victim, transforming the offender, and healing the relationship is because no person is expendable in our quest for a just society. Yet to live out this spiritual vision of reality requires us to accept a different perspective on criminal law and procedure than the standard theoretical models that label, scapegoat, and sometimes perpetually condemn human beings. So the fundamental Christian precepts of repentance, forgiveness and reconciliation can point us in a different direction in regard to how we view and treat criminals and the criminal justice process. These sacred precepts can be found in most of these religious traditions, but are rarely manifested in meaningful ways in the societies where these religious systems dominate. So Restorative Justice is more than just another pathway through which lawyers can practice their faith as they practice law. It is an inviting pathway through which lawyers and others can rediscover their faith. So much of what we are spiritually charged to do has been covered up by what societies feel they are legally required to do. If Restorative Justice really takes root in our criminal justice and legal systems, we may be able to break loose from these schizophrenic patterns. Restorative Justice, at is core, is a spiritual pathway because it "requires all of us to come to grips with who we are, what we have done, and what we can become in the fullness of our humanity."[304]   The standard criminal justice process and procedures encourage us to distance ourselves from those who have violated social norms, and thus subliminally encouraging us to distance ourselves from our own vulnerabilities and imperfections. The more we can personalize, understand, and empathize with social harms, and the forces that cause them, the greater our chances of preventing them in the future, and healing ourselves in the process.

There are certainly other groupings of lawyers who are following the path of the river and do not fall within the four movements I just reviewed. Many refer to themselves as holistic justice practitioners and embrace and employ various aspects of these practices and perspectives. This review was not intended to be exhaustive of all of the many streams and tributaries that now flow into this great river. Hopefully it reflects the flow of sacred waters in new and uncharted directions, as lawyers engaging in these healing practices connect with each other on a regular basis and exchange ideas, insights and failures so that they can widen the river and draw more lawyers and clients to its banks.

Practicing Your Faith as You Practice Law

For those lawyers who are deeply religious or who strive to be serious about their walk of faith,[305] it can be a challenge trying to reconcile one's spiritual belief system with the practice of law. Some individuals have chosen to avoid the profession of law because they believe it is "too ungodly" and unacceptable for a true believer. The historical practices of certain religious traditions sometimes served as a barrier to the observant believer who was considering becoming a lawyer. Admonitions about the role of lawyers contained in the Pirke Avot, the ethical teaching of the Jewish Talmud, served as a barrier for some Jews, though many found ways to reconcile these differences.[306] Some leave the profession because once they get exposed to the challenges, ambiguities, contradictions and unholy culture of the profession they conclude that there is no way to reconcile their faith with their profession. Others remain, but decide that certain aspects of the profession are inconsistent with their religious beliefs.[307]

Nevertheless, many lawyers have chosen to remain in the profession and accept the dueling realities that exist between their Christian, Jewish, Buddhist or Islamic faith, and their professional lives. They have accepted the wall that exists between what they do on Friday, Saturday or Sunday, and what they do on the other days of the week. Though certain aspects of their spiritual belief system seep into their week, and certain values of the profession, such as the pro bono work,[308] are consistent with their faith, a clear separation exists for the most part. Many of their colleagues are not even aware of their religious beliefs, and religious or spiritual discussions are considered inappropriate in the firm or office. Though the separation of church and state is a fundamental constitutional principle that should be respected, the separation of one's faith from what one does on a daily basis is an unfortunate and debilitating path for lawyers to travel. It creates a dual reality that permits one to be pious at worship, but vengeful at work. It relegates religious belief to the status of a hobby [309] that we can embrace for awhile and put away when it no longer serves our needs. It also places our work on a pedestal, beyond the reach of our innermost feelings, emotions and yearnings. Our daily activities, responsibilities and interactions are devoid of many of the values, insights and spirit that give true meaning to our work. Though many lawyers and other professionals have

330

learned to live comfortably with this artificial and limiting division of labor and life, [310] many others now are seeking a more harmonious path for their vocation and their faith.

Those who seek this harmonious path find various ways to view and articulate this joining of worlds. Some see their faith as a redemptive force for an otherwise corrupt and spiritually baseless profession. They attempt to interject into their daily practice the values and attributes of their religious belief system. Law and the practice of law are viewed by them as an unholy set of activities and processes that can be redeemed by interjecting the holiness of Christianity, Judaism or Islam into their work. Thus, they call upon their religious practices, such as prayer and meditation, to keep them centered, balanced and whole as they, like missionaries or crusaders, encounter the infidels and unsaved within the profession. Their religious beliefs require them to look at their clients, adversaries and judges differently. These practitioners of faith earnestly try to live their faith in the courtroom, offices and classrooms by demonstrating compassion, love and peace as they do their work. The shortcoming of this approach to the reconciliation of faith and the practice of law is that it still views the practice of law as this unholy enterprise that is acceptable for believers to participate in as long as they come with "the whole armor of God"[311] to protect them as they walk and work in this secular arena.

Some who take this approach look to their faith and religious texts for justification for some of the actions in which they have to engage, or some of the positions which they have to take as practicing attorneys. In response to the question, "How can you represent a guilty person?" Michael Schutt, a Christian lawyer stated:

> Moral lawyers may represent guilty clients. First, not all guilty people can be held accountable to human legal systems. An obvious example is found in the Sermon on the Mount. Jesus tells those gathered, 'You have heard that it was said to the people long ago, Do not murder, and anyone who murders will be subject to judgment. But I tell you that anyone who is angry with his brother will be subject to judgment'. He continues, 'You have heard that it was said, 'Do not commit adultery,' But I tell you that anyone who looks at a woman lustfully has already committed adultery with her in his heart.[312]

In the view of this attorney and law professor, we all are guilty and have "fallen short of the glory of God," and just because some acts fall within the jurisdiction of human courts while others fall within the province of God, does not make one less worthy of defense. He also justifies the defense of the guilty by citing the "two witnesses" rule found in the old and new testaments. "The Lord told Moses, 'One witness is not enough to convict a man accused of any crime or offense he may have committed.' Jesus later applies this provision to himself before the Pharisees: 'In your own Law it is written that testimony of two men is valid. I am the one who testifies for myself; my other witness is the Father, who sent me.'"[313] So procedural safeguards are not only consistent with the scriptures, but are also demanded by them.

332

The story of the woman accused of adultery in the New Testament by a group of men who were her accusers is another example of the consequences of failure of process, and of the need to seek mercy for those guilty of crimes. "When Jesus said, 'If any one of you is without sin, let him be the first to throw a stone at her,' he may have been referring to their sin of allowing the man to go free, in violation of the process required under the law. Since the process required for stoning had been violated, no one threw a stone, and Jesus did not condemn her, though she was almost certainly guilty." [314] This compelling and classic biblical story is used to demonstrate that it is morally and spiritually defensible for a defense attorney to insist upon the state following the rules in convicting the guilty, just as the defense attorney would in defending the innocent.

Furthermore, this passage is often used as evidence that even the guilty are entitled to mercy. Jesus was asking the men standing around to look inside their hearts and see this woman through the window of their personal frailties and vulnerabilities. He was creatively pleading to them to combine the power of the law, with the power of compassion. Since defense lawyers today are not restricted to the laws of the court, but can plead for mercy for their clients, this permits some lawyers to reconcile their faith with their practice.

A Jewish prosecutor finds reconciliation between Judaism and his role in the court in the following manner:

> The Jewish religious tradition speaks highly of those who work to cure the ills of society thorough the legal process. The Talmud states that, 'A judge who decides

a case properly is considered, as it were, a partner with
G-d in creation, because justice sustains the world.'
Similarly, the Mishna in Avoth teaches that the world's
existence is dependent on three conditions, one of
which is justice. Rabbi Jacob ben Asher, a leading
Medieval authority on Jewish law and author of the
Code of Jewish Law, commented on these statements
in his introduction to the section of the Code dealing
with the judicial process. He explained that G-d
created the world with the purpose of nurturing a
peaceful and productive society. When criminals
commit acts which lead to the destruction of societal
peace and order, these acts counteract G-d's purposes.
Thus a judge who properly brings a criminal to justice
is remedying society's evils and helping further the
purpose of G-d's creation. The judge is thereby a
partner with G-d in creation. .. [315]

In his prosecutorial role, this adherent to the Jewish faith not
only sees his prosecutorial work as being consistent with his
religious tradition, but also sees himself as a partner with God
in making the world a better place. Other legal scholars
approach this issue of integration more broadly. Robert Cover
writes that the "basic word of Judaism is obligation...,"[316]
asserting that one's religious beliefs compels one to be a moral
actor in the world through law and legal processes. Seth
Kreimer argues for an even deeper integration of law and
spirituality. He states:

As Jewish lawyers, we cannot act in a moral vacuum.
At a minimum, we must recognize that our

> professional acts have morally freighted
> consequences...(E)very choice we make as lawyers, in
> will contests, divorce proceedings, products liability
> actions or proxy fights, has an impact on the lives that
> are lived by the victims or beneficiaries of our actions,
> and the integrity of the system of justice in which we
> participate. We cannot claim indifference to those
> effects because we act on the behalf of clients.
> Our...tradition requires us to be alive to the moral
> dimensions of the choices we make in our professional
> lives.[317]

From these perspectives, the lawyer's faith is so strong and compelling that it demands adherence in every aspect of one's personal and professional life. These lawyers have broken through the wall that separates faith from profession, and see their faith as a guiding light for their legal work.

Joseph Allegretti in his book, *The Lawyer's Calling*, which analyzes the practice of law from a Christian perspective, places the connections between law and spirituality into four categories. Using H. Richard Niebuhr's classic text, *Christ and Culture*, he applies Niebuhr typology to the practice of law. He argues that there are four possible approaches a Christian lawyer could take to reconciling her faith and the practice of law. The four approaches are: Christ Against the Code, Christ in Harmony with the Code, Christ in Tension with the Code, and Christ Transforming the Code. The first three categories all lead to a separation between one's faith and the practice of law. This separation is grounded in various beliefs. The first suggests that law and Christianity are too different to be reconciled (Christ Against the Code). The second category (Christ in Harmony with the Code) permits reconciliation, but a lawyer's primary obligation is to the Code (law) with no moral mandate to practice one's faith as the lawyer practices law. The third category (Christ in Tension with the Code) recognizes that the lawyer is obligated to follow two different authorities that are in conflict. In none of these categories does law live in harmony with the lawyer's faith. Either there is an impenetrable barrier, or there are inherent internal conflicts which force the lawyer to forsake one part of reality for another.

It is the fourth category that Allegreti believes provides a healthy and holistic answer to the lawyer's dilemma. Christ Transforming the Code empowers the lawyer to use faith directly in the practice of law. "The task of the Christian lawyer, then, is to bring his religious values into the workplace, with the hope and trust that God will work through him to revitalize and transform his life as a lawyer, his profession and ultimately the wider community as well."[318] Though there is a major breakthrough in category four, there is also a spiritual limitation to this approach. Even from this enlightened perspective, law is still viewed as a sinful, secular enterprise which can be redeemed only by the pouring in of spirit from the outside.

All of the above examples that attempt to bridge the gap between law and spirituality still embrace a perspective that religion is the source of good in the world and through it we can make the world a better place. Even though these authors and lawyers argue for integration, it is still combining the sacred with the secular. Quoting Rabbi Hutner, one of the writers above captures the essence of this approach with the following words: "A religious individual who engages in a secular career has the opportunity to live a 'broad life,' one in which religious values are central not only to the overtly spiritual activities in life, but also to the more mundane activities that are part of a secular career." [319] Under this perspective, the spiritual things in life are juxtaposed to the activities of the profession. Thus, the day-to-day activities of the lawyer are still viewed as mundane and unholy. It is only through the application of spiritual beliefs and practices that these activities and practices become divinely meaningful. Even when they are meaningful it is only because they are in service of the ideals of the religion. The professional activities are merely a means to a holy end, but they do not appear to contain an independent, internal or inherent spiritual virtue.

Those who find their spirituality in non-religious sources also position law and spirituality as emerging from separate wells. Carrie Menkel Meadow, in a short but provocative commentary on conflict resolution, states, "... 'secular humanism'...is itself a source of spiritual and moral values that inform both the practice of law generally and the practice of conflict resolution particularly."[320] She, like traditional religious lawyers and scholars, looks primarily at places outside the law to find the values that sustain the work. Political movements for many lawyers have been their spiritual support to sustain them in their legal practice. Because organized religions did not always practice what its leaders preached, many lawyers became disillusioned with them, and the civil rights movement, the women movement, the anti-war movement and various other political activities instructed them on how to view and use their legal skills. Professor Menkel Meadow affirms that "there were moral teachings in these movements: people were to be treated as ends, not means; oppression of one person or one class by another was wrong; individuals should be free to self-define their destiny, and human resource allocation should be just and fair."[321] Though these political moral teachings were, and are, critical for many lawyers, they have their limitation.

The spirituality of political movements tends to focus primarily on the external aspects of spirituality. The goals of equality and justice instruct participants on how to treat others, but does not consistently instruct participants on how they should treat and view themselves. More importantly, these goals do not consistently provide methods for restoring the soul and spirit of those who do the work. There is an assumption that the work itself will provide the rejuvenation and spiritual strength to continue. There is also the assumption that those who choose to do this work already have good values, so the focus should be on the work and not on the individual. Despite the power derived from believing deeply in, and working hard to create, a better world, there needs to be an internal process that sustains and rejuvenates activist lawyers. Thus it should not be surprising that many activist lawyers eventually begin to look to other sources for their internal spiritual strength. Professor Menkel-Meadow describes this dynamic from a longitudinal perspective: "After the political and cultural revolutions of the 1960's dissipated...a different form of spiritualism arose, one that drew us inward. ...[activist lawyers and law professors] seeking spiritual enlightenment sought solace and different religious experiences in the religious and meditative practices of the East, particularly various forms of Zen Buddhism and a variety of "New Age' eclectic forms of mindfulness and reflective practice."[322]

This evolutionary quest for external transformation into internal enlightenment is a common pattern that highlights the dual nature of spirituality. Whatever source we look to for our spiritual strength must feed both aspects of our spiritual needs. One limitation of "secular humanism" as a source from which lawyers can practice their faith is that it tends to focus primarily on the external spiritual dimension. Though how strongly we advocate for justice for those around us is a powerful aspect of a lawyer's spiritual responsibility, it does not capture the complete picture. We also are charged to look within constantly to insure that we are nurturing the spirit that dwells within us, and living according to our highest values on a daily basis. Political goals, as important and redeeming as they can be at times, are often not enough to provide and sustain the balance, peace and meaning that is required over the long journey of life and lawyering. Over time these political aspirations can become the stones in our lives instead of the river. Our quest to change the world is often reduced to legislative enactments, unsuccessful political campaigns, and legal decrees or judgments. The underlying vision gets lost in the process, and so does our soul. The struggle can weigh on us until we become as heavy as the political burdens that we carry. So for some, political movements alone are insufficient sources of spiritual power unless they derive their meaning from a deeper spiritual well. One of the unique characteristics of the Civil Rights Movement was its strong connection to the church. Not only did the church provide an organizational structure within which the movement could operate, but also gave spiritual life and meaning to the movement. The prayers, songs and sermons were more than external trappings to justify political gains. They were the internal strength of those who led and participated in this historic and meaningful social transformation process. It was a classic example of the dual nature of spirituality. Within one movement was a command to change the world as you nurture your spirit and soul.

Another limitation of secular humanism as a source of spiritual power for lawyers is its negative perception toward the practice of law. Law is often viewed as an unholy tool to bring about a holy end. Because many activist lawyers are so keenly aware of how law has been used to create, promote and sustain oppressive structures, it is often difficult to see it as a source of spiritual enlightenment. Law is viewed as part of the problem, and those activists who choose to become lawyers are willing to soil their hands in order to rectify the serious injustices which they have witnessed. Their political aspirations provide the moral and spiritual motivation to practice law. Thus, once again the spiritual authority lies outside the profession as opposed to within it.

A less prevailing but more compelling perspective of reconciliation is to view the practice of law as an inherently holy enterprise which seeks individuals who are willing to work constantly on perfecting their faith in order to carry out the mandates of the profession, and to live up to its high, holy standards. This is the approach and perspective of this book, but it is not easily found in the literature or in practice. This perspective suggests that we practice our faith as we practice law, as opposed to practicing our faith through the law. This may appear to be splitting hairs but there is a profound distinction. To practice our faith through the law, as the approaches described above suggest, means that law is the object that our faith redeems or transforms. To practice our faith

340

as we practice law means that law is the <u>subject</u> of our faith. It sits at the center of our understanding of what we are called to do as human beings who are striving to become one with the river. If we understand the spiritual foundation of law, and see law as spirit, then the practice of law is not in opposition to our faith. To the contrary it is one of the most profound arenas in which our spiritual quest can be realized. James Pike in *Beyond the Law,* captures one aspect of this connection. He describes "true" religion as consisting of three characteristics: the profound humiliation of man, the boundless love of God, and an endless striving born of gratitude. He understands that a legal code of ethics does not capture these qualities, but that the all encompassing moral demands of lawyering can contain them. He writes:

> If this is true religion, then lawyers should be among the most religious people. For the very grist of their mill presents more ambiguous situations calling for decisions than most persons are faced with. More than most people, they are bound to be involved in ethically mixed situations, where choices between shades of gray have to be made – with or without 'purity of heart.' Since they more than the representatives of most callings should feel the need of grace, they more than most should be able to experience the fresh motivation that comes from a grateful response.[323]

Though Pikes elements of religion are not universal and certain eastern religions might reject one or more of his three characteristics, his understanding of the ambiguity of life and this inherent connection to spirituality and to the practice of law is profound. The above quote describes the essence of our work as lawyers as spiritual, not because we have clear holy choices facing us everyday, but because we have numerous opportunities each day to experience and witness compassion, love and grace. The morally ambiguous nature of the work we do provides a laboratory for spiritual growth or stagnation. Pike recognizes that most lawyers do not understand or embrace the profession from this perspective, but that does not distract from or destroy the spiritual arena within which lawyers operate on a daily basis.

Many lawyers still see law and spirituality as two separate and distinct realities as described by Norman Lamm in the following passage from *The Shema: Spirituality and Judaism.* "The contrast between the two -- spirituality and law -- is almost self-evident. Spirituality is subjective; the very fact of its inwardness implies a certain degree of anarchy; it is unfettered and self-directed, impulsive and spontaneous. In contrast, law is objective; it requires discipline, structure, obedience, order...But how can two such opposites coexist within one personality without producing unwelcome schizoid consequences?"[324] Yet Lamm goes on to demonstrate that these two realities are not separate, but encompass some of the same qualities and purposes in life. He writes:

> The life of the spirit need not be chaotic and undisciplined; the life of law, similarly, need not exclude the pulsing heart and soaring soul of the religious individual. In Judaism, spirituality is not antinomian, that is, the opposite of law and a structured approach to our duty under God. Halakha, a "way of life," does not preclude the participation of the heart

and a deepening of inwardness. In Judaism, each side -- spirit and law -- shows understanding for the other; we are not asked to choose one over the other, but to practice a proper balance that respects and reconciles the demands of each.[325]

If there is a spirit that exists within law, and if law is essential to spiritual growth, then not only is there no separation between them, but each springs from the same source – the river. This approach is also more comprehensive because it encompasses the work of those who are not coming from a particular faith tradition. If we only believed that those who adhered to a particular faith tradition could bring something special to the practice of law, then we could ignore the spiritual dimensions and attributes of those who do not adhere to an organized religious tradition. Those who, for whatever reason, chose not to believe in a divine reality, can still contribute to the enhancement and enrichment of the profession, and also can do tremendous good in the world.

The principles and values of lawyering that give life to the law are not limited to those who follow a particular religious or spiritual path. The atheist lawyer with the right heart and mind engages in spiritual work even when disclaiming spirituality with pride. James Pike argues, "as to those who claim with pride or regret that they are not religious, there is a failure to recognize that every man is religious, that is, operates on a basis of premises taken on faith."[326] Their faith may not be clothed in religious doctrine or principles, and they may not pray three times a day, but they are still being asked to address the ambiguities of the profession with compassion, love and grace. If their eyes are open, they will see these qualities manifested by those around them. Within their calling to be lawyers is a spiritual command which they cannot eliminate, even if they disclaim the source of the calling. Their rejection of spiritual and religious labels cannot take the spiritual dimensions and foundations out of the practice of law. A lawyer can operate inconsistent with them, but these qualities are inherent to the nature and structure of the profession. Having a religious tradition can certainly enrich and enhance one's ability to operate within the legal arena, but it is not a prerequisite for embracing the spiritual dimension of law as law is practiced.

This approach does not suggest that law is a religion or that a lawyer does not need or cannot benefit from a faith tradition. Law does not supplant Christianity, Judaism, Islam or any of the various Eastern religious traditions. It serves as a companion to them, as a reciprocal body or forum that has similar objectives. The practice of law is to the lawyer, what the church is to a minister, the temple is to a rabbi, and the mosque is to an imam. It is the place where the principles, values and spiritual insights are realized and given life. It is the sacred arena in which we strive to transform our individual and collective shortcomings, and remove internal and external structures that inhibit growth. Piety and internal peacefulness is sometimes obtained in prayer and isolation from others, but the true challenge of our goodness and our faith is when they are put to the test of human circumstances and conflicts. The legal system is a temple that is filled with spiritual choices, commands and dilemmas, for all who participate. Part of the calling of lawyers and judges is to ensure that this place and this process consistently embrace the highest ideals, and consistently enhances its search for its deepest meaning.

Since the thrust of this book is that the legal profession is an ideal arena to practice one's faith, it would be a serious oversight if I did not mention that there are some professional obstacles to lawyers of faith practicing their religion. The same Model Rules that I pointed to earlier which empower lawyers to bring more than the law to their work, has been interpreted to restrain them from exercising what they believed was a fundamental tenant of their faith. In an opinion issued by the Board of Professional Responsibility of the Supreme Court of Tennessee, an attorney who was assigned a case before the Juvenile Court was asked by the client to seek a waiver of the statutory prohibition against abortion without parental consent. Though Tennessee law permitted the request for a waiver, the attorney, who described himself as a devout Catholic, indicated that he could not, "under any circumstances advocate a point of view ultimately resulting in what he considered to be the loss of life."[327] He asked the Board a series of questions, including whether he could decline to accept the appointment based on moral and religious grounds. The Board, being concerned about not giving lawyers easy justifications for declining assigned cases, held that "religious and moral beliefs" were not a "compelling reason" to decline the case. [328]

Furthermore, the Board indicated that it was improper for the lawyer in his counseling role to advise the client to talk to her parents or others who could give her a different opinion.[329] Some have argued that in a pluralistic society the legal profession has to make more room for lawyers to practice their religious faith within the boundaries of their official duties to the state.[330] Clearly the lawyer in this case felt that he was being asked to compromise a cardinal part of his religious belief system by having to "zealously" seek a waiver so that this minor could have an abortion without parental consent. This opinion stands as one of those instances where the profession puts the religious lawyer in a moral straightjacket. Not only does it preclude the lawyer from declining an assignment that is inconsistent with his religious beliefs, but it also restricts the use of the lawyer's ultimate spiritual role of counselor. The Board put the lawyer into a "hired gun" role that assumes that the only good the lawyer can provide is securing what the client thought she wanted. Certainly the Board was justified in being concerned that the lawyer's religious views could compromise his zealous representation, or diminish his undivided loyalty to the client, but it should have been equally concerned that his client would not be counseled on the various consequences and ramifications of her choices. The lawyer must ensure that his religious beliefs are not controlling his advice and decisions, and that he is giving a balanced and equally sensitive assessment of all options. Because the lawyer was prevented from doing this, from the perspective of the overall well being of the legal profession, this decision constituted a loss.

There are certainly numerous times when religious lawyers encounter conflicts between their religious beliefs and their professional obligations. What makes the above case and opinion significant is the fact that the case was assigned to the lawyer by the court. In many other instances the attorney can decide whether to represent a particular client or handle certain types of cases. Even when the attorney is not a solo practitioner and thus accountable to others for her decision, especially partners and supervisors, there is still more latitude than what exists with judicially assigned cases. In all of these scenarios the lawyer's decision to decline a case is not without consequences. There is the possibility of lost revenue, decreased standing in the organization, and even dismissal, but living a moral and spiritually centered life sometimes comes with a price attached. It is this price tag that prevents so many lawyers from remaining true to their values or religious beliefs. If more lawyers were willing to make these sacrifices, the integrity of the profession would be greatly enhanced. While the goal of the profession should not be to eliminate all of these consequences, it also should not be to erect unnecessary barriers for lawyers who are striving to live spiritually or religiously centered lives.

In practicing our faith as we practice law, we should not assume that the only spiritual answer is to refuse to represent an individual who has engaged in a crime or act that our religious beliefs would condemn. At the foundation of all true religions is the command of love. Through this powerful mandate we can serve, inspire and comfort even those who have engaged in acts that are contrary to our belief system. Lawyers who practice their faith as they practice law must be willing to critically examine their faith tradition. Everything that we label as a religious command and practice may not pass the spiritual test of time or rigorous moral analysis. There were certainly times in this country when certain religious traditions would frown upon a lawyer representing an interracial couple seeking to be married in a state that had anti-miscegenation statutes. Likewise, certain religious beliefs would frown upon a lawyer who represents a gay or lesbian couple seeking a marriage license or civil union in a state that did not provide for these arrangements. There are religious beliefs and practices that still preclude women from occupying certain leadership positions in the church, synagogue or mosque. Sometimes what we label as spiritual commands are no more than a reflection of cultural or political norms. Thus the enlightened spiritual advocate must be willing to wrestle with these subtle and not so subtle distinctions.

The worst thing that could be done in the name of "practicing our faith" is to have a closed mind and heart to those who are different, or who have committed acts which our faith tradition would condemn. The enlightened spiritual advocate recognizes, as one faith tradition instructs, that "we have all fallen short of the mark." Therefore our posture should never be that of self-righteousness, but of humility and compassion. This does not suggest that we throw our beliefs out the window, or retreat to a place of moral relativism, yet we must be willing to wrestle with the ambiguous nature of moral decision making. The training that lawyers receive prepares them for a life of ambiguity. That same process must be applied to that part of our lives that prefers black and white, right and wrong, answers. When we choose to practice our faith as we practice law, then we are choosing to bring the benefits, limitations and awareness from both traditions to our daily living. Sometimes this will produce pressure and strains for our faith tradition, and other times it will create a tension within our vocation. Yet, if we travel this road with love and honesty, then in the final analysis we should have a wiser and stronger faith, and a more honorable profession.

Lawyers in Sacred Text

It is not uncommon to find lawyers in various scriptures, spiritual parables and other religious texts. In order to see them it is sometimes necessary to take the veils and scales from our eyes and not just look for the word lawyer, but embrace the essence of what lawyers have been called to do in society. Sometimes they are described as examples of the force that was not in line with the right spiritual path, or as antagonists to a holy movement, or even as the embodiment of the purest manifestation of advocacy for freedom and justice. While there are different and sometimes contradictory interpretations of the roles that lawyers were playing in these scriptures and sacred texts, there certainly are lessons contained within and between the lines for modern day legal advocates. These lessons do not condemn lawyers to any particular status in society, or in heaven for that matter, but open up various possibilities as to how we can view our calling and pursue our craft. I share these examples and analogies not to place lawyers on a religious pedestal, but to emphasize the longstanding connection between lawyering and spirituality.

Some people come to religion seeking laws, and some come to the law seeking God.[331] Both groups of seekers often leave unfulfilled however because the things they seek have been stripped from their source. Small remnants of what they sought are still there because law and religion are so embedded in each other that it is impossible to touch one without touching the other, but due to our concerted efforts to deplete or strip each source of its inherent strength, it is difficult to see the connections, and even more difficult to embrace the power generated by these connections. This brief journey through sacred text and writings will hopefully reveal these connections. This is not a journey into substantive law connections between religion and law, but focuses on those who were legal actors within various religious traditions. Though most of them would not define themselves as lawyers, the roles they played in the development of their religious tradition and in the world are extremely similar to the role that lawyers have been assigned, or should assume, in today's world.

Judaism

The word lawyer is not found in the Torah,[332] but the laws that created a covenant between God and Israel and defined their relationship serve as the foundation of Judaism. There is a sincere reverence for the law, and its sacredness serves as the foundation upon which one's ethics and moral obligation rest. It is through the fulfillment of the law that one serves God. Historically, the law was dispensed and conflicts resolved through Moses, the prophets, and eventually the rabbis. They assumed the role of judge, questioning believers and probing for truth as they applied and interpreted the law. The essentialness and sacredness of the "law" are so embedded in Judaism that one could argue that to be a true observant of the religion one has to be a "lawyer" in order to fulfill one's obligation to the religion, as well as to fulfill the commands of the law. I use the word "lawyer" here in its broad sense, which embraces being a "student of the law." There is evidence that this was the original religious usage of the term. [333] Since law and the instructions in law were the anchor and catalyst for spiritual development, mastery of the law or at least full dedication to its understanding was what distinguished this religious path from many others. This indispensable nature of law with respect to Judaism should not be interpreted, however, as a straight jacket restricting the believer or blindly judging conduct. The Jew must live within the law, but the law also must live within the Jew. For the law to live within, one must understand the spirit of the law and not just its words. This tension between law and spirit is captured in the words of Rabbi Abraham Heschel. He writes:

> The glorification of the law and the insistence upon its strict observance did not lead the Rabbis to a deification of the law. ... There is nothing more important, according to the Torah, than to preserve human life...Even when there is the slightest possibility that a life may be at stake one may disregard every prohibition of the law...The ultimate requirement is to act beyond the requirement of the law...To fulfill one's duties is not enough. One may be a scoundrel within the limits of the law.[334]

Thus, one must become a "student of the law" – hence, a lawyer, not only to understand the commands of the law, but also to reconcile its inconsistencies, search for its deeper meaning, and apply what is found to one's life and to life in general.

Though the word lawyer is not present in the Torah, there are important prophets and leaders in the scriptures who assumed the role and employed the skills of a lawyer. Various scholars have embraced this broad interpretation of the role of the prophets. Yochana Muffs in *Love and Joy: Law, Language and Religion in Ancient Israel*, states:

The prophet is thus the instrument of divine severity, the attribute of divine justice...He is also an independent advocate to the heavenly court who attempts to rescind the evil decree by means of the only instruments at his disposal, prayer and intercession. He is first the messenger of the divine court to the defendant, but his mission boomerangs back to the sender. Now, he is no longer the messenger of the court; he becomes the agent of the defendant, attempting to mitigate the severity of the decree.[335]

From this perspective, the prophet is "standing in the breach," [336]embracing the role of advocate on behalf of a collective client. An early example of this type of divine lawyering is found in Genesis, as Abraham advocates on behalf of the residents of Sodom and Gomorrah. [337] By asking the Lord if He would destroy the righteous with the wicked in Sodom, Abraham is subtly engaging in the ancient lawyer's technique of "distinguishing cases" in order to secure justice for those who have lived according to the commands of God. He is reminding the Lord that these two groups are not "similarly situated," do not have the same motive and intent, and therefore should not be subjected to the same punishment. Abraham also appeals to moral precedent when he offers a hypothetical of "fifty righteous within the city." He argues, giving deep reverence and respect to the heavenly court, that to destroy the righteous fifty along with the unrighteous city is against the Lord's standards and prior actions, and "far from thee to do."[338] When the Lord concedes that Abraham's point is a valid one and agrees not only to spare the righteous fifty if they exist, but also to spare the entire city "for their sake,"[339] Abraham puts down his

352

lawyer/advocate hat, and picks up his lawyer - negotiator hat. Since Abraham evidently is not confident that there are fifty righteous persons in the city, he begins to bargain with the Lord. Unlike many lawyers do today by opening with an extremely low number, Abraham first seeks to reduce the fifty to forty-five. Seeing and experiencing the Lord's mercy, he continues to suggest smaller numbers until he reaches ten. With each request for a reduction, he displays great deference to the divine "Court," stating "Oh let not the Lord be angry, and I will speak."[340]

Through the use of moral persuasion, sophisticated argumentation, pleas for mercy, and skillful negotiations, Abraham is able to develop an order, a divine decree, to govern the inhabitants of Sodom. One might argue that Abraham was motivated by a desire to save the life of his nephew, Lot, who lived in Sodom. [341] Yet this fact, if true, does not detract from the power of his advocacy or the agreement that was reached. Though his advocacy did not prevent the city from eventually being destroyed, it did invoke a moral standard between God and man, and it did provide for a "mercy opening"[342] that allowed Lot and his wife[343] to escape the destruction of the city. Through this story and interchange we find a wonderful and compelling example of a lawyer in sacred text. There was no retainer agreement between Abraham and the people of Sodom, nor was he hired to defend them in this particular situation. Yet Abraham believed his calling eclipsed contractual arrangements. His command to seek justice and mercy derived from a greater covenant – the relationship between God and him. His lawyering skills and advocacy required him to defend even those who he did not know or to whom he owed no allegiance.

The greatest advocate in the Torah is Moses. The initial role he was called to fill in the life of Israel was that of advocate. When approaching Pharaoh to secure the freedom of the Israelites, he was, in essence, serving a habeas corpus petition upon the authority that unjustifiably confined human beings. "Let my People Go" was the opening line of a divine writ that was served not only on the Pharaoh, but also on all oppressors in the future. Moses was a precursor of the abolitionist lawyers who sought through legal means to bring an end to the unjust system of slavery in America. This was not an insurgent movement that Moses was conducting. He made a direct and public appeal to the highest authority in the land to secure the justice he sought. Though his petition was denied on numerous occasions, he continued to engage in his advocacy. He was confident about the outcome because there was a divine power supporting his request. Though contemporary lawyers cannot turn rods into serpents or rivers of water into rivers of blood, they should still see themselves as the caretakers of the highest ideals of the society. When those ideals are trampled, threaten or ignored, lawyers, in the face of adversity, must be that voice which reminds the society of the serious consequences which result from unfulfilled ideals.

The promised land is also a legal metaphor which represents the inherent virtues that come with the pursuit of noble ideals such as liberty, equality and justice. One may argue that few advocates get an opportunity to make such a compelling appeal as the one that was presented by Moses. Though there is much truth to this point, too few advocates seek spiritually and morally compelling causes, or embrace them when they are presented.[344] Moses went to see the Burning Bush and found his calling in life. We often ignore the burning legal and moral appeals that exist within our midst, and thus our legal lives are consumed with the mundane as the sacred continuously eludes us.

It was not the eloquence of Moses' appeal, but the moral and divine authority behind the appeal, that gave strength to his advocacy. In fact Moses described himself as someone who did not have strong oratory skills[345] Too often we equate strong advocacy with superficial oratory skills, but the swiftness and beauty of words used are not the full measure of an advocate. It is the logic, sensitivity, compassion and knowledge which encompass the appeal that give power to the advocate. Moses exemplified these traits in many of his other advocacy roles. After leading the Israelites out of Egypt he often was required to defend them before God for their misconduct and disbelief. In the incident of the Golden Calf, the people had grown impatient during their long journey through the desert, and had fashioned an idol god which they worshipped. Moses interceded on their behalf with the following words when God indicated he would "consume them" for their misdeeds: "...Lord, why doth thy wrath wax hot against thy people, which thou hast brought forth out of the land of Egypt with great power, and with a mighty hand? Wherefore should Egyptians speak, and say, For mischief did he bring them out, to slay them in the mountains, and to consume them from the face of the earth? Turn from thy fierce wrath, and repent of this evil against thy people."[346]

This advocate of slow speech, quickly found a compassionate, moral, and practical ground upon which to stand and defend the Israelites. He sought a compassionate connection ("thy people") between the decision maker and the defendants.

He pointed to the moral inconsistency between bringing a chosen people out of captivity and then destroying them. He also made the Judge aware of the possible damage to the reputation of the Court if the wrong punishment were imposed, and how it would be mocked by the Egyptians. Being the careful, comprehensive advocate that he was, Moses added an additional legal ground for his appeal. He argued, "Remember Abraham, Isaac, and Israel, thy servants, to whom thou swarest by thine own self, and saidist unto them, I will multiply your seed as the stars of heaven, and all this land I have spoken of will I give unto your seed , and they shall inherit it forever."[347] In his final argument on this matter, Moses reminded God that the people he was about to "consume" were the beneficiaries of the contract between God and the Israelites, and to "consume" them would be a breach of that contract.

Other writers have seen the analogy between Moses' appeal contained in the scriptures cited above, and the role of lawyers in contemporary courts. Yochanan Muffs describes his actions in the following manner:

> Pay attention to the strategy of the defense attorney who avails himself of all the rhetorical devices of argumentation, legitimate as well as spurious, to save his client. How clearly the ancient authorities saw the irony in the tension between 'And the Lord spoke to Moses saying, Go down, because your people has behaved deceitfully' (Exod 32:7) and 'Why, O Lord are you angry at your people which you took out of Egypt?' (Exod 32:11). Suddenly the Children of Israel are no longer the people of God - they are the people

of Moses. But the defense attorney reminds the Lord
that Israel is not Moses' people, but God's. It is as
though Moses is saying, 'Don't blame me for their
sinful behavior. If they have sinned, they are Your
people, not mine. If You want to get rid of them, do so,
but don't try to erase your connection to them.' The
prophets know that their God is a God of truth, and
therefore they do not flatter Him. [348]

In the sacred tradition of the advocate, Moses spoke truth to
power, "stood in the breach," and preserved the life and future
of the Israelites. Exodus 32:14 enshrined the Court's verdict for
time in memorial: "And the Lord repented of the evil which he
thought to do unto his people." Though Moses was not a lawyer
in the classic understanding of the concept, he was truly a
lawyer in the spiritual, holistic and natural understanding of an
advocate's role – the role that many of us are called upon to
assume today.

Throughout the "TaNaKh," [349] the Hebrew Bible, there are
examples of major figures or prophets who assumed roles that
are similar to the role of an advocate. Within the context of the
sacred law tradition, these individuals served to warn the people
of the consequences of their deviation from God and the sacred
law.   The primary role of a prophet was to be a divine
messenger who brought guidance and instruction to the people.
Prophets also were able to see into the future and predict
spiritual events, catastrophes and punishments that awaited the
people if they did not change. Yet, at various times, they were
advocates to God on behalf of the very people they were called
upon to warn. Prayer was their primary mechanism for
intercession on the people's behalf, but the form of their

intervention took on similar structure to the arguments made by attorneys today. More importantly, many of them raised ideals and concepts that have become cornerstones of the legal system. The prophets promoted justice, righteousness and fair treatment for all, as much as they predicted calamities. This concept of "Prophetic Justice," as Jerold Auerbach indicates in his revealing text, *Rabbis and Lawyers,* has had a tremendous impact on the transformation of Jewish tradition and life, and on the American political and legal landscape. "...[T]he prophetic denunciation of oppression, exploitation, corruption, injustice, and war has remained an enduring inspiration to our own time. Throughout the twentieth century, the most conspicuous spokesmen for American liberalism - from Louis Brandeis to Martin Luther King, Jr.- have cited the Hebrew prophets in framing their indictment of social ills and their pleas for reform. American Jews still hear in prophecy these timeless truths of social justice that are embedded in their democratic faith and, they imagine, in historic Judaism."[350] Under this interpretation, the prophets were not only carriers of sacred scrolls, but also carriers of the sacred seeds [351] of the legal profession. This ideal of justice is as indispensable to the lawyer's craft as the ideal of wellness is to the physician's. If we are not seeking these ends in our work, then what justifies our existence? Though the prophets did not bring their seeds to the courts, they did attempt to plant them in the hearts of the people. To carry, plant and invoke the seeds constitute the essential and sacred work of advocacy and lawyering. The enlightened lawyer of today must likewise look for ways to plant these seeds into the landscape of the legal profession and the society.

Though this tradition of Prophetic Justice contributes much to our understanding of the special role of lawyers and the legal system, it is also a source of contention. Just as some can argue that the message and the seeds of justice which the prophets carried were universal and intended to be everlasting, others have found a narrower application. Auerbach meticulously makes the point that the prophets only can be understood within the covenantal relationship between God and Israel. He eloquently argues that this universalizing of the prophets and their message was part of a major movement among American Jewry to assimilate and embrace the values of their new homeland. The social justice message of the prophets became a mechanism for reconciling their religious faith with their political allegiance. This is significant because as the sub-title of Auerbach's book suggests, this process led American Jews on a "journey from Torah to Constitution," and lawyers began to replace rabbis as the major source of authority and meaning in American Jewish life. Auerbach warns that, "[I]t may be tempting to abstract the Prophets from history and nationality, accepting at face value the modern universalization of their role and message. But the temptation should be resisted, for there is little prophecy to sustain it. The Prophets were exclusively concerned with the relationship between God and Israel...Not only were they bound by time and place, but also by sacred law tradition." [352] Even if one accepts Auerbach's thesis that the only task of the prophets was "to call Israel to obedience of sacred law,"[353] it still does not take us away from the prophet-lawyer nexus, for the prophets remain the preservers and caretakers of the law. They may not have been invoking principles which had universal applicability, but they were embracing a methodology that is universal. Though the focus is on the sacred law of the Torah, it still demonstrates the reverent role that law plays in a person's life, and thus in society, and the reverence that should come to those who are called upon to safeguard and preserve the law.

We must not overlook the fact that judges are a fundamental part of the legal profession, and the lawyer's role is a natural extension and outgrowth of their work. Both are caretakers of the sacred art of dispute resolution; they just engage in the process from different angles and positions. When viewed from this perspective, the Torah and other Jewish sacred texts are filled with examples of those who carried out the functions which lawyers and judges do today. Moses begins a long line of individuals who not only served as caretakers of the law, but also interpreted and applied it to individual and collective disputes and conflicts. Exodus 18:13 captures the role and the burden that Moses assumed in regard to this calling of the law: "And it came to pass on the morrow, that Moses sat to judge the people: and the people stood by Moses from the morning unto the evening." After witnessing the amount of time that Moses and the people had to devote to this process, Jethro, Moses' father in law, advised him to delegate this judicial process to other worthy individuals so that he and the people would not "wear away."[354] Jethro suggested a judicial process of lower and higher courts, where small matters would be decided by those appointed by Moses to judge the people, and great matters would still be decided by Moses. Moses embraced this suggestion and established a system of dispute resolution that has lasted unto this day, with rabbis fulfilling the function that he and others performed in their day.

The inquisitorial technique used by those who served as judges in their search for truth, fulfilled one of the roles that lawyers later assumed. This process of inquiry was not intended to badger the parties, but was used to gather insights about the individuals and their situation so that the judge could decide the case wisely. It is this quest to discover and apply "practical wisdom"[355] to complex disputes that exemplified this period of legal development. This power of discernment was enhanced by the answers given to the judge's questions. One of the great exemplifiers of this ideal of practical wisdom was Solomon. The "wisdom of Solomon" is often used to describe the standard by which decision should be made in perplexing situations. Despite his own personal failings and indiscretion,[356] he still stands in the religious and secular world as a symbol of the illusive and hard to define concept that captures the essence of what judges and other decision makers are expected, but often fail, to possess.

The Scriptures, Talmud and Midrash contain examples of Solomon displaying his wisdom in difficult situations. These stories and parables contain lessons for today's lawyers and judges about this illusive quest for wisdom. In the story of the two mothers who were both claimed the same baby, he tested their hearts in order to discern the truth.[357] He knew that his proposal to split the baby in half would reveal the true mother. In the parable of the two-headed heir who was contesting how the father's estate should be divided, he used common knowledge of how one head would respond to having hot water sprayed on the other head in order to determine if the person should get one portion or two portions of the estate.[358] And in the parable of the stolen money buried by three travelers on the eve of the Sabbath, he shared with the disputants a story and sought their opinion in order to discern which of them stole the money. By asking them to pick the person in the story who was the most "praiseworthy," he was able to discern from their responses who the least "praiseworthy" of the travelers was."[359] Likewise in the riddles that the Queen of Sheba posed to Solomon to test his wisdom, he was able to provide the answers because of his knowledge of things, people and their behavior, and because he understood the deeper meaning behind symbols, events and acts.[360]

Though certainly understood and interpreted as a divine gift from God, Solomon's wisdom also was cultivated and enhanced by insights that are still available to us today. Wisdom, in this context, was a combination of his striving to understand the heart of those who came before him, using the common knowledge that he possessed about life and people; exploring the underlying meaning of acts and events, and asking key questions in an effort to reveal something about the parties and their dispute. These insights and approaches are not profound, nor do they constitute a grand theory of law. These gems of compassion, common sense and creativity do not spring from the mind, but reside in the heart of those who use them. As such, wisdom is defined and acquired, "not through exercising one's intellectual powers but rather through cultivating truth from one's experiences...[and] developing a clearer, more truthful sense of the world." [361] Solomon's request of God and his gift, as described by God, related to the quality of his heart: "Lo, I have given thee a wise and understanding heart...."[362] This is what sets Solomon apart from those who proceeded him in this role, and it is what lawyers and judges of today must seek and cultivate if the profession is to rise above the mundane application of rules to facts. We must seek and cultivate wisdom by pursuing the river, for therein lies the heart of the profession.

The Talmud captures this profound truth and employs the same metaphor: "All the streams run into the sea. All of man's wisdom is nowhere other than in the heart. 'Yet the sea is not full –the heart is never filled to capacity.' You might suppose that when a man lets his wisdom go forth from his heart, it will never flow back again. Hence the Scripture says, 'Yet the streams flow back again.'"[363] If the profession, like Solomon, cultivates and imparts wisdom, we will see it return to us in the meaning and satisfaction we derive from our work, and from the genuine respect that the public bestows upon us. The point of this brief exploration of Solomon is not to assume that the above examples in any way compare with the type of complex disputes, conflicts or cases with which lawyers are confronted today. Nor does it suggest that lawyers and judges will be able to determine innocence or quilt by praying or reading the Bible or Talmud. Like much of what is contained in this book, it is there to remind us that wisdom is an indispensable tool of the profession, and can be better understood and cultivated through our spiritual development along with our mental development. It also serves to remind us that knowledge alone is limited in its ability to provide us with wisdom, because "the spirit conceived and gave birth to wisdom." [364]

One cannot have a full and complete understanding of Jewish law and culture without venturing into the sacred waters of the Talmud. This ancient repository of oral law and scriptural interpretations is fundamental to Judaism and to this exploration of the intersection of law and spirituality. As one scholar states,

"If the Bible is the cornerstone of Judaism, then the Talmud is the central pillar, soaring up from the foundation and supporting the entire spiritual and intellectual edifice."[365] This majestic collection of legends, laws, stories and parables was the primary method through which rabbis kept the religious culture of Judaism alive and well. These materials date back to the Middle Ages and there are two versions; "the Jerusalem Talmud, a product of the academies of Israel, and the Babylonian Talmud, a product of the academies in Babylon."[366] This primary source of Jewish law is studied incessantly by the true believer. Not only does it apply answers to the resolution of difficult legal, social and religious issues, but also stands as a source of wisdom that sharpens the mind and soul of the student. The study of the Talmud is required for all serious believers. It is not written or interpreted in absolute terms, but raises questions, contains ambiguities, and invites the students to raise their own questions as a process of living the Talmud. This is not an easy world to enter and master, for the Talmud's "unique system of logic and involved argumentation often baffles the inexperienced reader." [367] What is relevant about this text for this exploration is that while it stands as an embodiment of Jewish law and culture, it also is an excellent example of legal analysis and exploration. To immerse oneself into the Talmudic process is akin to immersing oneself in the study of law. It contains laws, analysis, interpretation, varying opinions, hypothetical cases and situations, ambiguity and overarching principles. This is the stuff that law schools are made of. This is what consumes the time and intellectual energy of so many lawyers. The Talmud attempts to address the changing realities of Jewish life and culture, just as secular courts throughout this country and the world attempt to address evolving patterns in society. Instead of looking to the Torah as the foundational document, they look to state and federal constitutions.

These similarities are not coincidental, but reflect the religious origin of so many of the world's legal systems. They also remind us of the sacredness within which the legal process was originally encased. The secularization of law and legal method does not mean that its inherent sacredness should be stripped away in the process. For lawyers who adhere to a faith tradition, this is a powerful reminder of the synergy between what is observed within the faith and what is practiced within the profession. Many Jewish lawyers understand this and strive to make those connections through the practice of law. Yet the legal profession has a way of driving a wedge between the desires of our faith and the objectives of our practice. The Talmud speaks profoundly to this tension, and scholars in related fields are attempting to embrace these admonitions. The following quote by a contemporary Jewish accountant has enormous applicability to law firms and the legal profession:

> Making a profit is certainly important, but so is living the way of the pious. As Hillel said in the Babylonian Talmud, in Avot, "If I am not for myself, who will be for me? And if I care only for myself, what am I?' (1:14). Firms that are only for themselves may one day have to answer the question 'what am I.'

The Torah, Talmud and other sacred text do not only contain examples of individuals who served in the roles of lawyer and judge. They are more than mere compilations of laws and sophisticated and highly intellectual examples of legal interpretations and developments. They embody the sacredness of the legal process, and they emit sacred values and principles into the river, to guide all travelers in search of truth, love and justice.

Christianity

The word lawyer is found at various points throughout the New Testament. Generally, lawyers assumed the role of antagonist or questioner of Jesus and his mission. Yet hidden within their role and the exchanges are profound contributions to the growth of spirituality and direct guidance to today's practitioners. The first example is found in the Bible in Luke 11:46, where Jesus responds to a lawyer saying, "Woe unto you also lawyers, for ye lade men with burden grievous to be borne, and ye yourselves touch not the burden with your fingers." Captured in these words are a condemnation and a challenge. This description, whether factually accurate for all lawyers today, certainly demonstrates the dilemma that our present legal system fosters. Lawyers are expected to make clients aware of the options, choices and consequences that the law creates for them, but also are told to keep their distance from their clients. The burdens that clients carry when they enter our offices are not ours. The detached lawyer does not see himself as embracing emotionally or spiritually his clients or their situations. We, the caretakers of law, feel obliged to saddle our clients with the law, but do not feel spiritually empowered to help lift the burden that the law sometimes creates for them.

Lifting the burdens does not mean that we can make the problem go away easily. The burden is not just a legal problem, but also the manner in which the client has emotionally and spiritually internalized the problem. We touch the burdens with our fingers, by having compassion for the soul of the person we are serving. To touch the burden of others we must provide more than our skills and knowledge. To touch means to feel, to be able to embrace that which others are experiencing. We touch their burdens by being able to touch their souls. We gain access to their souls by first being in touch with ours. Touching the burden means that we see it as our burden, because we know that our legal shoulders are broader. Touching the burden means that we feel the problem in our hearts as we tackle it with our heads. It does not mean we become so emotionally involved that we become ineffective, but this scripture reminds us that we cannot be true servants of people or of justice from a distance. The spirit in law demands that we give the essence of ourselves to life and to the people we serve.

We also lift the burden of our clients when we can stand under the problem with them and provide a new perspective on both the problem and their lives. Jesus was not calling for lawyers to stop being lawyers, but challenging them to see their calling differently. Fundamentally, he was asking them to see it not as a self-serving craft, but as a calling to help heal others. "Woe" is a warning, not a condemnation. Jesus was sorrowful and concerned about how the law was being used to imprison the soul. Lawyers today occupy the same powerful and important position that can be used for self-aggrandizement, or can be used for healing, change and service. Touching and lifting burdens is a holy act, reserved for those who are courageous enough to bathe in the river. This scripture can be interpreted to mean that if one is not willing to be baptized in sorrow and pain, then one is not fit to be resurrected in joy and love. This is the spiritual challenge and beauty of lawyering.

Within that same chapter in Luke, we find another admonition to lawyers. Jesus states, "Woe unto you, lawyers, for ye have taken away the key of knowledge: ye entered not in yourselves, and them that were entering in ye hindered."[368] Jesus was reacting to the misuse of religious law and scripture by some who were learned in the law. This scripture and warning have spiritual relevance for lawyers of today. Often as lawyers, we use our knowledge and experience as a shield, and not as a door. We overly complicate matters through language and terminology that make it difficult for others to find the answers they seek and need. Unfortunately, one aspect of any profession is to justify and rationalize what its members do so that they can justify the cost of their services. The new movement around the "unbundling"[369] of legal services is an attempt to respond to Jesus' admonition. We have made it difficult for many to have access to justice or to handle their problems because of the over-complication and ownership that lawyers try to exercise over certain matters. Individuals who believe they can handle their own legal matters are often hindered by complicated procedural rules which may serve a purpose, but can also stand in the way of justice. The self-help and *pro se* movement has not been our banner cry as lawyers. Certainly it appears to go against our self-interest, especially if we are serving a category of clients who are likely to avail themselves of the process. Yet, from a spiritual perspective, we always should be on the side of making justice accessible to all who seek it. As one of my law students once stated, "lawyers should be in the business of putting themselves out of business."[370] Though that may be too radical and threatening for most lawyers to embrace, it does capture the essence of our spiritual calling. We should not desire or relish conflicts, suffering and injustice. We should not want people to feel disempowered when confronted with difficult personal challenges. However, many of us have benefited so much from the suffering and conflicts of others, that we would be disappointed if they went away. Should the bankruptcy attorney yearn for businesses to fail, or for individuals to lose their jobs? We should be yearning for their success and helping them prepare to succeed. Because conflicts and disaster seem to be a pervasive part of social reality, it is unlikely that lawyers will have to worry about not having a role to play in society. But we should see our practices as a calling to prevent conflict, suffering and misfortune, as much as a calling to serve those who find themselves in these situations. We enter the spiritual door of knowledge that Jesus mentioned, when we realize there is a deeper meaning to our calling than just our monetary rewards. Behind that door rests a deep reservoir of understanding about our purpose in life. We must constantly seek that door and what lies behind it for us. We give the key to others when we conduct our practices in such a manner that we empower our clients, instead of helping to make them dependent upon us. We serve humanity better by opening wide our insights and making our knowledge accessible.

One of my favorite examples of lawyers in scripture is found in both Mathew and Luke, where there is a conversation occurring between Jesus and a lawyer.[371] In Luke's version, the lawyer asks Jesus "What shall I do to inherit eternal life?." Jesus responds by pointing him to the law, and asking him for his interpretation of what the law demands. This prompts the lawyer to provide what has become the classic Christian summary of the Ten Commandments. The lawyer succinctly reduces all Ten Commandments into two critical precepts of loving God and loving "thy neighbor as thyself." After Jesus has indicated that this is the right answer, the lawyer asks for a clarification of the word neighbor. He asks, "Who is my neighbor?" Instead of answering the question directly, Jesus provides the lawyer with a beautiful and often recited parable of the "good Samaritan." The parable depicts a man who is robbed and badly beaten on his way to Jericho. Two religious men, a priest and a Levite, both choose to go past the suffering man without helping him. Then a Samaritan, representing the non-religious, distant stranger, chooses to assist him and pay for his care at a local inn. At the end of the parable Jesus then asks the lawyer, "[w]hich now of these three, thinkest thou, was neighbour unto him that fell among the thieves?"[372] The lawyer responds, "He that showed mercy on him."[373] Having made his point, Jesus instructs the lawyer to "go and do thou likewise."

This passage is often discussed as an example of how lawyers were always trying to trick or confuse Jesus, but were always outsmarted. Yet this exchange also demonstrates an important value that lawyers provide with respect to our intellectual and spiritual development. Because of this simple question from the lawyer, the world was given one of the most central parables of the Christian faith. We sometimes want to believe that faith is a passive process that does not permit questioning, doubts or scrutiny. But in asking the question, though possibly with negative intent, the lawyer provided an opportunity for future generations to have a better and more profound understanding of the spiritual mandate of love. Without this explanation, it may have been easy for some to interpret this mandate of "loving thy neighbor" as being limited to loving those who lived within close physical proximity. Yet the response through the parable that Jesus provided demonstrated that love was not restricted or limited by geography, status or ethnicity.

So the spirit in law does not demand that we accept all answers, nor does it mean that we should be less intellectually rigorous. Our minds are important to our hearts, and it is often through the probing of our minds that our spirits are enlightened. Taken in this light, the lawyer's classic tactics and techniques of probing and pushing should not be considered as anti-spiritual. When conducted in their most honorable manner, they are our worthy attempts to understand the river at its deepest and profound level. The analytical tools which we carry with us are not antithetical to the river. The pushing back and forth between the river and the stones provides a special movement to the river as it flows through our lives and the lives of those we serve. This engagement captures the essence of wholeness. "When a personality (stone) is in full balance, you cannot see where it ends and the soul (river) begins. This is a whole human being."[374] When the stones and the river meet and exist in harmony with each other, the lawyer's personality, as in the parable of the good Samaritan, is transformed from antagonist to healer.

In addition to His warning and conversations with lawyers, Jesus embodied and symbolized the highest attributes and ideals of a lawyer. First He was knowledgeable and well versed in the sacred law of his times. The Gospel writers capture His mastery of Jewish scripture and law even at a young age.[375] It was this knowledge that allowed Him to promote a new understanding of these commands and precepts. Second, Jesus was a reformer of the existing law. He believed that the religious leaders' interpretation of sacred scripture had limited and disempowered the people. Thus He set about trying to personalize people's relationship to the law and to God. The most powerful example is contained in the Sermon on the Mount.[376] Jesus realized that there was a limitation to the ability of law to change people's hearts, so He set about to provide an interpretation of the law that would infiltrate the hearts of men and women. This early law reformer lifted the veil from over the law so that people could see that its violation was not just an act of murder, but included anger against others without a cause.[377] He wanted them to know that reconciling with one's brother or sister was a prerequisite to being reconciled with God.[378] He wanted people to take responsibility for the root causes of legal violations by suggesting that adultery was as much an act of the head and heart, as it was of the bed.[379] Jesus was a radical forerunner of the restorative justice movement, as He attempted to redefine justice to mean more than "an eye for an eye." In this vein, justice encompassed love for a wrongdoer, love for a stranger in need, and love even for an enemy.[380] As a law reformer He understood that one's attitude toward law, people and life was vastly more important than one's superficial compliance with the law. Yet Jesus attempted to engage in this reform in a manner that respected tradition and precedent. Knowing how important and sacred the law was to the people, especially the religious leaders, He stated often that He came not to destroy the law, but to fulfill it.[381] Third, Jesus often was put in a position where He had to interpret and explain the law as it related to His mission and His insights about God and the kingdom of heaven. He demonstrated the wisdom of a seasoned jurist in trying to avoid the traps and tricks of the religious leaders of his time, and yet resolve some very thorny and difficult legal and moral questions.

Like Abraham and Moses, Jesus also was an advocate on behalf of His disciples and the people. The most profound and compelling example of His power as a defense attorney was His petition on the cross. His plea on behalf of those who were crucifying Him is captured in the words, "Father forgive them for they know not what they do."[382] Captured within these lines is the essence of the lawyer's understanding of the role of mercy in the decision making process. Jesus was advocating not on behalf of those who supported him, but on behalf of those who were in the process of killing Him. Yet He realized as a moral advocate that people should not be punished out of ignorance. Though certainly the soldiers and others in authority knew that to take someone's life was wrong, they also had to understand, as one of the thieves crucified with Him indicated, that Jesus had not committed a wrong worthy of death. Yet Jesus, the supreme defense attorney, could touch and articulate, even in the moment of His own agony, this place of innocence that existed within his tormentors. Their innocence did not derive from the law, but from the spirit of mercy and forgiveness which at times can supersede the law and is always available to be invoked by legal advocates. Part of our agony as contemporary lawyers relates to our inability to touch that place of innocence which exists within those we suspect are guilty, and to balance and reconcile that place with the wrong and violation which have occurred. When we insulate ourselves so much that we cannot see or touch that place of innocence within others and within ourselves, we lose the ability to fashion an appropriate remedy, which is the essence of justice.

Jesus, as advocate, takes on an even deeper meaning after the resurrection. In Christian theology, He now sits on the right hand of the Father, interceding on the believer's behalf. The Apostle John captures this role when he writes, "My little children, these things write I unto you, that ye sin not. And if any man sin, we have an advocate with the Father, Jesus Christ the righteous." [383] Jesus petitions on behalf of believers in every aspect of their lives, and certainly with respect to their acceptance into heaven. I grew up in churches where Jesus was often described within His advocacy role. In the midst of his prayer, my father would often in a rhythmic cadence usher words of praise by saying, "Jesus is a lawyer who never lost a case." Noted legal scholars also have recognized this analogy between Jesus and advocates. William Stuntz in his review of the book *Christian Perspectives on Legal Thought*, stated, "For if the Christian story is true, each of us is a guilty defendant, without hope save for a divine advocate. That is precisely Christ's role in this supernatural litigation: the accuser becomes the advocate, and the client is acquitted not by his own merit, but by the merit of his lawyer."[384] Jesus' advocacy is rooted in law, but also in the same reservoir of mercy which He petitioned on the cross. As a believer journeys through life, Jesus occupies the role of counselor, as the believer grapples with decisions, conflicts, callings and mistakes. As a wise counselor[385] of law would, He is not there just to advise the client of all the options available, but to point out the wisest path to take, while always recognizing that the ultimate decision is the client's. Like a trusted lawyer, Jesus remains available even when the client rejects the advice and pays the cost for a bad decision. His love turns not on His need to be right, but on His desire that the client live a blessed and prosperous life. So during His earthly mission and His heavenly existence, Jesus identifies strongly with the legacy and role of lawyers in society. He is scholar, reformer, jurist, defender, and supreme advocate, and He continues within a long line of religious personalities who were the forerunners of this sacred craft. There are many insights and attributes for lawyers to extract from the life of Jesus, and the manner by which He fulfilled his calling and perfected his craft.

Islam

Law is central to one's understanding of Islam. There are four main tools for developing and understanding Islamic law. The Koran serves as the direct source of law and is the ultimate sacred text of Muslims. The Hadith is a compilation of the oral tradition of the sayings of the Prophet Muhammad. Law is also discerned through consensus reached by religious scholars and Imams, and through analogies where rulings are derived or inferred from similar situations contained in the Koran. Prophet Muhammad, who is the central figure and founder of the religion, embraced the role of legislator, judge and advocate. It was through his revelations that the entire Koran, and thus the laws which are the foundation of Islam, came into existence. These laws and their interpretation govern every aspect of a person's life. They are the path not only to a better life on earth, but also to a glorious reward in the hereafter. Prophet Muhammad was the consummate legislative vessel through which divine law was given to Muslims. He also served as a judge when disputes arose between people. The Koran is full of examples of the Prophet applying the law and seeking revelations in order to resolve disputes. He was also an advocate for those who were being denied justice by existing law. His advocacy was directed sometimes toward Allah (God) in order to secure favor for the people.

From a jurisprudential standpoint, the Prophet Muhammad is an awe-inspiring figure. Not only was the entire body of Islamic law, which governs just about every aspect of a Muslim's life, revealed to him, but his clarification and interpretation of the Koran became the next authoritative body of law. In addition, these various sayings, traditions and interpretations, were often repeated and recorded by his followers, but the weight they carried depended on how closely connected the recorder was to the Prophet. The recorded traditions of those who lived during the time of Prophet Muhammad are more binding and influential than those recorded by his successors. The various jurisprudential schools of Islam developed more around disputes in regard to his successors than around the differences in regard to the sacred text. Therefore the various levels of authority and interpretation of Islamic law all lead back to one person – Prophet Muhammad. One Islamic legal scholar described this judicial influence in the following manner:

> After the death of the Prophet Muhammad, every case that came up for decision had to be referred either to the Holy Qur'an or to some judgment or saying of the Holy Prophet, which judgments or sayings, therefore, obtained a wide reputation. There are a number of numerous cases on record in which a right was claimed on the basis of a judgment or saying of the Holy Prophet, and evidence was demanded to the authenticity of the saying.[386]

Prophet Muhammad was also instrumental in creating and influencing the judicial process for the resolution of disputes. In addition to serving in this role himself, he appointed judges and taught them how to conduct their judicial responsibilities. They were instructed on the seriousness of their role, and the need to be honest, God-fearing and sincere men of integrity.[387] He also instructed them on the importance of treating all litigants the same, regardless of their wealth and status in life.[388] The Prophet enshrined procedural rights of the defendant and the plaintiff into Islamic law, and both were required to appear, testify and take an oath.[389] Though Islamic law is often criticized for the harshness of some of its penalties, the founder of this judicial system encouraged judges to err on the side of innocence. It is reported that the Prophet said,

> As far as possible, refrain from awarding Hadd punishment to a Muslim. If there is found slight excuse (or doubt), leave him alone because it is better for the judge to err in acquitting the accused rather than erring in awarding him punishment. [390]

The consultative nature of decision making was critical to the Prophet's jurisprudence. The idea that a decision maker could render a judgment without consulting and hearing from others, especially those directly involved in the matter, was repugnant to this system of law. Even though the Prophet received divine revelation, he too was required to consult before major and minor decisions were made.[391]

For a casual observer of Islam, it may be hard to grasp fully the centrality of the role of law and the caretakers of the law, to the individual and to society. Law is not a companion or parallel

System that is drawn upon only at critical times in one's life.

system that is drawn upon only at critical times in one's life. The law gives meaning and purpose to life itself. Imbedded within the contours of the law is a system of living that affects not only one's daily activities, but also one's soul. Jurisprudence, from this perspective, is more than a study of the compilation and interpretation of various statutes and court decisions. According to the great Imam Abu Hanifa, "Jurisprudence is the soul's cognizance of its rights and his obligations."[392] Law is not only a vessel through which spiritual matters are poured, but all social thoughts, insights and actions dwell there as well. The following quote by an Islamic scholar captures the profundity and centrality of law to Muslims:

Islamic Law is the epitome of Islamic thought, the most typical manifestation of the Islamic way of life, the core kernal of Islam itself. The very term, Fiqh (knowledge) shows that early Islam regarded knowledge of the sacred law as the knowledge par excellence. This is an admitted fact that the Muslim world from early times has given more importance to the study of Islamic law and its science which deals with the principles. ... 'The methodology of all Islamic thought finds its true expression in the principles of Fiqh and once this methodology has been understood and applied in the realm of law, its extension into ethics, education, economics and all others aspects of man's many sided personal and group activities becomes far nearer to realization.'[393]

Therefore, those who are given the law and the responsibility for internalizing, understanding, interpreting and applying it, occupy a sacred position in society.

Through this lens, lawyers, judges and students of law are engaged in a holy and all encompassing enterprise. Certainly this does not fully translate to the role of lawyers in a secular legal system, since the foundational law was not revealed directly from God, as is believed by Muslims in regard to the Koran. Yet the impact that secular law can have on the life, health and souls of members of a secular society is the same. An argument thus can be made that it should be viewed, studied, understood and applied with a similar sense of seriousness and sacredness. This brief glimpse at the role of jurist and the role of law in Islam serves to remind us of some of the historically spiritual roots of law and procedure. Yet it also serves as another reminder of the spiritual nature of law, and how this vessel has been used consistently to instruct human beings about correct conduct and living righteously. Whether one agrees or not with the laws and precepts of any particular religious tradition does not distract from the central role which law played in the creation and development of most of the world's major religions.

Buddhism

There are numerous Eastern religious texts and traditions. Their diversity will make it difficult for me to describe them all, and that goes beyond the goals of this book. I have selected several common themes from some of the Eastern religious and spiritual traditions as a way to compare and contrast these approaches with those from the West. In Buddhism, like

Judaism and Islam, everyone is a student of the law and thus a lawyer. However, unlike Judaism and Islam, the ultimate law is not etched in tables of stones or in sacred text, but in the hearts of every believer and every person. The goal of this spiritual path - and of life - is to seek and discover these universal laws.

There are numerous sacred Buddhist texts that contain writings and even speeches of "enlightened" leaders of the religion, including Siddhartha Guatama Buddha, its founder. The Four Noble Truths and the Noble Eightfold Path are the central guides on the journey to enlightenment. As with certain western religions, the "law" is central to the Buddhist spiritual journey. The word Dharma, which means "law," is so fundamental to this belief system that some adherents refer to themselves by this name. It is the search to understand universal laws that motivates the believer on the path to enlightenment. Just as lawyers in western courtrooms, Buddhists are engaged in an ultimate search for the truth. But in this context the truth is not hidden within facts and disputed accounts of events; it is hidden within the heart and within the universe, waiting to be revealed to the students who diligently seek it and are prepared to receive it. Though most lawyers are not confident that the adversarial process always produces the truth, one could argue that its legitimacy is not even dependent upon that determination, since truth seeking is still a fundamental part of the lawyer's calling.

Just as lawyers have rules, guidelines and procedures to lead to the discovery of truth, so does the Buddhist. The Noble Eightfold Path, which are fundamental and sacred to Buddhism, are not mere rituals to be blindly followed, but well thought out procedures and guides intended to lead the believer to the truth. In addition, the various components of the eight fold paths are divided into three general categories that are very analogous to the areas that most lawyers should master in order to be technically effective and ethically sound. Wisdom, morality and mental discipline are the three major areas that must be mastered and obtained by the Buddhist adherent. The right understanding, action and mindfulness that each of these categories demand are similar to what law schools should be striving to teach their students. Lawyers must discipline their minds to focus on minute details about rules and facts in order to understand the case before them. They must conduct themselves in a manner that is "appropriate" to their calling and role in society. They must have a right understanding, - "practical wisdom" - in order to see beyond the facts and comprehend the deep meaning of the situation. Unlike the Buddhist who has a daily ritual to guide him along this eightfold path, most lawyers attempt to master these skills and values on their own. The Middle Way, which all Buddhists are encouraged to follow, represents the merger of the attorney personality and the lawyer's soul. "Buddhism seeks the Middle Way, the right balance between extremes. The opposite poles...can be characterized in various, interrelated terms: mind and body, thinking and doing, reason and instinct, theory and practice. However you express the two coordinates, each one needs to be given its proper weight and attention in our lives. Jeopardy lies in favoring one too much and the other too little."[394]

Though the Middle Way is a place that some lawyers aspire to occupy as they engage in their craft, most of us fail to achieve it. Within the law we are constantly pulled between various extremes - between law and justice, between truth and procedure, between theory and fact, between loyalty to the client and loyalty to the court, and for some, between wanting to do well and wanting to do good. Those who attempted to master Dharma were in essence practicing a sacred craft of reconciliation and finding middle paths. For most lawyers today, this process has been turned into a mundane exercise in compromise. When we can't find answers that satisfy both sides we tend to try to find a place in the "middle" where everyone can feel comfortable, or at least, can accept the decision. Though there is enormous benefit to this approach, what it also does is deplete many decisions of any meaning and any meaningful function. The middle way that this religion prescribes is not "splitting the difference," but finding the "right path" or appropriate way to resolve a conflict or to live one's life. Lawyers are not called to just split differences, but to seek what is appropriate for the parties before them, not just in a legal sense, but with respect to the whole situation and the various aspects of the needs which are presented.

Eastern religions, especially Buddhism, have much to teach us about the role of law and those who are students of the law. Western religions start with the premise that if laws are carved on stone or recorded in a text, they will be internalized by members of the society. From a Buddhist perspective, the search and discovery of laws is an individual, internal process. Others can assist by providing a framework and certain practices and rituals, but each person must find the law for herself. The external realities, conflicts and trials are not the place where laws will be discovered. These are merely means that can bring the person to a place of discovery and realization.

The jurisprudence of Buddhism is individualized. The focus is not so much on a corpus of laws to be collectively interpreted, passed down and followed. Each person's life journey provides the corpus which serves as the medium through which laws are discovered and universal truths are revealed. This religion's focus on wisdom reminds us that insights often exist within the crevices and nuances of life, and not within the mastery of external constitutions. It is the search for an internal constitution that provides wisdom to the adherent.

Bhagavad-Gita

There are other sacred texts such as the Bhagavad-Gita of the Hindu tradition that are not discussed above, but convey similar connections between spirituality and the practice of law. The majestic context for this spiritual classic begins with a dialogue between Prince Arjuna and Krishna, an incarnation of God. Krishna counsels Arjuna as he faces the greatest battle of his life. Krishna's counsel is more than mere technical guidance about why Arjuna should engage in a battle against his relatives, but is timeless spiritual advice about how to live a righteous and meaningful life. Through the various chapters the counselor in the Bhagavad-Gita guides the client to a deeper understanding of self-enlightenment, selfless service, faith, freedom and renunciation. These poetic passages not only speaks to lawyers in their role as counselor, but also reveal an aspect of the lawyer's responsibility to the client as she struggles with conflict, crisis and disbelief. The Gita reminds us that, "You have the right to work, but never to the fruit of work. You should never engage in action for the sake of reward, nor should you long for inaction. Perform work in this world, Arjuna, as a man established within himself - without selfish attachments, and alike in success and defeat."[395]

Though intended for all, this passage from the Gita speaks volumes to the challenges of modern day lawyers. Lawyers are often so focused on outcomes and results that they are willing to manipulate rules and people to achieve them. Clients are so often attached to a particular outcome that they are not open to creative and fair solutions. The calling, integrity and attitude of the lawyer must be rooted in selfless service and not in particular outcomes. Certainly lawyers must achieve results for their clients, but the result should always flow from a pure well of authentic service that is not contaminated by the "fruits" of the lawyer's labor. Poor and rich clients should receive the same quality of care. The guilty and the innocent are entitled to the lawyer's wisest counsel. The pro bono mandate of the profession can be drawn from this sacred well. Lawyers are asked to give away their services to the poor because they have the right to serve, but not a right to demand payment in every situation.

To be "established within ourselves" instructs lawyers to resist putting their values, integrity and skills out to the highest bidder. The temperament of the lawyer must remain anchored in a set of sacred principles that can be used in the midst of victory and during moments of devastating losses. To be free of "selfish attachment" does not mean that lawyers should distance themselves emotionally from their clients. To the contrary, this spiritual principle instructs lawyers to pour all of themselves into the cause of goodness and justice without regard to their remuneration. This does not mean that lawyers should not get paid for their services, but getting paid should not be the primary motivation for the work. This privilege that is bestowed upon lawyers carries with it an obligation to connect the essence of their energies and activities to the pursuit of the highest ideals of the profession and life. In the words of the Gita it "means the yoking of the body and the mind and soul to God."[396]

What does this journey through sacred religious texts teach us about the role of lawyers in today's world? It is not intended to simplify the very complex challenges and dilemmas that lawyers and judges face today, for they confront problems that the prophets, spiritual advocates and lawyers in the scriptures did not encounter. Yet in our quest to master this sophisticated and highly technological new world, we have lost sight of many of the fundamental insights, practices, rituals and wisdom that these forerunners of the profession possessed. Hopefully this journey has revealed and reminded us of the treasures we trample daily under our feet. As we strive to rebuild the profession and return it to a place of sacredness, we must ensure that we place those treasures at the foundation of this new temple.

Hopefully this journey has served to inspire us about the mantle and legacy with which we have been entrusted. Though these revered religious figures did not all see themselves as lawyers, they carved a path and a process that paved the way for the work we do each day. The American lawyer of today is heir to a rich tradition that goes further back than just the Constitution. Our legal arena is certainly different, and the structures of our appeals to justice are more formalized, restricted and rule bound. Yet the spirit that we must embrace as we do our work is the same spirit that was cultivated in ancient sacred text. It is a spirit of passion, reverence, humility and honor, and it encased everything the ancients did, as it should inspire everything we do. It is not the type of work we do, or the type of matters we are asked to handle, but the spirit with which we approach and embrace the task. We are not "called" to a particular firm or to a particular case, rather we are "called" to a grand and hallowed tradition. We should be honored to be associated with this tradition and should see our participation in the profession as a continuation of a sacred craft. This journey subtly suggests that if religion is a sacred calling, then lying right next to religion is the sacred calling of the law. They are two parallel streams, which flow into the great river, feed the same human desires, and serve similar aims in life.

This journey also should serve as an invitation to those lawyers who follow a religious path, to search more diligently within their texts for insights about their professional roles. Our religious traditions offer us guidance for carrying out our vocation, but we will never benefit fully from our religious commitment if we do not diligently search the text. Simple truths, wisdom and inspiration can be found within the various religious traditions, and within their sacred texts. For those who prefer not to search scripture, these same truths can be found in nature, which is the basis for the river metaphor. And, for those who chose not to seek the truths in nature, these insights can be discovered through an inward journey of self. All of these paths can be traveled simultaneously. The path is up to us, but the journey is non-negotiable for those who seek a spiritual revitalization of the legal profession.

New Wine in Old Bottles: Transforming Legal Structures

The changes for which I have been advocating relate more to personal transformation than to institutional change. I start and focus there because without the personal changes, the institutional and structural ones will be meaningless. However, the personal changes also have their limitations if there is no change in the overall structures that house our approaches to teaching and practicing law. There is a spiritual warning that it is unwise to "put new wine in old bottles." [397] If wine represents the revitalized spirit and perspective that lawyers hopefully will embrace, then the bottles are the various institutional forms and practices within which we work each day. The message behind this spiritual warning is not that we need new structures just because the wine is new. The concern is that this new spirit embraced by lawyers will be damaged, destroyed or wasted if it is not supported by the profession.

When we begin to see law as spirit and practice from the river, it is difficult to go about our daily work in the same way. The things that we settled for in the past no longer feel comfortable. The patterns of behavior that we tolerated from those around us and from ourselves, are more difficult to ignore. This new found energy and perspective cannot be contained easily within existing structures and practices. If we want this new spirit to permeate not only individuals but also to be reflected in our legal institutions, then they must change as well. As with any individual, I am not suggesting that a complete overhaul should occur. There are various structures and practices that should not be abandoned. However, we should be willing to examine what we do so that we can better align that with our values and aspirations. Most law firms and offices will not reconfigure themselves in the way some holistic practitioners have transformed their practices; however there are some basic things that all organizations and institutions can do so that there are more expansive bottles to contain the new spirit of law.

We acquire more expansive bottles when we are willing to examine our reward systems to ensure that they are aligned with the values and spirit of the organization. If there are no incentives and rewards for pro bono work, then it will not become a fundamental or defining aspect of the organization. Those who do it for their soul's sake will eventually pay for it out of their own hides. If there is no partnership track for less than full-time associates, then our bottles will not be able to contain the wines of motherhood and parenting. The reality that most lawyers still struggle to strike a balance between their work responsibilities and their family obligations will remain an individualized challenge and not an organizational concern. If we do not create legitimate and meaningful opportunities for the organization and the individuals within it to refresh and retool themselves, then not only will the bottles look dusty, but the wine will become bitter.

One of the cherished old bottles that must be seriously reexamined is the accounting practice of "billable hours." This is especially challenging for large firms that must systematically account for the time and activities of hundreds of lawyers. The American Bar Association in 2002 issued a comprehensive report on billable hours.[398] In addition to reminding the profession that this sacred cow has not always been the standard method for charging clients, the report identified and analyzed the "corrosive impact" of the over reliance on billable hours. The report cited fifteen [399] negative consequences from this accounting practice. It stated that over reliance on billable hours by the legal profession:

- Results in a decline of collegiality of firm culture and an increase in associate departures
- discourages taking on pro bono work
- does not encourage project or case planning
- provides no predictability of cost for client
- penalizes the efficient and productive lawyer
- discourages communication between lawyer and client
- encourages skipping steps
- fails to promote a risk/benefit analysis
- does not reward the lawyer for productive use of technology
- puts client's interest in conflict with lawyer's interest
- clients run the risk of paying for
  -the lawyer's incompetency or inefficiency
  -associate training
  -associate turnover
  -padding of timesheets
- results in itemized bills that tend to report mechanical functions, not value of progress
- results in lawyers competing based on hourly rates.[400]

The analysis given in the report regarding the culture of law firms is very disturbing and confirms the belief that many have held for years that fundamental values are being destroyed. The report stated, "the increased need for billable hours has caused the pace of law practice to become frenetic and has had a negative effect on mentoring, associate training and collegiality. Lawyers no longer are being recognized primarily for the quality of their work and their talent. As a result, the quality of the culture in law firms is in decline and the pressure for hours makes it impossible for many lawyers to achieve balance in their lives." [401] It is this lack of balance that contributes to more serious problems confronting the legal profession such as high rates of divorce, alcoholism and depression. Though we cannot ascribe these problems solely to the billable hour procedure, it does appear to distract from the overall health of the profession.

Some scholars see the decline in the health of the profession, which they believe is caused by billable hours, in purely spiritual terms. M. Cathleen Kaveny argues that the use of billable hours forces lawyers to view time in a way that is antithetical to spiritual development. She argues that billable hours treat a lawyer's time as a commodity that is entirely extrinsic and fungible, and locks the lawyer into an endless present while alienating her from colleagues, family and community. [402] The new spirit that we are urging lawyers to nurture and cultivate demands time for introspection and reflection. Every moment in life is a special opportunity to experience the divine presence in life, and fulfill our unique purpose on earth. Though each moment and every day may appear to be the same, spiritually each moment is different and provides us with a different opportunity either to heal or hurt to the universe. The moments for healing are not fungible. Sometimes our colleagues and family need us to sit with them as they struggle with life's challenges, even though we cannot bill our clients for those moments. The good we do does not always engender immediate results. Sometimes the lesson we learn or the wisdom we plant in the lives of people around us will take years to root. Many lawyers forego or dramatically shorten these moments because of the inherent pressures of a billable hours system.

When we are selfish with our time and view it as something that belongs exclusively to us, then we frustrate the spiritual goals of our calling. Our pro bono obligation grows from an understanding which suggests that our time and our lives are collectively owned. The divine has leased us a period in these mortal bodies so that we can pursue sacred deeds on earth. When we share love, cultivate compassion, demonstrate trust, live by faith, seek truth, and unselfishly serve others in need, then we have placed a drop of pure water in the river that will last long after we leave this physical plane. If a billable hours regime precludes or discourages lawyers from carrying out this obligation, then it is negatively altering the content and flow of the river. Certainly a lawyer's time is there to produce revenue for the organization and a salary or income for the person. but it is also the means through which the lawyer fulfills a higher calling of this profession and life. To fulfill that higher calling one must not be limited to billable hour productivity, nor view time as belonging exclusively to the lawyer or to the firm. From a spiritual perspective we are not "giving away" time to the pro bono client, we are "giving back" a portion of time that was divinely given to us. The beauty and balance of the divine understanding of time is that we are not expected to use all of our time in the service of others, though certainly some have followed this path. We are expected to take some time for ourselves. Those moments are blessings for which we should be thankful as we prepare to fulfill our responsibilities to the river. So the lawyer's time and the lawyer's view of time is understood very differently when viewed from a spiritual perspective. Professor Kaveny analyzes a lawyer's time from a Roman Catholic perspective and finds a deeper understanding which does not fit neatly with a billable hours regime. He writes:

> Here time is perceived to have intrinsic value rather than merely instrumental value. Time is viewed not as a commodity valued in terms of its ability to satisfy human desires, but as a prism that is revelatory of the way those desires should ideally be directed (i.e., toward fellowship with God and one another). It is not fungible, but marks points of unique importance in the lives of individual persons and the broader community. It is not an endless, flat extension, but an integral spiral that encompasses decisive moments, including reversals of direction, as it moves toward an ultimate goal, which is evoked by the metaphor of the kingdom of God. Finally, at its very core, time on a Catholic view does not lead to isolation, but calls for the creation of community on many levels and among many different persons." [403]

So certain faith traditions invite lawyers to view their time in a manner that is more consistent with their faith and more humane. If we truly want lawyers to practice their faith as they practice law, then the practice of law must embrace a view of time that is more consistent with law's spiritual roots. The billable hours system is standing in the way of this change. This is very disheartening when, as the ABA Report indicated, there are numerous viable alternatives that other firms are using. These include contingent fee arrangements, flat fees, result-based premiums, retainers, stock in exchange for fees. Smaller firms with fifteen or fewer lawyers tend to use these alternative methods more often; however, these methods have not made their way into the accounting rooms of some large firms. [404] Spiritually, these alternative methods are also subject to abuse and could have similar or different corrosive effects upon the profession. Each method has obvious benefits in comparison to billable hours, but also has disadvantages and would not be appropriate in every situation. What the alternatives offer for this discussion is evidence that there are other flexible skins within which these new spiritual wines of enlightened legal practice may be housed.

Those things that many lawyers and legal organizations have considered fundamental to their practice can be reexamined from a spiritual perspective. If something as fundamental and guarded as the method for billing clients can be examined, then every aspect of the practice of law can be viewed through a spiritual prism. This examination does not mean that it will lead automatically to less revenue or productivity. Even the most spiritually engaged lawyer among us is still concerned about the fundamental issues of revenue and compensation. These concerns are not inconsistent with our calling as spiritually centered professional or as spiritually centered human beings. On the other hand, if we cannot approach these issues with candor and a critical eye, then we will remain prisoners of our earthly needs. Our quest for financial security will become the stumbling block to our quest for spiritual peace. It is written, "what does it profit a man to win the whole world and lose his own soul." [405] If we become too obsessed with our material gains to the point that we lose touch with our spiritual needs, we will never hear the rustling of the river's sacred waters and never fulfill our calling to transform this profession.

Another major structure in need of new thought is the way many legal organizations make hiring decisions. Many of the limitations we face are due to the fact that we continue to hire people with the same type of skills and perspective. Legal organizations are very risk averse, and are reluctant to take "chances" hiring someone who does not fit the standard profile. Yet the standard profile does not always provide the diversity we seek, the creativity we need, the values we deserve, or the chance to look at ourselves through a different lens. If we want to attract a different type of lawyer to the profession, we must send a different message about what we want, and we must develop more expansive criteria and methods to determine if the person possesses those traits and attributes. To do this does not require that we abandon our search for excellence, but does demand that we expand our definition of excellence.

When we attempt to place new wine in old bottles, the powerful fermenting nature of the new wine forces the old bottles to break, and we lose the precious wine that we have spent so much time cultivating. If we are serious about revitalizing the profession, we cannot expect this to occur on the backs of the new entrants and reborn lawyers. Without some change in our fundamental structures we will produce only

394

more frustration and disillusionment. Their spirits and energies will be wasted trying to remove barriers that were constructed by people who designed them for a different space and time. We must cherish the past, but we must not be trapped by its limitations and boundaries. We must honor those who paved the way for us, but we must not condemn ourselves to traveling the same road without any thought of going the scenic route.

We have spilled the spirit, idealism and passion of too many lawyers on classroom floors and on courthouse doors. They came believing that this was their calling, and hoping to make a difference in the world through law. We subtly told them that there were more important things to do like mastering the law and learning to think like a lawyer. Once they did that, we told them that it was premature for them to change the way things were done in the workplace because they first had to become partner or get tenure. When they did that, we told them that there was no time to think about re-imagining the practice or the world, because our competition was eating our lunch and we needed everyone to work harder and think less. When good times arrived again, we told them to start thinking about investing those bonuses and windfalls because retirement was right around the corner. When they retired we gave them a classic watch with the organization's name engraved on the back. At their funeral, we spoke so highly about how they gave so much to the organization and how much we will miss them. Sadly, no one remembers their dreams. No one speaks to their vision for their lives and the organization. Their voices and their dreams, their passion and idealism, have been hushed by the winds of consistency and normalcy. The old bottles were not willing or able to contain this new wine so it spilled on the floor of the institution, or it was purposefully extracted from the veins of this idealistic lawyer. Too many lawyers have spent their careers going through the motions of feeling fulfilled. Even those who have found certain levels of fulfillment have wondered about how much more meaning they might have achieved if they had been willing to keep their spirit within alive and engaged, and if the institution had been willing to fully embrace what they had to offer. So it is time we stop wasting the wine and start embracing the challenge of change. Transformation is always a challenging and unnerving process, yet we have so much more to gain if we are willing to change not only ourselves but also the institutions and organizations to which we give so much of our time and energy. We then will produce a fine wine that inspires the souls of our clients, and we will have designed beautiful and sacred bottles able to hold the best dreams and aspirations of this profession.

The Courtroom of Divine Guidance

A major concern that always arises in a book of this nature is the perennial question, "how do I practically achieve what you are prescribing?" Even those who are willing to lay aside their skepticism about the utility of spirituality in the practice of law are still at a loss as to how to put these insights into practice. Despite the appropriateness of the need underlying this type of question, there is a major danger in trying to prescribe a particular formula or path for spiritual enlightenment. In a strictly religious approach to this question there are numerous ways in which individuals are able to nurture their soul and find the peace they seek in life. Prayer, fasting, meditation, reading sacred scriptures, obeying codes and laws, attending religious services, and performing various rituals become the standard means, and there is an understanding that spiritual journeys are uniquely personal. I often hear ministers and others in the churches I attend echoing the admonition that "you have to find God for yourself." Embedded in this admonition is a warning against assuming that one person's path, approach or technique will work for everyone else. Thus to prescribe a formula is to deny the serendipitous nature of the spiritual quest, and place our experience on a pedestal upon which no one experience belongs. So this chapter will attempt to answer the question without violating the admonition. What makes this answer even more complicated and challenging is that our broad definition of spirituality embraces religious believers and those who do not follow a religious path. The approaches taken by those of us who fall into these two categories differ, overlap and intersect. Therefore contained in this section are some guideposts for those who choose to follow the flow of the river. There is no set pattern to the flow of the river, and it never stands still. What follows are sketches of its movement and the outlines of its power. We must take what works for us and weave it into our own personal spiritual journey.

For many who strive to live a whole and centered life, there is a deeply held belief that there is a divine force that provides guidance, insight and wisdom. If one does not believe that there is a divine reality beyond what can be seen, heard and felt each day, then the later part of this chapter provides some additional insights about this spiritual journey. If one embraces this reality, and certainly if one deeply believes in the divine, then one's quest is to draw near that divine source daily and to utilize its powers in everything that is done. This, in a nutshell, is the courtroom of divine guidance that religious believers seek and strive to operate from on a daily basis. This is not a courtroom where decrees are rendered, but where revelations, wisdom and insights are received, and where instincts are finely tuned.

Many lawyers and legal academics are more accustomed to believing that all we need to know and understand can be accessed through traditional forms of learning and life experiences. We want to feel that the wisdom, insight and knowledge we need is within our control, or at least within our reach. Though on the mental level this is true, on the spiritual level we have to accept that we are not all knowing. We have to accept the fact that the universe is structured and designed in ways that exceed our capacity to understand completely, but that it invites us to partake of the wisdom and insights that abound within it. Most religious believers, regardless of the path they pursue, accept that there is divine wisdom and guidance which they must seek in order to live a whole and pious life, and to fulfill their calling in the world. They may follow different paths, invoke different rituals, submit to the teachings of various intermediaries, but they all subscribe to the belief that there is a good, loving, righteous, and all knowing source which they must seek and embrace. Some seek this guidance not only in their religious activities, but also in every aspect of their lives, including their work. However, for many lawyers there is often a separation between the guidance they seek in their personal lives and the guidance they seek in their work.

We have constructed a barrier between the world of the spirit and the world of work. We spend so much of our time in the world of work, and yet while we are there we limit ourselves to only a certain type of wisdom and guidance. We make some of the most critical and long-lasting decisions at work, and yet feel that those decisions must be made without the benefit of all of the wisdom and insight that is available to us. We also tend to think that we can leave those decisions and their consequences behind us when we go home, but in reality, they seep into our home conversations, our thoughts and even into our dreams. Our inability to make peace with our decisions at times forces us to bring back to the workplace unnecessary hostility and lingering emotional pain. So if we have a reservoir of insight and peace that we can tap for our personal lives, then it behooves us to seek this guidance in all the things we do. This does not mean that we should try to impose our religious belief into all the secular decision we face. It means that we must seek the attributes of our faith, "the fruits of the spirit," as we wrestle with complex and challenging decisions. Wise decisions are not just the product of slavishly following a text, but are the end results of a process where decision makers are informed, centered, thoughtful, sensitive, self-reflective and at peace with themselves. They are certainly not the product of individuals who are motivated by unfounded fears, political gains, and other negative forces that compromise our integrity and our judgment.

In order to remain centered in our values and calling as we work, it is crucial to believe, seek and embrace the spiritual guidance that exists all around us. In order to tap into our own sources of power, it is vital that we seek the source that will move our rivers. As we face difficult meetings, decisions or trials, we must be able to tap into a deep well of peace and wisdom so that we can bring something special to the encounter, and so that we do not lose sight of our values or our calling. In order to tap into our personal passions, and fully empathize with the suffering and challenges of others, we must seek a source that goes beyond our intellectual boundaries.

So much of what lawyers do requires them to go beyond the limits of their personal experience and embrace, understand and articulate the experience of others. We certainly can do that in a factual manner by knowing the dates, places and circumstances surrounding our clients' lives. But to know them as whole human beings, and to tell their story in such a way that others can feel and touch their pain, is a special skill that derives more from the depths of our emotional and spiritual wells, than from our intellectual domain. So much of what lawyers describe as instinct, hunches, experience or luck, derives from their ability to access another source of power which they or others could not see with their eyes. This happens to religious believers and non-religious believers alike. The divine wisdom and guidance of the universe is not hidden in a closet so that only those with special keys can enter. It is embedded into every living and non-living thing. If we can quiet ourselves long enough, we are able to access and receive what is there. Scientific discoveries are a product of this same phenomenon.[406] Though hard work and dedication are essential for major breakthroughs to occur, there is generally a moment when the light bulb goes off inside and what appeared cloudy becomes crystal clear.

This is the experience of walking down an intellectual path that appears to be leading nowhere, but because of our faith we discover that the path has much to offer the world and us. "To walk by faith and not by sight," suggests that we are comfortable letting go because we believe in the eternal goodness of God and the universe. It does not mean that we stop trying to improve ourselves and enhance the quality of our lives and the lives of others, but it does mean we can appreciate the reality that progress and change may not happen the way we planned or predicted. There will be openings which we must take even though we do not know where they will lead. There will be people whom we must embrace even though they do not fit our preconceived categories of friends and essential others. We must be willing to let our creativity flow so that it can lead us in directions that we never intended to pursue. Just as we come into the courtroom believing that there will be a decision rendered from a higher power, we must see our spiritual lives through the same lens. If we are willing to trust and respect the wisdom of judges with whom we vehemently disagree, then we must also be willing to believe that wisdom and direction can come to us from a court of divine guidance. We may not be able to see this courtroom or judge, but for many the experience is as real and meaningful as an opinion from the U.S. Supreme Court.

We should not seek this guidance only in small things, such as what type of approach to take to a particular case, but we should seek it for guidance in addressing the fundamental question of our calling in life. Each of us has a special mission in this world. We were not born just to be a number in someone's database. We were not born just to indulge ourselves in the pleasures of life. We were born to bring more beauty and understanding into the world. The path through which we can do that varies, but the calling remains. Some of us will figure this out during our lifetime. Some of us do not even pause long enough to ask the question, but the universe still beckons. One of our greatest challenges in life is to strive to live our lives in a way that is consistent with our calling. Each of us must find the flow of our river. In the *Seat of the Soul*, we find the following passage that describes this understanding of our life's journey. It reads:

> Each soul takes upon itself a particular task. It may be the task of raising a family, or communicating ideas through writing, or transforming the consciousness of a community, such as the business community. It may be the task of awakening the awareness of the power of love at the level of nations, or even contributing directly to the evolution of consciousness on a global level. Whatever the task that your soul has agreed to, whatever its contract with the Universe, all of the experiences of your life serve to awaken within you the memory of that contract, and to prepare you to fulfill it. [407]

Yet some of us are not awakened, because we constantly ignore the signs and urges. We embrace a small part of our calling, but ignore the greater aspects of our contract. One of the primary reasons we do not awaken to our calling or fulfill it is because we do not constantly seek it. We make decisions about our lives based on formulas and patterns. We follow career paths that have been ordained by those who traveled them to get where they are now and where we think we want to be. We sometimes take cases and stay in jobs that we know are inconsistent with our deeper desires and aspirations because we have stopped seeking our special calling. We have trained ourselves to put those desires and urges to rest. We have anesthetized them with money, praise and status - but the contract still stands, and the yearning still lies dormant within us.

We can find our calling and tap into the divine guidance the same way we carry out our tasks as lawyers. Lawyers are uniquely trained in the language and procedure for divine invocation. Just as we petition a court for relief, we must petition the divine for our calling and guidance. Though divine guidance and wisdom are all around us, and can be received and accessed even without a major request, our greatest power comes when we earnestly and consistently seek it. We would never expect a judge to rule in our favor without first submitting a brief or making an oral argument, and we should not expect answers to our calling and guidance in our lives without petitioning the source. The process of the court, in some respects, mirrors the spiritual court of order. Through prayer we are able to invoke the grace of God, and gain a deeper understanding of life and ourselves in the process. Lawyers for centuries have written and invoked the words, "I pray the court...," when they have sought relief or a judgment for a client. In our daily lives we must make fervent requests for the guidance, grace and understanding that we need and desire. For those who believe, this is a universal path to peace and self-fulfillment, not a ritual for the weak and unintelligent. "It is impossible for you to come full circle in this way of empowerment without prayer. It is not enough to want or intend or to meditate. You must pray. You must talk. You must ask. You must believe. That is partnership." [408]

We petition the court because we want the judge or jury to see us. We want to enter into a personal relationship between the decision maker and our client. We want them to know our client, feel our client's suffering or situation, and assist our client in creating a new reality. We do not leave it up to chance and we do not expect the other side to make our case for us, though at times that does happen. While there is standard language we use as we engage the court, we strive to paint our client's picture using our most beautiful and captivating voice. The same principles and process applies in the spiritual world. The fulfillment of our calling will never be imposed upon us; we must seek it and embrace it willingly. The divine source must know that we want to receive what is available and what is uniquely for us. We make a claim on this power, creativity and peace through our personal engagement with the source. It responds to our personal pulls and tugs, and it creates a personal partnership of co-creation based on our consistent and fervent requests.

There are numerous lawyers who have discovered the power of prayer and through it seek divine guidance for their lives and their practices. The most compelling description of this relationship and process which I have heard comes from John McShane, a flamboyant Texas lawyer. He describes his practice as a "partnership with God." [409] God is the senior partner in the firm and he is the junior partner. From his perspective, God is responsible for long- range planning and making sure the bills are paid, and he is responsible for striving to "do the right thing" each day. What John is conveying is his surrender and trust in the goodness of the divine. Of course, on a practical level he has to write the checks to pay the bills, but he has a deep faith that his practice and his work would be prosperous. He trusts God to insure that he would be cared for, that if he practices law with love and compassion, he would be rewarded in material and non-material ways. John, through his personal struggle, found his calling and thus was relieved from trying to be in control of every aspect of his life and work.

So much of the stress, mean spirited behavior and cut throat tactics in which lawyers encounter come from an obsession with winning and being in control. Even with our ethical training in law school we easily embrace the culture of "win at all cost." When we see ourselves as the sole creator of our destiny and status in life, we believe that we must control every part of the journey, and manipulate people and circumstances along the way so that we can reach our desired destination. But when we "take our hands off the steering wheel,"[410] and earnestly and honestly say to God, "Let thy will be done," then we have started down the road to finding peace and meaning in our lives. This is hard for those who have been trained to hold tightly to the wheel, and to create the rules of the road, but by letting go, we gain more control over our lives. In surrendering we become victorious, and by abandoning our defined roles, we become authentic actors on the stage of life.

One of my most compelling experiences of seeking and receiving divine guidance in my professional life occurred when I was a relatively new professor at Northeastern University School of Law. I was attracted to the school for its progressive politics, innovative curriculum, urban location and genuineness of the students, staff, faculty and dean. Things were going along nicely from my perspective, and I was developing very positive relationships with students across various racial and ethnic lines. In February of my second year the Black Law Student Association decided to create a display of Black Leaders for Black History Month on a very visible bulletin board at the entrance of the law school. They solicited pictures, speeches and other materials from various members of the law school community. I gave them African artifacts, various pictures and an album cover with a picture of Minister Louis Farrakhan. Being aware of how many people felt about him, I indicated that to include him might be very controversial, but that I did consider him as an important contemporary Black leader. I remember passing the bulletin board one day and feeling proud and embraced by the numerous pictures and images of my people. Some of the materials were very heart wrenching, like a picture of a Black man being burned with a crowd of whites standing around smiling. I also noticed that they had included the picture of Minister Farrakhan and I felt proud that they had the courage to include him. It did not take long, however, before I was visited by students, mostly Black, who made me aware of the reaction of others within the law school, especially members of the Jewish community. Minister Farrakhan, because of statements he had made, some misinterpreted, others accurately reported, was considered by some to be anti-Semitic. Yet for many in the Black community, especially the youth, he was considered an important leader who was willing to "speak truth to power." Though I was aware of how controversial he was, I never imagined that the impact on the institution would be so negative and so hostile. The dean, various faculty members, and students were extremely concerned, and some outraged. The emotional temperature in the building was at an all time high, and tremendous pressure was being placed on the Black students to take down the picture. Though some discussions and negotiations occurred, the Black students stood their ground under intense criticism and pressure.

As the controversy began to unfold, I was approached by one student who was in a state of panic over the situation. Her nervousness, anxiety and fear began to seep into my spirit. Though I was calm and thoughtful at the start of the conversation, by the end I was a total wreck internally. I felt as if the walls were closing in on me and that the peace which I had known inside, and in the institution, had been taken away. Once the student left, I knew that I would be of no help to anyone as the institution grappled with this situation. I was shaking internally and externally in ways that I had never experienced before. I felt as if I was responsible for the situation which was making life unbearable for all involved.

Though I had from childhood sought divine guidance, I was probably at a spiritual low place during this time in my life. While prayer was still a part of my life, many times it was very ritualistic. Fortunately, I still had a deep belief in the power of the river, so immediately after the student left my office I stood up in the middle of the room, with arms open wide and head toward heaven, praying for relief and an answer. Though I cannot recall my exact words, the essence was a sincere request for peace and guidance. I knew that I could not emotionally make it through this situation in my present state, and I needed some divine guidance. My prayer was probably the most earnest and sincere prayer I had ushered up in a long time. In an instant, as I stood there, a spirit of peace descended upon me. My shaking stopped and I felt at peace with myself and with the situation. Shortly afterward, with the help of many others, I was able to engage the law school community in a thoughtful and candid conversation not only about the bulletin board, but about what the institution really stood for and how it should treat and respect all points of view. The peace that came at the end of that prayer stayed with me throughout those conversations and meetings. I had noticed at the end of the day of that prayer that I had not used any of my daily asthma medication. This had happened for brief periods before, but usually following an extended fast. This time it lasted for months. Not only had I received some peace and guidance for this difficult situation, but also had embraced a spirit of healing. Moreover, this same spirit of peace continued to guide my life, for within two months of this experience, I met in church the woman who was to become my wife, Marilyn. Fifteen years and two children later, I remain at peace in the most loving and spiritually centered relationship of my life.

Scientifically, I cannot describe or prove this experience or its consequences. Yet many of you reading this have had similar, and certainly more profound, experiences. We keep them to ourselves, we share them with a limited circle of friends, but we do not always embrace their full meaning and impact on our lives. Some of us are willing to seek the assistance of the divine in our private lives but are not willing to petition for guidance in our role as lawyers and law professors. It is dangerous to compartmentalize our existence on this earth. We are whole beings who are more than flesh and blood. We are spirit. We are connected to a divine spirit that can assist and nurture us on this journey, but if we do not acknowledge the relationship, at least to ourselves, and earnestly explore the connection, we will not experience fully the joy and beauty of life. We will limit our own power in the courtroom and classroom, and fail to unleash the healing that our clients and students need.

Sometimes we break through earthly imposed prisons, like
the one above, during moments of intense struggle and conflict.
In the midst of the storm, we wish there was no storm. We
yearn for the days before we or others placed this new challenge
into the universe and into our lives. Yet in the midst of the
storm, we can find new levels of peace. We can discover new
parts of ourselves and of those around us. As we climb to the
top of the mountain in pursuit of our calling, there will be
moments when we want to turn back. There will be moments
when we question whether this is the right path. Yet the joy and
healing that we can discover at the top makes the climb
worthwhile. The view from the mountaintop is awe inspiring.
As we pause and breathe in the air and take in the sights, we
must remember that there are other mountains to climb and
higher peaks to ascend. Spiritual growth is a never ending
journey. There is a greater wisdom to embrace and there are
different challenges to overcome. Because we are not perfect
and will continue to make mistakes and use poor judgment, we
will need the presence of grace in our lives. But if we think that
chance and our intelligence are the sole means of our good
fortune, then we will not see the residing grace or give it due
reverence. If we earnestly and sincerely enter into the
courtroom of divine guidance, petition the ultimate keeper of
enlightenment, and give reverence to the only judge of our soul,
then the fulfillment we seek in our practice of law and in our
lives will be ours to claim.

For those lawyers who seek a non-theist form of spirituality,
there are approaches and practices that contribute to this
integration of wholeness into the practice and teaching of law.
Steve Keeva in his groundbreaking book, *Transforming
Practices*, suggests a series of activities that allow attorneys to

find more balance in their lives. Most of these can be used by those who have a non-theist understanding of life. His eight suggestive points can be incorporated easily into one's daily routine. They include spending time "thinking about what parts of yourself you're neglecting"; taking "ten minutes each morning to think about the big picture"; taking "time to become aware of your concept of the divine and its place in your life"; mapping out a "balanced day, with time allotted for your financial, physical, emotional and spiritual needs"; "doing nothing for five minutes at least once a day"; and being reflective about how you could spend your day in ways that make you excited.[411] He argues against waiting for major vacations or quick getaways to rejuvenate oneself, but to seek it everyday as one engages in the decisions, challenges and stresses of the day. Though his list does not provide any novel concepts or techniques, it serves as another reminder that the wisdom and insight we need as lawyers lay dormant inside us and all around us, but we cannot avail ourselves of them in the hectic life styles we have embraced as a fundamental part of being lawyers. To slow ourselves down will require a major adjustment in our daily routines. The time it takes for us to do this is far outweighed by the benefits we will reap.

Another interesting "how to" book is *Lawyer Life, Finding a Life and a Higher Calling in the Practice of Law*, by Judge Carl Horn III. In this book, published by the American Bar Association, Judge Horn offers a Twelve Step process for finding fulfillment in the practice of law which any lawyer could embrace and follow. These steps are: 1. Face the facts, 2. Establish clear priorities, 3. Develop and practice good time management, 4. Implement healthy lifestyle practices, 5. Live beneath your means,   6. Don't let technology control your life, 7. Care about character - and conduct yourself accordingly, 8. "Just say No" to some clients, 9. Stay emotionally healthy, 10. Embrace law as a "high calling," 11. Be generous with your time and money, and 12. Pace yourself for a marathon. [412] Judge Horn does not label these as spiritual steps although he indicates that some of them as have a spiritual dimension; however, a closer examination of the twelve steps would place them all within the spiritual category.

For example, facing the fact that the profession is in crisis and not representative of the ideals and expectation of many lawyers is the first step on most spiritual journeys of healing. One cannot become whole through denial, nor can one tap into the wisdom and insights that exist within and around, without first accepting the fact that something is "not right" or missing. In order to establish clear priorities or "put first things first" we must first have a spiritual awakening that reminds us of what is first in our lives. Lawyers will continue to neglect their family and themselves until they realize that some things are more important to them than financial rewards and status. Implementing a healthy life style is clearly spiritual advice, and it is in this section that Judge Horn references *Transforming Practices,* which is a very spiritually centered approach to the problem of lawyer dissatisfaction. To live below one's means is primarily a values question which most lawyers and others are not able to do effectively, unless they have first developed the internal fortitude to curb their desires, and the faith to accept the social stigma that may emerge from this decision. To stay emotionally healthy, to free oneself from the technology trap, to embrace lawyering as a high calling, to be generous with one's time and money, and to pace oneself all require a spiritual development and practice that are not easily found in textbook and operation manuals. Even good time management, has a spiritual dimension. As stated earlier,[413] from a spiritual perspective time is sacred and we manage it better only when we see it as more than a commodity. So when Judge Horn advises lawyers, in a very secular way to find fulfillment, he is in essence advising them to pursue spiritual ideals, clothed in professional rhetoric.

What Keeva's and Horn's lists suggest to us is that lawyers must go beyond the code of professional responsibility in order to find answers to the moral and practice dilemmas they face. They must go beyond their training in law school in order to find answers to how to practice law in a fulfilling and meaningful way. And they must seek the court of divine guidance in order to better operate in the courts of justice.

Chapter Seven:
Voices From The River

The river speaks to all of us if we are willing to listen. It softly and quietly communicates with our very being. If we listen to the river with our hearts, we will hear it reflecting the essence of how we should be as lawyers. If we listen carefully, we can hear the yearnings of generations of lawyers who had visions that were not fulfilled, who had dreams that were not realized. If we listen to the river with our hearts, we will feel the pain and the joy of those who touched its sacred waters and tried to change their lives and their practices. Listen to the river. Hear the voices, spirits and dreams that flow subtly between the ripples. Listen to the river and you will hear yourself. You may not hear or see what you and the profession are today, but you will feel what you and the profession are becoming.

The voices from the river let us know that we are not mere cogs in someone's wheel; we are dream weavers assisting someone's quest for a better life. We have been placed at the center of the lives of people, close to their aspirations and hopes for the future. If we touch them with our hearts and not just our hands we can help weave their dreams. We can turn despair and disappointment into hope. As lawyers we have been given the keys to their locked-up dreams. The river allows us to unleash the power of possibilities in impossible lives and situations. The river will guide us if we are unsure or lack direction, and it will calm us when we are caught in whirlwinds of uncertainty and chaos. The voices from the river will give us insights when we have nothing left in the recesses of our minds. The river is our ultimate source of creativity if only we would listen and yield.

As a profession we have known rivers. We have watched great lawyers perfect their craft and lead this profession. We have gazed at their movements and stood in awe of their advocacy skills. Yet our strength and beauty are greater than a Brandeis brief, or the oratory genius of a Clarence Darrow or the eloquent moral and social reasoning of a Thurgood Marshall. We are the keepers of a flame that some would like to blow out. We are the bearers of a light that can lead individuals out of darkness and loneliness, to the fulfillment of their dreams, and lead nations out of the caves of injustice and oppression, into the sunlight of justice and peace. We do this not just with our finely tuned intellectual skills; we do it with what we draw from the river. We do it with our compassion and tears, with our hearts and wrinkled hands; with our unconditional love for those who have been rejected and despised.

We are chasers of illusive dreams. We know in our hearts that many of these dreams may never be realized, yet we chase them just the same. The river tells us that it is not just the attainment of justice and love that separates us from the animals, but our constant pursuit of these ideals in the face of stones and obstacles which we and others have placed in the river. The societies and organizations that we strive to create through our legal magic may never fulfill their missions and goals. Some will turn into the very thing which they were created to replace, but we cannot be restrained from giving away our magic, for it is not ours. The true magic resides at the bottom of the river. It sits there, anchored, waiting for some courageous soul to dive deep, and ask for permission to make the world a better place. So we must never stop pursuing dreams. Out of that chase this profession found its birth, meaning and ultimate calling. This illusive river, divinely created to be the source and sustainer of life, called this profession into existence.

Despite the fact that this profession has moved far from its original dream and original calling, the river still calls us. It beckons daily for us to see ourselves as the river sees us and not as we have been trained and programmed. Every thing we do and touch can have more meaning if we would listen to the river's voice inside us. Every aspect of our practice and our teaching is laden with possibilities that we have not explored. There are gems all around us that we trample in our haste to get to court, to meetings, and to class on time. When we write our briefs we are not just cutting and pasting words, and citing ancient rulings for contemporary answers. We are holding within our hands the lives and stories of trusting people. We are weaving delicate threads of life into whole cloth, trying to capture the essence of not only the present case, but also the dreams, fears, vulnerabilities, and latent powers of our clients. We are not just dropping off lengthy documents to court clerks; we are passing on sacred texts that may have the power to help blind men and women see. When we see our work through this lens it gives us the meaning we seek, even if it does not give us the results we sought.

When we look into the eyes of our clients and students, we are gazing at more than "revenue producing units," for we have been given the privilege to glimpse inside their souls. What we see, and how we treat what we see, will determine what good derives from each encounter. If we see them in their spiritual essence, as the river would instruct us to do, then we can serve them in ways that they had never been served before. If we allow them to see us in our spiritual essence, then we will and gain more from the crossing than just our compensation. This is the true joy of lawyering and giving. The reason it is "better to give than to receive," is because the river always returns back to us more than we cast in.

At times the voices from the river are crying. They cry for a profession gone astray. They cry because some of the streams of hope they created have been turned into cesspools of greed. They cry because the natural fluid movement toward justice has been diverted and replaced by the fixed stone of gamesmanship. They cry because many who they thought might have listened have closed their ears and hearts to their inner voice. The voices from the river cry not for themselves, but for us. These voices saw law as a way to bring justice to the earth, to bring order to chaos, to give trees rights, to serve hope on shining platters to those denied. That dream has been passed down to a generation of lawyers who as heirs stand at a crossroad and in crosswinds. We can choose to follow the river, or to seek the path that has been so brightly paved. No one is sure which direction the lawyers of today will follow. The paved path is alluring and proven. It provides security and distance. But, oh! how the river still calls us. With its uncertainty and turbulence, it still calls us. Knowing we will sacrifice and suffer, it still calls us. For the voices in the river lived long enough to understand that every shell does not contain a jewel inside, and that every paved path is not free of traps. The voices from the river still call because they have experienced the calmness and peace of the river and made it theirs. They have grown accustomed to the rapids because it helped them to grow.

The voices call because they know that the river is the only way out of this present state. They, too, tried to address the problems of the profession through rules and regulations, and addictions and denial. But they awakened one day to realize that all that mattered was the river. They awakened to discover that the trinkets which they had been chasing were not as valuable as the diamonds buried inside of them. Through pain they discovered peace; through a crisis they found love. Like all sojourners who at one point lost their way, they have become the voices "crying in the wilderness," trying to save us from ourselves. If we only would hear them, we could rescue ourselves, and in the process, save this profession from itself.

The river even calls out to lawyers who stand at a far distance from its source. These lawyers faintly hear the voices calling them and their practice to this ancient and divine place. They have become so secure standing on the rocks that the river and the voices seem strange and irrelevant. Lying dormant within them, however, is a place that yearns for the things that the river offers, but which has been overshadowed by ambition, greed and fame. The yearning for financial security, advancement and acceptance has silenced the yearning for the river. Even the illusive quest for excellence has become a holy symbol in a secular existence. They incessantly believe that the next brief, merger or judgment will provide the recognition, security and status that they seek. The enormous fixation over the correctness of every detail has become an end in itself. Excellence, in its narrowest sense, has become a shrine at which the profession worships, but it does not encompass the whole needs of the client or the lawyer. The true meaning behind the work is lost in the frantic pace to get it out on time, and to please the idiosyncrasies of the client or those in charge. The river and the voices fade over the years until they cannot be seen or heard anymore. These lawyers have created a world unto itself, ruled by a language that most people cannot decipher. There is much to be envied in this world, for there is much power bestowed upon those who stand on privileged stones on the riverbanks. But there is much remorse in the river, for there is so much more that these guardians could have secured for others, and themselves, as well as for the profession.

There are other lawyers who stand on the banks at the edge of the river, and listen often to the voices from the river and from within. Sometimes they are even willing to dip their feet into the water, but only briefly. They are reluctant to relinquish their positions on the banks. They are concerned about what others, who stand so seemingly secure and erect on the banks with them will think if they give themselves fully to the forces of the river. Little do they know that those confident, secure and experienced attorneys who stand next to them have similar yearnings and feelings of uncertainty as they contemplate what it would be like to live their lives and practice law from the river. Time on the stones has made it difficult for them to realize that it is not the stones that give them security, but their unwillingness to leave the stones. There is nothing certain or fixed about this profession. A number of prestigious law firms that were secure and financially prosperous have disappeared from the landscape of major cities. Retired lawyers have been stripped of their pension funds in the same manner that employees from the corporations which these lawyers represented were stripped of theirs. Many law school graduates have had to hang out their shingles as soon as they graduated, because they could not find other employment. And even though a select few will continue to have salaries and bonuses that rival corporate executives, the vast majority of lawyers worry constantly about how to take care of their families at a middle class life style. The financial allure of this profession is greater than the reality it presents to most who pursue this path. The only thing that is certain about this profession is that it will continue to exist. How it will exist, and the quality of justice it will provide for those who seek it, and the quality of life it will offer to those who work within it, are very illusive questions. The stones cannot remove this uncertainty or provide any answers. These answers lie deep in the river of our calling.

Can you feel the river? Do you sense and appreciate its omnipotence? It moves so gracefully and majestically inside us. It is there in ways that we do not fully understand or dare imagine. Yet, if we are true seekers, the river will find us; "for the whole purpose of every experience, every activity, every faculty, is to turn the human being inward and lead us back to our divine source."[414] In our most overwhelmed and confused state, the river will be there to lighten our burdens without removing them. On those days when we would prefer not seeing clients or students because we feel we have nothing to offer, it will give us what we need. When we sense that our values and ethical moorings are being tested by violent winds, we are secure in the knowledge that they are connected to an immovable anchor at the bottom of the river that can always hold and sustain us.

Our journey reminds us that the certainty we seek in law is merely an illusion. In the life and work of the lawyer there are many shifting sands. Cases we rely on today will be overturned tomorrow. Judges whose decision we think we can predict and gauge render decisions and write opinions that are utterly inconsistent with what they have done in the past. Clients who always pay on time stop paying. Areas within our practice that are so lucrative dry up as the economy and other forces beyond our control shift and change. To do the work of a lawyer requires us to live with a high level of uncertainty and ambiguity. Some have argued that it is the existence of ambiguity in words, facts, law and policy which serves as the foundation for the existence of lawyers and the legal profession. Yet that same ambiguity and uncertainty serve to disturb our sense of balance and slowly erode our values. We learn to manipulate words, situations, rules and people so much that we begin to feel as if it is all a game. The culture within which we operate not only embraces these patterns as acceptable, but also rewards those who do it very well. If we are not careful we can lose sight of what drew us to the profession in the first place.

If there is not a place where we can consistently go inside ourselves to find clarity, meaning and purpose, then we will be engulfed in a whirlwind of ideas and practices that gives us no ultimate meaning, despite providing us with monetary rewards. The place we seek for guidance and centering must not be something that we visit only in moments of crisis. It cannot be a marginal part of our existence. The river does not work that way. Dipping our feet into it once in a while just to make sure it is still there, will not provide us with the clarity, rejuvenation or insight that we seek. We must know the river, and the river has to know us. Whatever path we pursue must be pursued seriously and with reverence. Once we discover its benefits we will seek it constantly as so many of the lawyers I described in this book do. They seek it daily for sustenance and strength. They bathe in it in order to cleanse themselves of the "stuff" that people dump on them everyday. They wash their sinful clothes on the banks of the river when they make mistakes, violate trusts, deviate from the path, disappoint loved ones, or forsake the river. They stand in amazement as the river washes their sins away.

When we make the river a part of our lives it can become a part of our work. We will give more of ourselves to what we do and those we serve will intuitively sense the power of our calling and actions. If we travel this path throughout our career then we will leave a lasting and precious imprint on the sands of life. There is no guarantee of riches or fame. There is no promise of bonuses or partnerships. There is only one thing that we will receive and surely never lose – our souls. The following passage from The Bhagavad Gita captures the essence of the lawyer's spiritual reward. "At the beginning, mankind and the obligation of selfless service were created together. 'Through selfless service, you will always be fruitful and find the fulfillment of your desires': this is the promise of the Creator."[415] When we have done our work, we will know that it was done from our hearts. We will know that it touched the lives of others and that we left the profession and the world in a better state – at least that part of the profession and world we occupied. And when we come to the end of our journey and turn in our last brief or grade sheet, the river will say, "well done thy good and faithful servant of justice. The battles are fought, your faith was preserved, now enter into the everlasting joy that you have fashioned with your heart, refined by your choices, and cleansed by your time in the waters of life."

My Journey in the River

I have listened to the voices from the river and they have served as the source of my calling in law. It is because of these majestic yearnings and voices that I first chose to pursue this path. They reminded me of the suffering of my people as I grew up in a segregated south that questioned my self-worth. The voices showed me the "strange fruit" that hung on southern trees and looked like me. The voices were with me when I raked the lawns of wealth and power; they remained with me as I returned home to the yards of deprivation and love. These voices created images of justice and change that I did not fully understand but knew I had to pursue. I would dream about a different reality than the one in which I lived, and somehow magically believed that I could make a difference. The voices led me to believe in the power of law to change, and the impotence of law to love. I listened to the voices though I questioned my own ability to master law or to swim in the river.

Attending segregated schools created a sense of doubt in my ability to compete against those who were different from me. Like many Black children in the segregated south I grew up with an inferiority complex. Despite the confidence and pride that my teachers instilled within me, I still had lingering doubts about whether I was good enough to succeed in the white world at its highest intellectual levels. Even when I attended an integrated university, I knew that I was there more because of my athletic talent than my intellectual ability. So I continued to wear the inferiority badge of segregation on the inner lining of my mind, though the outward appearance sent a different message. The voices continued to speak to me as I tried to maneuver through college and incorporate new ideas into my world view. They never stopped speaking to me, but there were times when I stopped listening. I was confused about what the river was saying and what it had to offer. Yet life and all of its uncertainty and chaos has a way of driving us back in the direction of the river. I began to listen again, though not ready to dive in fully, and certainly, not knowing how to swim.

Since I had been taught about the river long before I was introduced to the law, I walked into law school wearing sandals of faith. I traveled where my mother and father dared not dream about traveling, because my mother never went to school and my father never finished grade school. Yet they gave me these sandals of faith and these blankets of love, and pushed me out into the world. The struggle and flow of the river toward justice opened up a new passageway so that I could enter law school through the back door. When I initially applied to the University of Oklahoma Law School, I was told that my LSAT score was too low to be admitted. About nine months later I was contacted about a new admissions program which the law school had developed as a result of litigation that questioned the fairness of its traditional admissions policies and procedures. It was in this summer program that I finally threw off those badges of intellectual inferiority. In the field of my dreams, I saw myself excelling, competing against white students whom I initially thought knew more about the law than I. This pattern continued when the traditional admits arrived in the fall. I made the Dean's list at the end of my first, year and I knew then that the summer experience was not a fluke - and that the river was calling me to a higher place.

In my second year the currents led me to Derrick Bell's first edition of *Race, Racism and American Law,* and I was reminded of my purpose and given more tools with which to work. I used his seminal text to teach an undergraduate course entitled, "Law and the Black Community." Not only did this process deepen my understanding of the legal quest of my people for justice and equality, but also began laying the foundation for my future career in legal education. Rumors began to circulate around the law school that the faculty was preparing me to join them one day. Though I had thrown off the badges of segregation, this seemed like a farfetched idea, but the power of the river in my life made it feel real and possible. Confirmation of the river arrived in my third year when I was approached by one of the visiting professors, Tom Mason, who inquired about my interest in applying for a teaching position at his law school, the University of Mississippi. Though I already had accepted an offer to work as a staff attorney for the Federal Trade Commission in Chicago, I could tell from this encounter that the river was drawing me in a different direction. That spring, the institution which I entered through the backdoor proudly awarded me my degree through the front door.

I eventually ended up teaching at the University of Mississippi School of Law, but that farfetched rumor became a reality when five years after graduation, I was offered a position at the University of Oklahoma Law School. The river renewed itself when I was asked to teach in the same summer program which had opened the door for me to enter this profession. The voices from the river kept guiding me through places, to positions and into lives that at first were strange to me, but became my home. This little Black boy who grew up in a segregated town, surrounded by visible and invisible signs of restraint, inferiority and doubt, rode the river to become an attorney, law professor, dean, provost and U. S. presidential appointee to the Board of Directors of the Legal Services Corporation. There were many stops, dams, and treacherous waters along the way, but my deep faith in the power of God and the goodness of the river allowed me to continue on this journey. The majestic flow of the rivers has guided me through divorces, the tragic deaths of loved ones, life long illnesses and emotional pain. The internal balance and blessings of its waters have brought me love, enduring friendships, an inspiring church family, wonderful children and grandchildren, and a magnificently beautiful, loving and supportive wife.

I spoke back to the river once and it smiled at me. I knew then that I could continue to speak truth to the river, as others spoke truth to power. The river is my power. It is what I offer to those who are willing not only to listen, but also to hear its calling and feel its power. I offer it not because it belongs to me, but because I believe so deeply in its righteousness, goodness and eternal movement. I offer it to the legal profession because I believe it offers a way back home. I offer it because it is what this profession so desperately needs. I offer it because it is the only thing I feel completely confident about in the law. I have finally learned how to swim, and the water is fine.

ENDNOTES

[1] Harold Berman, *Law and Revolution: The Formation of the Western Legal Tradition* (Cambridge:Harvard University Press, 1983).

[2] See infra page 24 for a list and description of the values that I believe are most important for the legal profession.

[3] *Everson v. Bd of Educ.*, 330 U.S. 1 (1947); *McCollum v. Bd of Educ.*, 333 U.S. 203 (1948); *Zorach v. Clauson*, 343 U.S. 306 (1952); *Engel v. Vitale*, 370 U.S. 421 (1962); *School Dist. v. Schempp*, 374 U.S. 203 (1963); *Wallace v. Jaffree*, 472 U.S. 38 (1965); *Epperson v. Arkansas*, 393 U.S. 97 (1968); *Walz v. Tax Com'n*, 397 U.S. 664 (1970); *Lemon v. Kurtzman*, 403 U.S. 602 (1971); *Committee for Public Educ. v. Nyquist*, 413 U.S. 756 (1973); *Meek v. Pettinger*, 421 U.S. 349 (1975); *Stone v. Graham*, 449 U.S. 39 (1980); *Larkin v. Gendel's Den, Inc.*, 459 U.S. 116 (1982); *Lynch v. Donnelly*, 465 U.S. 668 (1984); *Aguilar v. Felton*, 105 S. Ct. 3232 (1985); *Edwards v. Aguillard*, 482 U.S. 578 (1987); *Zobrest v. Catalina Foothills School Dist.*, 509 U.S. 1 (1993), *Locke v. Davey*, 540 U.S. 712, 124 S.Ct. 1307, (December 2003).

[4] Gretel Ehrlich, *From Islands, The Universe, Home* http://www.rivernetwork.org/newsites/quotes.txt (last updated May 2003).

[5] *Streamscapes: Aquatic Education and Information.* <http://www.streamscapes..org/newsites/quotes.txt (last updated May 2003).

[6] *Id.*, p. 2.

[7] Leonardo da Vinci, www.rivernetwork.org/newsites/quotes.txt (last updated May 2003).

[8] Langston Hughes, *The Negro Speaks of Rivers* (1922), http://www.eecs.harvard.edu/~keith/poems/rivers.html (last updated May 2003).

I've known rivers ancient as the
world and older than the flow of
human blood in human veins.
My soul has grown deep like the rivers.

I bathed in the Euphrates when
dawns were young,
I built my hut near the Congo and
it lulled me to sleep,
I looked upon the Nile and raised
the Pyramids above it,
I heard the singing of the Mississippi
when Abe Lincoln went down to
New Orleans,
And I've seen its muddy bosom turn
all golden in the sunset.

 I've known rivers;
Ancient, dusky rivers;
My soul has grown deep like
the rivers

[9] Maulana Karenga and Jacob Carruthers, eds., *Kemet and the African Worldview* (Los Angeles: University of Sankore Press , 1986), p. 90.

[10] William Stuntz, "Christian Legal Theory," 116 *Harv. L. Rev.* 1707, 1741 (2003).

[11] Abraham Heschel, *God in Search of Man: A Philosophy of Judaism* (The Noonday Press, 1955), p. 296.

[12] Love, P.G. & Talbot, D. "Defining Spiritual Development: A Missing Consideration for Student Affairs", *NASPA Journal* (1999), p. 361-375. As cited by Bryant, Choi, Yasuno, M., "Understanding the Religious Dimensions of Students' Lives in the First Year of College", *Religious and Spiritual Dimensions* 44 (Nov. 2003), p. 724.

[13] *Id.*, p. 724.

[14] Hill, Pargament, Hood, McCullough, Swyer, Larson. Zinnbauer, "Conceptualizing Religion and Spirituality: Points of Commonality, Points of Departure", *Journal for the Theory of Social Behavior* 30 (2000),: p. 66.

[15] *Id.*, p. 64-67.

[16] Emile Durkheim, *The Elementary forms of Religious Life* (New York: The Free Press, 1965), p. 31.

[17] *Supra* note 14 at 65, 67.

[18] *Id.*, p. 20.

[19] *Id.*, p. 67.

[20] *Id.*, p. 68.

[21] This approach to and definition of spirituality is very similar to that of African Spirituality "...It is an expression of African spirituality, which here means intense emotional and rational appreciation for the highest ideals and values of humankind, i.e. the transcendent and ultimate." *Supra* note 9 at 21.

[22] *Id.*, p. 297, "Spirituality is the goal, not the way of man."

[23] W. Bradley Wendel, *Professional Responsibility, Examples and Explanations*, (Aspen Publishers, 2004),.p. 4.

[24] Thomas Nelson , *Strongs' Concise Concordance and Vines' Concise Dictionary of the Bible*, 1997, p.226. "Christian love, whether exercised toward the brethren or toward men generally, is not an impulse from the feelings, it does not always run with the natural inclinations, nor does it spend itself only upon those for whom some affinity is discovered. Love seeks the welfare of all..."

[25] Robert C. Solomon, *A Passion For Justice*, (Addison-Wesley Publishing Company, 1990)

[26] *Id.*, p. 244.

[27] Hon. D. Brooks Smith, *"The Lawyer as Peacemaker"* 63 U. Pitt. L. Rev. 909, (2002).

[28] Anthony Kronman, *The Lost Lawyer: The Failing Ideals of the Legal Profession*, (Cambridge: The Belknap Press of Harvard University Press, 1993), p. 17.

[29] See discussion Infra at 348, Lawyers in Sacred Text.

[30] William Stuntz, *Christian Legal Theory*, 116 Harv. L. Rev. 1707, 1741 (2003).

[31] *Id.*, p. 1745.

[32] Jeffrie G. Murphy and Jean Hampton, *Forgiveness and Mercy*, (Cambridge University Press 1988), Martha Minnow, *Between Vengeance and Forgiveness: Facing History After Genocide and Mass Violence* (1998); *Burying the Past: Making Peace and Doing Justice After Civil Conflict*, (Nigel Biggar, ed., 2003); *Dimensions of Forgiveness: Psychological Research and Theological perspectives*, Everett L. Worthington, Jr., ed. (1998);); Luis Perez Aquirre, *Reconciliation, Justice, and Forgiveness, in Impunity: An Ethical Perspective: Six Case Studies From Latin America*, (Charles Harper, ed., 1996).

[33] Id., 37.

[34] *See infra* page 153, The Lawyer as Healer.

[35] Certain jurisdictions have adopted mandatory reporting rules in regards to the pro bono obligation of lawyers. *See, e.g.* Rules Regulating the Florida Bar 4-6.1(d). "Each member of the bar shall annually report whether the member has satisfied the member's professional responsibility to provide pro bono legal services to the poor. Each member shall report this information through a simplified reporting form that is made a part of the member's annual membership statement…The failure to report this information shall constitute a disciplinary offence under these rules." Among many other jurisdictions, Maryland has also adopted a mandatory pro-bono reporting requirement (see MD Rules of Prof. Conduct 16-901, 16-903). In the criminal areas there is an understanding that lawyers will accept judicially assigned case for indigent defendants.

[36] The Bible (Deuteronomy 15:11, New International Version), "There will always be poor people in the land. Therefore I command you to be openhanded toward your brothers and toward the poor and needy in your land."; Matthew 5:42 (New International Version), "Give to the one who asks you, and do not turn away from the one who wants to borrow from you."; Psalms 74:21 (New International Version), "Do not let the oppressed

retreat in disgrace; may the poor and needy praise your name."; Proverbs 14:31 (New International Version), "He who oppresses the poor shows contempt for their Maker, but whoever is kind to the needy honors God."; Proverbs 22:22-23 (New International Version), "Do not exploit the poor because they are poor and do not crush the needy in court, for the Lord will take up their case and will plunder those who plunder them."; Proverbs 31:9 (New International Version), "Speak up and judge fairly; defend the rights of the poor and needy."; Ezekiel 16:49 (New International Version), "Now this was the sin of your sister Sodom: She and her daughters were arrogant, overfed and unconcerned; they did not help the poor and needy."; Luke 14:12-14 (New International Version), "Then Jesus said to his host, 'When you give a luncheon or dinner, do not invite your friends, your brothers or relatives, or your rich neighbors; if you do, they may invite you back and so you will be repaid. But when you give a banquet, invite the poor, the crippled, the lame, the blind...'"

[37] See Infra page 148, Faith.

[38] Mark Perlmutter, Why Lawyers (and the rest of us) Lie and engage in other repugnant Behavior, (Bright Books, 1998), p. 30.

[39] Id., p. 157-204.

[40] Id., p. 189.

[41] Id., p.191.

[42] Id., p.192.

[43] Id., p.38.

[44] Id., p.196-199.

[45] Id., p.199-202.

[46] Id., p. 161, In defining courage Perlmutter states, "Courage is not so much an emotion as it is the product of a conscious choice, a way of being. Although the word courage comes from the Old French for 'heart,' I believe that courage depends on our ability to draw energy from the heart and collapse it into the region of the abdomen where we are centered. My own experience of operating from this place is that I feel powerful, safe,

invulnerable- at peace, loving. It is the former feelings that permit the latter; when we feel secure we are free to love."

[47] "God, give us the grace to accept with serenity the things that cannot be changed, courage to change the things which should be changed and the wisdom to distinguish the one from the other." Originally part of a 1943 sermon of Reinhold Niebuhr, cited in *Simpson's Contemporary Quotations: The Most Notable Quotes since 1950*, Compiled by James B. Simpson, Houghton Mifflin, Boston MA (1988).

[48] *See infra* page 53, Spiritual Challenges.

[49] The Bible, (Luke 21:19, King James Version).

[50] *Supra* note 30 at 1726, This concept can be found in most religious text, including Islam, which, like Christianity, has been labeled and used to impose beliefs. The Quran states, "There is no compulsion in religion..." 2:256. This perspective is articulated from a Christian perspective very eloquently by Professor Stuntz when he states, "My faith makes me less confident about my views, legal and otherwise, not more so. Christian belief is not a club to be wielded against those who do not share that belief. If anything, the club threatens those who hold it – the belief commands that believers see themselves as half-blind fools who are constantly tempted both to act in their own interest and to think too highly of themselves. Far from being a chilling threat to democracy, invoking a faith like that is something to be welcomed in a pluralist legal order."

[51] Martin Buber, *The Way of Response*, edited by N. N. Glatzer, (Schocken Books 1966), p.76.

[52] This list of resistances was created and recorded at the Equal Justice Conference in Portland Oregon in April 11-13, 2003, during a workshop on Spirituality and the Law.

[53] Harold G. Koenig, "Spiritual Assessment in Medical Practice" *American Family Physician*, January 1, 2001, citing Harold G. Koenig, M.E. McCullough, D.B. Larson. *Handbook of religion and health: A Century of Research Reviewed*. (New York: Oxford University Press 2000),

432

[54] G. Anandarajah, E. Hight, "Spirituality and Medical Practice: Using the HOPE Questions as a Practical Tool for Spiritual Assessment" *American Family Physician*, 63:81-88 (January 2001).

[55] *Id.*, p.48.

[56] R. Slaon and E. Bagiella, "Spirituality and Medical Practice: A Look at the Evidence," *American Family Physician*, (January 2001).

[57] Supra note 54.

[58] James Sass, "Characterizing organizational Spirituality: An Organizational Communication Culture Approach" *Communication Studies*, 51: 3, 195 (2000).

[59] *Id.*, p.200.

[60] http://www/abanet.org/litigation/lawyers, (last updated April 2002). In a 1993 study commissioned by the American Bar Association only 22% of people interviewed thought that the phrase "honest and ethical" describes lawyers; in fact, 40% specifically said this description does not apply to lawyers. Almost half (48%) said that as many as 3 in 10 lawyers "lack the ethical standards necessary to serve the public." Gary Hengstler and R. William Ide III, *Vox Populi – The Public Perception of Lawyers: ABA Poll*, A.B.A. J. 60, 62 (Sept. 1993). In a more recent ABA study, 40% of those polled disagreed or strongly disagreed with the statement, "Most lawyers do what is right for their clients, and still do what is right for the public." See American Bar Association Report *Perceptions of the US Justice System*, Opinion: Lawyers Being Civic Minded, released 2/24/99, available at www.abanet.org/media/perception.html. According to a 2002 ABA study, "Americans say that lawyers are greedy, manipulative and corrupt" and Americans believe that lawyers do a "poor job of policing themselves." *Public Perceptions of Lawyers: Consumer Research Findings*, prepared on behalf of ABA Section on Litigation, April 2002.

[61] http://www.abanet.org/yld/satisfaction_800.doc. *American Bar Association, State of the Profession*, p.52; M. Fisk, *A measure of Satisfaction: What America's Lawyers Think about the Profession and Their Peers.* The National Law Journal, May 28, 1990; supp at p.2 . According to the ABA Young Lawyer Division's 2000 survey, 19.7% of the more than 2000 young lawyers who were interviewed reported being somewhat or very dissatisfied with their current position, and 24.9% reported being somewhat

or very dissatisfied with the practice of law in general. ABA Young Lawyer Division Survey: Career Satisfaction (2000). According to an informal survey of members of the California bar in 1992, only 40% of lawyers reported being reasonably satisfied with their careers, while 36% reported being so unhappy they'd change careers, 16% were unhappy but inert, and 8% felt indifferent. Patrick J. Schlitz, *On Being A Happy, Healthy and Ethical Member of an Unhappy, Unhealthy, and Unethical Profession*, 52 Vanderbilt L. Rev. 871, 881 (1999), citing *It's Become a Miserable Profession*, Cal. Law., 96 (Mar 1992); A 1996 study of University of Michigan law graduates of the classes of 1990 and 1991 found that among lawyers working in firms of fifty or fewer lawyers, the percentage of graduates who were quite satisfied with their careers was only 37% for; for those working in firms of fifty or more lawyers, only 30% were "quite satisfied."

[62] Peter Riga, *Spirituality of Lawyering*, 40 Catholic Law 295, 304 (Spring 2001).

[63] Huie and Spilis, *Alcoholism and the Legal Profession,* 16 Law and Psychology Review 113, 118 (1992), cited by Boston, *Alcohol, Drugs & Law Practice: Chemical Dependency in Legal Education: Problems and Strategies*, 76 MI Bar J. 298, 298 (1997). The ABA's Commission on Impaired Attorneys once estimated that 50 percept of all disciplinary problems are rooted in chemical dependency. Studies in California, Minnesota, New Jersey, and Massachusetts found that up to two-thirds of the disciplinary actions in those states stem from chemical dependence. Cushman, *Substance Abuse in the Legal Profession: Facing Facts*, Ohio Lawyer (Sept 1989); Hennessey, *The State of the Judiciary*, 69 Mass. L. Rev. 1, 2 (1984), cited by Boston, *Alcohol, Drugs, and Law Practice: Chemical Dependency in Legal Education: Problems and Strategies*, 76 MI Bar J. 298, 298 (1997). More recent statistics reflect that the problem has not abated; according to the L.A. Times, between 30% and 40% of the California bar's discipline cases involve substance abuse in some way. Alex Gronke, *The State Assembly Oks Bar-Funded Rehab for Lawyers Health*, L.A. Times, B8, June 22, 2001. Another indicator of unhappiness with the legal profession is public admission of lawyers' unwillingness to recommend the profession to others. In a 1993 speech, Judge James Hill recounted this story:
"A lawyer in the grand tradition gave a talk some days ago. Here is how he commenced: 'How sad it is to hear myself say that after more than forty

---

years of making my own living practicing law, I would hesitate to recommend the profession to my son.'" Hon. James C. Hill, *Special Contribution: Remarks made at the 1993 National Conference of Law Reviews*, 45 Mercer L. Rev. 577, 581 (1994); "...And lawyers are an unhappy lot, leaving the profession in droves, or languishing in jobs they no longer enjoy, refusing to recommend law as a worthwhile calling for their children." Lawrence J. Fox, *A Nation Under Lost Lawyers: The Legal Profession at the Close of the Twentieth Century: Article, Money Didn't Buy Happiness*, 100 Dick. L. Rev. 531, 532 (1996). Finally, in a 1991 North Carolina Bar Association poll, over 40% of lawyers queried admitted that they would not encourage their children or other qualified persons to enter the their profession. North Carolina Bar Ass'n, *Report of the Quality of Life Task Force and Recommendations*, 4, (1991).

[64] Benjamin Sells, *Soul of the Law*, (Element 1994) p. 42-43

[65] Randy Lee, *Faith Through Lawyering, Finding and Doing What is Mine to do*, 11 Regents U.L. Rev. 71,79-80 (Month and Date).

[66] *Supra* note 28.

[67] *Id.*, p.17.

[68] *Id.*, p.109-162.

[69] *Id.*, p.109.

[70] *Id.*, p.375-376.

[71] *Supra* note 64.

[72] *Id.*, p.176.

[73] *Id.*, p.178.

[74] There are numerous examples of prosecutors calling defendants animals or likening them to animals during criminal trials. For example, a Texas prosecutor and District Attorney drew objections from defense counsel when they compared defendant Raymond Gonzales to an "animal" and likened Gonzalez's actions to that of Osama bin Laden. J. R. Gonzales, *Gonzalez Gets Life in Prison for Murder*, Corpus Christi Caller-Times (Texas), 4/16/02, B1. During the New Jersey trial of Frank Pennington, in his

opening statements the prosecutor called the defendant "a jackal," "a stranger to humanity," and "cold, calculated, implacably evil." P.R. Chenoweth, *Digest of Recent Opinions*, New Jersey Law Journal, 7/26/90, p. 51. In Anthony Nightengale's Chicago murder trial, prosecutors referred to him as "a debased animal" and "scum." Charles Mount, *Judges Order New Trial, Cite Prosecutors' Misconduct*, Chicago Tribune, 4/14/88 4C. During a Florida trial, prosecutors called defendant Willie Jasper Darden "an 'animal' who should not be let out of his cell without 'a leash' held by a guard." Philip Hager, *4th Ruling Issued in Death Sentence; Trial Held Fair for Man Called 'Animal' by Prosecutor*, Los Angeles Times, 6/24/86, Part 1, page 19. There are also many examples of prosecutors referring to criminal defendants as devils and using other grim epithets. In California, a prosecutor called defendant Luis Martinez "a mastermind of evil" during trial in 2003. Alex Roth, *Prosecutor Calls Kidnap Defendant 'A Mastermind of Evil*,' San Diego Union-Tribune, 2/7/03, B-3:7, B-2:1. Defendant Leroy V. "Tino" George, Jr. was called "the 'Grim Reaper'" by the prosecutor during his 1997 murder trial in Louisiana. Christopher Baughman, *Defense Says Suspect in Five Deaths was Trying to Flee Beating, Gunfire*, The Advocate (Baton Rouge, LA) 3/23/01 1-B, 2-B. Capital murder defendant Ryan Fincher was described by prosecutor Fred Rabalais Jr. as "a devil" during his trial. Eric Farcia, *Prosecutor Calls Defendant 'Devil' as Trial in Torture-Slaying Begins; Man Accused in Killing in Kennedale in '96*, The Dallas Morning News, 11/19/97, 33A. During Scott Cobb's murder trial in New York, the prosecutor called him an "agent of death." *Prosecutor Calls Defendants in Byrne Killing 'Agents of Death*' New York Times, 2/22/89, B1.

[75] See Discussion Infra in Spiritual Basis of Law, p. 71

[76] *Supra* note 64 at 16.

[77] *Supra* note 65 at 88.

[78] Graham, Furr, Flowers and Burke, "Religion and Spirituality in Coping with Stress," *Counseling and Values*: 46. 1. p 2 (2002), citing P.S. Richards, A.E. Bergin, "A spiritual strategy for counseling and Psychotherapy,"*American Psychological Association.*

[79] *Id* citing T.G. Belavich, Address, *The Role of Religion in Coping with the Daily Hassles,* (American Psychological Association, copy on file with ERIC Document Reproduction Service No. ED 393 042).

[80] *Id.,* p.61.

[81] D.R. Hodge, P. Cardenas, H. Montoya, "Substance Use: Spirituality and religious participation as protective factors among rural youth." *Social Work Research,* 25: 3 p. 153 (2001)

[82] C. Brooks, C. Matthews, "The Relationship among substance Abuse Counselors' Well Being, Values and Self Actualizing Characteristics and the Impact on Clients' Spiritual Well – Being" *The Journal of Addiction & Offender Counseling.* 21: 1: p. 23 (2000). The connection between spirituality and the recovery from substance abuse is an important part of organizations that work specifically with lawyers who are suffering with alcohol and drug abuse. Lawyers Concerned for Lawyers, which exist in numerous jurisdictions throughout the country provide counseling to lawyers and judges who are in crisis. The 12 step program for recovery served as the founding philosophy for many of these organizations.

[83] Supra note 28 at 165-270 for a complete discussion of how other theoretical movements within the academy contributed to this same problem.

[84] "For my own part, I often doubt whether it would not be a gain if every word of moral significance could be banished from the law altogether." Oliver Wendell Holmes, *The Path of the Law,* 10 Harvard L. Rev. 457, 464 (1897).

[85] The American Heritage Dictionary , Second College Edition, (Houghton Mifflin 1991), p. 967; *See also* H.L.A. Hart, *Positivism and the Separation of Law and Morals,* 71 Harv. L. Rev. 593 (1958).

[86] For example, Natural Law theory holds that universal principles should guide human behavior and legal systems. These principles are discoverable through divine inspiration and/or human reason, and the legitimacy of laws depends upon the extent to which they preserve inherent rights of human nature. Such rights are immutable and normative. R.L. Hagman, Jr., N. Levit, and R. Delgado, *Jurisprudence Classical and Contemporary: From Natural Law to Postmodernism,* pp. 1-2 (2002). As Aristotle once said, "There is in nature a common principle of the just and unjust that all people in some way divine, even if they have no association or commerce with each

437

other." *Id.* at 3, citing *Aristotle: On Rhetoric: A Theory of Civic Discourse*, Book I, Ch. 13, at 102 (George A. Kennedy, trans., 1991).

Legal Realism also measures the legitimacy of law according to external precepts, but within a Realist conception; the measuring device is one of experience. Hagman, Levit, and Delgado, *supra*, at 157. According to Oliver Wendell Holmes, Jr., "The life of the law has not been logic, it has been experience." Cited by Mark DeWolfe, *The Common Law* (1963), p. 5. To the Realist, the law is a multi-disciplinary realm in which all aspects of experience can and do assist legal problem-solving. Hagman, Levit, and Delgado, *supra* at 157. Accordingly, legal rules as such are of very little value to problem solving, as they are essentially political interests and are therefore relevant only in the way they align with the legal interests in the dispute. *Id.* Realism insists that politics is integral to the decision-making process, and that an appropriate balance of political interests help bring about a more just society. *Id.* at 158.

The most recent challenge to positivism and formalism, Critical Legal Theory (also known as Critical Legal Studies) developed in the mid to late 1970's. Critical Legal Studies (CLS) is a thematic critique of traditional legal and political thought. Like Realism, it challenges the idea that law is objective and politically neutral. *Id.* at 402. CLS attempts to expose the belief structures that are created and perpetuated by law as essentially political and subjective ideologies. *Id.* But CLS goes further; CLS scholars argue that traditional legal doctrines are socially and historically contingent, arbitrary, hierarchical, alienating, and often destructive. *Id.*, at 403. CLS scholars therefore attempt to explore alternative visions of law and society, thereby improving and reshaping current law according to more humanistic, communitarian, and democratic principles. *Id.*, *see also* Roy L. Brooks, *Structures of Judicial Decision-Making from Legal Formalism to Critical Theory*, Durham NC: Carolina Academic Press (2002).

[87] *Supra* note 28 at 165-270.

[88] Id., p. 182.

[89] Proponents of nihilism (from the Latin root *nihil* or *nil*, meaning nothing) maintain that there is no objective truth, and thus no rational justification for moral principles. *See* Black's Law Dictionary, 7th Ed., 1999. If nothing is true, then legal reasoning is indeterminate and its claims to objectivity are false. *See* Joseph William Singer, *The Player and the Cards: Nihilism and Legal Theory*, reprinted in *Jurisprudence: Classical and Contemporary:*

438

From *Natural Law to Postmodernism* (Robert L. Hayman, Jr., Nancy Levit, and Richard Delgado, Eds., 2002).

[90] The Critical Legal Studies (CLS) movement has at its heart the belief that lawyers and judges use legal reasoning as a means to make legal and political institutions appear natural and neutral when, in fact, they are historically and socially contingent. Id., at 429. Law, in the view of CLS scholars, therefore becomes "a mechanism for creating and legitimating configurations of economic and political power." Id., CLS does this by "exploring the relation over time between the legal system and the social structure." Id. at 429-430.

[91] As Justice Oliver Wendell Holmes said, "The first requirement of a sound body of law is that it should correspond with the actual feelings and demands of the community, whether right or wrong." Reprinted in Robert S. Sommers, *Instrumentalism and American Legal Theory*, (Cornell University Press 1982), p. 41. Justice Holmes was one of the early instrumentalists, who, like many other theorists, believed that the goal of legal rules and theory derived from society's prevailing needs and interests, rather than from some other source. Id., 43.

[92] *Supra* note 1.

[93] *Supra* note 62 at 306-307.

[94] The use of water hoses by the officials in Birmingham Alabama to halt the civil rights demonstrations in 1963 is a classic example of this negative use of water. *See* R.T. Weisbrot, *Freedom Bound, A History of America's Civil Rights Movement*, p.105, WW Norton, NY (1990).

[95] *Supra* note 11 at 47.

[96] Critical Legal Studies can be credited with eloquently and persuasively making us aware of the contradictions and conflicting ideals within law, language and legal processes.

[97] *See infra* page 296, discussion of Therapeutic Jurisprudence.

[98] http://www.LawLady.com (last updated February 2005).

[99] SARS (Severe Acute Respiratory Syndrome) is a viral respiratory illness that was first reported in Asia in February, 2003; over the next few months,

the virus spread and cases were reported in over two dozen countries in Asia, North America, South America, and Europe. During the 2003 outbreak, the World Health Organization estimated that 8,098 people became sick with SARS and 774 of these died as a result. All of the people afflicted with SARS had traveled to parts of the world experiencing a SARS outbreak prior to contracting the disease. Department of Health and Human Services, Centers for Disease Control and Prevention, *Fact Sheet: Basic Information About SARS, 1/13/04.* Available at www.cdc.gov/ncidod/sars/factsheet.htm ; *see also, Understanding SARS, One Year Later,* Connecticut Post, Latest Health News (1/27/04).

[100] For example, in the words of Ohiyesa, a Santee Sioux writing in the late nineteenth century: "The elements and majestic forces in nature – lightening, wind, water, fire, and frost – are regarded with awe as spiritual powers, but always secondary and immediate in character. We believe that the spirit pervades all creation and that every creature possesses a soul in some degree, though not necessarily a soul conscious of itself. The tree, the waterfall, the grizzly bear, each is an embodied force, and as such an object of reverence." Charles Alexander, *The Soul of An Indian and Other Writings From Ohiyes,* (Kent Nerburn, ed. 1993), pp. 4-5.

[101] In his 1905 paper introducing the Theory of Special Relativity, Albert Einstein demonstrated the equivalence of matter and energy. A. Einstein, *Zur Elektrodynamik bewegter Körper,* Annalen der Physik 17 (1905).

[102] See, e.g., Johannes Kepler, *De Harmonice Mundi,* translated by Charles Glenn Wallis in *Epitome of Copernican Astronomy & Harmonies of the World,* Promethus Books, Amherst NY 1995; Fritjof Capra, *The Tao of Physics,* Shambala Pub., Boston, MA 1975; Sunny Y. Auyang, *How is Quantum Field Theory Possible?* Oxford University Press 1995; David Bohm and B.J. Hiley, *The Undivided Universe,* Routledge 1995; Niels Bohr, *Atomic Physics and Human Knowledge,* Wiley Press, NY 1958; John L. Hitchcock, *The Web of the Universe: Jung, the "New Physics" and Human Spirituality,* Paulist Press, NY 1991; and John L. Hitchcock, *Atoms, Snowflakes, and God: The Convergence of Science and Religion,* Theosophical Pub. House, Wheaton IL 1986.

[103] *See infra* page 255, Chapter on The Social Justice River.

[104] I have purposely chosen to use attorney in regards to the personality of the lawyer because the word attorney is generally defined more narrowly than lawyer. "Attorney is often used interchangeably with lawyer but in a narrower sense refers to a legal agent for a client in the transaction of business. In a still narrower sense, attorney denotes anyone legally appointed to transact another's business." American Heritage Dictionary 2nd College Edition, Houghton Mifflin 1991 p. 718. On the other hand I have purposely used lawyer to refer to the lawyer's soul because it is generally defined to encompass a broader understanding and responsibility. "Lawyer is the general and most comprehensive term for one authorized to manage the legal affairs of client, give legal advice, and plead cases in court." Id.

[105] These personality traits have been identified in various empirical studies involving lawyers and the general population. Professor Susan Daicoff has developed an extensive list of sources and studies under the banner "How Lawyers Differ From the General Population." These are located on her website at http://www.fcsl.edu/faculty/daicoff/scla99.html

[106] Some argue that many law students come to law school with these tendencies already, yet these traits are intensified due to the structure and values of legal education. http://www.fcsl.edu/faculty/daicoff/scla95.html

[107] At a conference of federal judges, Judge Helen W. Nies described some of the hardball tactics some lawyers have adopted: "Nevertheless, an uncivil lawyer is known as a Rambo litigator. ...In hardball litigation, every request by the other side is opposed with paper, with briefs, and requests for argument, even a request for a two day extension of time. Discovery requests are made deliberately ambiguous and sweeping and no matter what reply is made, there's a charge of non-compliance. Depositions are scheduled at inconvenient times and mail is sent by slow boat to shorten the other side's time to respond. At depositions, there are senseless objections, bickering and delay and depositions are endless in numbers, whether there's anything under the next stone or not. Many stones do not have to be turned over. If a minor motion is lost, there's a demand for sanctions for a frivolous pleading." Tenth Annual Judicial Conference of the U.S. Court of Appeals for the Federal Circuit, 146 F.R.D. 205, 216-217 (1992).

[108] Gary Zukav, The Seat of the Soul, (New York, Fireside Books 1989), p. 140.

[109] Kenneth "Bear Hawk" Cohen, *Honoring the Medicine: The Essential Guide to Native American Healing*, (One World 2003) p. 38. "To say of two related spiritual phenomena 'A symbolizes or represent B' is not always accurate. The Bear does not simply represent the West, he is the West. The healer does not dance like the Eagle, she is the Eagle dancing. The swan feather on the altar does not represent the swan; it is the swan medicine power."

[110] John S. Mbiti, *African Religions and Philosophy* (Heinemann, 1969) p. 57.

[111] G. W. Curtis, from Lotus Eating: Hudson and Rhine: recorded in River Network, www.rivernetwork.com (last updated February 2005).

[112] Roderick Haig-Brown, recorded in River Network

[113] *Supra* note 108 at 37. "*It* has no beginning and no end but flows toward wholeness."

[114] The Bible (John 7: 38, King James Version).

[115] In her article *Lawyers and Substance Abuse*, Jennifer L. Reichert cites a fact sheet from the American Bar Association's (ABA) *Commission on Lawyer Assistance Programs*, which found that "over 56,000 ABA members will have a lifetime dependency disorder; over 30,000 will have a lifetime drug disorder (other than alcoholism); and over 100,000 will have a lifetime substance abuse disorder." 36 Trial 6, 76 (2000). Further, a Washington state study found that "18% of lawyers who practiced anywhere between two and twenty years had developed a problem with alcohol and that number increased to twenty-five percent among lawyers who practice more than twenty years." Nathaniel S. Currall, *The Cirrhosis of the Legal Profession – Alcoholism as an Ethical Violation or Disease Within the Profession*, 12 Geo. J. Legal Ethics 739, 741 (1999). Other studies have estimated that nearly 70% of lawyers are likely to have an alcohol problem at some point in their career, and 15-18% of lawyers were "problem drinkers." Connie J. A. Beck et al., *Lawyer Distress: Alcohol-Related Problems and Other Psychological Concerns Among a Sample of Practicing Lawyers*, 10 J. L. & Health 1, 3, 5-6 (1995). One 1992 study estimated that the occurrence of substance abuse in the legal profession ranges from 10% to 20%. John V.

McShane, *Disability Probation and Monitoring Programs*, 55 Tex. B. J. 273, 273 (1992).

Equally chilling was a study done at Johns Hopkins University in 1990, which found that lawyers were more likely to suffer from Major Depressive Disorders than members of 103 other occupations. William W. Eaton, et al., *Occupations and the Prevalence of Major Depressive Disorder*, 32 J. Occupational Med. 1079 (1990), cited in Schlitz, *supra* fn. 42 at 874. A study of Washington lawyers found that 19% suffered from significantly elevated levels of depression, while a study of Arizona lawyers found that two years after graduation from law school, 17% of lawyers suffered from depression, roughly double that of the general population. *Supra* note 42, at 874-875. The Arizona study also found elevated levels of anxiety, hostility, and paranoia among law students and lawyers as compared to the general population. *Id.* at 876. The Washington study found "alarming rates," of anxiety, social alienation and isolation, obsessive-compulsiveness, paranoid ideation, interpersonal sensitivity, phobic anxiety, and hostility. *Id.* In an interview with Carol Burnett of the National Institute for Occupational Safety and Health in Cincinnati, Ohio, one author learned that law graduates rank 5th in incidence of suicide. Krieger, *Supra* note 46, at 115.

Further, studies suggest that women who have completed six or more years of post-secondary education (which includes lawyers) have substantially higher divorce rates than women generally, and of these women, the divorce rate for lawyers was twice the divorce rate for female doctors and 25% to 40% higher than for female professors. Teresa M. Cooney and Peter Uhlenberg, *Family-Building Patterns of Professional Women: A Comparison of Lawyers, Physicians, and Post-Secondary Teachers*, 51 J. Marriage & Fam. 749, 751 (1989), *Supra* note 42, at 879. These results were supported by a study done drawing information from the 1990 census which found that the percentage of lawyers who are divorced is substantially higher than the percentage of doctors who are divorced, and the difference is more pronounced in women. *Supra* note 42, at 878-879.

[116] Barbara Bowe, Bonnie Waters, Nancy Brown, Jeffrey Fortang. This statement was offered by one of the above members of the staff of the Boston Office of Lawyers Concerned for Lawyers during an interview conducted by the author. Boston, MA, 10 June, 2004.

[117] The Boston Office of Lawyers Concerned for Lawyers describes itself; "...a private, non-profit Massachusetts' corporation...the state's sole lawyer assistance program, LCL assists lawyers, judges and
law students who are experiencing any level of impairment in their ability to function as a result of

personal, mental health, addiction or medical problems."
http://www.lcl.com (last updated June 2004).

[118] *Supra* note 117.

[119] Id.

[120] Id.

[121] Id.

[122] Id.

[123] *Supra* note 108 at 147.

[124] Some of them are the International Alliance of holistic lawyers,
Association of Collaborative Lawyers, Renaissance Lawyer, Contemplative
Law Society, and various peer group discussions sponsored and coordinated
by local Lawyers Concerned for Lawyers organizations.

[125] http://www.RenaissanceLawyer.org (last updated June 2004).

[126] Unknown Author, *Negro Spiritual*, Arranged by Jimmie Abbington (GIA
Publication, Inc).

[127] *Model Rules of Professional Conduct*, (Foundation Press, 2004).

[128] Deborah L. Rhode, *Ethics by the Pervasive Method*, 42 J. Legal Educ. 31
(1992).

[129] Supra note 108 at 144.

[130] This view of temptation is captured in the New Testament book of
James. Paul writes, "My brethren, count it all joy when ye fall into divers
temptations; knowing this, that the trying of your faith worketh patience."
The Bible (James 1:2-3, King James Version).

[131] Supra note 108 at 144. discussing the metaphor of temptation as a
magnet.

---

[132] Id.

[133] Derek Bok, *Access To Justice: The Social Responsibility of Lawyers: Markets and Mindwork*, 10 Wash. U. J.L. & Policy 1, 7 (2002). See also R. J. Sheran, D. K. Amdahl, *Minnesota Judicial System: Twenty-five Years of Radical Change*, 26 Hamline L. Rev. 219 (2003). Derek Bok comments on the lack of civility in the legal profession: "For example, in the legal profession, formal rules cannot bring about genuine civility in the way lawyers interact with one another. It is therefore hardly surprising that as law firm competition has increased, most lawyers of my generation would regretfully agree that standards of civility have declined."

In Bok's book several Minnesota lawyers and judges comment on the topic of civility in the legal profession over the last several decades:
"The two most significant changes in professional courtesy in the law the last two decades are the lack of trust between lawyers and the lack of respect or civility. When I began practicing law, I was able to trust the word of a lawyer on the other side of a deal or in litigation. Along the way, I've had the experience of being "burned" such that for the last decade, any understanding with another lawyer has to be in writing. The other change is the lack of respect. Lawyers should at least have the professional courtesy to be polite and civil to each other. Too much grandstanding."

"Is it for the lawyer's ego or for show for the client? I recently had the experience where a lawyer would not even shake my hand when I extended it." *Lynn M. Anderson, Vice President and General Counsel, Holiday Companies.*

"I believe that about twenty years ago, we entered an era which has been marked by a lack of civility among lawyers, a civility that obtained when I first entered the practice of law in 1956." *William S. Fallon, St. Paul attorney; former Assistant U.S. District Attorney*

"Professional courtesy has diminished sometimes because of the lack of mutual respect shown in written and oral comments made by the bench and bar about themselves. It is common to hear lawyers disparaging the work or inferior life of other lawyers. All too frequently it may be a judge (temporarily removed from viewing him/herself as a lawyer) who makes public pronouncements on such issues. ...In the recent past, I've wondered, often and sometimes out loud, what makes some lawyers so angry, so early in life or in the day. Their stomachs won't last if they continue to see every disagreement as Armageddon." *Theodore J. Collins, St. Paul attorney;*

former President, Ramsey County Bar Association and Minnesota State Bar Association

[134] Id., p. 151.

[135] Joseph Jaworski, *Synchronicity, The Inner Path of Leadership*, (Berrett-Koehler Publisher 1996), p. 127.

[136] *Supra* note 64 at 34

[137] See Chapter *Infra* at 279 on "New Streams and Old Dams, where various forms of Holistic practices are discussed.

[138] John McShane, (Paper presented at the Seventh Annual Conference of the International Alliance of Holistic Lawyers, Marathon, Fl., Nov. 4-7, 1999).

[139] *Supra* note 65 at 94 - 95

[140] Joseph Allegretti, *The Lawyer's Calling, Christian Faith and Legal Practice*, (Paulist Press, New York, 1996) p. 52.

[141] *Supra* note 65 at 94.

[142] *Supra* note 65 at 94

[143] *Supra* note 65 at 94 -95

[144] For an overview of the various philosophical perspectives on truth, See Fredrick F. Schmitt, *Truth: A Primer*, (Westview Press, 1995).

[145] *Supra* note 85, The American Heritage Dictionary, p. 1300 n.6, one of the definitions of truth is God.

[146] The Bible, (John 8:32, King James Version).

[147] Rule 1.6 (a), ABA Model Rules of Professional Conduct (2003). Commission on the Evaluation of the Rules of Professional Conduct, ABA Executive Summary: Changes the Commission Proposed (2001). Available at www.abanet.org/cpr/e2k-exec_summ.html The Model Rules of

Professional Conduct, defining attorney-client confidentiality, have been adopted in 42 states. States that have not adopted these rules have often used them as a guide when creating their own rules of professional conduct.
"A lawyer shall not reveal information relating to the representation of a client unless the client gives informed consent, the disclosure is impliedly authorized in order to carry out the representation or the disclosure is permitted by paragraph (b)."

[148] Rule 1.6(b), ABA Model Rules of Professional Conduct (2003). *Id*, "A lawyer may reveal information relating to the representation of a client to the extent the lawyer reasonably believes necessary: (1) to prevent reasonably certain death or substantial bodily harm; (2) to secure legal advice about the lawyer's compliance with these Rules; (3) to establish a claim or defense on behalf of the lawyer in a controversy between the lawyer and the client, to establish a defense to a criminal charge or civil claim against the lawyer based upon conduct in which the client was involved, or to respond to allegations in any proceeding concerning the lawyer's representation of the client; or (4) to comply with other law or a court order."

[149] *See infra* page 153, The Lawyer as Healer.

[150] Although there is no uniform federal rule governing the evidentiary privileges pertaining to priests and psychologists, the Federal Rules of Evidence state that privilege is, "...to be governed by the principles of the common law as they may be interpreted by the courts of the United States in light of reason and experience. However, in civil actions and proceedings, with respect to an element of a claim of defense as to which State law supplies the rule of decision, the privilege of a witness, person, government, State of political subdivision thereof shall be determined in accordance with State Law." *F.R.E. 501*
While some states rely on common law for all or most evidentiary rules, other states have codified evidentiary rules regarding privilege. For example, California has specific rules regarding the psychotherapist-patient privilege *(Sec. 1014 of the California Evidence Code)* as well as penitent-clergy privilege *(See Secs. 1030-1034 of the California Evidence Code).* Similarly, *Sec. 505 of the Texas Rules of Evidence (Article V)* provides an evidentiary privilege for communications to members of the clergy, while *Sec. 510 of Article V* protects the confidentiality of mental health information in civil cases, including communications between patients and mental health professionals.

[151] Bill van Zyverden, the founder of the International Alliance of Holistic Lawyers, operates his practice out of a Holistic Justice Center in Middlebury Vermont.

[152] *Supra* note 108 at 106.

[153] The Bible, (Hebrews 1:11, New King James Version), "Now faith is the substance of things hoped for, the evidence of things not seen."

[154] Author unknown

[155] Justice Warren Burger, *Annual Report on the State of the US Judiciary*, American Bar Association Journal, Vol. 68, pp. 274-277 (March 1982), "The obligation of our profession is, or has long been thought to be, to serve as the healer of human conflict."

[156] http://www.healingandthelaw.org (last updated February 2005).

[157] *Supra* note 85 at 599.

[158] Bill Van Zyverden, telephone conversation with author, 16 March 2004.

[159] See *infra* at page 283 Chapter on "Holistic Forms of Practice."

[160] CNN's *Larry King Live*, (broadcast September 2002).

[161] Ed Shapiro, telephone conversation with author 23 March 2004.

[162] Id.

[163] Maureen Holland, "On My Litigation Practice" (Paper presented at the Tenth Annual Conference of the International Alliance of Holistic Lawyers, Lake Tahoe, California October 2002),

[164] Stefani Quane, (Paper presented at the Annual Conference of the International Alliance of Holistic Lawyers, Lake Tahoe, October 2002); See also http://www.Ladylaw.com (last updated October 2002).

448

[165] Phil Penningroth and Barbara Penningroth, *A healing divorce: Transforming the end of your relationship with ritual and ceremony*, (First Books Library, 2003), p. 265-364.

[166] Some common United States business rituals include opening business meetings with the shaking of hands and small talk unrelated to the immediate business, the notion that negotiation is problem-solving through "give and take" based on strengths and weaknesses, and the ritual of extracting an oral agreement at the first meeting. *See* "Let's Make a Deal! American Business Culture", http://www.executiveplanet.com (last updated February 2004).

[167] Laurel J. Sweet, "Drunken Driver Sentenced; Woman to Serve Three Years for Killing Cyclist", *Boston Herald*, 17 October, 2002.

[168] David Hodge, "Spiritual Assessment: A review of Major Qualitative Methods and a New Framework for Assessing Spirituality." *Social Work* , Vol 46. Issue 3 (2001): 203.

[169] Steven Covey, *Seven Habits of Highly Effective People*, (Fireside Books, New York 1990).

[170] *Supra* note 135 at 1

[171] source unknown

[172] The Bible (Jeremiah 8:22, King James Version).

[173] Supra note 108 at 44.

[174] Id., p. 45.

[175] *Supra* note 85 at 787.

[176] Andres G. Nino and Peter Lang, "Spiritual Quest Among Young Adults," *Education as Transformation*, 2002), P. 54.

[177] Jack Maguire, *Essential Buddhism*, (Pocket Books, 2001), p. 112.

[178] Susan Daicoff, *Lawyer, Know Thyself: A review of Empirical Attorney Attributes bearing on Professionalism*, 46 am. U. L. Rev. 1337 (1997).

[179] Id., 1349.

[180] Id., 1365.

[181] Id., 1372.

[182] Id., 1377.

[183] Id., 1372-73.

[184] Id., 1426.

[185] Id., 1378, 1380.

[186] Id., 1381.

[187] Id., 1426.

[188] Id., 1409, "...(F)or example, recent studies reveal that while law school may have no effect on male students' approach to morality, it dramatically shifts female students' orientation from an ethic of care and compassion to an orientation similar to that of men, which typically emphasizes a right and justice orientation."citing Sandra Janoff, *The influence of Legal education on Moral Reasoning*, 76 Minn L. Rev. 193 (1991).

[189] *Supra* note 8.

[190] Ken Wilber, The *Holographic Paradigm and Other Paradoxes, Exploring the Leading Edge of Sceince*, (New Science Library Shambhala, Boulder CO. 1982).

[191] *Ordorizzi v. Bloomfield School District*, 264 Cal. App. 2d 123 (1966).

[192] *Supra* note 85 at 1109.

[193] This course and project has been cited by other authors and writers. See Steven Keeva, *Transforming Practices*, (Contemporary Books, 1999), p. 82, 178; *See also* Linda Kulman, "Redefining the American Lawyer – Ethics, Values, and Professional Fulfillment", *U.S. NEWS AND WORLD REPORT*, 2 MARch, 1998, p. 77.

450

[194] Joseph Allegretti, The *Lawyer's Calling, Christian Faith and Legal Practice*, (Paulist Press, New York, 1996).

[195] Parker Palmer, *The Courage to Teach*, (Josey-Bass Publisher, 1998), p. 76.

[196] Parker Palmer, *To Know as We are Known: A Spirituality of Education*, (Harper San Francisco, 1983), p. 115.

[197] Id., p. 115.

[198] *Supra* note 195 at 83.

[199] Id., p. 11.

[200] *Supra* note 195 at 125.

[201] This is attributable to an anonymous saying.

[202] *Supra* note 196 at 124.

[203] Christopher Columbus Langdell "A selection of cases on the law of contracts with references and citations (1871)" (Harvard University School of Law , photocopy).

[204] Steven Glazer, The Heart of Learning, Spirituality in Education, (Penguin Putnam, 1999), p. 35. quoting Rachel Remen, "Educating for Mission, Meaning, and Compassion."

[205] Id., p. 41.

[206] Id., p. 34.

[207] Id., p. 35.

[208] *Gratz v. Bollinger*, 539 U.S. 244 (2003), *Grutter v. Bollinger*, 539 U.S. 982 (2003).

[209] David Hall, *The Spirit of Reparations*, 24 Boston College Third World Law Journal 1 (2004).

[210] Perceptions of the U.S. Justice System. 1999, American Bar Association

[211] Id., p. 246.

[212] J. Deotis Robert, *The Black Theology in Dialogue*, (Westminster Press 1987), p. 74.

[213] Thomas Schubeck, "Ethics and Liberation Theology," *Theological Studies*, Vol. 56, Issue 1 (1995) p. 107.

[214] Id.,p. 170.

[215] Dennis P. McCann, *Christian Realism and Liberation Theology*, (New York: Paulist, 1986); Michael Novak, *Will It Liberate? Questions for Liberation Theology*, (New York: Paulist 1986).

[216] Id.,p. 177.

[217] Id.,p. 181.

[218] Peter H. Van Ness, *Spirituality and the Secular Quest*, (Crossroad Publishing, 1996).

[219] Id.,p. 381.

[220] Id.,p. 370.

[221] James Cohen, *Martin & Malcolm & America*, (Orbis Books, New York, 1991), p.62.

[222] *Supra* note 212 at 80-81.

[223] This includes, but is not restricted to legal service lawyers, public defenders, certain prosecutors in urban or poor rural areas, and attorneys who do pro-bono work that affects the poor.

[224] The Bible (Matthew 25: 40 & 45, King James Version).

[225] Dennis Warren, "Using Meditation processes to Enhance the practice of Law," *New Jersey Lawyer*, August 2002 p. 35.

452

226 *Supra* note 85 at 219.

227 The Bible (Ephesians 6:11, King James Version).

228 Theme of Equal Justice Conference co-sponsored by the ABA Pro Bono Committee and the National Legal Aid and Defenders Association in Portland, Oregon, April 10-12, 2003.

229 Classic examples of these approaches include; Legal Realism, Critical Legal Studies, and Humanist Legal Education.

230 The Renaissance Lawyer Society was founded in Las Vegas, Nevada, where the eight-person team dubbed "the Leaders Circle" met for a meeting and planning a retreat in June, 2001. The Society had its early roots in 2000 through the work of J. Kim Wright, J.D. The Renaissance Lawyer Society is a non-profit [501c 3] educational organization created to support innovation and transformation in the legal profession. Some of the goals of the Renaissance Lawyer Society the education of the public about the healing power of the law, respectful conflict resolution, to help legal professionals experience satisfaction and joy in the law, to provide a platform for exchange of ideas promoting understanding and collaboration in the legal community, and to help lawyers achieve, "...personal, spiritual, and intellectual growth while developing a higher level of respect for themselves and their role in society." The Renaissance Lawyer Society identifies their underlying values as integrity, flexibility, dignity, peace, love, compassion, leadership, quality, community with inclusiveness, diversity, and life-long learning. *See http://*www.renaissancelawyer.com (last updated April 2003).

231 *Supra* note 178.

232 http://www.collabcan.com/lawyers/development.shtml (last updated April 2003).

233 http://www.collaborativelawatlanta.com/ (last updated February 2005).

234 James Lawrence, *Collaborative Lawyering: A New Development in Conflict Resolution,* 17 Ohio St. J. on Disp. Resol.43, 442 (2002).

235 Rita Pollack, interview with author, Boston, March 2004.

[236] http://www.collaborativelaw.com (last updated February 2005); *See also* http://www.collabgroup.com (last updated February 2005); and http://www.collaborativelawatlanta.com (last updated February 2005).

[237] Marilyn Beloff, "Archetypal Jewish Divorce Rituals (The Get): Witnessing the Voices", Ph.D diss., Pacifica Graduate Institute, May 2, 2001).

[238] Rita Pollak, interview with author, March 2004.

[239] Id., p. 281.

[240] Id.

[241] *Supra* note 234 at 442-443.

[242] Comments of J. Kim Wright in regards to a draft manuscript.of this book.

[243] *Supra* note 233.

[244] *Supra* note 234 at 444.

[245] Rita Pollak, "Beyond the Code of Professional Responsibility: Can Spiritual Values Be our Compass?" (Paper presented at Suffolk University Law School, Boston, MA, 1998).

[246] Id.,p. 287.

[247] Id.,p. 288.

[248] Id.,p. 288.

[249] Julie MacFarlane, interview conducted by author, Boston, MA, 12 May, 2004; In conducting interviews with numerous collaborative lawyers and asking them why they chose collaborative law, she summarized their comments as a kind of "coming to Jesus language," a "coming home or finding of inner serenity."

[250] David B. Wexler, (ed) *Therapeutic Jurisprudence: The Law as a Therapeutic Agent.* (Durham: Carolina Academic Press 1990); Bruce J.

Winick, *Therapeutic Jurisprudence Applied: Essays on Mental Health Law*. (Durham: Carolina Academic Press 1997); Bruce J. Winick and David B. Wexler, (eds). *Judging In a Therapeutic Key: Therapeutic Jurisprudence and the Courts*. (Carolina Academic Press 2003); The International Network of Therapeutic Jurisprudence list over 600 articles, books and monographs that have been published on this topic http://www.law.arizona.edu/dept/uprintj (last updated Februarr 2005).

[251] David B. Wexler, *Therapeutic Jurisprudence: The Law as a Therapeutic Agent* (1990); Wexler and Winick, *Therapeutic Jurisprudence as a New Approach to Mental Health Law Policy, Analysis and Research*, 45 U. Miami L. Rev. 979, 981 (1991).

[252] David B. Wexler, *Therapeutic Jurisprudence and the Culture of Critique*, 10 J. Contemp. Legal Issues 263, 271 (1999).

[253] http://www.law.arizona.edu/depts/upr-intj (last updated February 2005). Excerpt from a lecture given by David Wexler at the Thomas Cooley Law School.

[254]Kay Kavanagh, "Don't Ask, Don't Tell: Deception Required Disclosure Denied, in Winick, Bruce J. & Wexler, David B (eds). *Judging In a Therapeutic Key: Therapeutic Jurisprudence and the Courts*. (Carolina Academic Press 2003).

[255] Mary Berkheiser, *Therapeutic Jurisprudence/Preventive Law and Law Teaching*, 5 Psych. Pub. Pol. And L. 1147, 1150 (1999).

[256] *Id* at 1149-1150.

[257] *Supra* note 253.

[258] Marjorie A. Silver, *Love, Hate, and Other Emotional Interference in the Lawyer/Client Relationship*, 6 Clinical L. Rev. 259, 276 (1999).

[259] *Supra* note 255 at 1156, footnote 69.

[260] Bruce Winick, *Client Denial and Resistance in the Advance Directive Context: Reflections on How Attorneys can identify and deal with Psychological Soft Spots*, 4 Psychol. Pub. Poly. & L. 901-923 (1998)

[261] *Supra* note 258 at 276.

[262] Id. For an excellent overview of the literature in the legal academy on this topic *see Silver 259-276.*

[263] Michael Perlin, *The Law of Healing*, 68 U. Cin. L. Rev. 407, 433(2000).

[264] *Supra* note 255 at 1155.

[265] Kerri Gould and Michael Perlin, *Therapeutic Jurisprudence: Issues, Analysis, and Application: Johnny's in the Basement, Mixing up His Medicine: Therapeutic Jurisprudence and Clinical Teaching,* 24 Seattle University L.R. 339, 355 (2000).

[266] *Supra* note 255.

[267] Rev. Ray Hammond, (Paper presented at the Black Achievers Banquet, Boston MA, 30 January, 2003).

[268] *Supra* note 255.

[269] Lucia Ann Silecchia, *Integrating Spiritual Perspectives with the Law School Experience*, 37 San Diego L. Rev. 167, 179-170. (Winter 2000).

[270] *Supra* note 14.

[271] Id., p. 304.

[272] Id., p. 54.

[273] Id., p. 304.

[274] *Supra* note 251 at 983.

[275] *Supra* note 252 at 276.

[276]

http://www.preventivelawyer.org/main/default.asp?pid=brown_program.htm (last updated February 2005).

[277] http://www.law.fsu.edu/academic_programs/humanizing_lawschool.php (last updated February 2005).

[278] Though Contemplative Law is how this approach is generally labeled, some scholars find the label confusing, and prefer to focus on the development of mindfulness awareness. I have chosen to continue to use the term Contemplative Law because this is how the majority identify the approach.

[279] See Jon Kabat-Zinn, "Catalyzing Movement Towards a More Contemplative/Sacred-Appreciating/ Non-Dualistic Society," The Contemplative Mind in Society, Meeting of the Working Group, September 29, October 2, 1994, Pocanitico, N.Y., Jon Kabat-Zinn, *Coming to Our Senses: Healing Ourselves and the World through Mindfulness*, Hyperion 2005

[280] http://www.coontemplativemind.org (last updated February 2005).

[281] http://www.contemplativemind.org (last updated February 2005).

[282] http://www.pon.harvard.edu/hmii (last updated February 2005).

[283] http://www.law.missouri.edu/csdr/mindfulness(last updated February 2005).

[284] Leonard L. Riskin, *The Contemplative Lawyer: On the Potential Contributions of Mindfullness and Meditation to Law Students, Lawyers and their clients*, 7 Harvard Negotiation Law Review 1 (2002).

[285] Id., p. 47.

[286] Id., p. 56.

[287] Id., p. 57-59.

[288] Douglas A. Codiga, *Reflections on the Potential Growth of Mindfulness Meditation in the Law*, 7 Harv. Negotiation L. Rev. 109 (2002).

[289] Id., p. 124.

[290] Id., p. 113-114.

[291] William S, Blatt, *What's Special About Meditation? Contemplative Practices for American Lawyers,* 7 Harvard Negotiation Law review 125, 126 (2002).

[292] Michael L. Hadley, *The Spiritual Roots of Restorative Justice,* (State University of New York Press, 2001), p. 43.

[293] Strang and Braithwaite, *Restorative Justice, Philosophy to Practice,* (Ashgate 2000), p. 13.

[294] Id., p. 15.

[295] Id., p. 16.

[296] For example, in Alabama a Montgomery County Circuit Judge organized a voluntary victim conferencing program in her courtroom late in 2001 in an attempt to integrate restorative justice principles into her cases. By February, 2003, 82 victims had met with their offenders after they were found guilty or convicted. Todd Kleffman, "Program Lets Crime Victims Pursue Closure", *Montgomery Advertiser,* February 28, 2003, p. 2. In many states' juvenile justice systems, restorative justice sanctions are often handed down in the form of restitution to crime victims (including giving young offenders the opportunity to earn funds to repay victims), victim-offender mediation (where offenders, victims, and a mediator meet to allow the victim to express feelings, to develop a reparative agreement, and increase the offender's awareness of the physical, emotional, and material impact of the crime). Courts also order direct service to victims, service to surrogate victims (where offender work crews repair homes and businesses damaged during break-ins or vandalism), restorative community service, services chosen by the victim, payment to victims service fund, victim impact statements, and offenders' participation in victim awareness programs. From *The Balanced and Restorative Justice Project, The Fork in the Road to Juvenile Court Reform,* 564 Annals (The Annals of the American Academy of Political and Social Science) 81, 89 (1999).
Another example of restorative justice being incorporated into the formal legal system is the Navajo Peacemaker Court. Although the Navajo judicial system is separate from the American justice system, it is similar to the way several formal international systems have integrated restorative justice. The Peacemaker Courts started in the early 1980's as part of the Navajo Common Law Project. Cases may come before the modern Peacemaker Courts in one

458

of two ways: (1)a (Navajo) District Court judge may transfer a case when it is deemed to be in the interest of justice, or (2) the disputants themselves may seek the assistance of a Peacemaker by submitting a request to their local District Court clerk. The judge then selects a naat'aanii (Peacemaker) or the disputants, if they can agree, can select their own. The Peacemaker acts as mediator or arbitrator, may lecture the participants on traditional Navajo teachings relevant to the dispute, and has the power of subpoena to compel participation. Navajo tradition or custom provides a framework for the Peacemaking ceremony, but each Peacemaker may utilize a unique style or technique for each dispute. Generally, this includes giving participants the opportunity to talk things out, express their positions, and listen to each other; the Peacemaker also listens and tries to point out the causes of the dispute and the disputants' disharmony. Then, the Peacemaker helps the parties develop a plan to settle the dispute and return the parties to harmony. This agreement may be entered as a court judgment, if the parties so wish, and is enforceable as any other judgment. Howard Brown, *An Integrated, Community-Based Dispute Resolution Forum*, 24 Am. Ind. L. R. 297, 303-307 (2000).

[297] For example, Howard Zehr, a well-known proponent of restorative justice, was called to Denver, Colorado by Timothy McVeigh's legal defense team to discuss restorative justice and act as a liaison between prosecutors and victims. He was also involved with families of the Oklahoma City bombing, and organized an exchange program where Oklahoma families hosted the families of victims of Nairobi bombings. Todd Kleffman, "Program Lets Crime Victims Pursue Closure", *Montgomery Advertiser*, Section A p.2 February 28, 2003. Mr. Zehr has also witnessed many meetings between victims and offenders, with one resulting in a burglary victim and offender shopping together to replace the furniture that was taken during the burglary. *Id.* Another example is John Rylas' grass-roots juvenile crime prevention and community-building movement in Jefferson Parish, Louisiana, which is based on restorative justice principles. The program, introduced by Rylas in October, 2002, proposes several strategies for communities to participate in restorative justice, including creating diversionary programs for juvenile property offenses, creating child abuse and neglect planning for troubled families, establishing a speakers' bureau, requiring letters of apology to victims of crimes, starting truancy and neighborhood mediation, establishing peer mediation in schools, establishing community policing, and instituting victim offender mediation for serious offenses. Christine Bordelon, "Jeff Residents Urge New Strategy in Dealing With Juvenile Crime; Restorative Justice Gains Momentum" *Times-Picayune, Metairie Picayune* p. 2 November 17, 2002.

In an interview with Sun Magazine, Marshall Rosenberg told of his experiences in mediating victim-offender meetings in prisons, often involving victims of rape. He recounted that he generally asks the victim to express what she wants the offender to know, and then Rosenberg helps the prisoner connect with the pain, repeats back what he hears, and gives the victim empathy. Next Rosenberg asks the prisoner to explain what he is feeling, then to explain why he committed the crime. The final step is to ask the victim whether there is something more she would like the perpetrator to do in order to bring things back to a state of peace. D. Killian, "Beyond Good & Evil: Marshall Rosenberg on Creating a Non-Violent World" *Sun Magazine*, February, 2003, p. 6-7. *See also* http://www.thesunmagazine.org/326_Rosenberg.pdf (last updated February 2003). The Minnesota Dept of Corrections employs a Restorative Justice Planner, Kay Pranis, who uses "restorative justice principles concurrent with training, conferences, and peacemaking circles for individual and community healing." *Brenda V. Smith, Symposium: Battering, Forgiveness, and Redemption*, 11 Am. U. J. Gender Soc. Pol'y & L. 921, 941 (2003).

[298] "...power imbalances between parties...for example, between a violent man and his female partner – are thought likely to be replicated in restorative justice processes. But processes can be devised whereby power imbalances are minimized or negated through for example, providing support to the female partner and none to the violent man, or using shuttle approach instead of face to face meetings." *See* Strang and Braithwaite, *Restorative Justice, Philosophy to Practice*, (Ashgate 2000), p. 22.

[299] Id., p. 15.

[300] *Supra* note 292.

[301] Id., p.16.

[302] Id., p. 13.

[303] Id., p. 15.

[304] Id., p. 9.

[305] Faith in this context refers to a concrete spiritual belief system that one attempts to understand, articulate and practice. Though this term is

460

commonly used to refer primarily to established western religion traditions, I am using it as a label for various forms of spiritual beliefs and practices. However the examples used in this section are taken from individuals who adhere to various western religious traditions.

[306] Russell G. Pearce, *Reflections on the American Jewish Lawyer*, 17 J.L. & Religion 179, 180-182 (2002).

[307] Israel Gresman, *The Jewish Criminal Lawyer's Dilemma*, 29 Fordham Urb. L.J. 2413 (2002). A law student well versed in the Talmud concluded that the applicability of Jewish Law to secular courts would preclude a Jew from practicing criminal defense law.

[308] Pro Bono is a standard aspirational principle and practice within the legal profession that encourages lawyers to provide a certain amount of free legal services to those who are poor or cannot afford to hire a lawyer.

[309] Stephen Carter, *The Culture of Disbelief*, (Basic Books 1993), p. 23-43.

[310] *Supra* note 52 at 296. "I must admit that in all the Christian legal organizations which I have joined, seeking answers to these questions (why does the public disdain for lawyers exist) has proven futile. Generally what I received was a spirituality that goes along side of, collateral to, the profession itself, without actually reaching within."

[311] The Bible, (Ephesians 6:11, King James Version).

[312] Michael Schutts, *What's a Nice Christian Like You Doing in a Profession Like This?* 11 Regent U.L. Rev. 137, 140 (1998/99).

[313] Id.

[314] Id., p. 141.

[315] Author's name Levine, *The Broad Life of the Jewish Lawyer: Integrating Spirituality, Scholarship and Profession*, 27 Tex. Tech L. Rev. 1199, 1206 (1996).

[316] Robert M. Cover, *Obligation: a Jewish Jurisprudence of the Social Order*, 5 J.L. & Religion 65, 66 (1987).

[317] Seth Kreimer, "The Responsibilities of the Jewish Lawyer 2" (unpublished article on file with Howard Lesnick); cited in Author's Name, *The Religious Lawyer in a Pluralistic Society*, 66 Fordham L. Rev. 1469, 1485 (Date).

[318] Joseph Allegritti, *The Lawyer's Calling*, (New Jersey: Paulist Press, 1996), p. 21.

[319] *Supra* note 315 at 1201.

[320] Carrie Menkle Meadow, *And Now a Word About Secular Humanism,, Spirituality, and the Practice of Justice and Conflict Resolution*, 28 Fordham Urb. L. J. 1073, 1079 (2001).

[321] Id., p. 1077.

[322] Id., pp.1078-1079.

[323] James A. Pike, *Beyond The Law: The Religious and Ethical meaning of the Lawyer's Vocation* , (Greenwood Press 1963), p. 94.

[324] Norman Lamm, *The Shema, Spirituality and the Law of Judaism*, 6

[325] Id., p. 7.

[326] *Supra* note 323 at 95.

[327] *Board of Professional Responsibility of the Supreme Court of Tennessee*, Formal Op. 96-F-140 (1996).

[328] Supra note 317 at 1470.

[329] Id.

[330] Id., p. 1471.

[331] I use the term God in this context to symbolize a person's quest for a deeper understanding of life and a more rewarding and meaningful life. Some people have been drawn to law because they deeply believe that the use of law will allow them to create a more just, peaceful and loving world; a

462

world more reflective of the attributes they ascribe to God. Certainly many religions "seek law" as a way to bring them in closer compliance with God's will, and thus in closer connection with God. Others seek religion hoping that it will reveal to them the ultimate law of life that they should live by.

[332] The holy book of Judaism consists of the first five books of the Bible. These books represent the essence of sacred Jewish law.

[333] *Supra* note 24 at 215. "The word nomikos is said to mean "learned in the law,"...the term may be regarded in the usual New Testament sense as applying to one skilled in the Mosaic Law."

[334] *Supra* note 11 at 326-327.

[335] Yocanan Muffs, *Love & Joy: Law, Language and Religion in Ancient Israel*, (The Jewish Theological Seminary of America, 1992), p. 9.

[336] Id., p. 341.

[337] Genesis 18:23-33.

[338] Genesis 18:25.

[339] Genesis 18: 26.

[340] Genesis 18: 30.

[341] Rabbi Wesley Gardenschwartz, interview with author, (Newton, MA Day Month and Year).

[342] Genesis 19:16.

[343] Genesis 20:26. Lot's wife, as the narrative continues, was turned to a pillar of salt because she looked back at the city.

[344] Exodus 3:3.

[345] The Bible (Exodus 4:10, King James Version); *See also* Hayim Naham Bialik and Yehosua Han Ravnitzky (eds.), *The Book of Legends , Sefer Ha – Aggadah, Legends from the Talmud and Midrash*, (Schocken Press 1992); which contains the story explaining why Moses was "slow of speech and slow of tongue."

[346] Exodus 32: 11-12.

[347] Exodus 32: 13.

[348] *Supra* note 335 a 12.

[349] Barry W. Holtz (ed), *Back to the Sources: Reading the Classic Jewish Texts,* (Simon &Schuster 1984). "TaNaKh" is what the thirty- nine books of the Bible are called by Jews. These are initials that stand for the three main parts of the entire text. "Torah (instruction), Nevi'im (prophets, namely the historical and narrative Former Prophets, and the poetic and oracular latter Prophets), and Ketuvim (Writings)."

[350] Jerold Auerbach, *Rabbis and Lawyers: The Journey From Torah To Constitution,* (Indiana University Press 1993), p. 49.

[351] *Supra* note 11 at 239.

[352] *Supra* note 350 at 55.

[353] Id., p. 54.

[354] Exodus 18:18

[355] *Supra* note 28.

[356] Kings I 11:1:3:6:11. Israel was divided during his reign because of his violation of these sacred laws. Describing Solomon's weaknesses and mistakes, "But Solomon loved many strange women…and he had seven hundred wives, princesses, and three hundred concubines and his wives turned away his heart…(A)nd Solomon did evil in the sight of the Lord, and went not fully after the Lord, as did David his father." "Wherefore the Lord said unto Solomon, Forasmuch as this is done of thee, and thou has not kept my covenant and my statutes, which I have commanded thee, I will surely rend the kingdom from thee, and will give it to thy servant."

[357] Kings I 3:16-27.

---

[358] Book of Legends, 123-24:107. The relevant portion of the story reads as follows, "So they all went to Solomon and said, 'Our Lord, we are seven, but our two headed brother says that we are eight and wishes to divide our father's estate into eight parts and take two parts himself.' Solomon called together the Sanhedrin, whom he asked 'What is your opinion in this matter?' They kept silent. Solomon said, 'Tomorrow morning there will be justice.' (Jer. 21:12) At midnight Solomon entered the Temple and standing in prayer before him who is everywhere said, 'Master of the universe, in Gibeon, when you revealed Yourself to me. You said, 'Ask what I shall give thee, I asked for neither silver nor gold, only wisdom, in order to be able to judge men with equity. Now lend light to my eyes, that I may issue verdict that is just. 'The Holy One replied, 'In the morning I shall give you the wisdom you require. In the morning Solomon sent for and gathered the entire Sanhedrin, to whom he said. 'Bring the two headed man into my presence.' After he was brought, Solomon said, 'Observe-if one head is aware of and feels what I am going to do to the other head, the man is one person. If not, he is two.' Then Solomon said, 'Bring hot water.' Hot water was brought and sprayed over one head. The other head cried out, 'My lord king we are dying, we are dying!' When Israel saw the way Solomon arrived at the verdict, they were amazed and shaken, and all were awed by him."

[359] Book of Legends 46:233. The following are some excerpts from the story found in the "Sefer Ha –Aggadah. "It is told that in the day of King Solomon, three men were journeying on the eve of the Sabbath, just as the Sabbath day's sanctity set in. So, saying to one another. 'Come, let us hide the money in one place,'they went and hid their money in a place agreed upon. At midnight, one of the three arose, took the money, and hid it in another place....So they went to try the matter before King Solomon. ...He sat down and, with his wisdom and understanding, sought to figure out a response whereby he might catch them through their own words. When they came back to him, he said to them, 'I hear of you that you are masters of the Torah and masters of wisdom and law. So I beg permission to consult with you about a suit in law: a certain king sent me a request for advice on something that happened in his realm. A young boy and a young girl who lived in the same courtyard came to long for each other. So the young boy said to the young girl, 'come let us make a sworn stipulation between us that whenever anyone wishes to betroth you, you will not respond to him except with my permission.' She so swore to him. 'After a while, the young girl was betrothed, but when the groom came to her, she said to him, 'I will not respond to you until I go to So-and so and ask his permission, since this is what I swore to him. ...She went to her childhood sweetheart and said to him, 'Take much silver and gold and release me to him who is to be my

husband.' He replied, 'since you have been faithful to your oath, I release you to him who is to be your husband, and I will take nothing from you. ...So off they went. ..they were attacked by brigands. Among them were an elderly man who seized for himself the young woman, and all the silver and gold that she and her betroth had...further , he wanted to rape her." (She convinced the man not to rape her by letting him know that her betrothed)... "though in vigor of youth, overcame his impulse and would not touch me, how much more and more should you already on in years [restrain yourself]!" [He released her and returned all the gold , silver and ornaments he had stolen. Then Solomon said to the three men] "Now, the king has sent a request to me to explicate which of these people is the most praiseworthy. Tell me your judgment. The first of the three men spoke up and said, 'I praise the young woman who stood by her oath.' The second spoke up and said, 'I praise her betrothed, who conquered his impulse and did not touch her.' The third spoke up and said: 'I praise the brigand who despoiled them of their possessions and then returned all the possessions he had taken, denying himself the use of them.' Solomon immediately spoke up and said, 'If merely from hearing the story, the third of you, who was not there, thought about the material possessions he had not seen, how much more would he think of them in the present instance!' King Solomon ordered that he be put in fetters and flogged until he confessed in the king's presence and revealed the place where he had hidden the money. 'Then they saw that the wisdom of God was within him to do justice' (1 King 3:28)"

[360] Book of Legends 29:119. Two of the riddles that demonstrates this point reads as follows, "Then the queen brought before the king a number of males and females of the same appearance-the same height, and wearing the same garb-and said to him, "sort out the males from the females for me" At once he beckoned to his eunuchs, who brought him nuts and roasted ears of corn, which he proceeded to distribute among the males and females. The males, not bashful, put the nuts and corn into their robes (whose lower edges they lifted up to form a pocket); but the females, who were modest, put them into their head kerchiefs. The king said, pointing, "These are males, and those are females," To test him once more, the queen set another exhibit before him. She had a number of men, some circumcised, some uncircumcised, stand in his presence and said 'sort out for me the circumcised from the uncircumcised." The king beckoned to the high priest to open the Ark of the Covenant, whereupon those who were circumcised bowed their bodies to half their height- more, their countenance seemed to be filled with the

radiance of the Presence. But the uncircumcised ones fell on their faces. Solomon spoke up and said, These are circumcised, and those are not."

[361] Jack Maguire, *Essential Buddhism* (Pocket Books, 2001), p. 92-94.

[362]Kings I 3:12.

[363] Ecclesiastes 1:,7 which reads, "All the rivers run into the sea: yet the sea is not full; unto the place from whence the rivers come, thither they return again." Solomon is believed to be the author of this book of the Bible. *See also* the Book of Legends 470:14.

[364] Book of Legends 469:1.

[365] Chaya Galai, *The Essential Talmud*,trans. Adin Steinsaltz, (Basic Books, New York, 1976), p. 3.

[366] Hershey H. Friedman, *Biblical and Talmudic Basis of Accounting Ethics*, The CPA Journal, 72:9 (2002), p.12.

[367] The Talmud, The Steinsaltz Edition, (Random House, Hebrew Institute for Talmudic Publication).

[368] Luke 11:52.

[369] This process attempts to separate the technical aspects of a legal case or controversy that can usually only be handled by a lawyer from the more basic aspects which could be performed by a paralegal or by other non-lawyers. The goal of this approach is to reduce the cost for legal services so that they can be more affordable.

[370] Henry Ofori-Atta, interview with author (Boston MA, 1998).

[371] The Bible (Luke 10:25; Mathew 22:35-40, King James Version), In Mathew's version Jesus provides the summary of the greatest commandments. The follow up question from the lawyer and the parable from Jesus are not included.

[372] Luke 10:36.

[373] Luke 10:37.

[374] Seat of the Soul, 37.

[375] The Bible (Luke 3:46-47, King James Version), describing his knowledge of scripture at the age of 12 in the following manner, "..,they found him in the temple, sitting in the midst of the doctors, both hearing them, and asking them questions. And all that heard him were astonished at his understanding and answers."

[376] The Bible (Mathew 5-7, King James Version).

[377] The Bible (Mathew 5: 21-22, King James Version).

[378] The Bible (Mathew 5: 22-23, King James Version).

[379] The Bible (Mathew 5: 27-28, King James Version).

[380] The Bible (Mathew 5: 38-44, King James Version).

[381] The Bible (Mathews 5:17, King James Version).

[382] The Bible (Luke 23:34, King James Version).

[383] The Bible (John I 2:1, King James Version).

[384] William Stuntz, *Christian Legal Theory*, 116 Harv. L. Rev. 1707, 1732 (2003).

[385] The Bible (Isaiah 9:6, King James Version), Christians believe that the following passage from Isaiah was referring to the future coming of the Messiah, whom they believed to be Jesus Christ; "For unto us a child is born, unto us a son is given and the government shall be upon his shoulders and his name shall be called Wonderful, Counselor, the mighty God, the everlasting Father, the Prince of Peace."

[386] Abdur Rahman L. Doi, *Shariah: The Islamic Law*, (Ta Ha Publishers, London, 1984), p. 50.

[387] Id., p. 11.

[388] Id., p. 12.

468

[389] Id., p. 365.

[390] Id., p. 13, *See* Al-Malati, Abul Husain Muhammad bin Ahmad, Al-Tanbih wal Radd, Instanbul 1936, 44-63.

[391] *Supra* note 386 at 15-19.

[392] Mohammad Hameedullah Khan, *The School of Islamic Jurisprudence*, (Kitab Bhavan, New Delhi, India, 1991), p. 10.

[393] Id., p. 9, 11.

[394] *Supra* note 177 at 117.

[395] Eknath Easwaran, *The Bhagavad Gita*, (Vintage Books 1985) p. 13 (2:47)

[396] Id., p.xxxvii

[397] The Bible (See Mark 2:22, King James Version).

[398] ABA Commission on Billable Hours Report (2001-2002)

[399] Id., p. 5.

[400] Id., p. 377.

[401] Id., p. 377.

[402] M. Cathleen Kaveny, *Billable Hours in Ordinary Time: A Theological Critique of the Instrumentalization of Time in Professional Life*, 33 Loy. U. Chi L.J. 173 (2001).

[403] Id., p. 215.

[404] *Supra* note 398 at 15.

[405] The Bible (Matthew 16:26, King James Version), "For what is a man profited, if he shall gain the whole world, and lost his own soul? Or what shall a man give in exchange for his soul?"), Mark 8:36, "For what shall it profit a man, if he shall gain the whole world, and lose his own soul?".

[406] Walter Gratzer, *Eurekas and Euphorias: The Oxford Book of Scientific Anecdotes*, (Oxford University Press 2002). Historic examples of this include Archimedes' moment of revelation when he understood the principle of specific gravity while bathing in a public baths; Joseph Priestly's discovery of the fundamental properties of oxygen, and Alexander Fleming's accidental discovery of penicillin in his laboratory in 1929. This phenomenon is succinctly summed up by Louis Pasteur's quote that, "In the fields of observation chance favors only those minds which are prepared." Louis Pasteur, inaugural lecture as professor and dean of the faculty of science, University of Lille, Douai, France, 12/7/1854, cited by Suzy Platt (ed.), *Respectfully Quoted: A dictionary of quotations requested from the Congressional Research Service*, (Washington D.C., Library of Congress 1989).
Other scientists have researched the existence of the human soul. Two texts on this topic are Larry Dossey, M.D., *Recovering the Soul: A Scientific and Spiritual Approach*, (Bantam, NY) 1989, Richard Goss, "Biology of the Soul", *The Humanist*, Vol. 54, Issue 6, 21-25 (1994).

[407] *Supra* note 108 at 235.

[408] Id., p. 240-241.

[409] John McShane, "Law as a Healing Profession," (Paper presented at the Seventh Annual Conference of the Alliance of Holistic Lawyers, Marathon, Fl., November 4-7, 1999).

[410] *Supra* note 108 at 239.

[411] Steve Keeva, *Transforming Practice: Finding Joy and Satisfaction in the Legal Life (Contemporary Books, 1999) p. 47-48*

[412] Carl Horn III, *LawyerLife, Finding a Life and a Higher Calling in the Practice of Law*, (American Bar Association, 2003) pp. 76, 78-124.

[413] See *infra* page 386, discussion RE: Billable Hours.

[414] Supra note 395 p. xlviii

[415] Id., 3:10, p. 18

Selected Bibliography

Books

Allegritti, Joseph, *The Lawyer's Calling* (New Jersey: Paulist Press, 1996).

Auerbach, Jerold, *Rabbis and Lawyers: The Journey From Torah To Constitution*, (Indiana University Press, 1993)

Berman, Harold, *Law and Revolution: The Formation of the Western Legal Tradition* (Harvard University Press, 1983).

Buber, Martin, *The Way of Response*, edited by N. N. Glatzer, (Schocken Books 1966).

Cohen, James, *Martin & Malcolm & America*, (Orbis Books, New York, 1991).

Covey, Steven, *Seven Habits of Highly Effective People*, (Fireside Books, 1990).

Doi, Abdur Rahman L., *Shariah: The Islamic Law* (Ta Ha Publishers, 1984).

Easwaran, Eknath, *The Bhagavad Gita*, (Vintage Books 1985).

Gratzer, Walter, *Eurekas and Euphorias: The Oxford Book of Scientific Anecdotes*, (Oxford University Press 2002).

Ha – Aggadah, Sefer,*The Book of Legends , Legends from the Talmud and Midrash*, Edited by Hayim Naham Bialik and Yehosua Han Ravnitzky (Schocken Press, 992).

Hadley, Michael L., *The Spiritual Roots of Restorative Justice*, (State University of New York Press, 2001),

Heschel, Abraham, *God in Search of Man: A Philosophy of Judaism*, (The Noonday Press, 1955).

Horn, Carl III, *LawyerLife, Finding a Life and a Higher Calling in the Practice of Law* (American Bar Association, 2004).

Jaworski, Joseph, *Synchronicity, The Inner Path of Leadership*, (Berrett-Koehler Publisher, 1996).

Karenga, Maulana and Carruthers, Jacob, ed. *Kemet and the African Worldview* (University of Sankore Press, 1986).

Keeva, Steve, *Transforming Practice: Finding Joy and Satisfaction in the Legal Life (Contemporary Books, 1999)*

Khan, Mohammad Hameedullah, *The School of Islamic Jurisprudence* (Kitab Bhavan, 1991).

King James Version, *The Holy Bible* (Tyndale House, 1985).

Kronman, Anthony, *The Lost Lawyer: The Failing Ideals of the Legal Profession*, (The Belknap Press of Harvard University Press, 1993).

Maguire, Jack, *Essential Buddhism*, (Pocket Books, 2001).

Mbiti, John S., *African Religions and Philosophy* (Heinemann, 1969).

Palmer, Parker, *The Courage to Teach* (Josey-Bass Publisher, 1998).

Palmer, Parker, *To Know as We are Known: A Spirituality of Education*, (Harper San Francisco, 1983).

Perlmutter, Mark, *Why Lawyer (and the rest of us) Lie and engage in other repugnant Behavior*, (Bright Books, 1998).

Pike, James A., *Beyond The Law: The Religious and Ethical meaning of the Lawyer's Vocation* , (Greenwood Press 1963).

Robert, J. Deotis, *The Black Theology in Dialogue*, (Westminster Press 1987).

Sells, Benjamin, *The Soul of the Law* (Element, 1994).

Solomon, Robert C., *A Passion For Justice* (Addison-Wesley Publishing Company, 1990).

Strang and Braithwaite, *Restorative Justice, Philosophy to Practice* (Ashgate, 2000).

Strong, James and Vines, W.E., *Strongs Concise Concordance and Vines Concise Dictionary of the Bible* (Thomas Nelson, 1997).

Wilber, Ken, *The Holographic Paradigm and Other Paradoxes, Exploring the Leading Edge of Science* (New Science Library Shambhala, 1982).

Wexler, David B., (ed), *Therapeutic Jurisprudence: The Law as a Therapeutic Agent.* (Durham: Carolina Academic Press 1990).

Winick, Bruce J., *Therapeutic Jurisprudence Applied: Essays on Mental Health Law.* (Durham: Carolina Academic Press 1997).

Winick, Bruce J. and Wexler, David B., (eds), *Judging In a Therapeutic Key: Therapeutic Jurisprudence and the Courts.* (Carolina Academic Press 2003).
Zukav, Gary, *The Seat of the Soul*, (New York, Fireside Books 1989).

Articles

Anandarajah G., and Hight E., "Spirituality and Medical Practice: Using the HOPE Questions as a Practical Tool for Spiritual Assessment" *American Family Physician*, 63:81-88 (January 2001).

Berkheiser, Mary, "Therapeutic Jurisprudence/Preventive Law and Law Teaching,"5 *Psych. Pub. Pol. And L.* 1147, 1150 (1999).

Cover, Robert M., "Obligation: a Jewish Jurisprudence of the Social Order," 5 *J.L. & Religion* 65, 66 (1987).

Codiga, Douglas A., "Reflections on the Potential Growth of Mindfulness Meditation in the Law," 7 *Harv. Negotiation L. Rev.* 109 (2002).

Daicoff, Susan, "Lawyer, Know Thyself: A review of Empirical Attorney Attributes bearing on Professionalism," 46 *Am.U. L. Rev.* 1337 (1997

Gresman, Israel, "The Jewish Criminal Lawyer's Dilemma," 29 *Fordham Urb. L.J.* 2413 (2002).

Hill, Pargament, Hood, McCullough, Swyer, Larson. Zinnbauer, "Conceptualizing Religion and Spirituality: Points

of Commonality, Points of Departure", *Journal for the Theory of Social Behavior* 30 (2000),.:
Hodge, David, "Spiritual Assessment: A review of Major Qualitative Methods and a New Framework for Assessing Spirituality." *Social Work* , Vol 46. Issue 3 (2001).

Kavanagh, Kay, "Don't Ask, Don't Tell: Deception Required Disclosure Denied, in Winick, Bruce J. & Wexler, David B (eds). *Judging In a Therapeutic Key: Therapeutic Jurisprudence and the Courts.* (Carolina Academic Press 2003).

Kaveny, M. Cathleen, "Billable Hours in Ordinary Time: A Theological Critique of the Instrumentalization of Time in Professional Life," 33 *Loy. U. Chi L.J.* 173 (2001).

Lee, Randy, "Faith Through Lawyering, Finding and Doing What is Mine to do," 11 *Regents U.L. Rev.* 71,79-80.

Meadow, Carrie Menkle, "And Now a Word About Secular Humanism,, Spirituality, and the Practice of Justice and Conflict Resolution," 28 *Fordham Urb. L. J.* 1073 (2001).

Perlin, Michael, "The Law of Healing," *68 U. Cin. L. Rev. 407 (2000).*

Rhode, Deborah L., Ethics by the Pervasive Method, 42 J. *Legal Educ.* 31 (1992).

Riga, Peter, "Spirituality of Lawyering," 40 *Catholic Law* 295, (Spring 2001).

Riskin, Leonard L., "The Contemplative Lawyer: On the Potential Contributions of Mindfullness and Meditation to Law Students, Lawyers and Their Clients," 7 *Harvard Negotiation Law Review* 1 (2002).

Sass, James, "Characterizing organizational Spirituality: An Organizational Communication Culture Approach" *Communication Studies*, 51: 3, (2000).

Schubeck, Thomas, "Ethics and Liberation Theology," *Theological Studies*, Vol. 56, Issue 1 (1995).

Schutts, Michael, "What's a Nice Christian Like You Doing in a Profession Like This?" 11 *Regent U.L. Rev.* 137 (1998/99).

Silecchia, Lucia Ann, "Integrating Spiritual Perspectives with the Law School Experience,"37 *San Diego L. Rev.* 167, 179-170. (Winter 2000).

Wexler, David B., "Therapeutic Jurisprudence and the Culture of Critique," 10 *J. Contemp. Legal Issues* 263 (1999).

Index

480

482

483

Talmud, 13, 328, 332, 360, 362, 364

TaNaKh, 356

Teaching, 5, 11, 17, 21, 36, 57, 80, 116, 124, 137, 194, 198, 203, 204, 208, 212, 218, 221, 225, 227, 232, 233, 235, 238, 240, 247, 248, 250, 304, 305, 306, 308, 315, 328, 386, 408, 415, 424

Temptation, 11, 118, 120, 358

Therapeutic Jurisprudence, 13, 283, 296, 297, 298, 299, 304, 307, 309, 310, 311, 312, 314

Tikkun, 295

Time, 1, 5, 14, 18, 19, 27, 44, 51, 53, 59, 60, 61, 64, 68, 71, 80, 82, 87, 99, 101, 108, 109, 115, 119, 122, 126, 132, 134, 135, 138, 143, 146, 151, 162, 172, 198, 199, 200, 210, 216, 217, 218, 219, 220, 222, 223, 224, 225, 226, 232, 233, 240, 252, 259, 261, 266, 267, 273, 288, 289, 290, 291, 295, 303, 304, 309, 317, 319, 320, 338, 346, 356, 357, 358, 359, 363, 372, 375, 387, 389, 390, 391, 393, 394,

397, 405, 406, 409, 410, 415, 418, 420

Transformation, 108, 110, 111, 112, 113, 115, 122, 132, 161, 166, 172, 188, 192, 213, 225, 226, 227, 228, 229, 243, 247, 252, 257, 258, 261, 270, 272, 273, 281, 338, 357, 386

Troubled waters, 11, 108, 111, 113, 115

Truth, 11, 18, 20, 35, 42, 48, 69, 102, 103, 104, 105, 106, 138, 139, 140, 141, 142, 143, 167, 191, 192, 212, 250, 276, 349, 353, 356, 360, 361, 362, 365, 379, 381, 390, 405, 425

UCC, 202

Uniform Commercial Code, 202

Universe, 21, 23, 37, 41, 82, 83, 87, 93, 98, 107, 137, 149, 240, 326, 379, 390, 397, 399, 400, 408

Values, 2, 5, 7, 9, 11, 18, 22, 23, 31, 32, 33, 34, 39, 42, 43, 44, 46, 53, 55, 56, 57, 61, 64, 68, 74, 75, 77, 78, 81, 85, 94, 95, 96, 101, 104, 105, 106, 108, 111, 113, 116, 120, 121, 124, 125, 126, 127, 128, 130, 139, 146, 147, 149,

484

166, 175, 176, 177, 178,
179, 185, 187, 189, 190,
191, 193, 195, 198, 200,
202, 205, 207, 210, 212,
216, 217, 218, 219, 220,
221, 224, 234, 235, 236,
240, 241, 243, 250, 252,
254, 263, 268, 270, 275,
279, 282, 286, 293, 295,
297, 305, 307, 311, 329,
330, 335, 336, 337, 338,
342, 343, 346, 358, 365,
380, 386, 387, 389, 393,
398, 410, 420